LIFE REIMAGINED

THE SCIENCE, ART, AND OPPORTUNITY OF MIDLIFE

Barbara Bradley Hagerty

RIVERHEAD BOOKS
New York

RIVERHEAD BOOKS
An imprint of Penguin Random House LLC
375 Hudson Street
New York, New York 10014

First Riverhead hardcover edition: March 2016
First Riverhead trade paperback edition: March 2017
Riverhead hardcover ISBN: 9781594631702
Riverhead trade paperback ISBN: 9780399573323

Printed in the United States of America
3   5   7   9   10   8   6   4   2

Book design by Meighan Cavanaugh

Praise for *Life Reimagined*

"*Life Reimagined* paints a portrait of middle age that is far from grim and decelerating. Midlife begins to seem like the second big phase of decision-making. Your identity has been formed; you know who you are; you've built up your resources; and now you have the chance to take the big risks precisely because your foundation is already secure."

—DAVID BROOKS, *The New York Times*

"Please don't have a midlife crisis. But if you do (and you will), drop everything and read this book. It's like having coffee with a good friend who has been there—and also happens to be well versed in neuroscience, psychology, and much more. Barbara Bradley Hagerty has written a sharp-eyed, bighearted book destined for widespread dog-earing and underlining. Whether it's navigating the worlds of marriage or friendship or work, *Life Reimagined* offers boatloads of earned epiphanies. This generous, wise, and often funny book will leave you revitalized—and actually looking forward to life's second act."

—ERIC WEINER, AUTHOR OF *The Geography of Bliss* AND *The Geography of Genius*

"Barbara Bradley Hagerty is a wise and engaging guide through the possibilities (and occasional pitfalls) of middle age. With her deft storytelling skills and exhaustive research, she reveals a truth that should hearten millions of people: Done right, midlife can be a time of remarkable engagement, purpose, and love."

—DANIEL H. PINK, AUTHOR OF *To Sell Is Human* AND *Drive*

"*Life Reimagined* gave me hope that midlife, even with its struggles, can be a time of growth and deeper joy in relationships old and new." —*BookPage*

"Bradley uses the perfect mixture of anecdote and facts, and knows how to tell a story. Inspiring and reassuring, this book is guaranteed to shake up anyone who is coasting through middle age, reminding them that it's up to them to find their essence and shape their last years with purpose." —*Booklist*

"Insightful . . . This work is a joyous reminder that the middle years can be satisfying, resilient, and significant." —*Library Journal*

"Bradley Hagerty crafts a book that is part insightful analysis, part memoir, and all-around engaging and relatable. . . . [Her] own journey is by turns instructive, poignant, and funny as she puts the information she's discovering into practice. . . . [She] makes a compelling case that our choices—to seek novel experiences, to stay active, to invest in enriching relationships—can transform the middle years into vibrant ones, and also help us move forward into old age with a greater sense of possibility and purpose." —*Washington Independent Review of Books*

"An upbeat look at the joys of middle age . . . For midlifers eager to 'create a new habit of mind,' Hagerty is a rousing cheerleader." —*Kirkus Reviews*

"This book is destined to become the bible for boomers seeking to make the most of the bonus decades opening up in midlife and beyond, as well as for those younger generations on their heels."
—MARC FREEDMAN, AUTHOR, *The Big Shift* AND CEO OF ENCORE.ORG.

"Combining her great reportorial skills with personal stories and fascinating data, Barbara Bradley Hagerty provides here a blueprint on aging. She debunks the idea of midlife crises while recognizing midlife changes and then, through interviews with experts and individuals, points the way to move forward into life's next phases. This book is so engagingly told, I've been telling my friends to get this book as soon as they can."
—COKIE ROBERTS, JOURNALIST AND AUTHOR OF *We Are Our Mothers' Daughters*

"*Life Reimagined* is a powerful and inspiring book. Hagerty writes with wit, warmth, and scientific rigor. She shares her own experiences of the journey into midlife with honesty and humor and teaches us what science says about our brains, our resilience, and our relationships. *Life Reimagined* motivates us to delve into midlife with enthusiasm and reminds us that a life well lived requires thought and commitment—no matter what one's age."
—KAREN REIVICH, PH.D., COAUTHOR OF *The Resilience Factor*

"Grab this book, find a comfortable chair, and get ready to change the way you think about your life. Barbara Bradley Hagerty blends the latest science with rich personal reflections to create a work that informs, uplifts, and ultimately offers a wise guide to what keeps people happy and healthy. Beautifully crafted by a journalist at the top of her game, this is an exciting book that you'll find yourself talking about and sharing with the important people in your world."
—ROBERT J. WALDINGER, M.D., DIRECTOR OF THE HARVARD STUDY OF ADULT DEVELOPMENT

"*Life Reimagined* is arguably the best book on middle life ever written. Not only is it in beautiful prose, but it's also thoroughly researched. In order to feel understood and to anticipate the future, everybody from thirty to seventy should read this book. It is a joy."
—GEORGE E. VAILLANT, M.D., FORMER DIRECTOR OF THE HARVARD STUDY OF ADULT DEVELOPMENT AND AUTHOR OF *Triumphs of Experience*

ALSO BY BARBARA BRADLEY HAGERTY

Fingerprints of God:
The Search for the Science of Spirituality

For Devin

CONTENTS

1.

AN ENDING, AND
A BEGINNING

September 5, 2012, had been a trying day. I devoted much of the afternoon to crafting a response to a listener who disliked a story that had aired the previous day on *All Things Considered*. When you cover a beat such as religion, as I did for many years at National Public Radio, you brace for a hailstorm of outraged e-mails every time you file a report.

But I never grew used to them, and this one was particularly upsetting. Just after I sent off my response, I felt a sharp pain in my chest. My breathing became clipped and shallow. Heat radiated up my back. Panicked, I googled "heart attack + women." The results were not reassuring—are any health-related answers on the Internet reassuring?—and I called my doctor, Brad Moore, on his cell phone. I described my symptoms as calmly as I could.

"I don't like the shortness of breath," he said. "I want you to call 911 immediately."

I made it partway through "I can do that," when the room lurched and went black. When I opened my eyes, my colleague John Ydstie was tucking a soft sweater under my head. "An ambulance is on its way," he whispered. Then I heard Scott Simon's voice directing the medics to my cubicle. Dr. Moore, who also sees Scott, had called him when he heard me faint.

By the time the ambulance reached the George Washington University Hospital, I was feeling pretty good, well enough to go home, in fact. I explained to the nurse that I was a healthy woman who takes a six a.m. spinning class every day. I could not possibly have a bad heart. The nurse looked at me, handed me a hospital gown, and scanned her notes.

"You're fifty-three, right?" she asked, as if that number were a clinical condition, like diabetes. "I think we'd better keep you overnight."

It occurred to me then that I *was* suffering from a condition: a physical and emotional condition called "midlife." This condition presented as a disconnect between my thirty-something self-image and my fifty-something reality. I recognized it every time I passed a mirror and saw the lined face of my mother in her fifties staring back at me. I spotted it often at work, when my younger, ambitious self insisted that I clamor to cover that breaking story, while my chronological self shrugged, preferring a good night's sleep to another all-nighter. Sitting there in the thin hospital robe, I admitted there were moments, more and more frequent, when I seemed to be pushing a wheelbarrow full of dense, unfulfilled ambition up a steep gravel path. It was exhausting, but I didn't know any other way to live.

I was not left to my thoughts for long. Within minutes, my husband, Devin; my brother, Dave; Dr. Moore; and Marty Makary, a good friend and surgeon at Johns Hopkins, had arrived, creating a little party in our corner of the ER. As the five of us chatted and laughed, e-mails from NPR friends and colleagues began filling my iPhone; someone had sent an All Staff e-mail. My dear friend Libby Lewis called to say she would visit early the next morning. I felt loved, I felt cherished. Why hadn't I pulled this stunt before?

Eventually everyone left, and at two a.m. I was given a bed. I awakened with a dull headache a couple of hours later to a persistent beeping from the bed next to me. I gazed at the ceiling, reflecting on my family and friends and how desperately I wanted a cup of coffee. At six-thirty, I called Devin to see if he could bring me a double espresso. I reached him as he was leaving the house.

"You need to call Dave," he said.

"Why?"

"Just call him," he said uncomfortably.

Instinctively, I knew: Dad had died. As it turned out, he had died at five that morning, at age ninety-one.

That night, after I was discharged from the hospital, my family and a few friends collected at my brother's house for dinner.

"Turns out I was with the wrong relative last night," Dave quipped when he ushered us in, and it felt good to laugh.

We crowded around the kitchen table and began swapping stories about Dad. We remembered how he learned to swing dance when he was sixty-nine, and how at seventy-four, by then two years divorced, Dad spotted Nancy at church and courted her with such charm and devotion that she had to marry him. We talked about how Dad believed in me: When I was struggling in school as a third-grader, how he spent hours helping me with homework and with prayers written out on yellow legal pads. We recalled how Dad studied French every night between two and three a.m., teaching himself vocabulary and grammar. He never progressed beyond terrible at French, but he always insisted that some things are worth doing poorly. I think he meant that some things are so worthwhile that even if you have no talent, even if the results are mediocre, it is still worth your time and effort. In his final years, his mind and body had failed him—he was nearly blind, nearly deaf, and suffered from dementia—but to the end, Dad lived each day with verve.

After hearing that my father had died, Scott Simon sent me a note. He had known Dad. They belonged to the same health club and would occasionally share a cup of coffee, Dad no doubt clueless as to Scott's fame. Scott mentioned that he had told his wife, Caroline, about my health scare and my dad's death.

"Caroline said, 'Darling, I don't care how far gone someone is, they always feel a tug from their children. Gene wanted to go instead,'" Scott wrote. "We believe that Gene somehow knew that you needed a little help and he said to God, 'Barbie still has a lot of things to do. I'm ready. Take me,' and he said it with that incredible chiseled smile. And God said, 'Gene, you've got a deal.'"

Even now, several years later, these words make me cry. They remind me that Dad loved me fiercely and would have instantly traded his life for mine. Scott's words also illumined a larger truth: A page had turned, Dad was gone and I was here, ostensibly healthy but keenly aware that a hospital stay or worse was only one stressful event away. I saw it would not be too long before my brother and I would be next at bat, and that the next generation to fall was my own.

At fifty-three, I gained a new sense of my own mortality. Now, what would I do with that?

ONE MYTH AND THREE TRUTHS

For the next two years, I examined the middle stage of life. I traveled the country interviewing brain scientists and marriage therapists, psychologists and kidney donors, geneticists and elite masters athletes—well over four hundred researchers and ordinary folk trying to figure out how to thrive at midlife. As a result, I have come to believe that the forties, fifties, and sixties are the least understood and,

in some ways, the most critical phase of life. Midlife is not flyover territory. Midlife is O'Hare, midlife is Heathrow, midlife is a bustling
hub where the decisions you make today largely determine the rest of
your journey on this planet. What I have learned has been a happy
surprise. It has changed the way I try to approach every single day.

Midlife has gotten a bum rap. It has suffered guilt by association,
linked inextricably to the "c" word: *crisis*.

The ugly rumors about midlife began in the 1970s, when Gail
Sheehy and others stereotyped midlife as a cataclysmic period surging
with existential dread, flattened by malaise, tortured by one's failed
dreams, or any combination of the three. In her book *Passages*, Sheehy
wrote of the "forlorn forties" and the "resigned fifties." Eventually the
idea captured the popular imagination, becoming plot lines for Oscar-
winning (and lesser) movies, and often an excuse for bad behavior.
According to the midlife-crisis argument, certain stalwart or blessed
personalities could escape the mud pit, but most of us were drawn inexorably into the emotional mire. We have been socialized to think
this way about midlife, and—what do you know?—we all seem to have
"midlife crises."

In fact, there is almost no hard evidence for midlife crisis at all,
other than a few small pilot studies conducted decades ago. Researchers today who have examined people across their life spans, peered
inside their brains, uncoiled their hopes and fears, and observed how
they deal with love and alienation, trauma and death, good and evil,
say that midlife is about renewal, not crisis. This is a time when you
shift gears—a temporary pause, yes, but not a prolonged stall. In fact,
you are moving forward to a new place in life. This moment can be
exhilarating rather than terrifying, informed by the experiences of
your past and shaped by the promise of your future.

This is not to say that the middle-aged are a cheerful or carefree lot.
If happiness over the life span looks like a U-curve—and researchers

suggest that it does—then people in their forties and fifties occupy the bottom of the curve. They zigzag between demanding children and frail parents. They shoulder heavy responsibilities at work. They are under-rested, under-exercised, and overfed. Yet 90 percent of them are not in crisis. Midlife malaise is fairly ubiquitous, but let's not diminish a legitimate phenomenon with a stereotype.

When I launched into this admittedly self-serving project—after all, this is about me as well as you—I knew what to examine. It was like being a first-time tourist to the United States, equipped with a must-see list. When you arrive in Washington, D.C., you must see the White House; in Arizona, the Grand Canyon; in New York City, the Statue of Liberty. But even after roaming through those places, you would not truly understand the country unless you absorbed some of its overriding motifs: democracy, the pursuit of happiness, religious freedom, and eternal optimism.

In the same way, I had my must-see list of midlife monuments: the (tedious) career, the (distant) marriage, the need for investing outward, or "generativity," which psychologist Erik Erikson enshrined as a defining characteristic of midlife. But as I looked around, I also spotted three themes that are helpful, and I believe necessary, to living richly in one's middle years.

Engage with verve. Emotionally disengaging from any part of your life—your spouse, your kids, your work—cuts off the oxygen and the patient dies. That sounds dire—that's my point, actually—because this insight surfaced again and again: Autopilot is death. Choose where to invest your energy, and do so intentionally, because the clearest path to a robust midlife is purposeful engagement.

In some ways, the best role models for people over forty are people under eighteen. Children study hard, learn new skills, and throw themselves into new passions. They fail like beginners, until frustration yields to success. They risk making and tending to friends, even if that hurts. The lesson for midlifers is: Of course it takes work to inject zest and vulnerability into your marriage; it takes courage to reappraise your career for not just income but also meaning; it takes effort to sharpen your aging brain. But the research is clear: Engaging in those things you feel are important will lift your joy and satisfaction, in the moment and over the years.

Choose purpose over happiness. "Happiness is overrated," Carol Ryff told me. Ryff is a psychologist at the University of Wisconsin and director of an enormous project called Midlife in the United States, or MIDUS. For some twenty years, Ryff and other scientists have tracked thousands of people through their middle and later years, measuring their well-being in every possible way: physically, emotionally, psychologically, biologically, and neurologically. After sorting through piles of data, the researchers have concluded that pursuing happiness can backfire, but pursuing *eudaimonia* rarely fails.

Eudaimonia is the Aristotelian idea of human flourishing, pursuing long-term goals that give meaning to life, rather than short-term happiness that delivers a jolt of dopamine. It is the kind of satisfaction that comes from raising terrific children or training for the Olympics. It means figuring out your purpose in life, given your unique set of talents and capacities. It is the Holy Grail that all people seek, most acutely in middle age, when we can see the final horizon not so many years away.

It turns out that finding a deeper purpose and pursuing it carries an unexpected bonus: It makes you robust. Dozens of new studies show that if you have a reason to get up in the morning, you will live longer, you will enjoy a happier old age, you will better retain your memory, and you will be more likely to not only survive the scary diagnosis but thrive. Purpose in life is more important than education or wealth in determining long-term health and happiness. It isn't a panacea, but it's awfully close.

Your thinking is your experience. How you think can shape how you experience the world, your career, your relationships, your health, your happiness. Please note that I am *not* arguing that whistling a happy tune will make you healthy, wealthy, and wise; at least, not entirely. Much of your life and mine is shaped by biology and life circumstances. Genetics—who your parents are, whether you are susceptible to mental or physical disease, what your emotional "set point" is—this is the wind thrusting your little boat in a particular direction. Your environment steers you as well, with the force of a strong current: Did you grow up in a safe and nurturing home, or a divided or abusive one? Did you receive a decent education? Are you poor or wealthy? Are you married, employed, religious?

But there is also a mechanism called a "rudder"—that is, your thinking, your approach to triumphs and defeats, joys and pain and losses, the stuff no one escapes—that calibrates one's happiness. Experts believe that 30 to 40 percent of one's happiness is determined by how a person thinks or acts. That rudder won't shelter you from a hurricane as you venture across an ocean, but it will absolutely color how much you enjoy the trip.

Your thoughts and attitudes today chart your destiny tomorrow, and the day after that, and the day after that.

A CIRCUITOUS JOURNEY

If you are middle-aged today (roughly between the ages of forty and sixty-five), this isn't your parents' midlife. Chances are good you will live to eighty or beyond. You may have two marriages and two or more careers under your belt. You will experience better health longer, you will have more time and more physical and mental acuity to compete in triathlons, learn Mandarin, write a novel, or start a nonprofit. At the same time, the world is no longer brimming with unlimited possibilities; the choices you have made until now set boundaries on your future. You will be confronting a different set of questions, challenges, and choices than your parents did, and their wisdom is not enough. The answers will come from you.

Until recently, scientists have paid scant attention to the middle years. Researchers find people between ages zero and twenty-five endlessly fascinating. And why not? That is the time of life when neurological and social development are stampeding like wild mustangs. If you happen to live to seventy-five (or, better, one hundred), you will once again become the object of scientific scrutiny. But the middle years, when most of us are healthy and productive, when we are creating families and suffering midlife malaise (or not), those years have been a vast desert, a research wasteland.

A tsunami of research is moving this way, drawing from biology and genetics to psychology and neuroscience. Researchers are doing more than taking snapshots of the middle years. Using longitudinal studies, they are scrutinizing people who have aged successfully, and are gleaning their secrets for the benefit of our generation. Science is confirming what we all suspected instinctively: There are certain steps you can take to thrive during midlife and set the foundation for the later years.

Absorbing the cascades of new research felt at times like sipping from a fire hydrant. But as a reporter, whenever I am faced with telling a complicated story, I remember my favorite piece of journalism advice: *Chronology is our friend.* That is the blueprint for this book. I will describe how my year of researching midlife unfolded. During that time (and a little beyond), I experienced the themes of every single chapter in a personal way—sometimes when I didn't want to, sometimes when it hurt. Serendipity helped. Every month seemed to launch a unique midlife concept: It just so happened, for example, that March would begin my "brain" research and June revolve around "marriage." It was not that the investigation of those topics *ended* in those months (thank goodness), but it overshadowed everything else.

Learning the art and science of midlife felt more like bushwhacking through a dense forest without a compass than cruising the interstate with its numbered exits. The whole process was messy, unpredictable, and full of contradictions. During this time, I landed in the emergency room twice—well, three times, if you include the day I mistakenly took six Percocet instead of six prednisone. I trained for the so-called Senior Olympics—and got hearing aids. I helped care for my ninety-one-year-old mother after she shattered her femur—wanting her to live, and giving her permission to die. I reevaluated my friendships, revamped my career, developed intense and unrelenting pain in my throat—and used principles of neuroplasticity to try to relieve it.

Those who say life is boring have never been middle-aged.

On January 1, 2013, I drove from a sunny, chilly Washington, D.C., to a lonely, dark, bitterly cold Williamstown, Massachusetts. It was my first day of book leave from NPR, and largely, I fretted. I had envisioned this book as a personal march through the science of midlife, and I worried that I had promised too much. Training my brain to raise my IQ for my midlife brain chapter—I can do that. Learning the secrets of long-term marriage from online dating sites—that's doable. But for the chapter on midlife hobbies, I proposed *biking across the country!* Did it occur to me that riding just fifty miles a day would still eat up two months of book leave?

I arrived in Williamstown near midnight, when it was six degrees below zero, and lugged my suitcase, computer, printer, and three boxes of research articles up the icy stairs of the house I was renting. For the next four weeks, I would be teaching a writing class to ten students at Williams College, my alma mater. When you have no biological children of your own, you have to jerry-rig a way to invest in future generations—a signature of a healthy midlife. More than that, I hoped this class would push some seeds of transformation into my psyche, make me more instinctively generous, less focused on my stuff. In fact, my secret hope was that writing this book would change me.

My hunch on that frigid day of new beginnings was that people don't change much at all. I am the same girl, I thought, who toiled in the college library instead of eating dinner with friends, who fretted about letting down her teammates in the next cross-country race, who never sat back and said, "Yes, this moment right now, this is an extraordinarily blessed moment. I am happy." I am the same girl my kindergarten teacher called to the front of the room and introduced as the "class worrier"—a harsh assessment, but prescient. I am the same girl who, at seven years old, fell in love with horseback riding at a ranch in Colorado. Each morning, with a frown as dark as a thundercloud, I marched purposefully to the corral, where I would saddle up Stampede, the pokey white pony I rode every day, all day, for a week. I was in love, my young soul soaring with the thrill of horses, but from my anxious face, you would think I was about to be waterboarded. I was too busy focusing to smile.

Can we change, I wondered, even at the margins? Are we middle-agers destined by our wiring and half a lifetime of behavior to proceed along a route that feels more desolate than meaningful? Can we reset our expectations, renegotiate our relationships, take a compass reading and shift direction? *Can we reimagine our lives?* At that moment, I simply didn't know.

A year and a half later, Mom and I met for coffee on the outdoor patio at her favorite café. It was late July, a few days before her ninety-third birthday, and she was, as always, impeccably dressed in beige slacks, a long-sleeved black shirt, and a tan straw hat with a black ribbon. It must have been eighty-five degrees, but Mom didn't notice: She was too busy relishing the date with her daughter.

"I went to bed thinking about this moment, and I woke up thinking about it," she said, even though I see her almost every day.

After a few minutes, we were joined by Desiré Moses, a young journalist who was helping me with my research. Mom spent several minutes asking all about Desiré's life. Eventually I shifted the conversation to Mom.

"You know, Desiré," I said, "my parents divvied up the work, character-wise, when it came to my brother and me. Mom taught us integrity and Dad taught us deferred gratification."

I paused.

"Sometimes, I wonder when it's time to stop deferring and start gratifying."

Mom looked at me in wonder.

"It's *now*, honey!" she said, raising her arms like a referee signaling a touchdown. "*This* is the time to enjoy your life. Don't waste another moment!"

Something like a shutter clicked in my mind's eye, preserving the scene to be savored later. At that moment I recognized that I was unbearably fortunate: I was working on a book, was married to a very good man, and had won the lottery with my stupendous stepdaughter, Vivian. At that moment, I was sitting between two generations, Mom and Desiré—one with the wisdom of the past, one with the energy of the future—and delighting in both. *Remember this moment, Barb,* I thought, *life is very good.*

Research suggests that if you do this, if you frequently mark off mental milestones, life feels as if it slows down and takes on more meaning. And so I trained myself to take snapshots of moments and tuck them away. Sitting at that café, I realized that the months learning how to thrive at midlife had altered my emotional DNA. Not completely, but definitely at the margins. And the margins make all the difference.

2.

PLEASE DON'T HAVE
A MIDLIFE CRISIS

On a balmy night in May 2011, a small crowd gathered in my mother's church for the Wednesday-evening "testimony" meeting. The three dozen Christian Scientists sat quietly in the pews, listening to spiritual readings and then, one by one, telling stories of how their faith had helped and healed them.

My mother stood up and waited for the usher to bring her a microphone. The congregants stirred when they heard her voice, surreptitiously glancing in her direction and anticipating her metaphysical insights. Mom began her testimony, then faltered. She searched for words, but they had vanished. Nothing remained but white noise. After an achingly long pause, Mom lowered herself slowly back into the pew. No one really noticed—she was, after all, eighty-nine years old—but Mom was uneasy, without knowing why.

My mother eventually made her way home, where she lived alone. Another twenty hours would pass before my brother and I realized she had suffered a stroke. In the emergency room Thursday night, a doctor measured her blood pressure at 260 over 120. A brain scan revealed a bleed in her left frontal lobe, which scrambled her language and her ability to sequence, to do things in order, whether putting on her stockings before her shoes or removing her clothes before stepping in the shower. Evidence of three other, older strokes also appeared on her brain scan, and these compounded her problem.

Over the long Memorial Day weekend, I sat by my mother's bedside in the hospital's intensive care unit as Mom floated just at the surface of consciousness, occasionally popping up long enough to look at me mutely, lost in confusion. Were there words in there, trying to elbow their way through the maze of her broken brain, or was her brain an empty room, all thought, all memory, all personality swept clean? This mattered to me, for my mother's singular gift is insight, her ability to listen carefully to my tales and dilemmas, take a reading from her impeccable moral compass, and suggest a way forward. At her core, Mom's identity is her thinking. I feared that she had lost her identity, and that I had lost my mom.

A few days later, I stood at our kitchen sink, cleaning lettuce in the spinner. Outside the window, a neighbor trotted up the street with her dog. Another one set the sprinkler just right. It was a soft evening in my favorite time of year, when all of life bursts with the vivid beauty of the adolescent spring, when I could remember, if only for a few seconds, the exhilaration of youth.

I felt nothing. No surge of joy at being alive, no frisson of gratitude for witnessing another annual rebirth. I glanced at my husband, who was slicing tomatoes.

"I think I'm having a midlife crisis," I announced.

Devin put down the tomato.

"Don't do that," he said. "Please don't have a midlife crisis."

A CRISIS IS BORN

M om's stroke provided the spark for a combustible collection of small despairs waiting to ignite: the unremitting daily-ness of work, the minor but scary health issues, the unpalatable fear that this is as good as it gets and that life slopes downward from here.

A few days after Mom's stroke, I sat at my desk and pondered these suddenly urgent questions: What, exactly, constitutes a "midlife crisis," and is that what I am experiencing? Is it unswerving destiny, or can I drive around it with the choices I make? So many people I know are struggling through midlife ennui. Yet some people flourish. How do they do it? How can *I* craft a meaningful middle life? And is there any science that can give me pointers?

As I thought about these questions, I felt that tremor of elation that signals I have stumbled on a great story. I decided then to follow my journalistic training and began to research.

Let us begin at the beginning: the moment "midlife crisis" was born.

In 1965, Canadian psychoanalyst Elliott Jaques published a study and sparked a cultural revolution. In "Death and the Mid-Life Crisis," in the *International Journal of Psychoanalysis*, he posited that around the age of thirty-five, a man begins to glimpse the slanting shadow of death and recognizes that he would be dust long before he could fulfill the dreams of his youth.[1] (Jaques excluded women, explaining that menopause "obscured" the midlife transition.)

Jaques's theory rested on what he called a "random sample" of 310 "geniuses," including composers (Mozart), artists (Raphael), and writers (Rimbaud). He noted that many of these men died around the age of thirty-seven, whether of natural causes or by their own hand, fearing that their creative abilities were waning. Jaques allowed that some geniuses were able to avert the midlife crisis and the death of their creativity. Indeed, some talents only ripened with time: Dante Alighieri did not pen *The Divine Comedy* until the age of thirty-seven, and Johann Sebastian Bach was still a church organist and tutor until age thirty-eight, when he began composing his most ambitious works.

Jaques also saw evidence of midlife crises among more ordinary psyches: specifically, among patients in his own clinical practice. One might ask how typical these men were, given that they were seeking psychiatric therapy, but still, Jaques detected a pattern. He described, for example, one patient who was haunted by the fear that he had crossed a threshold and that there was likely more time behind him than stretching ahead. "For the first time in his life, he saw his future as circumscribed," Jaques wrote. "He would not be able to accomplish in the span of a single lifetime everything he desired to do. He could only achieve a finite amount. Much would have to remain unfinished and unrealized."[2]

Jaques's insight was little noticed until Daniel Levinson put the midlife crisis on steroids in his 1978 book *The Seasons of a Man's Life*.[3] (He got around to women a couple of decades later.) Levinson, a psychologist and professor at Yale University, argued that all men experience "transitions" as they move from one stage of life to another. The stages begin with pre-adulthood (from birth to age twenty-two), then move to early adulthood (from age seventeen to forty-five), on to middle adulthood (age forty to sixty-five), to late adulthood (sixty to eighty-five), and (if you're lucky) late-late adulthood (over eighty years old). Watch out for those transitional years, he warned: Emotional turbulence strikes—and in middle age, this can trigger a full-blown crisis.

According to Levinson's own account, the midlife transition held a personal fascination. "At 46," he wrote, "I wanted to study the transition to middle age in order to understand what I had been going through myself."[4] After he met with colleagues at Yale, it became blindingly apparent that they were all "personally struggling" with midlife. If they were struggling, these Yale professors reasoned, then surely other people must be as well.

To test his theory, Levinson interviewed forty men: ten biology professors, ten novelists, ten business executives, and ten industrial laborers. The men, all aged between thirty-five and forty-five, submitted to six to ten interviews, each lasting between one and two hours. From these exhaustive and no doubt exhausting interviews— who wouldn't confess to a midlife crisis by the twentieth hour?— Levinson concluded that between ages forty and forty-five, a man suffers the "agonizing" process of "de-illusionment," when he compares his youthful dreams with his present, grayer reality. This brings about a crisis for most men: "Every aspect of their lives comes into question, and they are horrified by much that is revealed. . . . They cannot go on as before, but need time to choose a new path or modify the old one."[5]

A man in this state often makes "false starts," and "tentatively tests a variety of new choices . . . out of confusion or impulsiveness," Levinson wrote. This is the time men seem to grieve lost opportunities and desperately try to claim new ones before it is too late, in the form of a younger wife, a dramatic career shift, the stereotypical red convertible. How many men, you might wonder, experience this existential angst? Ten percent? Twenty? No, Levinson claimed that *80 percent* of men suffer through a midlife crisis.

If Levinson developed Elliott Jaques's kernel of an idea into a carefully detailed psychological state, journalist Gail Sheehy turned Levinson's midlife crisis into a cultural phenomenon. In *Passages*, Sheehy wrote that men (again, the focus is on men) could expect a midlife crisis at age forty-two.[6] The midlife crisis had made its grand cultural debut, and would come to define the psyche of an entire generation.

There was one problem: Other researchers looked and looked, but they just could not find evidence of an inevitable—or even common—midlife crisis.

THE VANISHING MIDLIFE CRISIS

Midlife crisis is very rare," Susan Krauss Whitbourne told me.
We were standing in her "laboratory," a converted closet on the campus of the University of Massachusetts at Amherst. An athletic, petite woman who easily looks fifteen years younger than her six decades, Whitbourne was perched on a chair, pulling a box of IBM punch cards from the top of a gray filing cabinet. These data cards flung her into a long love affair with midlife and the phantom midlife crisis.

In 1977, when Whitbourne was a young assistant professor of psychology at the University of Rochester, she discovered a dissertation that would change the trajectory of her career. The dissertation analyzed a brief survey of some 350 students at the University of Rochester, asking them about their family backgrounds, their friendships, their goals and emotions. If she could only track down the original data, Whitbourne thought, she could follow up with those students and conduct that most prized treasure of social science research: a longitudinal study that followed people through their lives. She eventually located the punch cards in someone's basement in Poughkeepsie, New York. She sent letters to the students, who were then in their early thirties, and a fair number agreed to continue answering her questions.

Whitbourne also recruited a new group of Rochester students, setting up a table on the quad and bribing a few dozen with lemonade and cookies. Now she had groups that represented the leading edge and the tail end of the baby boomer generation. Every few years over the next three decades, the University of Rochester graduates, half men and half women, responded to her queries. Their answers gave her a window into the baby boomer's passage through adulthood, which she published in her 2010 book *The Search for Fulfillment*.[7] In another study, inspired by the longitudinal study, she conducted in-depth interviews to chart people's journey from young adulthood through midlife.[8]

"We really got into depth with identity, values, work, family, gender roles, everything," Whitbourne told me. "And I'm scrutinizing these interviews and saying: 'Where is the midlife crisis?' And I realized, it's not there! You ask people, 'Are you having midlife crisis?' And the answer was, uniformly, 'No!'"

Other researchers, too, searched fruitlessly for evidence of a vast midlife crisis. In 1989, two dozen scholars scoured all the literature on midlife and its supposed crisis. Was it universal, frequent, occasional? They concluded that about 10 percent of American men may undergo a midlife crisis.[9]

After that, Elaine Wethington, a sociologist at Cornell University, conducted detailed interviews with more than seven hundred people who were part of the Midlife in the United States (MIDUS) project. She found that more than a quarter of the participants claimed to have suffered a midlife crisis, most commonly between the ages of forty and fifty.[10]

That statistic vanished under scrutiny.

"People would say, 'Yeah, I had one,'" Wethington recalled. "But they were interpreting what was happening *to* them." Then the investigators followed up: Had these people suffered existential angst, had they experienced the kind of panicked dread of death and unattained dreams that can launch people on a fumbling journey to reclaim their youth?

"And they'd say, 'Oh no, it was nothing like that,'" she said. "And then if I followed up with 'But did you have anything that you *thought* was a midlife crisis?' they'd say, 'Oh yeah, you know, I lost my job when I was forty-five.'"

People labeled any significant, unhappy event—an accident, a sickness, a divorce, a parent dying, a child leaving for college—a midlife crisis if it happened in one's middle years. But those events can happen at other times of life, and research shows that the biggest upheavals—in career and in family—occur before the age of forty.[11] In the end, Wethington, too, estimates that only one out of ten people experiences a genuine midlife crisis.

It is not that she and other midlife researchers, such as psychology professor Margie Lachman at Brandeis University, believe that *nothing* is going on. They do, although Lachman prefers to call it a "midlife checkup." Lachman says that such a checkup is generally triggered in one of two ways. The first is "an external event that makes you take stock," the kind of commonplace assaults that Wethington describes: a divorce or losing your job; a health scare for yourself, a loved one, or someone your own age. The other examination wells up from within, she says, triggered by "a sort of introspection and inner turmoil."

"You're looking for meaning in your life," she says. "Something will happen, and people will just have a realization that they're not happy in their job. It's not that they lost their job or were fired from their job. But they realize, 'This isn't satisfying to me. It's not what I'm looking for. I wonder if I can do something different.'"

Now I was fully engaged. Now she was talking about me. I wanted to know if others were beset by the same sort of ennui. So I went—where else?—to the Internet.[12]

A TALE OF TWO MIDLIFES

In August 2013, I asked my colleagues running NPR's website to post a question on NPR's Facebook page: "How is midlife treating you? Tell us about your transition through midlife (forty-five to sixty-five) and how you've bounced back from life's curve balls." The solicitation was followed by my e-mail address.

Within five minutes, my iPhone was pinging like a pinball machine, a fact that initially delighted and soon alarmed me. By day's end, more than seven hundred people had sent me mini-essays about the joys and tragedies of their midlife journeys. No doubt, a professional polling company would throw the results out. After all, this group was self-selected and relatively homogenous: If NPR's listenership is any guide, they would be highly educated and predominately white. Also, I didn't know who did *not* write me: Was I missing a wide swath of people who were living a more typical midlife, neither deliriously happy nor desperately sad? I could not possibly know.

Here is what I did know, as I read the essays for two straight days. I knew that these were little masterpieces, stories of life and death, cancer and remission, losing love and finding it, searching for meaning when it seemed so elusive—the best and worst of a person's life boiled down to a few paragraphs.

"I used to be pretty and glamorous," fifty-one-year-old Alessandra Lanti wrote. "Men flirted with me at the grocery store. Now my kneecaps are sagging. I am not sure why that bothers me so much, but it does. I have become invisible to men. And along with my shifting appearance I have had to shift my self-image too. I went back to school, got a degree, got married, got stepchildren, got old. I think about what I did, what I didn't do, what I wanted to do and what is left to be done.

I didn't become a famous writer, or rich or wise, or a perfect step-
mom. I didn't save the world from suffering or travel to the Amazon. I
didn't even master the lotus position. Oh yes, and I am afraid to die.
And as my parents become more feeble and ready to depart, I know
that I am next and I am scared. I am acutely aware of the inexorable
passage of time and I feel a new sense of urgency in my days. I mourn
the beauty, vigor and power of youth and I do not think I can move on
until I have fully grieved. Then perhaps I will be proud that I finally
grew up. But not yet. Not until I let go of what I have lost."

This, to my mind, qualifies as a genuine midlife crisis, a life rup-
tured by awareness of aging and death, a flailing attempt to embrace
her youth in a bear hug as it dissolves into mist. A few other writers
described Hollywood-style crises. One woman, for example, left her
husband in Nashville, traveled the country on a BMW motorcycle, and
now lives with her girlfriend in San Francisco. Another, Linda Silver-
stein, quit her job (but not her husband) after reading *Eat, Pray, Love*:
"I definitely feel like I was (am) in a midlife crisis," she wrote, "asking
all the same questions I did at eighteen. Who am I? Where am I going?
Why am I on this earth?"

But for every writer who described anguish and dread, ten others
vowed they would never trade their physical and emotional trials for
the easy ascent of youth. Reading their stories felt like wandering
through a war zone before the bodies are reclaimed, so much death
and destruction. Almost no one escaped being touched by the death of
a spouse, a best friend, a parent, even, tragically, a child. Almost everyone had lost something precious: a long marriage, a cherished career,
a vitality felled by cancer or stroke.

And yet. And yet, most described these alloyed middle years as
their golden period, even when life hunted them down. "Life kicks the
shit out of me regularly," Victoria Gallucci wrote. "I'm a work in prog-

ress, a beautiful mess, and even on those days when I hate my life, I love every lousy second of it." Toni Shade was married to her high school sweetheart for thirty-three years until she awakened one morning to find he had died of a heart attack; a short time later, she was diagnosed with (and successfully treated for) breast cancer. "I refuse to be defeated," she wrote. "This may be the second chapter of my life but it is not the last. I've been tested in ways I never imagined, and it feels good to be a survivor, in every sense of the word."

Then there is Heather Pilder Olson, divorced, who lost her job as a communications expert and found herself waiting tables. Eventually she fell in love and married. "I have used up most of my savings. I am not sure where my next job will be. I am currently working a retail job and just wrote a TV pilot. I am having the time of my life."

"The kids are leaving home," Eric Zehr wrote. "Friends are starting to pass away. My eyes aren't as good as they once were. I can't stay out as late as I once could. I like all this. It feels normal to me. Midlife? I think of it as the prime of life." Usually, they viewed their failing bodies with a bemused humor. "My hips hurt after twelve-hour shifts on my feet, and my hair is thinning," Aileen Hayes reported. "My brain cells are shedding faster than my dried-up skin and my memory is a thing of the past. And you ask: How's midlife treating me? I *love* it."

As I pored over their stories, a few very clear themes emerged from those who were thriving during the middle third of life. Relationships moved into the foreground as career and other accomplishments receded into the distance. When happy, they dwelled on the moment— enjoying a languid dinner with friends, or cradling their newborn grandchild—keenly aware that the number of unburdened moments ahead was dwindling. After a loss, they allowed a respectful pause, took a compass reading, and then began the next leg of their journey. Gaylin Laughlin, who left a dismal marriage, lost a hundred

pounds, and climbed Mount Kilimanjaro, saw midlife as a time to recalibrate, not surrender: "It's not about how midlife is treating me. It's
about how I'm *living* midlife. I only get *one* shot, you know." The
contented midlifers enjoyed adventure but cherished the familiar. They
invested outward, in children or grandchildren, in causes larger than
themselves. They learned to redefine success. As Walter King, an artist
who suffered a spinal cord injury, wrote: "I still see myself painting
the Sistine Chapel or the modern equivalent. It'll have to be a much
smaller chapel."

This dichotomy between those who emerge from midlife in crisis
and those who emerge with humor and serenity can be explained by
what Margie Lachman calls "a tale of two midlifes."[13]

"We talk about this low point in midlife. But I really think it's important to know that, despite the demands, despite the crises that
some people do experience, many people see midlife as the peak,"
Lachman said. "It typically can be the peak of earnings, it can be the
peak in terms of respect and being looked up to and being able to reason and solve problems. So much experience can come to bear. You're
still at the point where you haven't lost your faculties, you haven't lost
your abilities and, physically, people are typically doing pretty well,
too. For many people, it really is the best years of life."

This, then, was the first big insight gleaned from the researchers
and my e-mail correspondents: Genuine crisis at midlife, with its angst,
its turbocharged car, and its wandering eye, afflicts few people. The
vast majority bump along, stubbing their toes, coping, and laughing.

Yet this is not unadulterated joy. Andrew Oswald has the statistics
to prove it. He has found that almost everyone suffers a dip in happiness at midlife. Not even apes are spared.[14] Welcome to your destiny,
in the shape of a U.

TWO SHADES OF WELL-BEING

Andrew Oswald may have been the first to spot the U-shaped happiness curve. Since 1996, the economics professor at Britain's University of Warwick has been asking people of all races, ages, and nationalities how happy they are. Study after study, not just his but others' as well, reveals the same insight: Midlife is a low point. This is not necessarily evidence of a crisis, but it does point to a common, recoverable malaise.

"There's overwhelming evidence that human happiness or well-being follows an approximate U-shape through life," he told me. "You are, loosely speaking, rather happy in your twenties, and then you follow this huge swoop down through life reaching a minimum generally somewhere around the mid-forties or so, and then you start to swoop up the other side of the U-shape like coming out of a valley."

"What accounts for the U?" I asked.

One theory, he said, is that "people start out with very high goals. In midlife, they realize on average that they couldn't be achieved—most people can't be CEO—and that's painful. But what are you going to do about that? You can either cling to them and be increasingly miserable, or you can adapt to your failures. And the standard theory has become that we learned to forgive ourselves and our weaknesses and gradually we could get happier."

For American women, surveys show the nadir comes around age forty, and for American men, around fifty. In one recent study, Oswald and his fellow economist David Blanchflower, at Dartmouth College, surveyed seventy-two countries and found that the U-shape rules no matter where you live.[15] Whether in the United States or Saudi Arabia, Zimbabwe or Moldova, happiness dips in the forties. Oswald said that you cannot blame middle-aged misery on circumstances, since the researchers controlled for factors such as unemployment, health problems, and divorce. Rather, he said, it is something "deep inside" that causes the malaise, almost as if "we're wired for misery."

This is not to suggest that two people in different circumstances—one living in affluence, another in an impoverished war zone—would experience the same level of dissatisfaction in middle age.

"They both have U's, and some U's are higher than others," Oswald explained. "If you have a happy marriage, on average you've got a higher U. If you're richer, you have a higher U. If you're unemployed a lot, I'm afraid you have a lower U."

But almost everyone's happiness follows the same path.[16]

The happy coda to this research is that people typically rebound after midlife, a phenomenon buttressed by a growing pile of surveys and even neurological studies. Arthur Stone, a professor of psychiatry and behavioral science at Stony Brook University, decided to explore not just the good but the bad, not just short-term happiness but dissatisfaction with life as well. He found the same pattern. He and his colleagues surveyed nearly 350,000 Americans, breaking down well-being into positive and negative feelings.[17] They found that short-term happiness peaks at age twenty, dips in midlife, and then peaks again around age seventy.[18] When they asked about stress levels, people reported stress rising from age twenty-two, but then falling off after age fifty. The same is true of sadness and worry: They peak at midlife, and then, mysteriously, people become more cheerful and relaxed. In other words, positive emotions increase, and negative ones decrease, creating a "net" happiness gain after one's middle years.[19]

How does one square this plunge in middle-aged happiness with the good-natured embrace of the reversals of midlife that other researchers and I witnessed? How is it that people are both unhappier and more satisfied? David Almeida offers a clue. The researcher at

Penn State argues that there is a distinction between midlife "stressors," such as managing children and aging parents, college tuition and demanding jobs, and true unhappiness. True, sometimes the stressors pile up into an "overload." But this does not automatically spell a crisis. It is usually evidence of a rich life.

This brings me to my second major insight about midlife: Meaning trumps pleasure. People in the thick of midlife chaos may not say that they are happy in the moment. But they will say that their lives are *meaningful*, a measure that has its eye on the long game.

Well-being at this stage has a different texture than the pure exuberance of youth. You cannot live a few decades without taking some knocks, without seeing some friends and family perish and some dreams die. All this creates a mixed happiness, a certain poignancy that recognizes that things are not perfect, nowhere near as perfect as you thought they'd be when you were twenty-one, but they are pretty good.

It happens somewhere along the journey from nightclub to maternity room, from the laser-like focus on building one's career to the scattered attempt to juggle demands coming from every corner, somewhere between playing pickup basketball at a moment's notice to pulling a muscle on a one-mile jog—at some point, people adapt, shift their dreams, redefine success. And much to their surprise, people told me, they were relieved to trade their large ambitions for smaller commitments to family and friends. Alex Hamlin was an aspiring chef in New York who jettisoned his dreams for his wife and children; now he sells high-end food products to other chefs, and never once looked back. Dan Kasten left a six-figure job in Ohio after a messy divorce and moved with his two sons to Texas, where he earns a fraction of his former salary. But reversing his roles—parent first, professional second— has brought immeasurable reward: "Five years ago, I would have never imagined that I would be in this place as a completely different person and in a different role," he wrote. "Today, I can't imagine being anywhere else."

Few captured this magical transformation better than forty-six-year-old Dawn Stults. She graduated from New York University's prestigious Tisch School of the Arts with "absolute certainty that I would be a working actress (probably a very successful one) for the rest of my life." Now, with a Ph.D. in toxicology, she helps develop and run lung-cancer trials at a clinical research institute. She married for the first time two months earlier, five days before her forty-sixth birthday.

"So far, midlife is the best life yet," she wrote. "If I could go back in time and tell my certain-that-she-was-fully-formed self that she'd wind up in the suburbs thrilled to have a nine-to-five job with a decent salary and benefits, a job that required great people skills and no small degree of judicious conformity, she'd slit her wrists (dramatically, no doubt, after a profound, brilliantly delivered monologue about a well-balanced existence being a wasted one). If you are lucky enough and careful enough to be free of major health problems by midlife, be grateful and be a good steward. Right now is pretty good. It'll get hard again, and when it does I don't want to look back and realize I didn't value this time enough."

A NEW SORT OF CRISIS

It is true that few people suffer a textbook midlife crisis, defined as an existential fear about impending death and lost opportunities. For many, midlife is more mountaintop than valley. I have also observed that those who flourish view their new aches and forgetfulness, the losses and indignities and tragedies that mark this stage, with the weathered perspective of survivors. Usually, they laugh at themselves and derive meaning from what they have, not what they lack or have not yet achieved.

But I would be wrong to sugarcoat this stage of life when there is a large swath of people who are miserable. And while an external setback does not necessarily begin as an existential crisis, it can end that way. The culprit these days is often the Great Recession of 2008, which confirmed what many baby boomers suspected: For some of us, fifty-five is the new sixty-five. Midlifers are losing their jobs to less expensive, technology-savvy people twenty or thirty years their junior, and many do not have time to regain the ground they lost.

This stark reality washed over me as I read some of the most tragic stories from the NPR listeners. The essays defy the assumption that the economic recovery favored the "haves" (the college-educated) with jobs and damned the "have-nots" (those without college degrees) to a life of underemployment. Most of these essays came from the "haves." Their Achilles' heel was not education but age.

For example, one woman left her job as an executive vice president of a construction company at age fifty-four to become a lawyer. She could not find work in a law firm, even though she passed the bar in both New York and New Jersey. She has since lost her house to foreclosure. "I still cannot believe this is happening to me," she wrote. "I was literally sitting on top of the world and now I am at the bottom of it, selling off my jewelry and anything else I have of value and wondering what will happen to me."

Another woman wrote that her life "is pretty much over" at age forty-six. "I have no spouse or kids, just my career, which is now worthless because I am now too old for corporate America." She was unable to find a stable job in her industry, graphic design, nor could she find the kind of secretarial job that she landed just out of college, even though she applied for dozens of jobs. At the time she e-mailed me, she was working at Lowe's for ten dollars an hour. When I checked back a year later, she wrote, "Unfortunately, my life has gotten worse." She had lost her home and moved into her mother's basement.

One man had a master's degree in urban planning and a job he loved as a transportation planner for the State of Oregon. After losing that job, he said he applied for more than a thousand others. He, too, did a stint at Lowe's. Now he drives a city bus in Portland. He is also an adjunct professor teaching geography at the college level, a job he loves but that pays very little.

"I often wonder what I did wrong," he wrote. "What choice did I make that put me on this path? I just cannot figure it out. I have done everything one is supposed to do: go to college; study hard; volunteer; give back; work hard; be sociable; have passion; but somehow I have fallen into an abyss which has no bottom and no top."

When I described these stories to Elaine Wethington, who conducted the seminal study on midlife crisis in 2000, she nodded sadly.

"If I were to redo the study now with a bunch of forty-to-fifty-year-olds, I think I might find an extraordinarily higher estimate of [people] having experienced a midlife crisis," said the sixty-three-year-old researcher. "I think the people fifteen to twenty years younger than I am have much higher expectations for their lives and for success. But also, I think they've had a lot harder time in the job market. Their lives have been eventful in a way my life has been very stable. So I think the estimates would be much higher for having had a midlife crisis."

Wethington and other researchers cannot be faulted for missing the new crisis. To design a study, go out into the field, analyze, and then publish the findings in a peer-reviewed journal takes years. But the research has a more serious flaw than simply being in a time warp. It seems to me that a major premise of midlife research—that a midlife crisis is not an external event, but an existential concern about aging and lost opportunities—seems to totter under the weight of the recent recession.

While an external setback such as losing one's job may not *always* metastasize into an interior crisis, it often does. This comes as no surprise. For many of us, particularly professionals, one's career often does become one's identity: What you do is who you are. But as I read through the e-mails of those who had been set adrift during the recession, I noticed a pattern. Some people crashed and suffered serious emotional injury after losing their jobs (or, more rarely, suffering a health problem). But others drove over the setback as if it were a speed bump. These resilient people lost their careers but managed to find other work, usually not in their field of expertise, and almost always with a lower salary. And—here's the clincher—many of these people were, if not happier, then content, and even excited about the new adventure.

What distinguished those people?

Most of them possessed a key emotional advantage: love. They had a partner who loved them, children who needed them and gave them meaning; they had close friends or family who filled their lives. The gift, and responsibility, of a relationship provided a shelter from the wind. In contrast, many of the most distressed writers had no spouse or partner or children; they were facing the storm alone, on the open seas.

When Paula Mackin divorced, for example, she resumed her legal career to provide for her two adopted girls. "Sometimes I do wonder how I managed to find the strength, but having a seven-year-old and a two-year-old means you have to get out from under the covers, like it or not."

Gene Romano fell into a full-blown crisis when he was forty-seven. He was bored in a job he could not afford to quit. His house in the

San Francisco Bay Area was worth half its value after the market crashed in 2008. He would lie awake at night "paralyzed with fear that we would lose our house and become poor." In 2011, Gene's husband, Cliff, was diagnosed with a chronic form of leukemia. Two years later, they absorbed, improbably, yet another blow: Both men lost their jobs. Sometimes Romano fantasized about faking his death so he could start over.

"This is when I realized that his diagnosis *and* my crisis could not live in the same house together," Romano wrote.

"I needed to grow up and put my big-girl panties on. I stopped worrying about the house and its worth, and realized that *what* I had was still valuable to me. I realized that I had a great man in my life who was now sick, and if I lost him, it would be untenable for me. My advice to people who are undergoing the vacuum of self-worth that is a midlife crisis is to really focus on what you have and how you would feel if you lost it all. Find the precious things in life and cling to them.

"I am at the intermission now, the lights are blinking on and off, so I have a choice, either flee the theater, or go in and enjoy the rest of the show."[20]

Thus, I deliver my third key insight with trepidation and a disclaimer. The disclaimer first: Sometimes events in midlife, such as unemployment or illness, truly overwhelm a person, and the last thing I want to do is blame the victim. Still, reading through the stories and interviewing many of the writers, I realized that having a wider perspective, an investment in those you love, a willingness to be identified by your passions and not by your résumé, allow some people to unclench their hands and drop the burning coal that is a midlife crisis. The assaults of life can spiral you into an existential crisis. But they don't have to. You have a choice.

CLUES TO THE FUTURE—FROM THE PAST

As a journalist, I am fascinated (and moved) by these stories of malaise, hardship, joy, and resilience. It is helpful to glean insights from my fellow midlife travelers. But they are on the same ocean liner. I would like to talk with those who have already crossed the sea and can tell me which way the trade winds blow, how long the doldrums stretch, where the barrier reefs are, when hurricane season begins. As someone in the thick of midlife, I want more than the wisdom of contemporaries: I want to peek into the future. Given that the old tricks, such as clocking more hours at work or starting another diet, do not work as well as they once did—at least, they don't for me—I think it is worth studying the charts left by previous travelers.

Some of the most useful clues come from people who were born eighty or ninety years ago. Longitudinal studies, which follow a group of people through their lives, are a little like a game of *Jeopardy!* Researchers have the answers: They know how their participants lived and how they died. From those answers, they ask the questions. What lifestyle choices, such as smoking or drinking, led to an early death? What steered people to a meaningful life? Was it marriage, career success, or living a stress-free life? What were the habits or behaviors of people who seemed to keep their memories intact and stave off dementia? What, according to these nonagenarians, should we youngsters know about the future?

In 1921, Stanford psychologist Lewis Terman and his assistants searched the California public school system for gifted eleven-year-olds. They eventually selected more than fifteen hundred boys and girls (remarkably farsighted for that era) with an IQ of 135 and above. They interviewed the gifted subjects every five to ten years from childhood through adulthood to old age. The study has provided fodder for five books and dozens of articles. The most recent, *The Longevity Project*, by researchers Howard Friedman at the University of California, Riverside, and Leslie Martin at La Sierra University, overflows with fascinating gems about how to live a long life.[21]

Many of the insights challenge conventional wisdom. For example, the personality trait that best predicted a long life was not extroversion or optimism, but prudence: The prudent shunned risky behavior.[22] Another counterintuitive finding should bring hope to the overworked: Stress can lengthen your days. This seems akin to recommending a breakfast of bacon and eggs over fruit and yogurt. And yet stress can be central to flourishing, because it can be transformed by *engagement*. The "Termites" (as they were called) who were engaged in demanding jobs lived longer than those who hated their work or were bored by it. As Friedman and Martin put it, "Striving to accomplish your goals, setting new aims when milestones are reached, and staying engaged and productive are exactly what those following the guideposts to a long life tend to do. The long-lived didn't shy away from hard work for fear that the stress of it would lead to an early demise; the exact opposite seems true!"[23]

But more than a prudent personality, more than an engaged work life, more than intelligence or privilege or genes or any other factor, Friedman and Martin found that *relationships* lengthened one's years. Marriage was optional. In fact, they found that marriage was a double-edged sword. True, men and women in happy marriages did live longer. But people (particularly men) who were unhappily married or divorced generally died younger than those who never married at all.

Rather, what mattered was a person's social network: friends at church or at work, guys getting together to play golf or women meeting in a monthly book club. It was not the quantity of social connections but the quality of those connections that added years to life.

"We saw that over and above the number of connections and the frequency of interactions," Leslie Martin said, "that when those connections involved helping other people, reaching out, being actively engaged to do things for others, that was an added bonus on top of what we already see as quite beneficial from the social contacts themselves."[24]

THE MEANINGFUL LIFE:
THE DECATHLON OF FLOURISHING

Living a long life, it seems to me, can be a dream or a nightmare. What if you have no close friends or family? What if you have little meaning or purpose? What if life is a painful chore whose end, you hope, comes quickly? Personally, I care less about a long life than one that remains emotionally abundant, even as your physical abilities grow inevitably more circumscribed. Are there behaviors, or mindsets, that someone in the middle years can adopt to increase the odds of a flourishing finale?

There are. And who better to guide us on meaning than the Harvard Class of 1939?

The Harvard study began in the late 1930s, when chain-store magnate William T. Grant donated $60,000 to Harvard University to answer a question that had never been put to a methodological test: What predicts success? Harvard professor and physician Arlen Bock selected sophomores from the classes of 1939 to 1944 who seemed particularly promising. They totaled 268 men and, for the purposes of the study, remained anonymous, although some names slipped out: John F. Kennedy and Ben Bradlee were selected for the study; Leonard Bernstein and Norman Mailer were excluded.

William Grant and Dr. Bock had two different but complementary aims. Grant wanted to figure out who would make excellent chain-store managers. Dr. Bock wanted to unlock the secret of long-term health. Is it a "masculine body type," or how fast a boy could run on a treadmill? What about the wealth and education of the parents, or the longevity of the grandparents? What torpedoes success: a father who drinks too much, or a boy obsessed with (or indifferent to) sex?

"And then along came World War Two and everybody was interested in what made a good officer," George Vaillant told me. Vaillant directed the study for nearly four decades until he handed it off to a colleague in 2003.

The war posed this intriguing question: If most men started the war as privates, who would remain a private, and who would rise to the rank of major? The researchers assumed that the athletic men, the smart men, the privileged men, the young men who played on the fields of schools like Exeter and Choate, would distinguish themselves.

That was the first surprise.

"The people who came out majors were the people who had had warm childhoods," Vaillant said, "which my friends who work at West Point tell me is exactly what they find contributes to good leadership. To be a good leader, you have to love your men, and it's a lot easier to love your men if people have taken the pains to love you first."

This was the first inkling that something was amiss with long-held assumptions about success. As the decades unfolded, the Harvard men answered long surveys and in-person interviews every few years. Eventually, from a million little threads of data emerged a complex tapestry of what leads to a successful and happy life. It is not biology. It is not genes. It is not social privilege. It is not even IQ.

"What is it?" I asked.

"Five words," Vaillant said. "Happiness is love. Full stop."

He leaned back and watched my reaction, as if to say: Sometimes the answer is very simple, sometimes academic research gets it right. At eighty, Vaillant remains a strapping, tall, silver-haired fox. His eyes are keen, he laughs easily, he speaks like the Boston Brahmin he is. He flirts like a pro and with obvious delight. For the next two hours, we sat in his large, Baroque-style parlor room in his home in Orange County, California, as he unveiled the secrets to living a meaningful life.

Vaillant created what he called the "decathlon of flourishing." The decathlon covered a range of factors that would be a hallmark of success for one who reaches his ninth or tenth decade: From a mention in *Who's Who in America* and career achievement, to good physical and mental health, to being happily married and close to the children, to giving back to society and enjoying life in the later years. Once Vaillant had defined what constituted a flourishing life, he could then look for "antecedents" of flourishing—that is, the elements that led to a healthy, meaningful, contented old age.

By now, the study has spanned more than seventy years. A surprisingly large number of men reached their late eighties or early nineties, and Vaillant could make some safe conclusions. He was surprised at what did *not* contribute to flourishing: For example, watching your cholesterol after fifty, or career success, or family wealth did not help much. He was even more startled at how wide and deep was the trace of love. Love colored *everything*.

"The most important influence by far on a flourishing life is love," he wrote in his book *Triumphs of Experience*.[25] "Not early love exclusively, and not necessarily romantic love. But love early in life facilitates not only love later on, but also the other trappings of success, such as prestige and even high income. . . . The majority of the men who flourished found love before thirty, and that was why they flourished."

And yet, he says, baby boomers whose first marriage has failed can take heart: Many men failed several times before they found love that lasted.

"When I first started studying the men, they were just entering middle life," Vaillant said. "Divorces were not uncommon and I saw them—having gotten divorced myself—as evidence of instability and neuroticism and just bad capacity for relationships. And my editor [Llewellyn Howland] said, 'George, you're being much too hard on divorce. It's loving people for long periods of time that's good. It's not divorce that's bad.'"

His editor was right: By the time Vaillant wrote his final book, he realized that some of the happiest, and most fulfilled, men had married two or three times before finding lasting love.[26]

HOW TO REWRITE THE MIDDLE-AGE SCRIPT

Through the stories of Harvard men who loved and flourished or retreated and withered runs a deeper truth: Life is long. Neither childhood nor midlife is destiny. Genes do not predict a long and healthy life, but lifestyle choices made at midlife do. Men who are socially anxious grow out of it. Men floundering or uninspired in the middle of their careers can flourish later on.

As George Vaillant put it, "Even a hopeless midlife can blossom into a joyous old age."[27]

This is an important finding for those of us in our middle years: Second and third chances routinely present themselves if you keep your eyes open. Many of the Harvard men rewrote their scripts midway into their lives. One man, with the pseudonym Daniel Garrick, gave up his dream of professional acting early in life. As a forty-year-old college professor, he saw himself as "mediocre and without imagination."[28] But in his fifties, Garrick left his tenured position for the stage, becoming a highly acclaimed Shakespearean actor, most famous for his King Lear.

Another man, whom the researchers called Godfrey Minot Camille, was an "intractable hypochondriac" at Harvard, later becoming a doctor who "hated his dependent patients." But in his mid-thirties, he developed pulmonary tuberculosis. During his fourteen-month stay in a veterans' hospital, he experienced a religious and psychological rebirth. The young man who was so unappealing in college became devoted to his children and invested in his patients. Once in a flat marriage, by seventy-five he had found his true love, he could whip men thirty years his junior at squash, and he died from a heart attack at eighty-two while climbing the Alps. The funeral for this once-friendless man filled Trinity Church in Boston.

"Almost nothing is set in stone," Robert Waldinger, who now directs the Harvard study, told me. Waldinger added that not everyone in the study changed. And deciding against change—an introvert who chooses to work as a librarian instead of pushing himself to become an actor—was often the better choice.

"The people who seem happiest are the people who feel like they're able to express aspects of themselves that feel vital to them, that make them feel alive. It's not any particular path you have to take, it's being able to express the core of who you are."

I gazed at Waldinger. He was tall, lean as a runner, with a gray goatee and a shy smile. I sensed that Waldinger himself had experienced a midlife transformation, a shift in perspective, seeded and nurtured as he pored over the lives of the Harvard men.[29]

"What's meaningful in life is not about me as an isolated, separate self," he said. "What's meaningful is this vast continuum of life that

I'm just a little part of—and a totally interconnected part of. So that when I begin to worry about individual things like *Did I get this award?* or *Is somebody not giving me the resources that I need for this research?* I can more quickly come to that larger perspective about what's important in life and in the world: It's not little me, and it's not even my little research project, but a larger effort."

"So what are the one or two or three big insights about what predicts fulfillment at the end of the life?" I asked.

"Engagement," he said instantly. "Maintaining engagement with the world."

His answer surprised me. This was a new concept for me. When asked the secret of flourishing at midlife, other researchers had spoken of brain games to keep your mind sharp, or novelty to keep your marriage alive, or seeking meaning to keep your career emotionally rewarding. But now Waldinger was offering an insight that threaded through all the elements of life.

"Maintaining that kind of engagement," he said, warming to his subject, "means you're going to be in relationships. You're going to have social support. You're going to probably be generative, because when you engage, you notice things that you'd like to perpetuate. You notice people you'd like to help and nurture.

"When we think about older people who are vital, it's often because they're still thinking about the world and the future. They're keeping up with current events. They're excited to tell you about the book they've read. They're thrilled about the way the garden is coming in this year. They're engaged."

Waldinger was talking about people like my mother, a razor-sharp nonagenarian who reads every page of *The New York Times* and *The Washington Post* each morning, who has outlived all her contemporaries but entertains a steady stream of friends a generation younger.

Five days after Mom's stroke in 2011, she was still unable to speak, although it seemed that she was aware of her surroundings. That Memorial Day morning, the neurologist walked into her hospital room, trailed by several residents. After introducing herself, the doctor pointed toward the window.

"Mrs. Bradley, I'd like to ask you a couple of questions. See those green things on the trees outside your window? What are those called?"

Mom looked at her worriedly, and shrugged.

"That's okay," the neurologist assured her, taking notes. "Now, those vehicles moving down the road, what do you call those?"

Mom gazed out the window, focusing. Then she shrugged again.

"Ask her what her favorite Sunday-morning talk show is," my brother suggested.

"Mrs. Bradley," the neurologist prompted, "what's your favorite Sunday-morning talk show?"

"Fareed Zakaria, *GPS*," Mom instantly replied, natural as daylight. Mom couldn't care less about cars or gardens, but foreign affairs? The Arab Spring? The mission to capture Osama bin Laden? These events engaged her, which is why Fareed Zakaria's name sliced clean through the aphasia.

It took another few weeks before Mom could speak in complex sentences, but now her memory and name recall are better than mine. I know that one obvious explanation is that Mom had a good kind of stroke, a brain bleed that the doctors stemmed before it caused lasting damage. But somehow I think that Mom's engagement—with world events, with her children, her friends, her church—is a clue to her recovery. It is a message from the future about how I, as one passing through midlife, can thrive.

I began my research a little anxious about what I could expect from these middle years. Could I offer hope, or would the research point to an inevitable, dreary decline? But the more I talked with those who are studying and living these middle years, the more I saw that midlife is all about choices. Some people suffer a midlife crisis, but most do not, even those whose lives are strewn with tragedy and loss. Those who thrive shift their energy and attention from seeking happiness to finding meaning, from achieving success to cherishing people and paying attention to moments.

Those of us in our middle years have arrived where we are because of a million choices we have made to this point. We can no longer be anything we want—an astronaut, a color commentator for the Mets, or for some of us, a mother. But we have far more choices than a midlife-crisis culture would lead us to believe. Happily, we can make more informed choices now than we could at twenty-five or thirty-five: We can gather all those experiences that have shaped us; we can be guided by decades of victories and failures, and steer toward a second half of life that has at its center the stuff we're good at, the stuff that has lasting meaning, the stuff that brings—dare I say?—joy.

A good midlife is an intentional one. And so we make choices about how to approach our partners and friends, how to rethink our careers, how to absorb the setbacks, how to leave a footprint. Let's begin with that part of your life that has allowed you to follow me thus far. Let's begin with your midlife brain.

3.

CAN A MIDLIFE BRAIN
REMEMBER NEW TRICKS?

MARCH

Saturday, March 16, 2013

By seven-thirty on this cold, grim, slushy morning, controlled chaos is raining down on the Con Edison building in downtown Manhattan. A dozen cameramen, soundmen, and producers from Science TV, all dressed in fluorescent orange, are frenetically setting up their equipment in the nineteenth-floor auditorium. Fifty or so contestants gather in twos and threes, between rows of long tables. Some are laughing nervously, others are studying sheets of paper. The young men (they are almost all men) look to be in their twenties and thirties, with a large contingent from a nearby high school. Welcome to the USA Memory Championship, where brain trumps brawn, and thought triumphs over action.

I scan the room. I am not interested in the young brains, tuned up like Porsches. I am interested in the '67 Chevys, the middle-aged brains that would try to accelerate fast and hang on for dear life.

I spot Brad Zupp, seated at the end of one table. He looks younger than his forty-four years, ramrod thin, with a boyish face and rimless glasses. You could imagine him as the precocious math whiz in a detective show. I hesitate to approach him as he works through a deck of cards, flipping one at a time. An hour before the contest is to begin, he is already wearing earplugs and cupping his hands around his eyes to keep the world at bay.

I overcome my reluctance and walk up to him. "My brain isn't focused," he says, miserable. "I'm definitely feeling a little bit stressed about not being in the right mind space."

Zupp represents my deepest hope for middle age: He placed fifth last year. The contest, which began in the United States in 1998, challenges "Mental Athletes" to perform such arcane feats as memorizing scores of names and faces, original poetry, long lines of numbers, and as many as three decks of cards in the space of a few minutes. A woman won the first three years, but since 2001, the contest has belonged to young men.

In an interview the day before, Zupp told me he had always had a terrible memory for names and numbers. "If I called directory assistance and they said, 'The number is . . . ,' I would have to write it down because I could not remember it long enough to hang up and dial the number," he admitted. "The same was true for names and faces."

On the cusp of forty, Zupp took defensive action. He bought a memory book. He began to practice, a few minutes a day at first, and he made quick gains. Now his once-failing memory is his livelihood: He teaches elementary school children the art of memory, adding juggling and vaudeville comedy to keep them engaged. He does the same (without the juggling) for parents, small businesses, or any group that wants to learn how one can sharpen one's brain.

Zupp can memorize a deck of cards in ninety-five seconds. (The world record is twenty-one seconds.) More practically, he no longer forgets his keys: He imagines them as exploding and burning a hole in the table where he has placed them, a trick I now use. He still has trouble with faces, but he never needs a pencil when you tell him your number. Age has nothing to do with memory, he says. Effort does.

"Imagine if it were uncomfortable to brush your teeth the first couple times. *Ah, that's not worth it, I'm going to be fine when I get older.* And then, all of a sudden, five or ten years later, you go to the dentist and he's going, 'Well, we've got to pull all of these, because you haven't taken care of them.' It's that same thing with our minds."

Now, on the morning of the competition, Zupp's confidence has ebbed. He glances down at the cards in his hands, anxious to cram just a little more before the contest begins. I leave him to it, and look up to see Paul Mellor waving me over.

Mellor, fifty-four, is the other middle-aged contestant I am following. He has reached the finals before, and believes he has a chance today. He's chatting with the defending champion, thirty-year-old Nelson Dellis. Dellis possesses an improbable constellation of qualities for a geek: brilliant, disciplined, a mountaineer—he is about to make his second attempt at Mount Everest—with the build of a swimsuit model. I suspect that his choice of T-shirt, which fits snugly over his muscular body, is no accident. Cameras will be trained primarily on Dellis. He can memorize a deck of cards in forty seconds, 310 digits in five minutes, and can match 193 names to faces in fifteen minutes. He has been the person to beat two years running.[1]

"Do you feel prepared?" I ask Dellis.

"I didn't get much sleep," he notes, "but I feel good, just calm and excited to get started."

I turn to Paul Mellor.

"I'm excited," Mellor says, and he looks happy. "The brain is working today. So we'll see. But I'm as ready as I'll ever be."

❧

The day before, I had driven to Williamsburg, Virginia, to watch Mellor work his memory magic before an audience of 150 sales and marketing executives on their company retreat. Lean, six feet tall, with a Roman nose and silver hair, Mellor demonstrated what the audience so fervently wanted to believe: The middle-aged brain is a thing of wonder.

He opened his presentation by asking a volunteer to write down twenty words and repeat them one second at a time. A few minutes later, after he had told some stories and cracked some jokes—enough time to forget, in other words—Mellor rattled the words off with the speed and precision of a machine gun. Then he asked the volunteer to circle every other word, going backward.

"So for twenty, you're circling the mug, correct?" Mellor asked, certain of the answer. "Then eighteen is the beer, sixteen is the cushion," he ventured, gaining speed until he ended, correctly, with "Two was the car."

The crowd sat silently for just a beat, then burst into applause.

For ninety minutes, without a single note, Mellor taught them the secrets of memory, as he has with dozens of audiences. He teaches policemen how to memorize license plate numbers and crime scenes. He trains trial attorneys to remember depositions, the faces of jurors, and closing arguments without notes. He speaks to bankers, politicians, postal workers, and salespersons, anyone who needs to attach a face to a name and a relevant fact.

What I appreciated about Mellor's presentation was its practicality. I would wager few people in his audience cared about memorizing a deck of cards or a string of digits. But remembering grocery lists, or putting names to faces—those talents are as precious as rubies.

"There were many times I would meet someone, as soon as they said their name, I couldn't recall it," he told the audience. "And you're thinking: *Darn it!* Has that ever happened to you?" he asked, as the crowd nodded knowingly.

If you want to remember a name, Mellor said, repeat it, and use your imagination. When he meets a Walter, he mentally throws him against a wall. Roxanne conjures up the Police song. Julie is draped in precious jewels. Tony is an award—but be careful not to call him Oscar.

"I truly believe that memory can improve with age," he concluded, and the room seemed to heave a sigh of relief.

Mellor's memory isn't perfect: He admits that he forgets where he puts his glasses and whether he set the security alarm when he leaves the apartment. He recalls once looking frantically for his cell phone before realizing he was talking on it.

And yet, when he concentrates, he will always remember your name. (I am *Barb*ed wire, Ben *Bradlee, Haggarty* pants.) He doesn't need a list for grocery shopping or paper to jot down your phone number. He remembers Bible verses, gives talks without notes, and of course, can memorize more than a hundred digits in five minutes.

"If you could swallow a pill that would improve memory, that line would stretch around the globe," Mellor said. "The answers to our memory deficiencies are already in our head. We have the greatest computer system that sits on top of our shoulders, but we're not taught how to apply it."

THE TRIUMPH OF THE YOUNG

At precisely nine a.m., the contestants are handed several sheets of paper with 117 faces and names under them. They have fifteen minutes to etch the names and faces in their minds; then they are given sheets with only the faces (no names) in a different order. Their mission is to fill out as many names as possible.

I watch my middle-aged contestants. Brad Zupp with his furrowed brow, slow but careful. Paul Mellor looking relaxed, pencil poised over a face. By contrast, Nelson Dellis scribbles names as fast as if he were taking down dictation.

"It's really comforting," Dellis tells me afterward, "when you get it perfect, it's like, so smooth, just like everything is in sync. It's a good feeling."

Mellor confesses he has performed better in the past. "I'm not going to be one of the top bananas," he predicts, laughing. "But there's always a free lunch, you know, so you can't beat that."

If Mellor is philosophical, Zupp is devastated.

"My processing speed has slowed down," Zupp confesses. "I know that I think more slowly than I did when I was in my thirties."

I watch as things go swiftly downhill for my middle-aged compatriots. By morning's end, after memorizing numbers and cards and poetry at breakneck speed, Mellor, Zupp, and all the other middle-aged contestants have been eliminated. Nelson Dellis is the runaway favorite as the competition moves into its final rounds.

The finals belong to the young, as one might expect in a competition that requires processing speed: two high school students, two college students, four other men no older than thirty-six. During the finals, the men memorize one or two decks of cards. Then, in what is probably the only made-for-TV moment, the contestants dramatically take turns announcing the cards one by one. Soon only two are left standing.

Much to everyone's surprise, Nelson Dellis names a card and immediately looks stricken.

"That is incorrect," the emcee intones, and the audience gasps. Really gasps, as in the movies.

Dellis's downfall was not processing speed, but ambition: He tried to memorize two decks and confused them. The crowd waits in stone silence as Ram Kolli, shaken by Dellis's fall, tentatively recites the final card.

"We have a new champion," the emcee announces, and Kolli grins. He is thirty-two.[2]

A few days ago, I was at home, preparing for my trip to New York City. In the late afternoon, I heard a tentative knock on the side door. One of the men who had been repairing our roof stood there, looking slightly embarrassed—for me, as it happens. He pointed to my car.

"Your car never stop," he observed.

I followed his gaze to the Honda. It was vibrating. I had left the car running for nearly four hours, burning through a quarter tank of gas and, since the radio was on, three NPR programs. *All Things Considered* was halfway over.

If this were the exception, I might have found it funny, as I did the first time I left the car running all day in NPR's garage. But these days, I am fighting a guerrilla war with a wily enemy: my forgetful brain. The little amnesiac in me is always finding a clever new way to forget; it is always one step ahead as I wage the last war. Leave my prescriptions in the hotel room in Phoenix? Fine, from now on, I'll scour the bathroom before checking out. Forget my coat when exiting the flight to Atlanta? Fine, I'll triple-check the overhead bins. Still, I could never predict the next forgetful move.

Two weeks ago, on the way from my office to my car, I misplaced my favorite black sweater vest, a gift from my sister-in-law, Katherine. When I locked my office door, the vest was draped over my arm, along with my computer bag and purse. When I got home, it was gone. I did not stop on my way home. The vest simply disappeared, escaping under the lackadaisical gaze of my mind's eye. Another victory for my wandering brain.

Brad Zupp told me that he used to be distracted all the time. But now, after steady training, he can memorize nine decks of cards in an hour. To which I say: *That won't get me back my vest.* But I take his point. I just need to challenge my memory a little bit each day: Learn three new words, perhaps, or retain the name of the person I just met for two minutes, and I will be smarter. Let's hope he's right. I'm willing to give brain training a try.

STOKING MY WORST FEARS

I have heard that one measure of intelligence is how far back in your childhood you can remember. I have deliberately chosen not to verify that theory. I do not want to know the answer, since one of my earliest memories dates back only to third grade. Yes, I had lived eight years with only one previous event leaving a permanent trace in my brain: the time I fell from the apple tree, which hurt. I was four. But most of the time, I daydreamed. The real world, involving times tables and SRA Reading Labs, was an overexposed photo.

Here's what I remember about that day in third grade. I am sitting in a classroom on a Saturday morning, taking the SSAT test to qualify for a private school. The principal of my public school had informed my parents that I was failing, and I might need a "special school." My parents refused to believe it. I just needed a smaller class size and a stricter teacher, they reasoned.

"You may begin," the proctor announced on that cold, early-spring day. I picked up my No. 2 pencil. I answered the first question, and the second. Then I noticed something out of the corner of my eye. *Is that a robin?* I wondered, gazing out the window. *And are those baby robins? I wonder if they'll try to fly . . .*

"Put your pencils down," the proctor ordered. I had completed two questions but had spent a marvelous hour spinning out the lives of my new friends, the robins.

I was fortunate that my parents resisted the principal's pleas to hold me back a grade or find a school more suitable for someone of my apparent IQ. I was fortunate because my father helped me understand my homework, believed in me, and prayed for me every day. I was fortunate, because Mrs. Sales, my fourth-grade teacher, would see me struggling, put me on her lap, and declare, "I *know* you know what nine times seven is." And soon I did. The fog dissipated, the daydreams receded, and I began to excel—but only because I outworked everyone else. I became convinced that any success I might have, in college or graduate school, at *The Christian Science Monitor* or NPR, boiled down to one fact: If I worked really hard, I could outperform my IQ.

This is the psychological baggage I brought with me into the laboratory at the University of Maryland one day in April. A few weeks earlier, I had read about the work of two Swiss brain researchers. Susanne Jaeggi and Martin Buschkuehl, who happened to be married, were teaching just a few miles from my home. In 2008, they had upended long-held convictions about intelligence. Most intelligence researchers believed that a person's natural or "fluid" intelligence is determined by genes and set at an early age. The Swiss researchers believed that a person's fluid intelligence is malleable and can be increased with training. I wanted to test out their theory. I wanted to see if brain training would lift my IQ.

They were game. They explained that I should come to their lab for a battery of intelligence tests. At the end of the day, they would give me a computer thumb drive with a brain-training game on it. I would practice for at least twenty sessions over the next month, and return for a second set of tests. These would show whether the brain training had raised my IQ.

I barely slept the night before my first visit, convinced that I would soon be revealed as a dim-witted impostor living in an intellectual house of cards. I failed the first (unofficial) test: finding my way to the laboratory. I had to call the lab manager, Ally Stegman, to find me.

Ally would guide me through a morning of cognitive tests. She was in her mid-twenties, petite, with long brown hair and bangs, and a wide smile that quickly put me at ease. She led me to a windowless room, and we began a series of anguishing tests that measured my reasoning ability, my ability to reorient objects in space, and my ability to remember increasingly long strings of digits and letters.

Two of the tests are seared in my mind. The Advanced Progressive Matrices, or Raven test, shows several boxes with patterns and one blank box; you try to figure out the pattern that is missing. It is the gold-standard test of fluid intelligence, a favorite of elementary schools and the military. As I struggled with this test of basic intelligence, all of my insecurities from third grade crashed down on me. I muttered to myself, reasoning out loud, hugely embarrassed at my performance.

Then Ally described a "more challenging" test, called the Bochumer Matrices Test (BOMAT). She pushed a small sheaf of papers in front of me, and when I flipped over the page for the first problem, I saw fourteen complicated designs, with one blank spot where a design should be. A dizzying combination of squares, circles, arrows, triangles, and crosses stared up at me. My task was to figure out the missing pattern. Ally explained that the problems could be solved horizontally, vertically, diagonally, or you could merely pull back and intuit the missing design. I looked at her blankly. I barely understood the instructions.

She stood up and walked to the door.

"Don't worry if you don't finish them," Ally reassured me. "They're quite difficult."

With that, she closed the door softly and left me with my nightmare. I had trouble solving the first problem—it took about two minutes—and was completely stumped by the second one. I kept muttering and berating myself. Ten eternal minutes later, I was just beginning number five, on the verge of tears. I almost got up and left. Then I thought, *What if my life depended on this? What if this were an episode of 24 and all that stood between the United States and an act of nuclear terrorism was my performance on these tests?* That kept me in my chair, but did not improve my performance. When Ally returned after twenty-five minutes, I had completed only fifteen problems. I suspected eleven of them were wrong.

"Are there any easy tests?" I asked.

"No," Ally answered, smiling ruefully.[3]

Between tests, Susanne Jaeggi and Martin Buschkuehl, the intellectual powerhouses who are changing our view of IQ, walked into the lab to meet me. Jaeggi's brown hair, parted in the middle, flowed down almost to her waist. She was wearing brown glasses and no makeup, a brown V-neck long-sleeve T-shirt and green cargo pants. She is forty. Her husband, Martin Buschkuehl, is four years younger, a six-foot-five-inch, powerfully built man with premature gray in his short wiry hair. He is classically handsome, with a square jaw and kind eyes behind his wire-rimmed glasses. We walked to the college coffee shop and chatted. He speaks slowly and softly; she speaks in rapid fire.

The two met at university in Bern, Switzerland, and have been collaborating on cognition ever since. One day a few years earlier, Buschkuehl read an article by a cognitive neuroscientist showing that young adults who trained on a brain game for a few weeks improved a critical type of intelligence called "working memory."

Buschkuehl was skeptical.

"I told Susanne, 'Well, I don't believe this will work.' And then we decided, 'Well, let's try to replicate it,'" he recalled. "And we tried this on a first batch of people, and it actually worked. So we were really surprised by that. And that's essentially how it all started."

Most brain researchers, they told me, divide intelligence into two categories: fluid intelligence and crystallized intelligence. *Fluid intelligence* is your ability to solve new problems, to reason, to figure something out without relying on your previous experience or knowledge. It is raw intelligence; it rises through the twenties, but the upper limit is thought to be bounded by your genes.

"It's very interesting to try to improve because of its predictive force," Jaeggi added. "It predicts scholastic and professional success."

Crystallized intelligence, on the other hand, is all the stuff you have scooped up in school, work, and everyday life: vocabulary, general knowledge, specific skills, math and reading ability. Crystallized intelligence continues to slope upward through midlife and, for many people, into their seventies. *Jeopardy!* champions have lots of crystallized intelligence: obscure capital cities, names of Russian ballerinas, 1950s movie stars. USA Memory Champions possess a different flavor of crystallized intelligence, not by being natural sponges but by training their brains to recall decks of cards. My own fluid intelligence should have put me in a special school. My crystallized intelligence saved me.

For years, people have known that you can improve memory and many other cognitive abilities by practicing specific skills. For example, you can learn to memorize hundreds of digits, or improve "perceptual speed" by shooting down enemy spacecraft on video games. The reigning wisdom has always been that honing one skill does not help, or "transfer to," another. This is why Memory Champions remember decks of cards but not pictures of snowflakes, or why *Jeopardy!* champions know facts but cannot match names to faces better than you or I.

Jaeggi and Buschkuehl used to believe that as well. But as they trained young adults on a particular computerized game, they began to suspect that one could, in fact, grow fundamentally smarter.

Specifically, the young people improved their "working memory." Working memory is the deluxe version of short-term memory: It is the ability to hold the information in your head as you manipulate, juggle, and update it. It is not simply reading words, but understanding what they mean when strung together in a sentence. It is a crucial ingredient in fluid intelligence.

"We describe working memory as our cardiovascular functioning of the brain," Susanne Jaeggi explained. "It's so fundamental. It's an underlying mechanism which then helps all sorts of different higher cognitive skills, including fluid intelligence, reading comprehension, math skills."

If you can figure out a way to improve working memory, Jaeggi and Buschkuehl reasoned, maybe you could make people smarter at a fundamental, fluid intelligence level, just as exercising in one way can make you fitter in other ways.

"If you go jogging and improve your cardiovascular functioning," Jaeggi said, "you might profit on some other tasks that rely on the cardiovascular functioning, such as biking or climbing stairs or swimming."

This is essentially what they did. They improved the cardiovascular system of the brain. They asked young adults to play a computerized game for twenty minutes a day. Some trained for eight days, others for as many as nineteen. They tested them on various measures of fluid intelligence—the tests I had just endured—before and after training on the computer game. To the researchers' surprise and delight, they found that the participants improved not only on the game but also on all sorts of fluid intelligence tests. There was also a "dose effect": The more days they trained, the higher their scores.[4] In a happy development for middle-aged adults who fear we face an inevitable intellectual precipice, the Swiss researchers have since found that brain training raises the fluid intelligence of older adults (average age sixty-nine). And, like young people, the more they trained, the greater the improvement.[5]

When the researchers published their results in the prominent *Proceedings of the National Academy of Sciences* in May 2008, the world of cognitive psychology tilted on its axis. Critics claimed it couldn't possibly be true, and insisted it could not be replicated. But some very big names in the cognition business took them seriously, and soon others replicated the results.[6]

At this point, the controversy about brain training rages on. I can only report what happened to me.

At the end of the day, Buschkuehl handed me a thumb drive with the training game on it. Over the next month, I would "play" the game five days a week and return to see if I had raised my intelligence. I did not know the torture and insecurity that awaited me. I looked uncertainly at Susanne Jaeggi.

"So, can I make myself smarter?" I asked.

"Potentially," she said.

I wasn't so sure. Maybe young adults could get smarter. But I doubted my fifty-three-year-old brain could learn new tricks.

Tuesday, March 26

This was the week I needed to complete all my background research for this book. But nearly four months into my book leave from NPR, the end seems as remote as Botswana. Life intervened.

Now my brother and I are sitting in the waiting room of Sibley Memorial Hospital. It is near midnight, and Mom has been in surgery for three hours. Yesterday morning, as she was walking down the corridor in her apartment building, she stumbled, fell, and shattered her thighbone, which is what happens with ninety-one-year-old bones, I suppose. They are impossibly fragile, and now the surgeon is trying to paste together her femur like broken porcelain.

Mom's is the last surgery of the day. David and I are alone in the dimly lit room, working. Every now and again, one of us looks up from the laptop to tell a story.

"Have I ever told you about my first surgery?" Dave asks. I shake my head and lean back. The operation took place years ago, when Dave owned a consulting firm that specialized in the health care business.

"It was on my foot, and they put me under local anesthesia. I was awake, but loopy, and later I had the feeling that I had talked throughout the surgery. When I saw the surgeon two weeks later for a checkup, I asked him, 'Was I talking during the surgery?'

"'Yes, you were,' he said.

"I said, 'Really? What did I say?'

"He said, 'You seemed to be making a presentation about the future of doctor income. We were all very interested.'

"'Did I talk the whole time?' I asked him.

"'Yes,' he said, 'and at the end, you opened it up for questions.'"

We both laugh and laugh, in giddy relief after two days by my mother's bedside. It is a brief respite from the certainty that we have passed another milestone in our mother's descent. In my mind's eye, I take a snapshot: This is a good moment with a brother I adore; it is a lull before the chaos surrounding old age, with its tubes and beeping monitors and painful physical therapy, begins in earnest.

I have missed, to my great regret, the inconvenience of children, their habit of shredding your careful plans on a moment's notice. But I am getting a small taste of it as my parents, first Dad, now Mom, appropriate more of my emotional and temporal real estate. I am surprised at how wrenching it is to watch Mom fail, to contemplate her dying, to wonder what is best. If she emerges from the surgery and never quite recovers, never walks again, is that a good enough life for one so fiercely independent? I want her to end well. I have witnessed the opposite, the dementia and yelling and petulance that must seem justified when your mind, your body, your memory, your sense of control are being stripped clean. I don't want this for Mom.

And—I am ashamed to admit this while my mother lies on the operating table—I worry about my own stuff, about meeting my book deadline, about having to reschedule my interviews and reporting trips. How will I write a manuscript in between caretaking? I feel churlish for begrudging my mother a single second. She is the dearest person I know, my longtime confidante, but I know we are facing a forced march of recovery and physical therapy, long days at the hospital advocating Mom's interests and, later, daily visits to her apartment that will last who knows how long. Even though I know this is a rite of passage for most middle-aged adults, I am breaking out in a cold sweat.

The surgeon, looking exhausted, walks into the waiting room. The surgery went well, he said, but she'll be kept in the ICU overnight.

"How many breaks were there?" I ask.

"More than I can count."

He sends us home. We will need all the rest we can get.

THE (MIXED) STATE
OF THE GROWN-UP BRAIN

If you have passed the thirty-year mark, your brain is beginning to hiccup and cough a little. By forty, it stalls every now and then, and by fifty, you just hope it will start up when you turn the key.

"Almost every important neural aspect is declining with age," observes Mark McDaniel, a professor of psychology at Washington University in St. Louis.

Do you feel slower? Well, your synapses *are* firing more slowly. Wonder why you walked down to the basement? Your default network has hijacked your brain. Forget the name of your longtime colleague? It is tucked in some deep, momentarily inaccessible crevice of your cerebral cortex, only to leap out when you no longer need it. Well, that's reasonable: Your brain *is* shrinking, after all.

"Neurochemically, physiologically, transmission interactions—all those things decline with age," McDaniel says. "So it makes sense that we should expect a bit of memory decline."

And yet, McDaniel and other brain researchers remain cheerful.

"I think midlife is the best time of all for your brain," insists Denise Park, a neuroscientist and director of the Center for Vital Longevity at the University of Texas at Dallas. "You've reached a stage in your life where you have both cognitive resource—that is speed, memory, working memory, sort of mental horsepower—but at the same time, you have knowledge, experience, and judgment. So I honestly believe, in terms of your overall cognitive abilities, there's this wonderful blending of knowledge and cognitive resource that makes it probably the most efficient, effective time of your life."

Wow. I feel a little better. But before we gaze upon the beauty of our well-used brain, let's explore the un-Photoshopped wrinkles.

The first wrinkle is the tip-of-the-tongue phenomenon, in which the word is there, you know it, but it lurks stubbornly just beyond your grasp.

"As we age, we lose proper names," says Henry "Roddy" Roediger III, a sixty-five-year-old psychologist at Washington University and coauthor of *Make It Stick: The Science of Successful Learning.*[7]

"I seem to have trouble with restaurants that I know well. I'll be able to imagine the place. I'll know where it is. I can't think of the name. It will come to me in ten seconds, and not in one second, like it used to."

What is happening, brain researchers such as Deborah Burke at Pomona College believe, is a failure of retrieval, the final step in the three steps of memory.[8] When you hear a name (step 1: input), your brain files it in short-term memory, until it can find a better place to store it (step 2: storage), where it should, theoretically, be on call for immediate retrieval (step 3). However, the sound of the name—say, Angelina Jolie—and the information about the person are stored in different places in your brain. Her profession may be tucked in a space for "movie star in films often featuring assault weapons." There might be a little storage bin for visuals: "Gorgeous, high cheekbones, and enviably thin." A third drawer might be relational: "Brad Pitt and a gaggle of children." As you age, and particularly if you don't think about Angelina Jolie very often, the connection between the sound of her name and the other pertinent information about her weakens. Further confounding the picture: Names are arbitrary. Why should Angelina Jolie be called Angelina Jolie, and not, say, Eleanor Roosevelt? To remember her name, try priming your memory by working your way through the alphabet. Or better yet, imitate a Mental Athlete: Slap a pair of angel wings on her; then at least you would have a mental image that connects to her name.

Another midlife wrinkle is inattention. What about all those times you walked into the kitchen, stopped, and wondered what you came for? Or those mornings you ran around the house, late for work, frantically looking for your car keys? Or the moments you simply lose your train of thought? Roddy Roediger says this mindlessness has as much to do with the demands of middle age as the brain.

"I think twenty-two-year-olds don't have as much to keep track of as somebody who is forty, married, with two kids and a job," he says. "Part of it could just be greater cognitive load, if you will. You just have many more things in life to attend to. It means you're going to forget some of them."

"I think that is probably part of it," neuroscientist Cheryl Grady at the University of Toronto tells me. "On the other hand, we do know that there are changes in the brain."

One change involves the so-called default network, a network in the brain that allows your thoughts to meander off the reservation, away from the task at hand to the internal world of *you*.

"Let's say you're reading a magazine, or watching TV, and you're focused on that," Grady says. "Then a few minutes later, you find yourself mind-wandering. You are now thinking, 'Tomorrow, when I get off work, I have to go to the market and buy *blah, blah, blah*.' The default network is involved in that mind-wandering."

Grady has watched the default network in action in her laboratory at the University of Toronto. In a series of studies, she has observed what happens when young, middle-aged, and older people are put in a brain scanner.[9] Sometimes they are given a cognitive challenge, such as trying to recall words or pictures they had just seen. Sometimes they simply lie still, staring at the crosshatch on the screen above them.

When the young person is asked to concentrate, one part of the frontal lobe associated with mental focus lights up, and another part associated with mind-wandering (the default network) grows dim. Grady says watching a finely tuned young brain switch from focused attention to daydreaming and back is like seeing two children on a seesaw. When one child soars up toward the sky, the other plunges down to the ground. But in an older person, the default network never turns off, and the happy seesawing comes to a halt as the two areas of the brain are suspended in the middle, flailing for dominance. The middle-aged brain is somewhere between the two, not overwhelmed with self-reflection but not as focused, either.

Worse, there is no shelter for the aging brain. Everywhere, inside and out, distractions are clamoring for attention. A text message arrives as you walk into the kitchen, or you remember you have to call your mother; these divert your focus, leaving you wondering what you were looking for in the kitchen. This happens much less frequently to the young. Grady says that as we age, the "fan of attention" grows wider. Instead of focusing on the laptop in front of you, you pull back your gaze to see everything on your desk. Older people really do see the big picture, which can be helpful when creativity and wisdom are required, but can be disastrous when you need to focus.[10]

All of these distractions could happen because the switch, like an indulgent maître d', is letting everyone in, those with reservations and walk-ins alike. In a way, the aging brain is a loud restaurant, when really what you want is a quiet candlelight dinner.

Thursday, April 25:
First day of brain training

After a few glitches, I managed to upload the brain-training game from Susanne Jaeggi and Martin Buschkuehl. It is called the "n-back," with "n" standing for a number. Here's how it worked. My laptop screen was filled with squares. One at a time, random squares would turn bright blue—one, then another, then another. The challenge is to remember when I had seen that particular square lit up before. For the 1-back, I pressed the "A" key if the square that lit up was in the same position as the square that had just been bright blue: that is, one square earlier. Otherwise, I pressed the "L" key. For the 2-back, I would press "A" if the bright blue square was in the same position as *two* squares earlier, and "L" if not. It's devilishly hard to describe; it is even harder to do.

I did not enjoy the game one bit, not for one second. My heart raced, my hands grew slick. I suffered through fifteen rounds of agony. I performed well enough on the 2-back that the computer advanced me to a 3-back. But I blew that level, so I was dropped back down to the easier one.

I kept thinking, *It's okay. If you do badly today, you'll look great by comparison on day 20.* But I simply could not take the game in stride. I could not let myself fail. I pressed those keys with a brow so furrowed that a liter of Botox would do no good. Mercifully, it finally ended. I hope tomorrow is a better day.

PLEASE LISTEN CAREFULLY, IF YOU CAN

Before moving to the good news—and there is much to celebrate— allow me to wallow in one more problem that will be familiar to a growing number of my middle-aged peers.[11]

The first time I realized I might have a hearing problem was a week after our wedding. I had just turned forty-three. It was Monday morning, I was making the bed, and Devin was standing in the bathroom, shaving.

"The monkey's [indecipherable] in the sink," I heard him say. I thought about this briefly, then began running through the possible permutations: What rhymes with "monkey"? Chunky, funky . . . money (sort of)! What rhymes with "sink"? Blink, mink, shrink . . . think! How about something like "The money's on the dresser, I think." Which seemed a random comment.

This took a few seconds, long enough for him to wonder at my lack of response, turn to me, and say, "Did you hear me?"

I looked at him and thought, *Houston, we have a problem.*

"There is evidence that hearing loss can have effects on your cognitive ability," says Sherry Willis, an expert on aging at the University of Washington, who directs the Seattle Longitudinal Study, one of the most extensive studies of people across the years.

Hearing experts told me that many people develop hearing problems in middle age. Most people don't notice they are a little deaf until they've lost twenty-five decibels. A person who cannot hear well has trouble encoding the information in her brain in the first place. Later, when it is time to retrieve that person's name or recall the driving instructions, the information isn't there. I told Willis that I have a hearing problem, which may be hereditary—my dad was pretty deaf— or an occupational hazard, since NPR reporters spend a lot of time with headphones on, turning the volume up as they play back the ambient sounds and interviews they have recorded.

"If you're only hearing parts of words, it's like having a bad Skype or phone connection," Willis sympathized. "So it looks like you're not as bright as you once were, but part of your ability to gain and process information has been limited."

Even mild hearing loss can wreak havoc as time goes on. Brandeis University researchers found that adults with mild to moderate hearing loss could not remember as many words as could those with good hearing. I felt as if researcher Arthur Wingfield was reading my mind when he observed: "The effect of expending extra effort comprehending words means there are fewer cognitive resources for higher level comprehension."[12]

Happily, a solution beckons: Buying hearing aids can solve most of your problems, from annoying your relatives to staving off future dementia. But to me, it is an ignominious surrender to premature aging. I do not want shrill whining sounds coming from my direction as my batteries run down. I'd rather learn to lip-read. Now, please don't bring up the topic again. Devin.

Wednesday, May 1:
Sixth day of brain training

This is getting embarrassing. The game has switched from squares to objects: Roman numerals, beach balls, action heroes (of which I can identify virtually none). I briefly ascended to the lofty heights of level 4. Apparently I have a good eye for remembering pine trees. Then I blew it when trying to sort through the English castles, and found myself at level 3. I feel as if I'm walking through water; I simply can't react fast enough. I feel naked, that one part of my identity, my ability to be quick and, above all, accurate is quickly vanishing.

NOW FOR THE GOOD NEWS

With our brains shrinking and synapses firing more slowly, how can midlife be the sweet spot for the brain? As codirectors of the Seattle Longitudinal Study, Sherry Willis and her husband, K. Warner Schaie, have monitored the lives of some six thousand people, starting in 1956. Every seven years, the Seattle residents, whose ages now range from their early twenties to over one hundred, submitted to cognitive tests that measured memory, reasoning ability, and processing speed. They added brain scans in recent years. In this way, Willis and Schaie could chart their subjects' mental acuity as they passed from young adulthood to middle age to old age.

Willis says midlife, which she defines as forty to sixty, is a wondrously stable period for the brain.[13]

"People don't believe this," she says, "but if you follow people longitudinally, their reading ability, memory ability, number ability are very stable during midlife, and it's only during the mid-sixties that you begin to see what we call formative age-related change."

Certainly, if you compare a twenty-five-year-old with a sixty-five-year-old, you will find the younger person has a faster and better memory.[14] But the picture brightens considerably when you compare the same person across the years. In four out of six cognitive measures, the middle-aged person outperformed his younger self. True, perceptual speed (the ability to compare numbers, letters, patterns, and the like) and processing speed start to drop off early in life. But the researchers could not *measure* an actual decline in those abilities until a person was in his fifties. Other abilities continued to improve through midlife. Inductive reasoning—solving a problem, understanding novel concepts, seeing patterns—held steady until one's sixties; so did spatial orientation and verbal memory, that is, remembering what one has read or heard. A person's vocabulary, on average, held steady right into the seventies.[15]

This may seem small comfort in a workplace that puts a premium on speed, technical savvy, or dexterity in updating Twitter feeds from one's iPhone. Neil Charness, who studies expertise at Florida State University, has found that when learning a new technology, a sixty-five-year-old takes twice as long as someone who is twenty-five. But there is something that the twenty-five-year-old cannot download onto his phone.

"Knowledge," Charness says. "Knowledge is absolutely a critical variable."

Sometimes slow outperforms fast. Joy Taylor at Stanford University studied the tests of 118 pilots, aged forty to sixty-nine, who were trained on flight simulators over a three-year period. Initially, the older pilots performed worse than the younger pilots, but over time they surpassed the younger pilots and avoided more crashes.[16] Older air traffic controllers also called on their experience, or crystallized intelligence, to help navigate tricky conditions.[17]

Neuroscientist Denise Park believes the secret may lie in the way the brain adapts. A young brain, she says, is a well-oiled, efficient machine. It uses fewer regions of the brain to learn a new word or avoid a midair collision. An aging brain, which over a lifetime can shrink by as much as 25 percent in some regions, compensates by using more brain regions, more circuits, and both the left and right sides of the brain. Think of that additional neural activity as a scaffold.[18]

"Scaffolds are not ideal," Park says. "I mean, preferably you would have the beautiful new building, just like the scaffolding has been removed from the Washington Monument. But the scaffolding offered protection and support to the building so that the building could continue along. And I think that's what neural scaffolding does."

That is why people don't see a precipitous decline as they age, she says.

Park notes: "When you look at the aging brain and see some of the neural degradation that occurs in people that are behaving admirably, without any problems, the question that I often have is: How do we maintain as well as we do? Not: Why are we showing these declines?"

Neil Charness and others argue that so-called crystallized intelligence (the knowledge and experiences one has accumulated over a lifetime) gives an older, slower-thinking performer a shortcut. He first noticed this in chess, which is by all accounts a young person's game. An older chess master may not be as quick as a younger player, but he has seen countless chess patterns and at a glance knows what to do.

"You're not wasting your time on moves which aren't going to lead anywhere," he says. "For instance, grand masters would instantly dismiss a move that I might think of because they know immediately that it would ruin the pawn structure in a way I haven't considered."

Charness and other researchers note that some professions *depend* on pattern recognition. Doctors who have seen these symptoms before; salesmen with their thick Rolodexes and vast network of contacts; writers and editors with their sense of cadence and phrasing; managers who have learned to negotiate problems and personalities; lawyers and judges (look no further than the U.S. Supreme Court justices)—all these people draw on the emotional and cognitive intelligence that can be cultivated only by years in the field.

I recalled the surgeon who operated on my mother after she shattered her thighbone. When he finished the surgery close to midnight, the man who walked out of the operating room looked exhausted and impossibly old—too old, I thought, to be wielding a scalpel. But everyone had assured my brother and me that he was the best.

"Who would you rather do your surgery," I asked Charness, "a thirty-five-year-old surgeon or a fifty-five-year-old?"

"The answer is reasonably clear in the literature: You want somebody who has done that surgery thousands of times," Charness said. "They know what to do when anatomical anomalies show up. *I've seen one like that, so I know what to do,* as opposed to an inexperienced surgeon who might not. If I had a thirty-five-year-old surgeon who's got the latest surgical techniques and can make use of the latest robotic surgery tools or something very effectively, if they aren't doing an awful lot of surgeries, they may not be as skilled at recognizing things before they go wrong."

Monday, May 13:
Fourteenth day of brain training

Have I mentioned recently the instrument of torture called the n-back? Have I mentioned how I dread the game each day? I can rarely get above 4-back—that is, remembering whether the thing I'm looking at was the same thing or a different thing four items ago. I performed adequately at flowers, improved at trees, did passably with flags, but I was hopeless at distinguishing between various seashells, mountains, and Roman numerals.

I'm not sweating anymore. I just have a dull loathing. The further you go into the test, the more confusing it is: After all, you see two hundred beach balls in a row, and you get a little mixed up about whether the purple beach ball appeared three or four beach balls ago. On those rare occasions when I did get to 5-back, it was dumb luck: *Hmm, that tree looks familiar . . . Sure, I'll press the "A" key . . . haven't seen that one in a while . . . Press "L" . . . Saw that one in the last six or so . . . Okay, what the heck, I'll select it . . .* And then I'd watch with almost detached curiosity how badly (or sometimes, luckily) I performed.

I have no idea whether my brain is becoming faster or more acute. Honestly, I'm dreading my second round of tests. But I'm also looking forward to it. Then I can give my poor brain a rest.

QUANTUM MECHANICS FOR NONAGENARIANS

When I arrived at Mom's apartment for a visit, I found her, as always, sitting in her white chair in the living room, finishing up her dinner.

"Honey," Mom said, setting aside her plate, "would you please explain quantum mechanics?"

I settled into another chair, not oblivious to the fact that my nonagenarian mother was asking about quantum mechanics. I suspected this curiosity was sparked by an interview she had read with neurosurgeon Eben Alexander, who wrote about his experience of near death in his book *Proof of Heaven*.

"Well," I began, "let me tell you about quantum physics."

"No, I want to know about quantum *mechanics*," she insisted.

"I know, but I think they're basically the same thing. Anyway, even if they aren't, they're in the same zip code."

"Okay," she said, relenting, "tell me about quantum physics."

I told her about Heisenberg's uncertainty principle, and that at the quantum level—

"What does that mean?" she interrupted.

"It means smaller, subatomic, smaller than an atom," I said. "At the quantum level, things behave strangely. At the size of people, or planets, things behave like billiard balls, there's a predictable reaction when one thing bumps into another," I said. "But at the quantum level—"

"You mean, smaller than an atom?"

"Yes, that's right. At the quantum level, they don't follow Newtonian laws of nature. There are probabilities that a particle will act a certain way, go in a certain direction, but it's not certain."

I paused, and she was looking at me, concentrating fiercely. I felt a rush of awe for my mother, hanging on for dear life to understand quantum physics. I told her then about quantum entanglement, and Einstein's prediction of "spooky action at a distance."

"So if you smash two light particles together and separate them by a hundred miles, when you change the spin or velocity of one, the spin or velocity of the other instantly changes, faster than the speed of light," I explained. "It's as if, once they are connected, they stay connected. It's like they become the same particle or something."

Mom looked at me, absorbing this. "And what does all this *mean*, honey? What are the *implications*?"

"Well, Mom, some would say that everything is connected. Some would say that the fabric of the universe that connects everything is God. Or, if you don't believe in God, then consciousness."

She thought for a moment. "That's what Christian Science says," she observed.

"I know, Mom."

"You're very smart, honey."

"No, Mom, I'm educated. *You* are very smart."

When I described the conversation to Yaakov Stern, a neuroscientist at Columbia University, he said with admiration, "That's exceptional aging."

It is also, no doubt, cognitive reserve.

INVESTING IN YOUR FUTURE BRAIN

Cognitive reserve is the brain's defense mechanism against the ravages of age, a buffer against memory loss and dementia. It's the answer to the question: Given two people with the same level of

Alzheimer's disease pathology (the same amount of plaques and tangles), why does one person enjoy lively debates about the Arab Spring or quantum physics, while the other fails to recognize his daughter, asking the same questions over and over again in a twenty-second loop? Cognitive reserve is one answer to that mystery, but it is a mystery in itself. Is it more brain matter, or more neural connections? Is it the brain's ability to find an alternate route for information to travel when the plaques and tangles block the way?[19]

At this point, we don't know, says Stern, who is director of the Cognitive Neuroscience Division at Columbia University's College of Physicians and Surgeons. But we do know this: You can build up reserve throughout your life, and, like your 401(k), it's good to invest early and often. Of course, a person's mental acuity at age eighty-five has much to do with the luck of the genetic draw. But in recent years, Stern and other researchers have found that you are not stuck with the brainpower you were born with. And while you may be biologically destined to have the physical plaques and tangles of Alzheimer's disease, you are not necessarily destined to lose your memory or, indeed, any mental acuity at all. In fact, about one third of people whose autopsies reveal they had Alzheimer's disease showed no signs of the disease.[20]

There are precisely three times in your life when you can build up neural defenses: the beginning, the middle, and the end. When you are in school, when you are working, and when you are retired. You fail to do so at your peril.

At the beginning of your life, education is the elixir of a healthy mind at eighty. In one of the earliest studies about cognitive reserve, Stern and his colleagues tracked nearly six hundred people over age sixty for four years in the early 1990s.[21] He found that people with a college education were half as likely to develop the symptoms of Alzheimer's disease as those with fewer than eight years of schooling (which was not unusual for that generation). Working at a complex job—a manager or lawyer rather than a construction worker or janitor—also reduced one's risk of dementia by half.

"And if you put them both together," Stern says, "the people with low educational and low occupational attainment versus those with high [educational and occupational attainment] had almost four times the risk."

Since then, other researchers have found that a college education staves off memory problems for a decade or more.[22] As I read these studies, I raised a prayer of thanks that my parents had seen beyond my abysmal third-grade performance and pushed me through private school and college. But I do think it seems a little unfair that the decisions your parents make when you are still eating dirt on the playground can chart the course of your cognitive reserve seven decades later. If education is destiny, large swaths of the population could fall into a funk.

But wait! Marcus Richards, a professor at King's College, London, says our mental reserves can be boosted, or drained, at any time in life.

"You can contribute to it or take away from it right across the life course," he told me. "The myth that the horse is out of the stable is simply not true."

Richards directs the so-called 1946 British birth cohort study. The British government asked mothers in England, Scotland, and Wales who were giving birth in one particular week in March 1946 if they could follow their children's lives from beginning to end. Seven decades later, the government has amassed details about those 5,500 children: from teething and primary school, to health problems and exercise habits, to career and (for some) retirement. Researchers jotted down the children's IQ scores at ages eight, eleven, and fifteen. They believed that IQ would drive their lives with an iron fist. They were wrong.

"There's sometimes a fixed idea that our IQ is set in stone at an early age," Richards said. "But it's not. Obviously IQ is at the greatest degree of malleability in early life. But it continues to be modifiable later on."

IQ—and cognitive function as people pass from middle age to old age—adapts to your lifestyle. Take an adult education course: Add a few points to your cognitive bank account. Take up a hobby, such as playing the piano or learning Spanish: Add a few more. You go for a walk each day? Excellent: Exercise turns out to preserve your brain more than any other thing. But watch out for those hot fudge sundaes or deep-fried fish-and-chips. They could drain your future acuity like a sieve. In fact, each experience of education, work, or leisure activity (I'm not including eating ice cream in front of television) adds a different sort of cognitive reserve.

"Now, that's very important, because it suggests that even later in life you might be able to continue to impart reserve," Yaakov Stern says. "Which is a very hopeful message. You're not stuck if you don't have a great education or a stimulating job."

Stern and his colleagues discovered that older people who are actively engaged in life were much less likely to show signs of dementia.[23] The most engaged had a 38 percent lower risk of developing dementia than the least active. They even ranked them: The best activities for your memory are reading, visiting friends or relatives, going to the movies or restaurants, or walking and going on excursions. It is also cumulative: The more activities, the merrier you will be when you are trying to follow the conversation with your grandchildren.

Since then, researchers at Brandeis have found that people who had only a high school diploma but exercised their brains in midlife (reading, writing letters, attending lectures, filling out crossword puzzles) had memories as sharp as college graduates later in life.[24] When Mayo Clinic researchers tracked nearly eighteen hundred older people, they discovered that people with less education could delay dementia by more than seven years by reading, playing music, playing board games, and engaging in other stimulating activities. They took up these activities not in childhood but in middle age.[25]

My mother is exhibit A for developing cognitive reserve at midlife and beyond. Mom did attend college, although she says she was "lightly" educated, graduating from Emerson with a degree in drama. She stayed home to raise my brother and me. But in her mid-fifties, she began to work with my dad in his small company, which put on conferences for business leaders. She vividly recalls a flight to Europe, where they were introducing European business leaders to some American officials, including James Schlesinger. Schlesinger, who was then Secretary of the U.S. Energy Department, was sitting four rows up, and Mom wanted to ask him a question.

"So I went up, and Dr. Schlesinger didn't have anyone in the seat next to him," Mom recalls, even to this day a little impressed by her own chutzpah.

"And I said, 'May I sit down with you, Mr. Secretary?' And he said yes. And he had *The New York Times* in his hand. And I said, 'What is the one thing that I could do to help my husband in his business?' And he picked up the *Times*, and he said, 'Read every word of this newspaper. Read it every single day.'"

Mom, whose deepest news interests at the time were found in the *Washington Post* Style section, began to read everything. At first, it was tough sledding—*the Middle East is so complicated!*—but soon no day would be complete without *The New York Times*, the *Post*, *The Atlantic*, the *National Journal*, and CNN. I never debate her on public policy. She always has the nuanced argument. She always wins.

The message for you and me is clear. Use your brain and the sun could shine until the end. Don't use it at your peril. Or take it from my mom: The Middle East isn't all that complicated once you really study it.

TURNING BACK THE BRAIN'S CLOCK

As baby boomers reach the age of dementia, the race to find the potion that will forestall losing our minds is as fierce as it is varied, from brain-training games, to a blueberry-rich diet, to transcranial direct-current stimulation. But neuroscientist Denise Park and a growing number of others are zeroing in on a very simple idea: engagement.

Park divides her time between her lab at the University of Texas at Dallas and Rockville, Maryland, where she is working with the National Institute on Aging. She moves fast and talks faster, fueled, I suspect, by the many cans of Diet Coke I saw in her wastebasket.

Recently Park has been consumed with rolling back the symptoms of aging. It is simple but not easy: Challenge your brain, make it perspire and toil, the way you did when you were a student learning the Pythagorean theorem or French grammar.

"You should not be on autopilot," she says. "When you're on autopilot, you're cruising."

Park recently decided to test-drive her theory.[26] She recruited 219 people, aged sixty to ninety, and asked them to engage in certain activities (or not) fifteen hours a week for three months. She divided them into several groups. Some lived their lives as before. Others listened to classical music or did crossword puzzles, pleasant but not particularly challenging hobbies. Others socialized, going on outings and to movies. Two groups learned a new and complicated skill that would stretch their minds. She briefly considered dance—that has been shown to boost cognition in the elderly—but worried about injuries. She considered bridge or chess; they were both "competitive and people would fight." Finally, she settled on digital photography and quilting.

"Quilting may sound like a homey, not very challenging activity, but that's absolutely not true," she said. It involves mentally rotating abstract shapes, for example. Digital photography involves learning massive amounts of technical information quickly and applying it. Both of these hobbies tapped working memory, long-term memory, and other high-level cognitive processes.

At the end of three months, only the people who tackled the challenging activities improved their memories. Digital photographers won hands down: They made significant gains in verbal and spatial memory. Quilters, too, improved their mental acuity, though not as much, probably because quilting is hard at first but then becomes procedural. A year later, both groups still had better memories.

"I don't think it's unique to digital photography or quilting. I think the issue is mental challenge," Park told me. "If you're an expert quilter, I would actually not suggest you quilt all the time. You may not be challenging yourself enough. You need to do something that's unique, challenging, and interesting to you to maintain the commitment. And that can even be work."[27]

All this speaks to the triumph of neuroplasticity, the relatively recent idea that a person can learn new skills, sharpen his memory, even grow new brain cells, to his dying day.[28]

Thursday, May 23: Final exams

I have been dreading this day.

Happily, I managed to find the laboratory in the basement of the University of Maryland's Biology-Psychology Building by myself, which I hoped was a good omen. Ally Stegman launched me on the tests immediately, so that the researchers could tally my scores by the end of the day. I did feel more confident during some of the block tests, although that could be due to the "test-retest" phenomenon that be-devils researchers: You perform better because the test is familiar, not because you have fundamentally improved.

But when she left me in the room to do the Raven test, I sensed an elemental shift. The seconds seemed to tick by more slowly, and I felt I had more time to consider each puzzle. I finished almost all of them and thought I had gotten most correct. Even the diabolical BOMAT had lost its power to make me cry. I was buoyed: Maybe the brain training worked after all.

After the tests, while waiting for the results, I said, "Out of curiosity, Ally, how many n-back can you do?"

She hesitated.

"Thirteen."

"*Thirteen!*" I laughed, as impressed as if she had swished a basket from center court. That meant when Ally saw a particular English castle, she could remember if that was the same castle she had seen thirteen castles ago. "How can you possibly do that?"

"I just memorize a set of thirteen and compare it to the second set of thirteen, et cetera," Ally explained, "and since at those higher levels there's a smaller number of sets to compare them to, it actually becomes a little bit easier in my mind."

Ally called Susanne Jaeggi and Martin Buschkuehl with my scores. Moments later, they walked into the lab, grim-faced. I thought my worst nightmare had come true: I had done worse the second time. It has been three decades since I have fretted over standardized tests. I was seventeen again, opening the envelope with my SAT scores.

"I'm really nervous," I told them.

Martin Buschkuehl permitted himself a little smile. He showed me bar charts of my performances on each test before and after my month of training. On average, I had scored 18 percent better.

"Is that good?" I asked, relaxing a bit.

"That is good," Jaeggi said.

"Next drumroll," Buschkuehl said, and now he was smiling broadly. He flipped over a sheet of paper to reveal the scores for the Raven test, the gold standard of cognitive testing, the one where it felt as if time slowed down. Apparently in some cognitive way, it had.

"You improved by seventy-five percent," he said, and he looked like a proud parent.

"So what does that show improvement in?" I asked.

"This is a prototypical measure of fluid intelligence," he said, "so it's reasoning performance, solving new problems you haven't seen before."

"Your ability to solve new problems without relying on previously acquired knowledge like vocabulary or other skills," Jaeggi elaborated. "So it's very close to what people describe as 'G': your overall mental ability, which people have assumed to be highly fixed. But you improved seventy-five percent. It's pretty good," she added, with some understatement.

They said that such dramatic results, along with a 26 percent improvement in the harder fluid intelligence test, the BOMAT, probably cannot be explained away by retest effects.[29] They also said this showed that the working memory task—the n-back—had transferred to other, nonrelated measures of fluid intelligence, which in the parlance is called "far-transfer." But, they added, this was not a scientific study: I was an experiment of one, an illustration, and until they trained more middle-aged people like me, they could draw no conclusions.

I asked if they had been nervous about my performance: After all, it was their test results on the line.

"I was not worried," Jaeggi said. "You really trained very conscientiously, and took it very seriously, and we know that engagement with training is related to how much you improve."

"Well, you know, that has always been true of me," I said. "I outperform my IQ. That's always how I felt about myself. I'm not that smart, but I've done pretty well just through hard work."

"I think, in the end, that that's kind of our message too," Busch-kuehl said. "When you work hard, you can get better. I think that that's the story of our training."

"Yes," Susanne Jaeggi agreed. "You have to put effort into that and you will improve eventually, but you have to do it. It's not coming for free. And I think that's really one of the messages that we want to convey. Nothing comes free. You have to engage. But if you do, you will get something out of it."

4.

THE SHIFTING SANDS
OF FRIENDSHIP

Friendships at midlife are a little like a smoke detector. You need them in theory, but they can be a nuisance to keep up, especially if you are juggling children, aging parents, and a career. So you let them run out of juice. You don't really miss them until the house begins to burn and you wish you had a few firemen nearby.

For growing legions of baby boomers, friends serve as lifelines, surrogate families, a new kind of shelter in the storm. Historic numbers of middle-aged people live alone, single or divorced, scattered across the country, disconnected from their families of origin. Many live a solitary existence by day as well. The new economy, which favors younger, cheaper, technology-savvy employees, leaves more of us working as independent contractors or freelancers, without a workplace where we see colleagues each day and commiserate about yet another Redskins loss over a cup of coffee. Now science is showing that friends are the surest defense against one of the most ruthless killers: isolation.

All the research converges on one unshakable imperative: If you want to live a long and healthy life, invest in friends, particularly at midlife. Every evolutionary instinct cries out for trusted companions, and the more the merrier, because the more friends you have, the healthier, happier, and more mentally acute you will be, now and in your later years. We are wired for friends.

Monday, April 29, Charlottesville, Virginia

Friendship is easy to spot, but harder to define. We know the look of it: rushing to the hospital after a friend has had an accident; knowing how he takes his coffee (milk, one Splenda); dropping off lasagna after her father died, and then staying to talk, or not talk, but just staying. It seeps in, effortlessly, in small moments when you pick up the phone to chat, or in long stretches that ebb and flow over the years. It is intense. It is languid. We know what friendship looks like.

What does friendship look like in the brain? That is the question Cherie Harder and I are aiming to answer as we arrive at the University of Virginia on a cold April day.

The mastermind for this uncomfortable experiment is James Coan, an associate professor of psychology at the university and the director of the Virginia Affective Neuroscience Laboratory. A few years ago, he discovered that people in good relationships—marriages, partnerships, with siblings or friends—exhibit a neurological quirk. When they face a threat, their brains behave differently, depending on whether they are alone, with a stranger, or with a trusted companion. In fact, Coan can often assess how close a relationship is by looking at the activity of the brain.

This is why I invited Cherie to Charlottesville. For the past fifteen years, she has been one of my closest friends. We met at a dinner party where we were marooned with another woman who insisted on telling us a series of embarrassing personal stories. That awkward night forged our friendship. Over the years, we had seen each other through career trials, bad relationships, and harder breakups. She was in my wedding. She, like me, is serious about her Christian faith. She is one of the smartest friends I have, and she is game for just about anything. Cherie is the perfect candidate for a brain study on friendship.

At UVA, we are greeted by Casey Brown, the project coordinator for the lab. She leads us to a room in the basement of the psychology building, where several research assistants and MRI technicians are prepping the brain scanner. One technician asks me to remove my socks and roll up one pant leg. He scrubs around my ankle, then straps on a black anklet.

"We hook shock electrodes on your ankle," he explains blandly, "which allows the electricity to conduct to your ankle."

"Don't worry," Brown reassures us. "It's just a basic static shock. Like walking across a carpet and touching an electronics device. It's meant to be unpleasant, but not painful."

Jim Coan enters at this moment, a tall, lanky man with an appealing smile and a ponytail that has just a whisper of gray. He promises us that all the kinks are out. Gone are the days when the electricity turned on, but not off, giving one lab assistant a "very long shock." Coan says he submitted himself to the experiment a hundred times when they were developing the procedure.

Before sliding me into the brain scanner, Jim Coan explains that after they take a baseline picture of my brain, I will see on the screen above me either an O or an X. The O means that no shock will be administered. The X means that there is a 20 percent chance of an electrical shock to the ankle. Coan is not looking for my brain activity when my ankle is shocked; in fact, my head would probably jerk and render the image fuzzy and useless. He wants to see how my brain behaves when I am *anticipating* the shock. Will it react differently if I feel I am facing the threat alone, with a stranger, or with a close friend? To tease these apart, he will zap me under three conditions: holding no one's hand, holding the hand of a technician I have never met, and holding Cherie's hand as she stands awkwardly just outside the brain scanner. How my brain behaves will indicate how much I trust Cherie to help me when I am feeling threatened.

They slide me in and the machine begins its deafening clanging. I am rather enjoying myself, unconcerned about the static shocks—how bad can it be?—when the first shock shoots electricity into my ankle for what seems like thirty seconds (although I was told it's less than a second). *Whoa!* my mind howls silently, as my electrified leg bounces up of its own painful accord. *That hurts like hell!* Now my brain shifts into serious threat mode, sparking an existential dread whenever I see the red X's. There are a lot of them, too. I thought it would never end.

Afterward, Brown and Coan try to hide their smiles as I walk into the control room with Cherie.

"I would like to say, for the record, that was not like walking across a carpet and touching a piece of metal," I observe, trying to regain a little dignity.

I fail at this: The researchers burst out laughing.

OUTRUNNING, OR OUTSMARTING, THE BEAR

Jim Coan began to wonder about the neurology of relationships as a young assistant in John Gottman's Love Lab. Gottman, a professor of psychology at the University of Washington, would invite couples into his laboratory, ask them to chew cotton balls to measure their cortisol (stress) levels, and wear sensors on their fingers so that the researchers could measure their physiological arousal. Then the researchers would introduce touchy subjects and provoke a fight, which was "shockingly" easy to do, Coan notes. After a few minutes' observation, Gottman and his colleagues, including Jim Coan, could predict with more than 90 percent accuracy whether or not a couple would divorce.

Coan says the couples that survived had learned a secret: In the heat of battle, one would soothe the other, break the tension with a joke, a gentle touch on the knee, or an apology. Once that happened, "their physiological arousal would decrease," Coan explains. That urge toward fight or flight simply dissipated when the person was with someone he or she trusted.

The central switch among emotion, biology, and relationships is, of course, the brain. Coan believed that the brain's reaction to a threat would vary depending on whether the person is alone or with someone else. It depended, in other words, on the way our brains respond to each other.

Several years ago, Coan developed an experiment to test his theory, the one I had just suffered through, with X's and O's and electrical shocks.[1] In the first part of the study, the brain acted according to script: When the person anticipated the electric shock alone, the parts of the brain that process threat or danger "lit up like a Christmas tree," and the prefrontal cortex, which regulates your emotions, worked overtime. When the person was holding a stranger's hand, the parts of the brain associated with mobilizing your body, such as heart rate and general physiological arousals, seemed a little quieter. The brain considered the situation less threatening because of the presence of another person. This is just what Coan predicted.

But when Coan looked at the brains of people holding a trusted partner's hand, all his predictions fell apart. He had expected parts of the prefrontal cortex to become more active, he says, "because that portion of the prefrontal cortex was going to be telling other threat-responsive portions of the brain to quiet down."

Instead, the reasoning part of the brain grew quiet, as if the brain did not think there was anything to worry about.

"It really caused a kind of crisis, because I had no idea what the alternative explanation might be," he says. "I was like, 'Well, it was good while it lasted, but I guess I should go back to roofing.'"

But as Coan slid more and more couples into the scanner and arrived at the same result each time, he had an epiphany.

"This one finding that we thought was a giant error is turning out for us to be a real discovery," he says. "It's really led us down a whole different path of how we understand the brain, how we understand the way that the brain evolved, and how we understand the way the brain is designed to function in a social context."[2]

Coan says we can trace this surprising brain response to our ancestors. Let's go back to the year 10,000 B.C. Your hunter-gather ancestor is strolling through the woods. He comes face-to-face with a bear. If he is alone, his brain is screaming *Run run run!*—because he is safe only if he can outrun the bear. If he sees a stranger from another tribe nearby, his brain relaxes a little—because now he is safe if he can outrun the stranger. And if his hunting buddy is with him, his brain says it is a whole new ball game. The bear is no longer a threat. The bear is tonight's dinner.

Fast-forward ten millennia, and people in midlife find their brains reacting similarly: There is comfort and safety in knowing that you are not alone when trouble (in whatever form) arises.

Coan says that, depending on what my brain scans show, it is possible Cherie altered the way I viewed the electrical shock, moving it from the *Get me out of here!* category to the *That's not so bad* class. My brain may be less rattled by the prospect of pain, he says, "not because you're regulating more effectively through the prefrontal cortex, but because you're not perceiving much of a threat at all."[3]

This all sounds a little neuro-technical. But doesn't it ring true?

Raising kids is simpler with a reliable partner, not just because two juggle logistics better than one, but also because you breathe easier knowing someone is in your corner. I greatly prefer reporting trips with a trusted producer: You split up the work, you share the burden, then you grab a glass of wine.[4] Life runs more smoothly with two, and now we know why: Our brains are wired to make us dependent.

THE TIMBRE OF LONG FRIENDSHIP

For the sake of argument—because no one has tested this yet— let us assume that friendship looks the same biologically and neu- rologically across one's lifetime. After all, it feels easier to face the schoolyard bully when you have a buddy, to survive the dramatic breakup in college if you have a loyal roommate, to approach the joy and terror of childbirth if you have a friend who has lived through it and can show you the way.

But friendships that survive into midlife acquire a different tenor. You hear more minor keys, and each year the score grows in complex- ity. These friendships no longer center on promotions and parties and new loves. If your friendships outlive the innocent days of your twen- ties and thirties, you will experience birth and death, love and betrayal, accomplishment and failure. This, at least, is what I have experienced.

Jody Hassett and I met twenty years ago, two thirty-something women trying to stay afloat in the dangerous seas of hard-news jour- nalism. Jody was traveling the world as CNN's chief foreign policy producer; I was mired in reporting on legal scandals, covering the Justice Department for NPR. We both wrestled with childlessness, hav- ing sacrificed practically every minute and drop of energy to the vora- cious appetite of the news business. My childlessness dilemma resolved when I gained a wonderful stepdaughter; Jody's, when she and her husband adopted a boy from Kazakhstan. Jody was the first to arrive at the ICU after my mother's stroke. I edited the eulogy she wrote for her father's memorial service. She trained me in the art of media interviews when my first book came out. Mine was the placeholder voice she used for her first documentary. We serve as each other's shock absorbers as we bounce through the transitions of midlife.

I detected this theme in the stories of scores of people who wrote me about their long-term friendships, thanks (once again) to a request I placed on NPR's Facebook page. Reading through the e-mails, I realized there was not a carefree story in the lot. Divorces, abusive husbands, death of a spouse, the murder of a child, attempted suicides, and a parade of illnesses, from cancer to Parkinson's to Alzheimer's disease—these shaped the landscape of midlife friendships. Indeed, what gave these friendships their staying power, what made them worthy of note, was the trauma, loss, pain, and in the middle of all that, the presence of someone who gladly shared the burden, even at personal cost.[5]

People also spoke of the singular nature of long friendships: They are voluntary, not obligatory, and in that lies their freedom and joy. Lee Lewis Hoegler met Lisa when they were fifteen. They both lost their mothers to cancer much too young; they walked together through marriage and divorce, legal troubles, health problems, and career shifts. Lee says friends like Lisa occupy a unique category.

"These people are not your relatives: They are not bound to you by genes, or contract, or marriage, or social convention," Lee wrote. "They have chosen you—and that makes all the difference. They know when to call and not text—that it's the voice that matters. They know what you need to hear and when you need to hear it, and when to just listen. They know exactly what scarred you and what healed you. But they also know every inside joke, every tic and twitch, every one-liner, and every memory that will make you well up and smile wide. Lisa and I joke about growing old together—two old chicks in a condo somewhere. It's not really a joke."

Midlife friendships also demand effort, because they are so easy to neglect. Chris Cook met his three best friends in sixth grade. Chris, Frank, Jeff, and Gregg spent the next six years sneaking beers and fighting over girlfriends, before three of them joined the Air Force together. They all returned to Oklahoma City, and their friendship was the one constant through the maze of adulthood, jobs, marriage, kids, divorce, and death of parents. "We'd been friends so long that it didn't make a difference if we saw each other every day or every week or every month," Chris told me.

On January 4, 2008, Jeff was driving to Chris's house for a party; on the way, he suffered a fatal brain aneurysm and drove off the road.

The three surviving friends "decided we weren't going to take our friendship for granted anymore," Chris said. "That was a kind of wake-up call that these people aren't going to be around all the time and you need to cherish the time you have with them." Now they meet most Friday nights, for dinner or a beer. They look out for each other. "My buddy Frank has been harassing me about getting healthier," Chris said. "He said, 'Dude, I want to grow old with you.'" Chris has lost fifty pounds.

These and other stories evince the yin-and-yang nature of close friendships, a light and dark I would soon experience firsthand. It's a gift to have a friend who braces you during the hard transitions; but that steadfastness can become a burden, and that friend a reminder of sadness and pain. Or, if the strength of friendship lies in its voluntary nature, so does its fragility. You can always walk away. And while the investment in a friend usually repays many times over, the care and feeding can be exhausting, and well, isn't life already hard enough?

Still, the real fruit of friendship is obscured at midlife. You see the early foliage—in the support, the companionship, the occasional sacrifice—but the crop is harvested later. Sickness, however, moves up the schedule. In sickness you catch a glimpse of how friendship enriches your soul—and your body.

IN SICKNESS AND IN HEALTH

For years, Lisa Howey Trevor drew up wills and estates as a partner in her Chicago-based law firm. Every now and again, she says, she would receive an urgent request.

"People would come in and say, 'Wow, I've just been diagnosed with cancer, and they gave me three weeks to live. I need to get my documents together.' I have been there with people and grieved with them and saw the shock in their eyes and the disbelief. It is hard to believe." She pauses. "Even now, even with the pain, sometimes I think: *Really? Can this really be happening?*"

Lisa is dying of cervical cancer. She looks healthy: athletic, slim, with shoulder-length brown hair, appearing younger than her fifty-three years—that is, until she moves, slowly and carefully. We are sitting in her home in Lincolnshire, Illinois, about an hour north of Chicago. Late tonight, Lisa and her husband, Richard, will drive to the Mayo Clinic, with the hope that her doctors will agree to a long-shot treatment. One by one, Lisa is running out of options. What she is not running out of is friends.

As we talk, five of her closest friends arrive. These women bonded in fifth grade. In one way, they defy the predominant model of friendship, which asserts that people befriend others who are like them, economically, socially, educationally, and politically; it's called "homophily." Career-wise, this is not a homophilous group. Among the five friends, Janet Larson delivers mail, Donna Smith coordinates curricula at Northern Illinois University, Lisa Eckert is a graphic designer, Mary Ellen Hull works at her church, and Kathy Konstan teaches fifth grade. Yet they do reflect another, powerful theme: At midlife, people gravitate toward those who knew them in their purest form, when they were children.

"Today, I was able to actually pull up the MRI results," Lisa says, as they settle around the family room. "So, the bad news is, they're seeing more cancer. The good news is, it seems like it hasn't grown a whole lot." Then she describes the various options, including a new treatment she's researched.

"This is what happens when you're this smart," Janet quips. "Me, I'd go: 'Doctor, could you draw a Pictionary kind of thing? Like, okay, here's the bladder and here's your ovary?' Honestly, Lisa, you're so amazing."

"I'm trying to save my life here," Lisa laughs, "so I figure it's worth the education."

The room falls silent for a beat. They can never escape it, this lengthening shadow.

The prospect of death can scare people away; it's too hard, too near. But for Lisa's elementary school friends, death pulled them into the center, and their shared history became the thing they clutched as the disease progressed.

"They weren't afraid of me," Lisa says. "There isn't anything you can say to make it right or make it better. But they didn't desert me. I think that takes real courage."

On May 11, 2013, unknown to Lisa, the women threw a fund-raiser at Janet's house. Vendors sold candles, jewelry, and chocolate fondue, putting their proceeds into a purple bucket with Lisa's name on it. They raised $2,500. With the money, Lisa took her family to New York, where they met Matthew Broderick after a Broadway show.

"It's bittersweet, because, in a million years, I wish we didn't have to do that," Janet says. "We all want Lisa to be healthy. I just wish we could . . ." She hesitates.

"Cure this," Mary Ellen says.

"It sucks," someone else mutters.

"Do you think your friends have prolonged your life?" I ask Lisa.

"Absolutely," she says. "There are days, if there weren't anyone in your ear saying, 'C'mon, fight!' you would just say, 'Okay. It's not worth it.' It's hard. Sometimes, you don't have it in you to even fight for yourself anymore, but you will fight for the others. What can be done, what other treatment haven't I considered? There are clinical trials at the first of the year, so if I can make it that long . . ."

Lisa was not healthy enough to participate in new clinical trials. A few months ago, she sent me a text, asking if I had written about her yet. I told her I was racing against my deadline. I would send it as soon as I could. I learned then she had moved into hospice. Tragically, her deadline would arrive first.

No one can possibly know if Lisa's grade-school friends gave her extra weeks or months. You can never tell in an individual case, but the evidence suggests they may have extended her life. They surely increased her happiness.

THE OVERLOOKED ELIXIR

For someone like me, who has not always been an attentive friend, who has often allowed career and family to consume most of her emotional resources, Rebecca Adams delivered some chilling news.

"It is much more important for people to have robust friendships than it is for them to have close family relationships," she told me.

Adams, a sociologist at the University of North Carolina at Greens-boro, is one of the few academics who have studied adult friendships. Friends are kind of the Swiss Army knife of relationships: They do everything, boosting your health, lengthening your life, preserving your memory, helping your career, gentling the aging process.

Initially, I had trouble believing this, given the evidence that hap-pily married couples live longer. How could friendships hold a candle to the overwhelming firepower of family relationships? But the deeper I dived into the research—which is, admittedly, still scant—the better friendship looked. Sure, it plays the role of Dr. Watson, plodding and unexceptional next to Sherlock Holmes. But remember, if Holmes was brilliant and charismatic, he was also a cokehead. In the same way, friends bestow a purer, less complicated emotional and biological re-ward than family does.

"Family includes a lot of people you might not get along with or you might not have chosen to have in your family," Adams explained, and that can lead to stress and other deleterious effects on the body. "But with friendships, you tend to keep the ones that actually benefit you, and so of course they have a bigger [beneficial] impact on you."

Here's what we know. Friends increase one's life span. In one of the earliest studies, Harvard researchers found that people who were not connected to others were three times as likely to die over the nine-year study period as those who had strong social ties.[6] In fact, people with healthy lifestyles and no friends died earlier on average than those who smoked, drank, and shunned exercise, as long as the latter had friends. Australian researchers following fifteen hundred older peo-ple for ten years found that those with a large circle of friends were 22 percent less likely to die than those with fewer friends. Family and children made no difference; only friends did.[7] Ditto for some three thousand nurses who developed breast cancer. Those without close friends were four times as likely to die from the disease over ten years as those with ten or more friends.[8] Husbands did not increase their chance of survival.

For their part, men who head over to the pub to hang out with friends and cheer on their football team face a much lower risk of heart attack. A study of middle-aged Swedish men found that only two traits seemed to influence whether they would suffer a heart attack: smoking and friendships. Being married did not move the needle.[9] Another study, looking at the effects of a beta-blocker drug, followed 2,300 men who had survived a heart attack. Those with strong social connections were only one quarter as likely to die as those who were not socially connected. It was also bad news for pharmaceutical sales: Having friends and family had a greater influence on survival than the drug being tested.[10]

Why would friends make you healthy? Jim Coan at the University of Virginia says that having friends (and other close relationships) prompts you to turn off stress hormones, lower your blood pressure, reduce your levels of inflammation, and boost your immune system.

"When you have more friends, you don't have to use as many of your own personal resources to deal with the world," Coan tells me. "You can use those resources to build yourself up. You'll grow hair, repair skin, you'll beef up your immune system, so you're more prepared to deal with what life can hurl at you. But when you have fewer friends, you have to take those resources and keep them free-floating in your bloodstream, because you never know when something's going to strike and you're going to have to do it all by yourself."[11]

Friendships soothe not just the body, but the soul and mind as well. A study of nearly seven thousand middle-aged men and women in Britain found that those who had fewer friends at forty-five experienced poorer psychological health at age fifty.[12] What about losing your memory, the night terror of every baby boomer I know? Harvard researchers tested and retested the memories of people in their fifties and sixties over six years. Socially active people had less than half the memory loss of those who were less engaged.[13] But quality, not quantity, of friendships matters most. If you have as many bad relationships as good ones, the stress of the bad cancels out the restorative powers of the good, suggesting your brain wants you to cull the herd to include only the happy and supportive friendships.[14]

SCORE ONE FOR FRIENDSHIP

M*ay 24, Washington, D.C.*
A month after I had dragged my friend Cherie to Jim Coan's laboratory at the University of Virginia, Coan had the results. I was a little nervous. I suspect he was as well, since studies usually aggregate many people's scans to ensure that outliers do not distort the findings. *What if I am an outlier?* I thought. *What if my brain declares that I am incapable of friendship, that I am a five-foot-three-inch female Hannibal Lecter?*

Mercifully, Coan opened his computer and revealed a reassuring slide. He pointed toward the threat regions of the brain, which glowed with activity when I was holding no one's hand, calmed down a little when holding the stranger's hand, and went almost dark when I held my friend's hand.

"Cherie was quite an effective regulator of your threat response," Coan said. "Probably more than most we've seen. These are strong effects."

I silently raised a prayer of gratitude that I was capable of such a connection. But there was more, he said: a truly remarkable result. He pointed to another image. Red dots lit up two areas, one involved with scanning for danger, the other with releasing stress hormones to catapult the body into fight-or-flight mode on a second's notice. Both of those areas quieted dramatically when I held Cherie's hand. Coan seemed particularly impressed with my hypothalamus, the region that dumps cortisol into the bloodstream.

"Typically, we only see an impact by hand-holding on the hypothalamus in really the best relationships," Coan said. "We typically don't see them with friend relationships. We tend to see them in marriage relationships, and only then among the highest-quality marriage relationships. So this suggests to me that whatever else is true about your relationship with Cherie, you trust her very much."

"So my brain was saying, 'Barb, this painful shock we're about to get—it's no big deal'?"

"You're saying, 'We are, in effect, in a kind of a partnership. We're close friends. We will do things for each other.' Your brain is assuming that part of the task that's involved in dealing with that threat, she will take on."

Once again, the Beatles were spot-on: We get by with a little help from our friends.

WANTED: FRIENDS IN A SPLINTERED SOCIETY

Maybe Hillary Clinton was right. Maybe it does take a village—not just to raise a child, but to survive in twenty-first-century America. Consider the math baby boomers face. Even as most Americans leave their hometowns and families of origin to follow their careers, more than a third of adults between ages forty-five and sixty-five are unmarried, compared with 20 percent three decades ago.[15] All these numbers add up to "one." More of us are on our own. Friends are no longer a luxury for those in midlife: They are a lifeline.

This brings me to one of my favorite wedding photos. It is a snapshot. It never made it into our wedding album, but it enjoys a prominent place in our living room. Eight women, including Cherie and Jody, surround my new husband. We are beaming from the sheer wonder that I, at age forty-three, am finally getting married. Now, as I study the photo, I suspect that some of that joy sprang in part from ignorance: We were blissfully blind to what the next few years would bring. At that moment, our lives were ascendant, fueled by the momentum of relative youth and energy. But one by one, as each of us entered her forties, we would hit turbulence.

We began meeting around 1998—two dropped out, two joined later—ostensibly for a Bible study. (In my church, regular meetings like this are called "small groups.") For the first four years or so, we met every Monday night and actually discussed theology. But the time we spent talking about our lives—about bosses and unemployment, about the sadness of infidelity, the addictions of relatives, the death of parents, the slow-motion agony of being single year after year, and the razor-sharp hurts of marriage—gradually nosed out theology. For me, at least, my small group was a shelter in the storm, a place I could confess my anxieties and celebrate my victories without being judged as weak or arrogant. Little by little, we knit together into a sturdy tapestry.

This is a high-octane group of women.[16] Most of us attended elite universities. We boast one Ph.D., one M.D., and three master's degrees. Two people run nonprofit organizations. Three of us have been journalists at major news organizations. We have a marketing executive and a project director. Of the current group of eight, only three are married, and with the exception of me, no one lives near her family.

We are it. Our group is a little like Walmart: one-stop shopping for career advice, logistical help, and emotional support.

We are even a proxy family. From her earliest doll-playing years, Beth told our group, she had wanted to be a parent. (I promised my friends confidentiality and changed some names.) As she watched her thirty-fifth birthday, then her fortieth, pass by without a husband or a child, she mourned, briefly, but then decided to adopt. It was painful for all of us as she gave us updates each Monday night, hearing how one adoption agency after another took her money in exchange for nothing: no child, no hope. Finally, she aged out of the process.

"When things didn't work out with adoption, I felt like people suffered with me," Beth recalled as we met one winter night. "And then when I switched to foster care, Sophia came quickly."

"That's an understatement," Jody remarked drily.

Sophia was born prematurely. Her birth mother was a drug addict, and her birth father was unable to parent. Beth was given forty-eight hours' notice to prepare for a radically different life with a premature infant. The hospital sent her home with one diaper.

"All I had was a car seat, a Pack 'n Play, and some newborn clothes," which Sophia was swimming in. "She was cold, and she was so little, and you can't put a blanket over her, because of SIDS. She was at high risk for SIDS. She needed clothes to keep her warm. So Samantha went out the first night."

"I did the baby sweep at Target!" Samantha said, and we all grinned at the incongruity: Samantha, with a Ph.D. and zero experience with infants, shopping for a newborn.

"I remember calling Beth from Target, saying, 'Okay, I'm in the baby section, tell me what you need,'" Samantha recalled. "I was looking for anything preemie, kind of wandering around with the cart. And I was like, 'Ooh! You need a Diaper Genie!' I think I bought one. I was just walking up and down the aisles, telling her whatever I was seeing, saying, 'Do you need this? Do you need this? Tell me what you need.'"

"Sophia was addicted to heroin, so she was in withdrawal," Beth said, picking up the thread. "She couldn't sleep, and she needed such care. Jody came and brought her whole family, [husband] George and [four-year-old] Beck. They brought a changing table, they brought all these toys."

Play mats. A bottle sterilizer. Clothes from friends with baby girls. Beth had not been able to decorate Sophia's room, and Jody, a former network news producer, took over.

"She took all the toys and she made it into a nursery by arranging all the pretty things she had brought," Beth recalled. George, an accomplished photographer, pulled out his camera. "George took photos, so I had a set of professional photos of Sophia and me. At that point, they told me she wasn't going to be able to stay more than thirty days, and so I felt"—she paused, wiping her eyes behind her glasses— "it was particularly touching to me then, because I didn't think she'd stay."

For the first few weeks, Beth could not take Sophia out of the house. She was too fragile. So someone was always bringing lunch, or dinner, or groceries.

"Everyone was calling and e-mailing. It was an overwhelming experience," Beth said. "I don't have family here. So you all were my family in a very, very profound way."

Two years later, Beth has adopted Sophia. The birth mother died of a drug overdose, the birth father is unavailable, the grandparents opted out of the picture. Beth has chosen a difficult road, since Sophia is facing a lifetime of developmental challenges. But Sophia is healthy and Beth is a mom. Beth tells us often: She could not be happier. Nor could we.

Monday, April 22

Mom came home from the hospital today, a month after shattering her femur. Her apartment was bathed in soft evening sunlight.

"I just want to look and look and take in all this beauty," she said, gazing down at the Potomac River, where rowers were gracefully inching their way downriver.

Mom has been weary—weary of the hospital, weary of the bed that vibrated every few minutes, weary of the poking and prodding and the physical therapy. Mostly, she worries that, in that thirty-second fall in the basement hallway, her independence crumbled like dry dirt in her hands. And selfishly, I worry, too, about our changing roles: I as the adult, my ninety-one-year-old mother sometimes helpless as a child. The shift has been occurring, slowly, for more than a decade, but now it is a fact, hard as concrete. Mom needs my full attention, and she deserves it. But that does not alter the fact that all my relationships will change as a result.

I hoped that being back in her own apartment would settle her. I hoped it would shove the conversation we had had a few days earlier into a remote corner of her mind.

"My biggest problem is I have to deal with you and David not wanting me to go on," she had said.

"You mean die?"

"Yes."

"You're right, Mom, we don't want you to die."

A pause.

"Do you want to die, Mom?"

"I'm curious."

"You're curious?" I said, hoping to levitate the mood. "Well, I think it's a pretty big gamble to satisfy your curiosity."

A pause.

"Is this because of that experience you had after your stroke?" I asked.

"Yes, it is, honey."

"Tell me about it again," I said, trying to divert her from gloomier thoughts.

"Well, it was the middle of the night, the room was completely dark. I looked toward the window and saw a light coming through the sides of the venetian blinds. And I walked over to it—I don't know if this was a dream or not—and I parted the slats with two fingers," she said, demonstrating the gesture gently, with awe. "And what I saw was a brilliant light. Honey, it was all peace, all love, all joy! And I thought, *This is the consciousness of God.*"

"Do you think about it very often?"

"All the time," she said, smiling for the first time in our visit. "All the time."

I realized in that moment, *I have to let her go.*

What I did not recognize is that I had to let my friends go as well.

THE FRAGILITY OF FRIENDSHIPS

The same thing that makes friendship so valuable is what makes it so tenuous," Tim Kreider writes in his book of essays *We Learn Nothing.*[17] "It is purely voluntary. You enter into it freely, without the imperatives of biology or the agenda of desire. Officially, you owe each other nothing."

I read Kreider's description of "defriending" with a slap of recognition. Recently my small group, which had lived through more than fifteen years of marriages and divorces, deaths and births, jobs lost and found, simply collapsed. It reminded me of lines in Ernest Hemingway's novel *The Sun Also Rises*: "How did you go bankrupt?" "Two ways. Gradually and then suddenly."

For some time, we had all sensed a certain centrifugal force. True, we had shared dinner and history for years; but during that time, all our lives changed in ways both large and small. Our jobs grew more frenetic, traveling encroached, as did the demands of children and parents. The force that had bound us together for so long—the habit of collectively navigating each week through the challenges and triumphs in our individual journeys—began to weaken. It was like a Graviton ride in an amusement park: We were spinning faster and faster, the centrifugal forces trying to fling us apart, but we were strapped in, not going anywhere because of our mutual affection and history. Then someone hit the wrong button and the sides fell away, shooting us on our different trajectories, away from each other.

That someone happened to be me. What I did—the button I pushed—was to ask my friends to share some of the highs and lows of their lives in this chapter. I thought they'd be game: Some of us had previously joked about which movie star would play their part in the film version. But I misjudged. We had all served as priests and penitents in this safest of places. They thought I wanted to breach our confidentiality and ask them to reveal their deepest insecurities and most troubling moments. This was not my intent, but they did not know that. And by the time I could recover from my surprise and explain, the damage was done. Individually, we all remained friends, but the fierce commitment to walking through life each week as a band of sisters, as it were, dissolved. I was, and am, heartbroken. Devin suggested, only half joking, that I title the chapter: "How I Lost My Closest Friends Writing This Book."

Obviously, the fault lines existed long before my query. We had been tottering for months. Not from disaffection, but from, well, middle age. And now I see the cause: Middle age itself is a centrifugal force, mentally, physically, and emotionally draining. It is like a bankruptcy proceeding, of sorts. We prioritize the creditors of our time—caring for partners and children and ailing parents, tending to work commitments—and if we need friends, then our colleagues at work will do in a pinch, grabbing coffee or drinks after a long day. But maintaining close emotional ties with people who do not share our home or DNA is difficult, and rare. Often when I tell people (particularly men) that I am writing a chapter on the importance of midlife friends, they respond: "Huh, that's interesting. I don't think I have any friends."

As it happened, a scientist would point to the cause of my small-group collapse—as well as the cure, if we were willing.

In the early 1990s, Robin Dunbar was contemplating the size of the social groups of monkeys and apes. Dunbar, now an anthropologist and evolutionary psychologist at Oxford University, noticed a relationship between the size of a monkey's brain and the size of his social network. The larger the brains of various species, such as chimps, gibbons, and great apes, the larger and more complex their groups. He wondered: What about humans?

A few years later, he arrived at an answer. Human beings can, on average, juggle about 150 people in their networks. This has been dubbed "Dunbar's number," a title he quietly relishes.[18]

"We then realized—this was about ten years ago—that this number really was just one of a series of layers," Dunbar explained in an interview.

The inner circle of people—friends or family you would call in a crisis—contains on average five people. The next circle, close but not intimate, is fifteen; the next, fifty; then a hundred fifty, then five hundred, then fifteen hundred. Why do humans gravitate toward such specific numbers? The answer lies in our brain: specifically, the way two parts of the brain connect.

In brain-scanning studies, Dunbar has focused on the circuit between specific areas of the frontal lobe and the temporal lobe. He says
the frontal-temporal lobe circuit, which is known as the "theory-of-
mind circuit," comes to life when you are trying to understand another
person's state of mind. He has found that the size of specific areas of
the frontal lobe seems to determine how many mind states you can
handle simultaneously without getting lost.

"Your competencies on that then determine how many friends you
have," Dunbar said. "It's a reflection of your ability to [manage] these
various individuals, like a juggler juggling balls in the air without
dropping them or causing them to bash into each other with, shall we
say, embarrassing and unfortunate consequences."

Let's take a closer look at your inner circle of five friendships. Dunbar said it usually includes two friends, two family members, and one
other person, friend or family. (This describes my inner core precisely.)
Over the years, friends move in and out of the inner circle: When a
new friend floats into the inner circle, he or she bumps another friend
down to the less intimate circle of fifteen. If you don't believe this, take
a look at your wedding pictures. How many of the bridesmaids or
groomsmen do you talk with every week?

Romance throws your network into a state of chaos. Your new love
shoos some friends out of the henhouse so he can create a nice, big,
comfortable space in your life. The beloved takes up so much of your
time and emotional space that he or she colonizes two spots in your
inner circle.

"Your close family will probably tolerate that, but friends won't,"
Dunbar explained. "They will sort of 'cool' toward you. You're investing less time, and they are naturally bumped down into the next layer,
where their perception of the emotional closeness in the relationship
will have deteriorated as well."

"What happens when you have children?" I asked. "Do you lose even more friends?"

"I think you lose almost all your friends," he said, laughing, "because you just don't have any time at all when they're very young."[19]

I described the plight of my small group.

"For whatever reason, we began missing meetings," I said. "Sometimes we'd go every other week, and sometimes once a month. The group that was so strong for all those years, living through everything with each other—suddenly it's collapsed."

Dunbar nodded. He has heard this before.

"The way you keep friendships going is that you're constantly updating each other on what's interesting," he said.

He has even calculated the numbers: at least once a week for the inner core of friends, at least once a month for the next layer of fifteen.

"If you don't have that constant updating time, then suddenly you find that you now only have so many things in common. Suddenly, there comes a point when it's dropped down from these close relationships to the next layer. At that point, you probably start to disinvest even more."

He paused, then summarized the problem—and the solution.

"It's all about time investment."

ONE: THE MOST TERRIFYING NUMBER

When you are old, loneliness is a careless stalker.[20] It leaves you crumpled on the curb. It is more discreet with the young and middle-aged. The bruises are better hidden. But don't be fooled, loneliness attacks every age. One national survey found that people between forty-five and sixty-five are the loneliest people in the United States.[21] Loneliness is capturing more and more territory, in part because we are 30 percent more likely to live alone than only three decades ago, in part because of the isolation of unemployment or the longer work hours, in part because technology has allowed us to avoid personal contact. When asked how many confidants he or she would feel comfortable discussing an important personal issue with in 1985, the average American could name three people. Two decades later, the number had dropped to two. A quarter of the participants said they had no one to confide in at all.[22]

I once believed *having* friends was a luxury. Now I know that *losing* friends can be lethal. Feeling lonely and isolated, no matter what your age, will shorten your life as much as smoking fifteen cigarettes a day.[23] It destroys your body as effectively as alcoholism. It is twice as lethal as obesity. Maintaining relationships with friends, family, or work colleagues increases your odds of survival by 50 percent.

Loneliness employs many methods to work its dark magic. It raises blood pressure and dumps stress hormones into your bloodstream, which can lead to tissue damage and all manner of disease over time, including heart disease.[24] Loneliness reprograms genes and attacks the immune system, making you more vulnerable to infectious diseases and to viruses, from the common cold to HIV.[25] Scientists believe that isolation increases your risk for diabetes and neurodegenerative diseases. Lonely people in midlife are more likely to develop dementia and Alzheimer's disease.[26] Isolation even seems to lower your IQ over the course of your life.[27] Scientists believe that it can make cancer replicate faster and make tumors metastasize more quickly. It robs you of sleep, it afflicts you with micro-awakenings, and when you finally rise in the morning, exhausted, your cortisol level is higher, suggesting you are bracing for another stressful, threatening day.[28] You never relax. And if you are over sixty, loneliness makes you far, far more likely to die.[29]

"Not to mention it makes your life miserable," says John Cacioppo. "That would be sufficient reason to want to do something about it."

Cacioppo, a professor of psychology at the University of Chicago, says loneliness is also a *psychological* tsunami, leaving broken lives in its wake. He ticks off some symptoms.

"It promotes social withdrawal. It promotes hostility. Meaning in life decreases. Your feelings of control over your life and your environment decrease. It's associated with a number of impulsive behavioral changes. When you feel lonely, you're more likely to binge drink or binge eat. It lowers your happiness, above and beyond what you would have expected by the increase in depressive symptomology."

Suicides are associated with loneliness. So are murders.

It was hypnosis that prompted John Cacioppo to wonder about the nature of loneliness. As a young professor at Ohio State in the mid-1990s, he knew that loneliness correlated with dying young and a host of other health horrors. At that point, the small tribe of scholars who studied it believed loneliness sprang from poor social skills or shyness. But at bottom, they thought, people have different personalities and introverts drew the short straw.

Then Cacioppo hatched an idea. He knew that colleagues at Stanford University had located and tested people who were highly hypnotizable. He flew out to Palo Alto and, with the help of some skilled hypnotists, put twenty of the subjects into a deep state of hypnosis.

"We made them feel lonely or connected," Cacioppo explained. "Half were made to feel lonely first and then non-lonely; the other half, the reverse order. What we were really surprised to find was their personalities changed, their outlooks changed, their social skills changed—just this dramatic transformation based on whether they felt connected or not."

Maybe, Cacioppo thought, loneliness "was not just a passenger on the bus, but a real important driver on that bus. And these other factors like shyness and social skills were really being carried along."

Maybe loneliness was *causing* the death and destruction, shaving off years and making people sick and unhappy. Maybe he should study this.

Yet loneliness is not without its redeeming features.

"Loneliness is a biological signal, just like hunger, thirst, and pain," Cacioppo noted. "It motivates you to care for yourself so you can have a genetic legacy."

Just as hunger and thirst tell you that you need nutrients and hydration, just as pain tells you to remove your hand from the stovetop before you do more tissue damage, Cacioppo said, "loneliness is an adverse signal that appears to have evolved to motivate you to care for your social body."

Social animals need each other to survive, whether as a helpless infant being fed by his mother or as an adult who needs the protection of the community to survive predators.

"It's dangerous being on a social perimeter," he told me. "If you think about documentaries where you've seen a herd of animals, the animal on the edge is the one most likely to be predated," that is, eaten. "If you look at fish, they swim in schools. When a predator comes up, it's the one on the edge that's most likely to be predated. It's not because they're the slowest or the weakest—they're just the easiest to access and separate from the group and eat."

Thanks to evolution, when you are lonely, when you believe you are on the social perimeter, your body rebels. *Get back in the game,* it yells, *get in the middle where you can't be singled out for lunch.*[30]

Over the next two decades, Cacioppo would chronicle the devastation of loneliness on the body, mind, and emotions. But a question remained: We know what loneliness does, but how does it work? How does it worm its way into one's very genetic code?

WHY THE FRIENDLESS DIE YOUNG

About the time that John Cacioppo was discovering that loneliness makes healthy people sick, Steven Cole was finding that loneliness was making sick people die faster.

When Cole was a postdoctoral fellow at the University of California, Los Angeles, he began to wonder how one's emotions, fears, and worldview change things at the molecular level. This was the mid-1990s, and as Cole pondered the question, he realized there was a large group of candidates to study: gay men who were HIV positive. Something about how the virus worked caught Cole's eye. HIV discriminated.

"Some people would stay healthy for decades without treatment, and other people would get sick and die within just a few years," he told me. "It made people ask, 'What's the difference between these people?'"

After a lot of testing, one thing jumped out: *closeting*. The virus replicated three to ten times as fast in men who kept their sexual orientation hidden as in men who came out, and killed closeted men two to three years earlier.[31]

Cole realized that these closeted men might have a lot in common with John Cacioppo's lonely people. Both seemed to die more quickly because they perceived the world as a hostile threat.

The two researchers collaborated on a pilot study.[32] What they found was that loneliness reprogrammed a person's genes in the same way that fear of being outed altered the genes of closeted men. Loneliness changes the immune system. Specifically, feeling isolated turns on genes for inflammation—which are the first responders to tissue damage or bacterial threats—and it puts the brakes on genes that stop inflammation. At the same time, loneliness seems to turn off genes associated with antiviral responses and the production of anti-bodies. This is a bad combination, making the body vulnerable to infectious diseases, to viruses (from the common cold to HIV), and to other conditions that are sensitive to inflammation, such as cardiovas-cular disease. Lonely people were not faking their symptoms. Their own bodies were reacting to loneliness at a cellular level, trying to nudge them to make friends and get back into the warm, safe center of the herd.

This is easier said than done. Lonely people perceive the world as more hostile, and they do not derive as much pleasure from connecting to other people. This is not something they try to do, or are even con-scious of doing: Their brains do it for them.

Cacioppo and his colleague Louise Hawkley discovered this by watching the brains of people who felt lonely and those who felt con-nected as they processed information (happy and sad pictures) in a brain scanner. The first glaring difference: The reward centers of lonely brains fail to light up when they are contemplating images of happy interactions between friends or family members. The second insight is that lonely people zero in when they see negative social inter-actions. Their brains go on high alert, because for a brain that sees danger around every corner, hostility is very relevant.

"When you feel isolated, whether you're with others or not, your brain goes into self-preservation mode," Cacioppo explains. "You're aware that you're sad. But you're less aware that you become ag-gressive."

Cacioppo says that society pushes the lonely grumps away, which is why it's so hard to break out of chronic loneliness.

"Say I have two coworkers, one who is this adorable person and this other who is kind of depressive, defensive, and hostile," he says. "Both of them come in and act in a grumpy fashion to me. To the first person, I say, 'What's wrong, how can I help you?' To the second person I say, 'Gee, I'd like to talk but I have a meeting. I have to go.'"

"And that just confirms that every interaction is going to be bad," I ask, "so every interaction is a threat?"

Cacioppo nodded. "That's what I call 'social spirals.'"

HOW I ALMOST FELL INTO A SPIRAL OF LONELINESS

I found this all riveting in a theoretical way, until the science got personal. I have always delighted in my friends, and seemed to have plenty of them from work, church, my neighborhood, as well as random people I like a lot. But when I took a leave of absence from NPR to write this book, I lost my daily dose of friendship.

During the first few months, my world continued to teem with relationships as I asked people to tell me their stories and explain their research. But as my reporting wound down and I dived into the solitary business of writing, as I carved out more time for my computer and less for my relationships, I noticed something sinister.

A little terrorist began to occupy my mind. I mulled over offhand comments or, worse, silence, turning them over like an oyster worrying a grain of sand. I sometimes fretted (for no reason) that my follow-up interviews would be prickly affairs, anticipating that the person on the other end would cut the interview off after two minutes, and I would be left alone with my unanswered questions. One friendship, a very close one, ran aground, and it was partly my hand that steered it into the shoals, because I had too much time alone to catalogue the (surely unintended) hurts.

My thinking appalled me. It reminded me of something ABC *Nightline* anchor Dan Harris wrote in his book about meditation, *10% Happier*. "The voice in my head," he observed, "is kind of an asshole."[33]

Now, being a PG kind of person (usually), I cleaned it up and smoothed it into a neat iambic pentameter: *The voice in my head is a bit of a jerk,* I would tell myself several times a day. *The voice in my head is a bit of a jerk*. Having read the research, I add: *Now quit acting lonely.*

I know that John Cacioppo would probably cringe at the comparison. I fall outside his definition of lonely: I see my husband each night, I call my mother each day, I have friends who do not, as far as I know, duck behind a pillar when they see me from afar. But I wonder: If Cacioppo slid me in his scanner, would he see the beginnings of a lonely brain? And given that so many people find themselves, at midlife, shed from the institutional workforce, consulting, operating in a virtual workspace (I am editing this book at Starbucks), or otherwise toiling alone, I wonder if loneliness researchers are about to reap a bumper crop of test subjects.

Monday, April 29

Yesterday, when I dropped by Mom's apartment, she looked lovely, sitting regally in her reclining chair, wearing a lavender housecoat and salmon lipstick. But the minute she saw me, her face crumpled. She was clutching a *Christian Science Journal* article, one she had been reading and rereading without much comprehension. I know from my research that hospital stays can dramatically erode cognitive abilities, particularly in the elderly.

"I just can't get it, I can't break through to the metaphysical truth," she said, and my heart sank, for her entire life rests on her mental acuity.

"Is it like a fog, Mom?" I asked, poised to explain that the anesthesia could still be making her cloudy but that it would lift.

She nodded, then reverted to the subject I dreaded: death.

"I told David that he just needed to let me go on," she said.

"Do you want to go on?"

"Sometimes," she said softly.

I looked at her, astonished. The Mom I knew never succumbed to circumstances, she never allowed herself to become mired in doubt. I recalled the day two years earlier when we were driving to her speech therapy session at National Rehabilitation Hospital. My eighty-nine-year-old mother had suffered a stroke; aphasia had robbed her of most of her vocabulary and, worse, her ability to complete a thought. At a stoplight, Mom began, "Mary . . ." Then the light changed, distracting her and dissolving any hope of expressing that idea. I thought, *That's the end of that sentence.* Mom put her head down, scrunched her eyes in fierce concentration, and whispered to herself, *"Push through, push through, push through to the other side."* She lifted her head and said: "Mary came to visit yesterday." A small idea, a giant victory. It was as if a lifetime of mental discipline had kicked in, overriding the aphasia; within weeks Mom had made a full recovery. She astounded her doctors, who called her a "career-changing patient" and wondered how she managed to recover her acuity when others her age could not.

Now, two years later, my unsinkable mother seemed defeated. And yet, who wouldn't feel helpless at ninety-one, with a shattered femur, facing her final years in a wheelchair. My independent mother had been stripped of the power to decide the course of her life, down to the most mundane details, relying on others to make her dinner, to give her a bath, to turn up the air-conditioning, to pick up the newspaper from the door stoop. I knew in that moment that Mom did not need to be bucked up. She didn't need a pep talk that glossed over the stark facts. What she needed was that power to decide—to consider death and choose life.

"Mom," I said, and my heart was racing, because I avoid hard personal conversations like the plague, "if you want to live and fight and walk again, there's no reason you can't. And Dave and I will do everything we can to make that happen."

Then I began to well up. "But if you want to go on, I'll be there for you in that decision as well. I don't want you to die, but I'm here for you."

Mom said nothing. Then she reached over and clutched my hand. We sat in silence for several moments, until she nodded and released my hand.

Today, Mom dressed for the first time since her fall, in a nice sweater and pants, fixed her hair with a ribbon, and went in her wheelchair to Dave's office a block away. I don't know if our conversation had anything to do with this, but she seems to have decided to live, and to live vigorously.

For much of the time I was reporting and writing about midlife, I enjoyed little bandwidth for friendships. As with many midlife professionals, work and family colonized all my time. I wondered how to regain the ground I had lost. It was in my interest, after all, to invest in relationships because those would be the engine of long-term health and acuity. But this motive seemed too strategic, too transactional; it didn't capture why I needed my friends: Outside the cocoon of my colleagues at NPR, I missed uncomplicated relationships that were less insistent than job or family.

One evening, I managed to spend some time with my friend Libby Lewis. Libby and I had become instant buddies almost twenty years earlier as nervous new hires at NPR. She is indirectly responsible for my marriage: Her beau, now her husband, insisted I try Match.com, until I finally relented and almost instantly met Devin. Every morning, Libby and I grabbed coffee at NPR's deli. We discussed story ideas and shared sources. We spent so much time together that we started to look like each other. People asked if we were sisters. I think of Libby as my "warp and woof" friend: Her absence left a hole in my day.

"You know, I've learned a lot about friendship theory in the past few weeks," I told her as we enjoyed a cup of tea at a French café near our homes.

I described the Friend Niche model, where you have a small number of friendship slots, which you fill with people who can help you survive.[34] For hunter-gatherers, your circle might include someone good with a spear and someone who could navigate the woods and bring you home. Today, it might include someone who understands your career, someone who can babysit your child in a pinch, someone who plays tennis at your level, someone who knows where the bargains are. You should also have someone who considers you hard to replace.

Another intriguing theory, I told Libby, is the Alliance Hypothesis, which says you need a friend who considers you as valuable as you consider him or her. Otherwise you can't count on absolute loyalty when you need it.[35]

"They're kind of academic explanations," I said, "but I did get one insight from a young sociologist at Stony Brook named Peter DeScioli. He's found that if you rank someone as your best friend, it's really disconcerting if you find out she doesn't rank you as high. There's a power imbalance. And he says if you're in an imbalanced friendship, you can do one of two things."

"Which are?" Libby asked.

"Either you work harder to become her best friend, or you find another friend."

"Or there's a third way," Libby observed. "You ask yourself: *Do I want that friendship or not? Is it important to me?* Then cut 'em some slack."

I realized that is what Libby had done with me. Maybe midlife friendship does not have to be that complicated after all.

IT'S THE THOUGHT
THAT COUNTS

Two of my mother's sayings threaded through my early childhood and shaped my thinking. The first typically came during long car rides, when my brother and I were buckled in the backseat. David, six and a half years my senior, would chant under his breath so that only I could hear him: *Barbie's a baby, and fat as a pig.* Eventually it would become too much; I would complain bitterly and demand that my mother intervene. Mom would swivel around and declare: "You have no right to spoil this lovely moment." The rebuke was always directed at me, never at David, who would fall silent and gaze serenely out the window the moment she turned her head. Even now, when I am on the verge of muttering a snarky comment or complaint, I sometimes think to myself: You have no right to spoil this lovely moment.

The second pronouncement penetrated even more deeply. "Your thinking is your experience," Mom routinely observed—usually, again, when I was complaining or fretting. This idea sprang from her Christian Science background. Whatever one's view of Christian Scientists and their resistance to medical treatment, they zeroed in on a key concept one hundred years before the scientists landed on the "mind-body connection." Christian Scientists believe that your thoughts, attitudes, and prayers largely shape how you will experience the world, and "correcting" your thinking can fix almost any problem, from the flu or a layoff to marital or financial problems.

I may have walked away from Christian Science two decades ago, but not this central idea. Now scientists are discovering that the way you think affects every aspect of your life: It can slice through the haze of Alzheimer's disease, even if your brain has plaques and tangles. It can add years to your life and protect you from all manner of disease. It can turn off genes that lead to inflammation and early death. It can even turn down the deafening roar of chronic pain. All this is true for the young as well as the old, but the way we think gains urgency in middle age, when we see the finish line not so far down the road, when we begin to touch the fringes of frailty—and we still have time to alter the pattern of our thoughts.

The new science brought me hope, since I carry the genes of my father, who succumbed to dementia. It showed me a path forward through chronic pain—pain that no medicine could cure but might, I fervently hoped, be tempered by my thinking. As researchers study the restorative or destructive power of thinking, they are also discovering nuances. Not all thinking is equal. One particular attitude seems to lift every aspect of your life: your mind, your body, your longevity, even your happiness. So indulge me, please, as we witness the subtle and cumulative power of thinking. Beginning with the dread of every middle-aged person I know: Alzheimer's disease.

Monday, May 6

Julie Schneider strides into the windowless, frigid room and scans her small kingdom.

"This is what we call the 'dirty lab,'" the neuropathologist says, although it looks pristine to me. You could eat off the floor. But not the countertop. There are slices of brains on the countertop, lined up like wedges of cauliflower ready to be grilled. She stands near the brains and waves me over, as if I were a shy child. I approach them with a squeamish fascination.

Schneider picks up one of the slices in her gloved hands, from the brain of a woman named Marjorie, and holds it up to the fluorescent light.

"We can't diagnose Alzheimer's disease by looking directly at the brain, but we can look for other things related to cognitive impairment," Schneider explains, turning the section over for closer inspection. "So far, looking pretty good . . . there . . . see that white area?" she asks, holding the brain slice uncomfortably close. "That white area is a plaque within a blood vessel. The vessel should look all blue."

The neuropathologist at Chicago's Rush University Medical Center is athletically slim, confident, and reassuring—qualities lost on these bits of brain tissue. Yet these specimens represent the hope of my generation, the fervent wish that we will not all slide into the quicksand of dementia. These specimens, and Marjorie's in particular, tell a wonderful story: We need not forget all that matters—even, yes, even if we develop Alzheimer's.

After a few minutes, I gratefully follow Schneider out of the frigid dirty lab to a sun-drenched room lined with microscopes. She settles in front of one and slips a slide with Marjorie's brain tissue under the lens.

"I'm scanning the cortex, and I'm seeing a moderate number of neuritic plaques, which is the hallmark of Alzheimer's disease," she says. She selects another slide. "I'm seeing enough plaques that we can make a diagnosis of Alzheimer's. Intermediate level of Alzheimer's disease."

"Would you expect her to have memory problems?" I ask.

"Well, knowing what I know through our studies," she says, "I know that a lot of people can have this much pathology and do not have memory problems."

"Why is that?"

"I think there's compensation in the brain. We don't understand what the compensation is, exactly. Is it more connections that occur early in life, or in midlife? Is it that some people are better at finding alternative connections? There are many reasons people could have reserve."

Five hours later, Betty Borman welcomes me into her home in Arlington Heights, twenty-five miles northwest of Chicago. I arrive with David Bennett, a man who has interviewed her many times as director of Rush University's Alzheimer's Disease Center. More than fifteen years ago, Bennett began recruiting healthy older people (sixty-five and over) in retirement homes around Chicago. The participants, now numbering more than seventeen hundred, agreed to regular cognitive tests and an autopsy of their brains after they die.

Betty is eighty-six, dressed casually yet carefully in her yellow polo shirt buttoned to the top and yellow cardigan with off-white pants. She possesses a gracious, erudite manner, punctuated by frequent and at first unexpected wry quips.

Betty joined the Rush Memory and Aging Project several years earlier, after watching a close friend descend into Alzheimer's disease.

"And at the end, she didn't even know me, and that really hurts," she says. "And I thought, *I've got to do something.* So here I am."

Betty is not just any participant. Her older sister was Marjorie, whose brain I had just viewed under the microscope.

The sisters attended Chicago Teachers College in the 1940s, an unusual path for women of their generation, who generally married right out of high school. Marge nearly earned a master's degree in history before marrying and having children. Both sisters taught middle school for years before and after raising their children.

"Marge had twenty-two years of education," Bennett adds, looking at his file and noting that the average amount of school was fourteen years. "We and others have found education to be protective."

"What do you mean, 'protective'?" I ask.

"Education delays the onset of dementia—the clinical signs and symptoms of dementia from Alzheimer's disease and other things," he explains.

The more education the better: A Ph.D. is better than just a college degree, which is better than a high school diploma—a point cheerfully volunteered by several university researchers (with Ph.D.'s).

"It turns out that if you get dementia, you'll get it later, but you'll also progress a little bit more rapidly" at the end, Bennett adds.

This "compression of morbidity" bestows two gifts, Bennett notes: It delays the symptoms of Alzheimer's disease until the plaques and tangles overwhelm the brain, and then you go downhill blessedly fast—so fast you may spend only a couple of years in a demented state. Bennett says education builds up that cognitive reserve, that buffer against memory loss.

"Marge was also a reader her entire life," Betty recalls, adding that after Marge's husband died, she developed a bad back that almost debilitated her. "The local library would send over a box of books that she had ordered and she would read a book a day. I mean, it could be seven hundred pages and she would read a book a day and call me up and say, 'Now you've got to read this. It's about the whole German empire.'"

"I would say, 'Yeah, Marge, I'm still trying to get my grocery list together,'" Betty says, laughing at the memory. "She read and read, and I believe that kept her going. She had a bad back. She had a lot of miseries in her life. She lost two sons out of three. She lost two husbands. She never complained."

"I want to comment on both of those things," Bennett says, jumping in. He pulls out Marge's files, wherein her personality scores and test results are numeric evidence of a mind that defied deterioration.

"One of the things that we assess is how cognitively active people are over their lifetime, including late life," Bennett says. Her lifetime of reading earned her high marks for cognitive activity: The average score among the participants is 3 on a scale of 1 to 5. Marge scored a 4.2.

The researchers measured other, noncognitive traits as well—and this is another feature that distinguishes the Rush study from all others. One personality trait of particular interest is "neuroticism," that is, how one responds internally to stress. You want a low number, Bennett says. The average score is 15.7. Marge scored 11.

"So when you hear about how she lived through the death of two children and two husbands," he says, "some people are resilient and other people aren't. This is evidence of a resilient woman."

Bennett then runs us through the other attitudes or propensities that may have buffered Marge from dementia. She scored much lower than average on the personal or stylistic traits that increase the risk of cognitive decline: harm avoidance (being shy and failing to engage in the world), anxiety, and perceived social isolation (loneliness). And she blazed to victory on the characteristics that appear to keep one's mind intact, such as social engagement, conscientiousness, and an attitude called "purpose in life."

Every year, Marge topped out on the standard cognitive test, called the Mini Mental State Exam, until she died at age eighty-seven. On a delayed-recall test—where she was told a complicated story, then distracted for twenty minutes, and then asked to repeat as many details as possible—Marge remembered sixteen of twenty-five details.

"Is that good?" I ask.

"You and I would be lucky to get that," Bennett laughs.

Recalling the many plaques and tangles I had just seen in Marge's brain, I turn to Betty. She had talked with her sister once or twice a week until the end.

"Did you notice any change?"

"Nothing!" Betty says emotionally. "When I heard about finding Alzheimer's evidence in her brain, I was shocked. I knew her better than anybody else did. I would have picked it up. And I saw nothing."

What is so stunning, David Bennett says, is not merely that Marge effortlessly navigated her cognitive tests while her brain was fighting through the thicket of Alzheimer's. What is remarkable is that this performance is so common. Fully a third of people who, as autopsies indicate, have the disease show no cognitive decline, no evidence of Alzheimer's.[1] At first, other scientists raised their eyebrows; now, after some five hundred autopsies, the finding is beyond dispute.

Bennett tells me that he and his colleagues are approaching Alzheimer's disease sideways.

"Most of the world is focused on 'How do we stop that pathology from developing, or how do we reverse it or get it out of your brain?'" he says. "We're interested in those questions, too. But on the flip side, let's assume for the moment that it's going to happen. Then how do you build a better brain so that *despite* the accumulation of the pathology, you don't lose your memory? Because that's what people want to preserve. People's memories are among the most precious things that they have."

ESCAPEES

Previous studies, including the so-called Nun Study of nearly seven hundred elderly Catholic sisters, had shown that some people have brains riddled with the plaques and tangles of Alzheimer's disease and yet show no symptoms.[2] They are called "escapees." These sisters were better educated than the average woman of their era, and lived intellectually rigorous lives, teaching well into retirement age.

David Bennett fell hard for the Nun Study, but he wanted more. He wondered: What about attitudes and personality? What if he and his colleagues look not only at what a person has *done*—completing crossword puzzles, walking every day, seeing friends and family—but at how he or she *thinks*? And what if they recruit people earlier, when they are still cognitively healthy, and follow them for decades, as they develop dementia—or escape it?

Beginning in 1994, Bennett recruited more than 1,250 Catholic sisters, monks, and priests, later adding some 1,750 laypeople of all races, education, and income levels.

"We wanted to capture the full range of things that were relevant to aging," he told me. He wanted to examine not only the usual suspects (education, family background, hobbies, social network, and exercise), but also personality traits and attitudes toward life.

Two attitudes seem to predict with astonishing precision whether or not someone developed dementia. The men and women who scored highest on conscientiousness—that is, who control their impulses, who were dependable and goal-oriented—had 89 percent lower risk of developing symptoms of Alzheimer's than the least conscientious people.[3] That remains true even after accounting for behaviors that go hand in hand with conscientiousness, such as taking one's medicine, exercising, and living a disciplined life.

But the big surprise—and almost a magic bullet—is "purpose in life." These people, Bennett explained, find each day meaningful. They have a reason to get up in the morning. "They're happy and they're looking forward to their next day when they're eighty-eight or ninety-eight."

Bennett said that these people are far, far less likely than those with low purpose in life to develop dementia or exhibit cognitive declines, even if their autopsies show that they had the pathology. In fact, people with little purpose were *two and a half times* more likely to develop dementia than those with a mission.[4] More than education, more than a happy childhood or a lifetime of learning, more than physical activity or eating right, more than any other thing, this engaged attitude toward life is the secret to a sharp mind right to the last day.

"It reminds me of my mom after she had her stroke," I said. "She was eighty-nine and she made a truly remarkable recovery. Later, I was talking to her speech therapist about it, and she said, 'You know, you never hear an eighty-nine-year-old talking about her future plans. But your mother did. She talked about going back to Nantucket for the summer.'"

"That's what we're talking about," Bennett said. "I remember my grandmother in her nineties was diagnosed with cancer. And the doctors said, 'We're going to send you home and make you comfortable.' And she said, '*The hell you are!* I've got a bar mitzvah in six months.'"

"Did she make it?" I asked, laughing.

"Yes. She danced at my younger son's bar mitzvah."

The benefits of a purposeful attitude grow bigger and bigger with time, Bennett added.

"Somehow, purpose in life is not just delaying your onset of Alzheimer's. It's affecting how your brain responds to the accumulation of the pathology."

How is that possible? I asked. How could an outlook on life, a nonphysical thing, make the physical brain more nimble, allowing it to work around those plaques and tangles and other neurological roadblocks?

"What makes the brain so different from any other organ is plasticity—its ability to respond to adversity," Bennett said. "Somehow, people with more purpose in life have brains that are more plastic. And therefore they're not just able to tolerate stuff because they're hardwired better; they're able to tolerate it better because they have other ways of dealing with pathology that people without purpose in life don't."

I sat back in my seat and absorbed this. The thought really does count. I realized that Bennett's research offers a clear piece of advice for midlifers like me: Develop thought patterns, particularly purpose in life, *now*, in one's forties, fifties, and sixties. Find a purpose beyond your career—because you will one day retire. Find a purpose in your children, and then your grandchildren, who will need you when your own progeny do not. Build momentum now, looking beyond the quotidian activities of today to something that will get you out of bed ten years from now and twenty after that—a new passion, a hobby, a cause that outlives you. I think about my seventy-seven-year-old neighbor who takes German classes on Saturdays (his seventh language) and my stepmother, who competed in hundred-mile horseback races until my father persuaded her to cut back to fifty-mile races when she turned eighty. They, like Bennett's escapees, developed their passions early on, and those passions carried them when their natural resources waned.

THE TWO FACES OF HAPPINESS

I find Bennett's work enormously satisfying on so many levels. The former Christian Scientist in me cheers at the idea that how you think—your attitudes, your mental discipline, your steely resolve—somehow holds dementia at bay, and who knows what other diseases? Then there is the conscientious egghead in me, the college student who did *not* get drunk on Friday nights, but went to bed early because she had a cross-country race the next morning. And finally there is my father's daughter, who learned that deferred gratification, sacrificing for the longer-term goal, may possibly be the *summum bonum* in the pantheon of human attributes.

But Bennett's findings also pose a dichotomy. For years, positive psychologists have credited happiness with all sorts of benefits, including a long and rich life. Yet happiness seems, if not the antithesis, then certainly a pretty distant cousin of "purpose in life." As I sat talking with David Bennett, a revelation washed over me. There are two types of happiness: short-term happiness and long-term meaning.

More than two millennia ago, the ancient Greeks spent considerable time and energy debating happiness, Carol Ryff told me. Ryff, a psychology professor at the University of Wisconsin, runs the Midlife in the United States (MIDUS) project, which has been following thousands of Americans from young adulthood through old age for the past two decades. In one corner was *hedonia*, as in hedonism, feeling happy, "satisfying appetites, having a good beer, a good meal, and good sex," Ryff said.

But at the same time, Ryff said, Aristotle was asking questions like What is the highest of all goods? What is the good life?

"He explicitly said it's not that kind of feeling good, contentment, satisfying of appetites," Ryff said. "In fact, he likened that to cattle standing out in the field, munching away. He said it's something more than that. He wrote that the highest of all human goods is the realization of our own true potential. So it's a really beautiful idea, in my view, that we all come into life with unique human capacities, something that he called the *daimon*. And our task in life is to figure out what those unique capacities are, and then to do our very best to bring them into reality."

Thus was born eudaimonic happiness.[5] It is about striving, working hard, purposeful engagement, the kind of effort that may be stressful or even painful in the short run but over the long run brings meaning and a wildly profitable return on investment. Think: raising children, or training for a marathon, or staying at work to finish that report, or pulling an all-nighter to file a story for *Morning Edition*.

Only recently has eudaimonia emerged from hedonia's shadow. In the past few years, psychologists have started peering closely into the two faces of well-being. As in so many things in life—who is the better long-term bet, the high school quarterback or the geek who would start Microsoft?—shy, diligent eudaimonia seems to garner better reviews in the long run.[6]

This seems counterintuitive at first. A life of meaning can be kind of a drag: It involves sacrifice, stress, sleepless nights to feed the baby, working long hours to put your child through college, sitting by your wife's side through the last stages of cancer, visiting your father even though Alzheimer's has stolen his capacity for a shared memory, a joke, a gentle word.

So what's the point of meaning, of eudaimonia, anyway? As it turns out, both our minds and our bodies prefer it. Researchers at the University of Rochester tracked some 150 recent graduates, dividing them into those who were seeking intrinsic goals (valuing "deep, lasting relationships" or "helping others improve their lives") or extrinsic goals, such as wealth, looks, fame. The researchers checked back two years later and found that the young people who achieved their extrinsic, image-related goals fared poorly: They reported more negative emotions like shame and anger, and more physical symptoms like headaches, stomachaches, and loss of energy. The intrinsic set, which valued relationships and personal growth, reported more positive feelings toward themselves and others, and fewer physical signs of stress.[7]

Let's drill down a little further, into our biology. Our bodies prefer selfless happiness to self-centeredness, and will reward eudaimonia with a longer life.[8] Scientists have discovered that people who pursue eudaimonic well-being also have lower particular biomarkers for inflammation that have been linked to a number of health problems, including diabetes, cardiovascular disease, osteoporosis, and Alzheimer's disease.[9] These purposeful people even had lower cholesterol.[10]

Drill down deeper still, and we find that even our DNA rewards eudaimonic meaning and punishes hedonism, Steven Cole told me. Cole, a professor of medicine, psychiatry, and behavioral sciences at UCLA School of Medicine, backed into studying eudaimonia. He has made a career of charting the bad effect of stress, threat, loneliness, and misery on the human body. Recently he became intrigued by the flip-side of the question: Could well-being reverse the ravages that disease has on a person's immune system? He had seen intriguing hints that women with breast cancer who were able to reduce their stress levels actually turned down the genes that bring inflammation and cancer. He wanted to know more.

"I thought, *I've got to find myself a happiness researcher.*"

At a conference, Cole bumped into Barbara Fredrickson, a famous happiness researcher at the University of North Carolina at Chapel Hill.

"Her first question was: 'What kind of happiness are we talking about?'"

From that threshold question, a wildly pioneering—and in some circles, controversial—exploration was launched.

Using a widely accepted questionnaire, they asked eighty participants to answer questions designed to pick up hedonic proclivities: Are you happy and satisfied? They also tried to pick up on eudaimonic tendencies: Do you have a sense of meaning and direction in your life? Do you contribute to society? Then the researchers drew blood, looking for something called the "conserved transcriptional response to adversity" (CTRA), which is academic lingo for the stress fingerprint on the genome.

From previous work, Cole knew that when people become lonely or stressed—when they are worried about their jobs or money, divorce or the loss of a loved one—their bodies bolt straight into threat mode. Their genes respond in a particular (and particularly harmful) way. The inflammatory genes turn on, and the antiviral genes turn off.[11]

"Our genomic programming to activate inflammation in response to stress is particularly troublesome," Cole says. "Inflammation is like molecular fertilizer for cardiovascular disease, metastatic cancer, and neurodegenerative disease."

But when Cole teased apart the two types of happiness—separating the people who seek short-term happiness from those who pursue long-term meaning—Cole discovered something astonishing. Those who pursued pleasure more than meaning had the bad genomic fingerprint profile, the one with the dangerous immune response. But those whose dispositions tipped toward eudaimonic well-being had the opposite response to stress: They were protected at a cellular level.

"I was like, Wow! That's almost too good to be true," Cole recalls. "That's what Aristotle would say! And apparently our genome is wired to agree."

After the study was published in the prestigious *Proceedings of the National Academy of Sciences*, headlines trumpeted what those buzz-kill psychologists had been solemnly arguing: It's better to be good than happy.[12]

Why would our bodies prefer meaning, the deferred gratification, the effort, the relative asceticism of eudaimonia?

Cole theorizes that these people feel less threat, and therefore less need to fight or take flight. "If I derive most of my happiness, my personal value, from hedonic well-being," he says, "if bad things happen to me, if bad things happen in my life, if I'm not feeling happy, that threatens everything that I derive my sense of happiness from. I am fundamentally at the mercy of life and my experience of it."

From your body's perspective, that is a precarious position to be in.

"If, on the other hand, the things I value most are this cause that I support, or these people, this community that I want to thrive and bloom, if it comes from this noble endeavor I am engaged in—*if my happiness comes from something outside me*—then if bad stuff happens to me, that may not threaten me very much," Cole says. "Because where my value is, is to some extent outside of my body and my own hedonic machinery, and it lies in this purpose, or this mission, or this community that can live on and thrive even if my body doesn't."

It is as if the body involved in eudaimonic pursuits—deeply engaged in a community, sacrificially committed to a family or to a cause—somehow knows that it is in a better position to fend off disease. Somehow that body knows it has other resources, friends, family, a web of people it can rely on. That body knows it is not on its own, forced to keep constant vigil against threats, predators, bacteria. *That* body can down-regulate all those genes and stress chemicals that, in the long run, could bring it to an early or miserable death. That body can take a deep breath and relax.

THE BODY'S SECRET WEAPON

In a way, the MIDUS project is one massive psychology experiment. Beginning in 1995, the researchers recruited some seven thousand people from ages twenty-five to seventy-four. They regularly came into clinics to give their blood and saliva samples to test for stress hormones, inflammation markers, and cardiovascular risks. They submitted to psychological exams and neurological tests, and answered questionnaires about all manner of things, from wealth and education to marital happiness, volunteering, exercise, and eating habits.

The researchers were making up for lost time: For decades, scientists have studied the young and the old and ignored the middle years of life. Now, under the direction of Carol Ryff, scientists could watch people, their bodies and their brains, as they passed from young adulthood to midlife to old age.

The researchers want to ferret out the connection between a person's demographics, psychological approach to life and behaviors, on the one hand, and health on the other. Ryff and her colleagues are taking a less traveled route than traditional medicine. Most modern research has focused on pathways to illness, disease, and dysfunction, trying to figure out how to cure cancer, manage heart disease, or remove the plaques and tangles from a person's brain.

"I'm not saying that isn't important," Ryff told me. "But we've given far too little attention to the factors that actually keep people healthy and well."

When you are watching thousands of people navigate through midlife, she says, you see every type of plague that can befall human beings: poverty and low education, cancer and dementia, losing a spouse, raising a child with mental illness.

"I mean, all of these things are part of the midlife journey," she said, "and what we are finding is evidence that many individuals have the internal and external resources that they need to actually hang on to their health and well-being in the face of these challenges. Some of those individuals in those kinds of adverse circumstances are doing well. And if so, Why?"

What are the "internal resources," Ryff wondered, the psychological ingredients, that make a person resilient and healthy in the face of challenges, rather than send him over the cliff of depression or disease? After much testing, she and her colleagues arrived at a cluster of six attitudes or mind-sets that seem to predict health and well-being:

1. Positive relations with others
2. Environmental mastery, or the ability to create or choose environments where you thrive and handle events as they come along
3. Self-acceptance, or knowing your strengths and weaknesses
4. Autonomy, that is, independence, controlling your own behavior, and not looking for approval from others
5. Personal growth, meaning that you keep evolving and learning throughout your life
6. Purpose in life, or the search for meaning in everyday life, even when things go (horribly) wrong; a sense of direction and a zest for life

Ryff seems to have a soft spot for "purpose in life," and for Viktor Frankl, the Holocaust survivor and modern intellectual father of this particular quality. In his 1946 book *Man's Search for Meaning*, the Austrian psychiatrist described finding a purpose in the Nazi concentration camps, places that stripped prisoners of their dignity, their health, their very humanness. One morning, when Frankl was worrying about a particularly sadistic foreman and fretting over whether he should trade his last cigarette for a bowl of soup, he suddenly realized that his thinking had become trivial, self-serving, narrow as that of a trapped animal. He realized that the key to his survival did not lie in the cost-benefit analysis of cigarette versus soup, or even in slinking out of the angry gaze of the foreman. The secret lay in seeking meaning and purpose every day. Frankl found that meaning by thinking about his wife, who had been moved to another camp and (unknown to him) had already died, and by imagining a time in the future when he could explain to students the psychology of concentration camps, and thus bring some meaning to almost unimaginable suffering.

"Life is never made unbearable by circumstances," Frankl is credited with saying, "but only by lack of meaning and purpose."

"His basic message," Ryff observed, "was, no matter what is happening to you, you have the opportunity, and indeed, I would say you have the responsibility, to actually find some meaning in it. And if you can do that, it will probably not only improve your subjective experience; our work is showing it may also have benefits for various aspects of your health."

Over the past decade, Ryff and other scientists tried to measure the health benefits of purpose in life through sophisticated analytical studies. What follows is hardly an exhaustive list, merely a representative sample. Older people who score high on purpose in life were twice as likely to be alive over a five-year follow-up period, according to David Bennett and his colleagues at Rush University.[13] The benefit isn't reserved for the elderly: Middle-aged and younger adults were more likely to be alive fourteen years later if they possessed that trait, prompting the lead researcher to note: "The earlier someone comes to a direction for life, the earlier these protective effects may be able to occur."[14]

Having a reason to get out of bed in the morning translates not only into longer lives but also into better health. In one study, American men who said they had a tangible purpose in life were 22 percent less likely to suffer a stroke than those with little purpose.[15] Studies of Japanese men found that those high in *ikigai* (sense of purpose) were less likely to have a stroke or heart attack[16] or die.[17] Not surprisingly, perhaps, middle-aged and older Americans with close family and meaningful work, those who invest in a hobby or in organizations outside themselves, such as their church or a cause or a political campaign, live longer.[18] Researchers found that a sense of purpose changes behavior: People are more likely to take care of their health, getting checked out for high cholesterol and for various cancers such as breast, prostate, and colon. They also spend significantly less time in the hospital. And as people age, researchers have found, purpose in life seems to lower the risk of multiple chronic conditions.[19]

The biggest surprise for Carol Ryff was that a person's psychological makeup seems to undo some of the effects of poverty and poor education (not just purpose in life but also the five other traits in well-being). She says the strongest predictors of one's health are, hands down, wealth and years of education. But a poor person who scores high in psychological well-being is by some measures far more healthy than her underprivileged peers.[20] Similarly, when researchers looked at the inflammatory markers of a psychologically robust person with a high school education, he seemed just as healthy as someone with a college degree—and much healthier than his less-educated peers.[21]

"It's unlikely that any of us are going to be able to wave a magic wand and redistribute wealth and educational attainment overnight," Ryff said. "But in the meantime, I think it's actually uplifting to know that—especially for people who don't have a college education, who don't have a high-status job—that doesn't inherently doom you in terms of your long-term health profile."

A HAPPIER BRAIN, NATURALLY

A t this point, a harried person in his or her middle years may be thinking: Sure, some people won the psychological lottery and are brimming with optimism, selfless instincts, and a sense of purpose. But what about the rest of us, frantically tending to the needs of a generation above and below, paying the mortgage and college tuition, all the while navigating a challenging career and impossible deadlines? You want to add a psychological makeover to my to-do list?

Happily, Stanford psychologist Laura Carstensen says, you don't need to actively cultivate eudaimonia or purpose in life to enjoy a happier brain. You just need to live a few decades.

Carstensen has revolutionized the way science thinks about aging.[22] The more she studied older people, the more they surprised her. Older people, with their ailments and their walkers, their faulty memories and their shrinking worlds, are the most contented of us all. She notes that midlife represents a black hole in research, since people in this stage are too busy rushing off to work, driving their kids to soccer practice, and taking their own parents to doctor's appointments to drop by the lab for testing. Most insights about middle age, therefore, are an extrapolation, the dotted line connecting the data points from the young to the old.

This dearth of research made Carstensen's ten-year beeper study a rare and valuable enterprise.[23] In 1994, Carstensen recruited nearly two hundred Northern Californians between ages eighteen and ninety-four to wear an electronic pager for one week. Five times a day, at random (sometimes inconvenient) times, she paged them, reminding them to write down the intensity of their feelings at that moment, choosing from one of nineteen emotions ranging from happiness and pride to anger, guilt, and boredom. She repeated the week-long experiment five years later, and five years after that. The participants came to the lab for psychological testing, underwent brain scanning, and chewed on cotton balls, allowing researchers to test for the stress hormone cortisol.

"What we see is this curve upward where negative emotions decline and positive emotions stay fairly stable," Carstensen told me, "so that the balance between positive and negative emotions improves with age."

The sweet spot for happiness arrives in the late sixties to early seventies, she said. It's well chronicled that people in their forties and fifties feel a dip in their hedonic, momentary happiness, but she, like others, believes a subterranean alchemy is taking place. During midlife, people begin to pivot, to stop and appreciate things both smaller and richer: primarily, relationships and the present moment.

"We think this is related to time running out, so that as people move through life, they see something positive, enjoy and experience it. You know, they imagine the face of an old friend with greater and greater knowledge of the fragility of life, and that makes emotional experience, I would argue, richer than ever."

A person's happiness curve rises sharply from around eighteen to forty, early midlife. Then it holds steady. It is the *unhappiness* curve where elders press their advantage: In general, the older you are, the more adept you are at managing your emotions. Compared with young people, middle-aged and especially older people tend to look at the glass half-full, and they seem to bounce back from adversity more quickly.[24]

Carstensen calls this the "positivity effect." In several studies, she and her colleagues asked young people and older people to inspect a series of photos, ranging from pleasant or happy (puppies, laughing babies, a sunset over the desert) to disturbing or sad images (a snake, an old man with his wife in the hospital). The younger people remembered more of the negative photos, while the older people remembered twice as many positive photos. When Carstensen included middle-aged people in one study, the midlife participants also recalled more positive than negative photos, although not as many as their elders, suggesting they are right on schedule for a happier outlook.[25]

Then Carstensen slid them into a brain scanner and observed their brains processing the information. The researchers found the older brains behaved in startlingly different ways than younger brains.[26] Carstensen was particularly interested in the amygdala, the emotion center of the brain. The results were stark: The amygdala of young people's brains lit up at both happy and sad photos.

"For older people, we saw no activation in the amygdala in response to the negative images, but we saw significant activation and response to the positive images," she said. "The amygdala is the part of your brain that says, *This is important. Pay attention.* And it appears that older people are not activating that region of the brain when you show them negative information."

In other words, their brains ignore, or "disattend," bad news. As you grow older, your brain, like a cheerful conductor, begins to orchestrate the various sections into a happier pattern. Gradually, your perspective becomes a glass half-full. Other researchers have shown that people with great purpose in life, no matter what their age, process negative information in the same considered, more positive way.[27]

What is the insight that middle-aged people can glean from these findings? I ask Carstensen.

"There are certain parts of life that are just going to keep getting better," Carstensen said. "Relationships seem to get better, and I think that's because when you let go of the trivial problems and you look at the big picture and stare across the breakfast table at that partner of many years and know it's not going to go on forever, but it's here today and you're focused on it and the sun is shining and you're okay."

Why do people grow more contented as they age? I wondered. Do older people become more chipper naturally, or is this a skill they have consciously cultivated over the years?

Carstensen believes it's a little of both. According to her widely accepted "socioemotional selectivity theory," people's motivation changes as they grow older. They are able to monitor time—not just according to the clock or the calendar, but according to their lives. Twenty-year-olds see the future "as absolutely limitless" and behave that way: trying out different jobs, dating wildly inappropriate people, because, well, why not? Fifty-year-olds see the end a few miles down the road and begin to shift their behavior; as Carstensen puts it: "Fifty-year-olds don't go on blind dates." Seventy-year-olds are keenly aware of their shortened time horizon.

"What we have found is that when time horizons shrink, that's what is related to these goal changes. People who see time as running out make shifts in motivation and goals to focus them on what really, really matters."

"Such as?"

"For most people, what really matters is other people."

While I have witnessed this in my ninety-something mother, I realized the foreshortened time horizon also shapes the emotions of those who are dying too young. In August 2013, after I sent out an inquiry to NPR listeners about the ups and downs of midlife, I received more than a dozen notes from people for whom midlife is the last station before death. The notes surprised me: Where I thought anger would colonize their lives, gratitude reigned. Where I thought there would be resentment or regret that they would miss their children's high school proms or wedding days, there was instead an unswerving attention to squeezing every particle of joy out of the moment. Before meeting

Laura Carstensen, this would have puzzled me; now I recognized her socioemotional selectivity theory as I read these tiny masterpieces of wisdom from the shadow of death.

Chuck Bryant's notes were perhaps my favorite, and we struck up a correspondence. He had been diagnosed with stage IV prostate cancer a decade earlier, when he was forty-seven.

"Two rounds of radiation and two regimens of chemo have knocked the little buggers back," he wrote in 2013, "although in recent months they've mounted a new offensive."

What was keeping him alive, Chuck quipped, was "evidently some biological predisposition to keep going." That, and relationships: with members of his church and, most of all, the woman he had married six and a half years earlier.

I, with my ostensibly long time horizon, let the correspondence lapse. I feared the worst when I wrote Chuck a year later, half expecting my e-mail to bounce back, a modern sign of twenty-first-century mortality. To my relief, he wrote back immediately.

Chuck's cancer was closing in on him, cutting off his options one by one. His PSA had more than doubled into the 300s; his bone scans showed his skeleton "lit up like a Christmas tree." His oncologist told him, "At this rate, you will die soon."

Then he described the events of the previous night: a concert at his church, featuring Beethoven's Moonlight Sonata and Schubert's "To the Distant One," followed by dessert with friends at their home.

"The best part," Chuck wrote, "was listening to the music with Jan's head on my right shoulder, her arm around me and touching my left arm. I closed my eyes and I felt every note. Maybe I'm physically oversensitive to stimuli right now, but it delighted me beyond words.

"Throughout the apparently inevitable approach of my final point on the bell curve, a crowd of devoted friends and family continue to support me vigorously and steadily. I aim to remain conscious and aware enough to experience the best of it all with the worst. I'm receiving ample bouquets while I live. Who could ask for more? All in all, I'm biased, but I can't imagine a life more blessed than mine has been."

Would that I, at fifty-five, with many more moments ahead, cease scattering them with the centrifugal force of my oh-so-busy life. Would that I, more than halfway through my time, pause, look one of these moments in the eye, and recognize, in that casual dinner at the neighborhood watering hole with Devin and Viv, that oft-repeated story from Mom, that inside joke with Jody, a little piece of grace. Blink, it's gone. I want so many more.

PAIN AS A LAUGHING MATTER

Tuesday, May 7

Welcome to laughter club," Katherine Puckett enthused. "This is a chance to laugh with each other, not at each other."

The crowd of a dozen or so people looked at her blankly. They formed a circle, some leaning on canes, several occupying wheelchairs or resting on gray metal chairs. One older woman was attached to her IV pole.

Puckett knew this was the hardest moment of her sell. She smiled, attempting eye contact with each one of the cancer patients. She knew it was premature to put on the red foam clown nose, but experience had taught her that even in this setting—a fluorescent-lit conference room at Cancer Treatment Centers of America (CTCA) in Zion, Illinois—the crowd would soon be roaring.

"Why do we do this?" she asked rhetorically. "Because laughter has a lot of health benefits, physiologically, psychologically, emotionally."

Katherine Puckett explained to these people with every sort of cancer and attendant pain that there are three laughter centers in the body. The hee-hee center—*Put your hands on your cheeks*—is the head center. The ha-ha center—*Hands on heart, please*—is the heart center. The ho-ho center is, you guessed it, the belly center. With unimaginable bravado, Puckett asked the quiet crowd to follow her lead. She began slowly chanting *Hee, hee, hee hee,* then, faster and louder, *HEE HEE HEE . . .* quickening the pace until her fake laughter turned into peals of real laughter.

I am so grateful I'm not doing this, I thought. Several patients looked at each other; I sensed they were thinking the same thing. But they politely complied. A minute later, people were *hee-hee*ing at the top of their lungs, at startling volume, given the circumstances.

"Now try *ha ha!*" Puckett cried. She had them in the palm of her hand. For the next hour, the patients shook hands, introducing themselves not by name but by *hee hee, haa haa, hoo hoo.* They sang "Happy Birthday" with the same vocabulary. They threw invisible snowballs at each other in slow motion, they rode an imaginary roller coaster and galloped on an imaginary horse, *whoa*ing and laughing and swaying in their wheelchairs. I watched, gobsmacked. It was like seeing people rise from the dead.

Puckett, a middle-aged woman in a tailored red jacket, with wire-rimmed glasses and an unruly mass of curly brown hair, told me she isn't a natural comic. But as the national director of mind-body medicine at CTCA, she felt obligated to do *something* after a patient came to her office one day more than a decade earlier and said, "You guys need some more fun around here."

Initially Puckett invited patients to bring in jokes, Mad Libs, and funny videos. Those flopped. Then she heard about laughter clubs, and she invited a certified laughter leader (yes, there are such jobs) to demonstrate. She began to catch on. Or rather, the laughing did. It's contagious, like the flu. Still, she resisted earning her own laughter leader certificate.

"I was really dreading it," she said, "because I thought, *Really, they're going to try to get me to be a clown. And I'm not a clown! I don't want to do that silly stuff!* But I loved this training. I could not believe it. I loved it so much!"

Improbably, the patients love it as well. They come in wheelchairs and walkers, and when they can't get out of bed, she takes the laughing to them.

"We had one woman there one day who was in a wheelchair and she had such a great time," Puckett recalled. "She said at the end, 'I'm going to take this home to my kids and grandkids. I love this.' The next day she died unexpectedly. I just had a brief moment of, *Oh my gosh! Did we stress her out in the laughter club? Was it too much for her?* Well, it really was unrelated. But then I thought: *She was laughing and having fun and making plans to go out and share it.* So I ended up feeling really good that she'd been able to have that experience on her last day."

Puckett isn't particularly bothered that the evidence for the healing powers of laughter is somewhat scant, at least by the standards of academic science.[28] Some studies suggest that laughing can help a person in the short run by regulating blood pressure, improving circulation,[29] and releasing endorphins,[30] the feel-good hormone. There is some indication that laughing may decrease stress hormones, and possibly boost a person's immune system. The strongest evidence of laughter's efficacy, however, involves pain.[31] And in a place where people inevitably focus on pain and death, a simple break from those primal thoughts is good enough.

"When we're laughing, that's really all the brain can handle in that moment," Puckett said, and she's right: Scientists have shown that distraction temporarily relieves chronic and acute pain.[32] "Even if we're feeling sad, even if we're feeling angry, if we start laughing, those other feelings get put aside. The brain can't handle all of those feelings at the same time. It allows us to take a break from those other feelings. We can go back to them later, but in that moment, that's all we can do."

Which is why, a decade after Puckett heard about laughter clubs, CTCA offers them at each of its five sites. Which is why the dozen patients in this small conference room seem momentarily transformed, radiant, smiling like children, moving with more agility, catching the breath their laughing has stolen. Somewhere between the penguin walk and their placing red foam clown balls on their noses, I stopped the action to ask a few questions.

Teresa Frioux (breast cancer) deemed the exercises "hilarious. I mean, your spirits are lifted in the middle of a humdrum day of appointments and you feel a lot lighter. Happier."

"I feel lighter myself," said another patient, leaning on a cane. This man, who suffers from prostate cancer, asked not to be identified. "You know, my foot's been killing me and then when I was in here, I didn't even feel it. So the pain has gone away."

Robbie Robinson (non-Hodgkin's lymphoma), who finished treatments a decade earlier, lives nearby and drops by the laughter club whenever he can. "I still deal with a lot of neuropathy and a lot of pain from my treatments and everything," he said. "I was really hurting when I came in here today, and I forgot about it. I'm feeling pretty good right now. The pain's still there but the laughter makes the mind forget about it. So that's as powerful as any drug."

I'd go with Percocet, I thought. But in the next instant, I had a deadly serious question: *Could I think my way out of pain?*

WE ARE FAMILY

Disease and pain sometimes ignore the boundaries of age. Cancer can strike a three-year-old, and diabetes often afflicts a child before her teens. But generally, it takes a few decades for our bodies to revolt and for stress to mutate into physical symptoms. Usually cancer or Parkinson's genes bide their time before switching on, hips wait awhile before lodging their arthritic complaints. My husband reached his forties before type 1 diabetes struck. For nearly five decades, I enjoyed perfect health, until my middle years brought first silence, then pain.

On May 4, 2009, at the age of forty-nine, I lost my voice. That morning I awakened with a cold, gave a twenty-minute talk at a conference, and that was it. Gone.

It is always a problem for an on-air radio correspondent to lose her voice, but this was a particularly inconvenient time. In less than two weeks, my first book would be published, and I was scheduled to speak on a number of radio programs, including *The Diane Rehm Show*.[33] I was putting together a five-part series for NPR. I had not finished writing the scripts, much less recording them, and for the edits and the final product, I needed to speak. Initially I reassured myself, *It's just a cold, I'll have my voice in a few days*. But as day unfolded into silent day and I could not even squeak, I began to panic. As one of my friends observed later, "You imploded from the stress." I thought my friend had a point.

My voice did come back, barely, with two days to spare, thanks to a heavy course of steroids. But my vocal cords had turned temperamental, grudgingly working overtime—then, suddenly, they would go on strike.

The uneasy détente lasted nearly three years, until one Monday in

April 2012. I came down with a cold and my vocal cords quit for two weeks. When they finally deigned to return to work, they complained in a new way. The pain began softly, just in my right vocal cord, then it turned up a notch before going to stereo. Within two weeks, the pain was truly all I could think about. I remember covering the trial of a priest accused of pedophilia, forcing myself to concentrate on the defense testimony, but all I could think was, *How do I escape this? How do I escape my own body?*

I realize how melodramatic this sounds. This was not cancer or MS or schizophrenia. Still, I had never encountered something that shaded my every moment. The pain pulsated, a spikey red living thing two inches in front of my eyes, blocking out my entire world except my peripheral vision, where my husband, my mother, my editor, and my deadlines clamored for attention. Short deadlines sent the pain soaring: Scrambling to get up to speed on a story, conducting interviews, frantically writing the story before airtime, editing (which required voice), tracking the script (which required voice), I would drive home catatonic with relief, and think about sleep, blessed sleep, the only moments I evaded the pain.

It was not that the pain was excruciating. It was that it was relentless. It was also boring. Who wants to hear about my vocal cords? But it narrowed my world to a pinprick.[34]

When the pain began, I finally connected it to my brother's voice problems. Around Christmastime 1988, my brother, David, was thirty-five years old, already a successful entrepreneur and married for two years to Katherine, his smart and exquisite wife. David was on a diet, came down with a cold, and lost his voice. When the cold lifted, he still could not speak. He was mute for the next four months, until he found the right voice specialist, who taught Dave how to retrain his paralyzed vocal cords so he could talk again.

Dave had good days and bad days for the next nine years. In October 1998, he went on another strict diet—he had not made the connection between diet and vocal cords—and lost his voice again. This is when the pain arrived, pitched its tent, and stayed. By now, he had met many of the nation's top ear, nose, and throat specialists. They recommended surgery.

"Their view was, if they keep perfecting the surgery so my vocal cords were straighter and had to work less hard, then the pain would go away," Dave recalled. "They were getting them straighter, but the pain wasn't decreasing at all."

They operated on his vocal cords ten times in the next five years.

In November 2014, we sat in David's sun-drenched Watergate office overlooking the Potomac River. I had brought graham crackers, our favorite comfort food and the only food that soothed our throats, and we happily munched through a packet. By now Dave had sold his companies and bought *The Atlantic* magazine. Dave's life looks enviable: He is wealthy, with a beautiful and accomplished wife, and three exceptional boys educated at Yale or Princeton. Yet I doubt anyone would trade their life for his, once they read the small print. Once they learned about his pain.

"The pain wasn't such that I couldn't get by," David said, "but it was such that I thought, *If I have to go like this for the rest of my life, I don't know that I would choose to go on.*"

"That's exactly how I felt," I admitted. "It wasn't like 'I'm going to kill myself tomorrow,' but I thought, *I can't do this for forty more years.*"

When my pain began in 2012, I had somehow forgotten that David was living with not only an unreliable voice but also pain. Nor did Dave realize the extent of my suffering. He thought I was simply terrified of losing my voice, given my career at NPR.

It was not for another few months, when Dave, Mom, and I were driving out to Middleburg, Virginia, on a Sunday afternoon, that we made the connection. I was sitting in the backseat, scrunched in the corner so no one could see me silently crying. When I finally told David, out of Mom's earshot, he pulled out his cell phone and texted his doctor. Dave describes himself as "assaultively empathetic" when he finds others in pain, especially his little sister. That week, I found myself in New York, talking to his vocal cord specialist, on my way to relief through a pain medication called Neurontin. In one of those flukes of genetics, we both had the same, extremely rare, vocal cord paralysis. His is worse—it went untreated for longer—but, well, as Sister Sledge has it, *We are family.*

At the end of our conversation, I told Dave that I had been looking through my journal for a specific entry about him. I used to keep a sporadic spiritual journal, and beginning in around 1999, I wrote a lot of prayers on yellow pads of paper—a habit I picked up from my father—about David's voice. I told him I recalled, but had not yet located, one particular prayer.

"I know I wrote it around 1999 or 2000," I said. "I prayed that I could take the burden from you and that I could have your voice problem instead."

David paused, absorbing this.

"I'm sorry you did that prayer because look what happened to you," he said. "I'm really sorry." Then: "Go pray that away. Withdraw that prayer!"

"I tried, later," I said, laughing. "In 2012. You know, *I was just kidding!*"

"Do you think that's causal?"

"I think it's partly genetic," I began.

"I came to the view that it has to be," he said.

"Yeah, I mean, what are the chances?" I said. "But I do believe that you have to be vigilant about your thoughts."

This surely springs from my Christian Science background: Your thinking is your experience. But while I had seen the healthful effects of thinking positively, I had never considered the possibility that thinking negatively could open the door to disease, or vocal cord paralysis. It seemed superstitious.

I broached this question with psychiatrist James Gordon. He has impeccable credentials: a graduate of Harvard Medical School and a clinical professor at Georgetown University School of Medicine. Because he is the founder of the Center for Mind-Body Medicine, I thought he would take my spooky mind-body question seriously. I described my voice problem and, feeling a little silly, told him about the prayer for David.

"We can't rule out some strong genetic factor," he said.

Nor could we rule out the mind, he said.

"If you were in a relaxed hypnotic state, as you may well have been when you were praying like that," Gordon told me, "if I put a piece of chalk in your hand and I tell you it's a lit cigarette, you will likely have a burn on your hand. The mind is enormously powerful, so by expressing that wish, that prayer, that hope, you may have taken it on. It's possible."

He reflected for a moment.

"There's a discipline in Buddhism called *tonglen*, in which you do take in the suffering of others. But it's part of a process of letting it go as well, and I think you haven't let it go."

Now painkillers have ridden to my rescue. But Neurontin makes me stupid: relieved of much of the pain, but slow, as if I am running through chest-high water. My own view is that I do not have sufficient intellectual buffer to allow for sluggishness, and while I am grateful for the basic relief of pharmaceuticals, they pose a dilemma: I cannot function without taking the nerve medication, and I cannot function well with it.

This, then, is how I arrived at that moment at Cancer Treatment

Centers of America, watching a dozen cancer patients laughing away the pain.

I did not believe laughter offered a long-term solution. But in that moment, I thought: *Could my mind reroute the pain messages? Could my thinking reduce the pain?*

Few questions seemed more pressing, or more hopeful.

THE DESERT OR OASIS OF MIDLIFE MARRIAGE

JUNE

Tuesday, June 25

It was bright and blazingly hot, topping ninety degrees, when we pulled up to the Cruise America office in Germantown, Maryland. I waited in line with Sandra Day (our eighty-pound Labrador–golden retriever mix), behind two customers picking up their RVs. Devin and Vivian ventured out to buy some soft drinks for the trip, waiting discreetly until two men completed their drug deal in front of the liquor store two doors down.

This was a dream—or an ordeal, depending on whom you are asking—more than eleven years in the making. From our second date in March 2002, Devin rhapsodized about traveling the country in an RV, stopping in small towns, camping in untouched forests, and at first light, pulling up stakes and hitting the open road. I could imagine few things as pointless, or as boring.

And yet, here we were, receiving last-minute instructions on RV living from the Cruise America manager. Jay was garrulous and theatrical as he showcased the amenities. He opened the narrow shower, apparently built with Kenyan marathoners in mind. He moved to the cabinets, filled with ceramic plates, mugs, and plastic glasses; these would all catapult across the RV when the cabinet doors flew open at the first turn. Looking a little like a game show model, Jay gestured toward the "double bed" in the space above the driver's seat (clearance: two feet), and then, with a flourish, opened the slatted doors to reveal the back bedroom with the "queen size" bed. He gave *no* guidance as to how to handle this behemoth. No tips for turning, except to look in the side mirror. No explanations about the generator versus the coach battery versus the gas-powered electricity versus plugging into an electrical outlet; no warning that the tap water was not drinkable, nor an explanation about gray water (from the shower) versus black water (from the toilet) or (most important) how to drain the dirty water from the vehicle. We were clueless. And we were too ignorant to ask.

We said goodbye to Vivian, who would pick us up back here in two weeks, and piled in. Devin climbed into the driver's seat and, in a scene that would replay itself several times a day, Sandra and I raced for the front passenger seat. She won. I pulled her off and settled in. We scanned the parking lot. Devin turned on the ignition. Before moving the gearshift from Park to Drive, he paused, looked at the traffic racing down the highway, and said, "There's a mobile home park across the street. Can we stay there for the night?" I still wonder if he was kidding.

LONG-TERM ROMANCE IN THE BRAIN

The person directly responsible for our driving down the Blue Ridge Parkway in a thirty-foot RV is Arthur Aron, a research psychologist at Stony Brook University. Aron has studied the psychology and neurobiology of romantic love and has pondered this conundrum: How can middle-aged couples keep their marriage fresh?

"When you fall in love," he told me, "it's exhilarating, it's exciting, you feel that your world has expanded. You share memories. Then it slows down."

That much I knew, having fallen breathlessly, rapturously in love with Devin eleven years earlier, spending every minute together and telling my closest friends shortly after we met that "you can get on board or off, but this train is leaving the station." He was forty and I was forty-three on our wedding day, my first marriage, his second. But too quickly, the stresses of merging the lives of two independent, seasoned adults began to drain the romance like oil leaking from an engine, a process accelerated by my long hours covering the Justice Department for NPR and Devin's lengthy commute to the University of Maryland, Baltimore County. And we had it easy. We didn't even have children living at home.

But some couples defy gravity, Aron insisted. About one third of couples in long-term marriages claim to be intensely in love.[1] He wondered if their brains would confirm it. He decided to find out.

The first task was to identify what romantic love looks like in the brain. To do that, Aron and his collaborator, Helen Fisher, a biological anthropologist at Rutgers University and the chief scientific advisor for Match.com, recruited people who had recently fallen in love, and asked them to gaze at photos of their beloved while lying in a brain scanner. What the scans revealed upended their definition of love.

"I had always felt that romantic love was an emotion," Helen Fisher told me. "But when I saw those brain scans, I realized, 'Oh my goodness, the basic traits of romantic love are produced by the reward system in the brain.'"

The emotional center of the brain was quiet, she said, while another area of the brain lit up. "It's linked with drive, motivation, focus, and goal-oriented behavior. Those are not emotions."

When you fall in love—romantic love, not the lust of a one-night stand—you feel the urgency of hunger after a day-long fast, the obsessiveness of thirst on a hot day, even the kind of craving associated with cocaine, since romantic love releases a flood of dopamine throughout the brain. Oxytocin—the cuddle hormone that bonds mother and child, and man and woman—spreads through your brain. Aron said this is not a luxury reserved for the young.

"People who are sixty and newly in love are like people who are twenty and newly in love. And like seven-year-olds having a crush," he added.

That is new love. What about seasoned love? Aron and Fisher found seventeen people in their fifties and sixties, married an average of twenty-one years, who insisted they still felt passionate love for their spouses.

"We looked at ourselves and said, 'Are they lying?'" Fisher recalled. "So we put them in the machine and, sure enough, we find the same activity in the [reward and drive areas of the brain] as we did among those who had just fallen happily in love. But we found some differences."

Specifically, they found that brain areas linked to attachment grew active in long-term couples, while they remained quiet in the recently besotted. This is the kind of marathon love that spells commitment and prompts two people to raise children together. If long-term love seems calmer, less painful, and less anxious than the frenzy of new love, there is good reason, neurologically. Gazing at a valued long-term partner ramps up areas rich in opioids and serotonin, which increases pleasure and reduces pain; in fact, doctors target these areas to moderate anxiety and obsessive-compulsive disorder. That twenty-year marriage is better than a pharmacy: cheaper, and with a few recreational drugs thrown in.

Good for them, I thought, but if your seasoned marriage is punctuated by distraction and exhaustion as much as fireworks and chemistry, how do you revive the romance? How do you navigate from Archie and Edith Bunker to Paul Newman and Joanne Woodward? You can do this, Art Aron says, by infusing one element into your life.

Novelty.

Long before brain scans told us that romantic love is a drive—something the brain considered a necessity for our ancestors to survive and procreate—Aron was thinking about date nights. He divided fifty-three seasoned couples (married on average fifteen years) into three groups. He asked a third of them to spend ninety minutes once a week doing something familiar and pleasant, such as going to a movie. He asked another third to go dancing, skiing, see a concert, or something else out of their routine. The third group was not assigned any activity. After ten weeks, the couples with novel date nights reported significantly more marital satisfaction than the couples who went to a movie or trundled on as before.[2] He followed this with another study that had some couples crawl across a room with their ankles and wrists Velcroed together, carrying a pillow between them, while other couples performed a boring task, in which one person rolled a ball across a room while on his hands and knees, while the spouse watched.[3] Those with the "novel" task reported more happiness with their relationship, as well as greater acceptance of their partner.[4]

Now we know why. The brain rewards novel activity and craves surprises. No wonder couples that infuse novelty into their relationships feel a little dopamine-driven reward, a little cocaine-like high, a little oxytocin-mediated closeness, all of which leads to romance.

As I considered how I could test this premise in my own marriage, I envisioned my husband, a Ph.D. from the University of Pennsylvania who specializes in understanding war, terrorism, and nuclear deterrence, crawling across a gym mat with a pillow between us. No, I realized, he would rather die on one of his beloved nuclear weapons. What to do? I knew instantly. I tried to strangle the idea before it could cry out, but then I let it live, for the greater good of science—and our marriage.

I called Cruise America.

When I told Art Aron that he had inspired our two-week RV trip, he sighed.

"The only thing I'd say from the research and from the theory, both, is that you don't want it to be overly stressful," he said, perhaps perceiving that an introvert (Devin) and extrovert (me) might do some damage in such close quarters.

"It's good to have excitement and novelty and challenge up to a point," Aron said, "but if it gets really stressful or difficult or upsetting, then it's not good."

But seeing that I was committed—we had put down a deposit—Aron offered to conduct a basic test. Devin and I should each draw a picture before the trip, which we were not to show each other. Each picture must include Devin and me, a car, a house, and a tree. We should draw another picture upon our return, put all the artwork in an envelope, and send it off to him for analysis.

That night, I asked Devin to draw a picture including him and me, a car, a house, and a tree. He looked at me for a long moment, as if I were speaking Dutch. I waited expectantly. He pulled out a yellow pad and began to draw.

Wednesday, June 26

Last night we rolled into Candy Hill Campground in Winchester, Virginia, a little past eight. The lanky, weathered manager took one look at our RV, with the vistas of the Badlands and the Grand Canyon painted on the sides, along with "800-RV4-Rent," and walked briskly inside.

"They shouldn't go in site seventeen," he said to the woman at the register, assigning spaces. "They have one of those *rented* vehicles," disdain surging through his voice. Apparently, *rented* RVs have short hoses for water and waste. We needed a space where we could snuggle right up to the "dump" holes and the water spigot.

He directed us to another site and we drove into it. We plugged into the electrical outlet and waited for the air-conditioning to turn on. Nothing. We began to perspire. Devin pulled out the manual. Unfortunately, it was written generically for numerous RV models, so none of the diagrams—of the water, refrigerator, heater, air conditioner— looked vaguely like what we saw in front of us. I just began pushing buttons.

By ten p.m., Sandra Day was panting hard, I had stripped down to shorts and sleeveless shirt, and Devin had thrown the manual back in the drawer. I envisioned the vacation unfolding before us, and it looked hot and muggy. But I knew what to do. I waited until Devin took Sandra for a walk, then darted to the plush RV next to us—even in the world of RVing, there is the 1 percent—and knocked.

"I'm so sorry to bother you," I said to the grandfatherly man who answered. "This is our very first night in the RV and for some reason we can't get the air-conditioning on."

He grabbed his flashlight.

"I'm Durham, as in Bull," he said,

"I'm Barb, as in embarrassed to ask you to help us at this time of night."

"No problem," he said generously. He walked to the electrical outlet by our camper, flipped the switch, and the RV came roaring to life.

"I guess you turned off the electricity when you plugged in," he said, embarrassed for us. I realized that all our advanced degrees and pointy-headed accomplishments would get us nowhere in this new world. We would need many Durhams as the trip unfolded.

That night, drifting off in our cool RV, I realized we had unwittingly demonstrated a key discovery about long-term marriage. Generally, marriage research is overwhelming and emphatic on one point: Opposites attract, then attack. People who share personality traits, worldviews, education levels, and conflict styles tend to have happier marriages than those who do not. I found this disquieting, since Devin and I often seem to inhabit different planets.

But there is a major exception relevant to midlife marriages—not always but often. After the first few years, couples who do *not* share traits report that they are happier than look-alike couples.[5] Early on, young couples are exploring the world together, and sharing personality traits such as extroversion, openness to experience, and conscientiousness makes the sailing smooth. Midlife, however, is about getting things done: raising kids, paying bills, juggling two careers, enjoying a social life if possible. Two conscientious people may fight over who handles the family finances better, while the kids' playdates go unscheduled. If a conscientious person is married to an extrovert, that family would pay the bills *and* see friends for dinner.

So it is in the Hagerty world. Devin is the Secretary of Transportation, figuring out the logistics of life, keeping the cars running, the bills paid, mapping out the best route from D.C. to Roanoke. I am the Secretary of State, calling the plumber, making appointments with the dentist, asking how to turn on the air-conditioning in the RV, and generally interacting with the world. We split up tasks: The quiet ones that require precision go to my introverted husband, the public ones go to me.

Our differences in style can create a little tension. But on our RV adventure, we reveled in them. Today I biked twenty-seven miles along the Blue Ridge Parkway, racing along the sun-dappled road until I was exhausted. Ever since arthritis in my right knee ended my running days a year ago, robbing me of a daily ritual that kept me sane and healthy for the past thirty-five years, I had discovered a new passion: cycling. Running mile after mile ground me down, but on my bike, I felt light as air. Today I could contain myself no longer. I burst into song:

"Jeremiah was a bullfrog [bah-bah-bum]," I panted. *"Was a good friend of mine [bah-bah-bum] . . ."*

In those moments, I was not a married fifty-something peddling up and down the Blue Ridge Parkway. I was in my friend Betsy's basement, two seventh-graders playing the record again and again, singing "Joy to the World," shouting harmony into imaginary microphones.[6]

For a few minutes, I sloughed off my middle-aged estate. For the length of that ride, I was twelve years old again.

Devin and Sandra Day drove ahead and waited, as they would do every day. When I rolled up, Devin was sitting in his $9.99 Walmart lawn chair, reading a book. We were both so happy we could burst. I realized that Art Aron was right. Venturing out of our familiar world could be just what our marriage needs. I suspect this may, just may, become The Best Vacation Ever.

BABY BOOMER MARRIAGE ON LIFE SUPPORT—OR NOT

If anything captures the confounding complexity of middle-aged marriage, it was Al and Tipper Gore's slightly R-rated, nationally televised kiss at the 2000 Democratic National Convention. When I saw it, I thought: *Here is hope. Here is visual evidence that you can keep passion alive.* And then, in 2010, the Gores announced they were separating.

The hard evidence suggests that midlife marriage is frayed and breaking. One quarter of all the people who divorce these days are over fifty—more than twice the rate of our parents' generation. Even as the overall divorce rate is tailing off overall, baby boomers continue to break records.

It is what Susan Brown calls the "gray divorce revolution."[7] Brown, a researcher at Bowling Green State University, says the revolution was sparked by a combination of trends. First, boomers started their (first) marriages during the 1970s and 1980s, just when states were making it easy to end a marriage. Later, in their second marriages, these couples were more likely to split up. Previously divorced people are far more willing—two and a half times more willing—to divorce a second time.[8]

"They know that life goes on after divorce," Brown says, "and so these individuals are willing to call it quits if they're dissatisfied."

Researchers say that midlife divorce has a different feel and character from an early breakup.[9] Those who split up in the first seven years tend to do so with pots, pans, and epithets flying. The fourteenth year of marriage sees another spike in divorces. But these couples are distant, passionless, and cool; they have suppressed their negative emotions and allowed their affection to shrink to a dust mote. These marriages are emotionally dead.

Which is where the "Viagra theory" comes into play, says Russell Collins, a marriage therapist in Santa Barbara, California. Baby boomers live longer and more vitally than any generation in history. Collins says he suspected his own parents were hardly thrilled with their marriage, but if you live only a few years after retirement, what's the point of divorcing?

"I think people see themselves living another twenty-five years and they feel vital and healthy, and so they're saying, 'You know, there's another chapter to be lived.'"

Most often, Collins says, the wives are the ones who envision a chapter without their current husbands; and for the first time in history, they can afford to. "Women are increasingly more likely now to say, 'I'm not happy. I've got plenty of dough in the bank. I've got my own career and I don't need you anymore,'" Collins notes.

But if health and financial independence are precipitating causes, many researchers see something else as the root cause, something unique to baby boomers: namely, the mind-set of the "me" generation. Today's marriages are in service to a larger goal of self-fulfillment for both husband and wife.

"If our marriage is not cutting it, divorce is an acceptable solution," Susan Brown says. "And the bar for cutting it has risen. So if, historically, being the traditional wife and mother was enough for a woman, and being a good provider and earner was enough for a man, that's not true today. Now women have to be good providers, too, and men have to be involved fathers, and do half the housework. And the spouse has to be your best friend. And you have to have a good sex life, and on and on the list goes. It's a high bar to achieve, let alone maintain for decades."

Not everyone, of course, is wringing her hands over the gray divorce revolution. Helen Fisher, for one, is "extremely optimistic about the future of relationships for many, many reasons."

Fisher argues that marriage had to be shaken up: It used to be a trap, especially for women, whose only career choice was to marry well. The divorce revolution is a correction, like losing two hundred points in the Dow. It will recover.

"One hundred years ago, the vast majority of men and women had to choose the right person from the right background, with the right kin connection, the right social attributes, the right economic background, and from the right religion," she says. "None of that is important anymore."

This may not be universally true, but she has a point: Externals such as money and religion now take a backseat to internals such as love and commitment. If the marriage doesn't stick, that is a good thing, too.

"People don't walk out of good marriages," Fisher says. "We're walking out of bad marriages and some demographers believe that we will now have much better marriages, because bad marriages can end."

So which is it? Is marriage in midlife dying a swift and agonizing death, or remaking itself in a newer, fresher form? Eli Finkel, a professor of psychology at Northwestern University, says marriages today are both better and worse. It just depends on one's level of privilege.

Finkel notes that divorces doubled between 1960 and 1980. In that time, professional couples with college or graduate degrees were almost as likely to break up as those with high school diplomas and blue-collar jobs. Since 1980, the divorce rate has steadied, but the divorce gap between the more and less educated has ballooned.[10] Those with only high school diplomas are three times as likely to divorce as the college educated.

Marriage, he says, has become a luxury good. Couples who can afford nannies or regular babysitters, who can go on frequent date nights or jet off for romantic vacations—those people have won the marriage lottery.

"Those few marriages," Finkel says, "are experiencing a level of marital bliss that people didn't have access to before."

What about the rest?

Finkel says middle-class marriages are under stress as well, not only because of economics but also because of soaring expectations. Gone are the days when marriage revolved around creating an economic unit to raise a family and provide food, shelter, and protection, as it did until around the 1850s. Gone, too, are the marriages that centered on companionship, love, and raising a family with specific gender roles, as was the case until the 1960s. Today's couples, Finkel says, want to be fulfilled emotionally, professionally, and romantically—and they want their partners to help them realize all their dreams. He compares it to the highest rung on Abraham Maslow's hierarchy of needs: You are expected to "deeply understand the essence, the psychological dreams and hopes and internal battles that characterize your spouse in a way that wasn't anywhere near as important in these previous eras."

It sounds exhausting. To create that kind of marital paradise, couples need lots of good quality time.

"The problem is that if you look at the evidence, on average, Americans aren't managing to do that," Finkel says. "People without children are working longer hours. People with children are parenting like maniacs, which is fine. I'm not judging it as negative, I'm just saying that if you're putting so much time into work or so much time into the children, you are finding very little time for your spouse. That state of affairs is uniquely bad for today's marriages."

DEPOSITS, WITHDRAWALS, AND MIDLIFE LOVE

I could throw a stone in any direction and find dissatisfied midlife couples that fit this description. A trickier feat is locating an exceedingly happy couple. I happened on one couple that has experienced both unhappiness and contentment across the course of two marriages, and could talk with me about their journey from the desert to the oasis of love.

Mary Lou O'Brian and Anton Struntz are sitting on their couch in

Gaithersburg, Maryland. She, at sixty-one, has improbably lustrous brown hair, the glasses of a cool librarian, and a gentle, wide smile. He, at fifty-nine, has no hair and a nicely shaped head, a wiry build, and eyes that seem to suggest an inside joke. Her arm is casually tossed over his leg, his arm around her shoulder. They fit together like two pieces of a puzzle; their sentences seem incomplete without a comment from the other, a small detail, a laugh, a memory, not in a competitive way, but elaborating, complementing, complimenting.

As I listened to them, I realized that this is the quintessential married couple in the twenty-first century: casualties of high expectations, and beneficiaries of the new science of marriage.

Anton's first marriage began to unravel almost immediately. He and his wife had both grown up in rural areas, but, he said, "that's where the similarities ended." Anton was "a softie," she was a little more hard-edged; he was laid-back, she was hard-charging. Adopting a seven-year-old girl with a troubled background brought more chaos into the already fragile marriage.

"My first marriage was always a struggle," Anton recalls. "I was exhausted all the time, wondering, What's it going to be like today?"

They divorced after eleven years.

Mary Lou's first marriage survived seven years. She was an extrovert with a large circle of friends. Her first husband, an introvert, focused on his career as an attorney. At first she could gloss over the differences. Then she couldn't.

"I was not confident enough in my first marriage to demand a person I was more compatible with," Mary Lou says. "He needed a support person. I took care of life so he could excel. It got to the point where I wanted more."

As Mary Lou and her first husband began to live socially and emotionally separate lives, she opened a calligraphy business, and he decided to move to New York for a job in another law firm.

"I thought, *Oh no. That's just the death of me*," she recalls. "And at that point I realized I must not really love this person anymore, because I would have followed him to the end of the world, and now I'm starting to see that if I go with him, that's the end of me. And I felt, Okay, I have to make a decision here."

These are twenty-first-century midlife divorces, as described by marriage researchers John Gottman and Robert Levenson: no physical abuse, no fatal explosions, just two people with diverging values and dreams, drifting quietly apart.

After her divorce, Mary Lou "spent the next fifteen years dating and crashing and burning, with young, buff men. It was my wild stage. And it was hard meeting someone at fifty."

One day, a friend sat her down.

"She said, 'Try eHarmony, because they don't let you pick your own people. They send you people who they think would make good partners for you.' I thought, *Oh, that might be good for me because clearly I'm not doing a good job on my own.*"

eHarmony's premise is that a marriage relationship is like a bank account. Similarities—or what it calls "dimensions of compatibility"—are like deposits. Differences are like withdrawals. Some differences are fine if you have a large enough balance, but too many, and you eventually overdraw your account. Some researchers consider that theory simplistic. And many adults looking for love consider eHarmony paternalistic, with its 240-or-so-question application (it varies) and its insistence that the company, not you, make the first pass at a match. But Mary Lou liked it. So did Anton.

"One of the things I liked about it was I had to take the time to really think about what I wanted instead of just saying, 'Oh well, I'm going to run into somebody and the fireworks will go off and there will be love forever after,'" Anton says. "No. I had to think: What do I want in somebody?"

When eHarmony matched them up, Mary Lou was puzzled: They seemed to have little in common. She grew up in Argentina; her father was an accountant for a mining company there. She assumed she would relate best to another expat. Anton rarely strayed from rural Maryland, where his working-class parents owned a bar. She was used to (although she didn't much like) operatic relationships; he preferred a "slow simmer."

But to their surprise—and this is one of eHarmony's key arguments—background and even interests do not create a good match. The secret is similar values and approach to the world.

"We're so much alike that oftentimes I joke we're the same person," Mary Lou says. "It's a good thing we happen to like ourselves because when we married each other, we married ourselves."

"We bought each other the same book for Christmas," Anton says, laughing. "We like a lot of the same things. We think the same things. It's never been a struggle."

I asked them how their relationship—married eight years, together for ten—differs from their first marriage.

"I don't ever feel any clashing," Mary Lou says. "There are no threats, no jagged edges. And it's so much fun with Anton. Everything is more fun with Anton."

When I left, they were working on the *Washington Post* crossword puzzle. Before they met, Anton had told me, they could each complete only half the Sunday crossword puzzle. Now they finish it together every week.

I wondered how to reconcile Mary Lou and Anton's simpatico relationship—with their shared values, styles, and even sentence structure—with the research suggesting that different styles and personalities bolster a marriage at midlife. I realized that differing styles and skills may allow a midlife marriage to run more smoothly in the midst of children and playdates, careers and aging parents, but it's not necessarily true that opposites attract after the chaos of midlife subsides. For this reason, Mary Lou and Anton's marriage looks like a young marriage, without children and the attendant complexities. In this they have much company among middle-aged people on their second marriage—my own marriage, for example.

Still, when I drove away, I remained a little skeptical. How many couples could boast this kind of frictionless marriage? And I had trouble believing this simple idea—*a bank account, for Pete's sake*—held the key to long-lasting love.

Wednesday, June 26 (continued)

It is 8:16 p.m. and I am writing in the near dark. We arrived two hours ago at the KOA Charlottesville campground. We have figured out how to hook up to the electricity and how to pour the gray water into the dump hole, although we have vowed never to use the bathroom in the RV so we don't have to dump the "black water." This will probably not last long, especially after we pick up our friends Jack and Beth, who will be traveling with us for eight days.

We have finished our dinner of Triscuits, cheese, and salami. I am no cook at home, much less in the wilds of RV living. Devin has a stack of magazines; my legs ache deliciously from my long, hilly bike ride. I feel totally at peace, our RV adventure spreading out before us, one languid day after another.

"Can we just live here?" I venture. "I bet we could get an excellent deal."

Devin looks at me a long moment.

"I wonder what it's like being Barb," he says.

"I wonder what it's like being Devin," I respond.

Even after more than a decade, we are a puzzle to each other.

Twelve years earlier, I was forty-two years old, with no time to date. Covering the Justice Department for NPR in the wake of the September 11, 2001, terrorist attacks left me few hours to sleep, much less plot my romantic life. It had always been this way. I had always privileged work above all else, and in this I am not much different from other news reporters. Except that they managed to find love, settle down, and have children. How did they do that?

A few days before Christmas 2001, I dropped by the house of my good friend Libby Lewis to deliver a present. Her fiancé happened to be there, although in retrospect it seems more calculated than that. As I was leaving, he said he had something serious to tell me.

"You need to increase your numbers," Jonathan said. "You don't have time for blind dates. You need to see the profiles of one hundred men, pick one or two quality dates, and ignore the others. You need to go on Match.com."

After some resistance—I dreaded writing a profile—I signed up. For six months.

Three weeks and several hundred e-mails later, I received a charming, self-deprecating, funny, and—this was crucial—grammatically correct note from an extraordinarily cute guy.

When we finally met, some six weeks later, Devin and I had developed an old-fashioned relationship based on well-crafted e-mails. From his profile, I thought Devin was an outgoing, gregarious man who, raised as a diplomat's son, had a taste for elegant parties. In truth, Devin generally avoids parties and loves nothing more than staying home with a good book. From my profile, Devin thought I was a low-maintenance, sophisticated news reporter who lived for deadlines. The truth is I love nothing more than hiking or biking in the wilderness, and deadlines make me break into a cold sweat.

We managed to keep up the pretense for many months. Only after the wedding did we fully recognize the chasm between perception and reality. When I pointed that out shortly after our honeymoon, Devin explained, paraphrasing Chris Rock: "Oh, that was just our representatives courting each other."

Not only were our Match.com personae nothing like the reality; we were nothing like each other, in terms of background and style. Devin spent most of his childhood in South Asia and Europe. I lived most of my life in the suburbs of Washington, D.C. Devin's international school barely mentioned SATs, much less college preparation and applications. My all-girls private school thought of little else but the Ivy League. Devin was raised without religion and was an accomplished partier at university. I was raised a Christian Scientist and ordered my first glass of wine at forty. Devin is an introvert, an observer. I am a reluctant extrovert (by necessity, not choice) whose first instinct is to grab the phone and ask questions. He loves watching sports; I don't see the point, when you could be playing the game yourself. Devin's careful deliberations can drive me to distraction. My lightning-fast reactions leave him feeling like a spectator at a rodeo, watching a bucking bronco.

You can imagine, perhaps, why I was not keen on research suggesting that similar couples are more likely to go the distance. Yet I knew I needed to enter the lion's den.

THE CALCULUS OF LOVE

I arrived at eHarmony's gleaming headquarters in Santa Monica for an eight-thirty a.m. interview with the company's founder, Neil Clark Warren. If anyone could offer me some twenty-first-century insights about lasting love, I thought, it would be this near octogenarian with an Internet dating service.

There has been surprisingly little research into what sustains marriage through the peaks, valleys, rough seas, and deserts of middle age. That research involves relatively few American couples: studies of two hundred couples at the most, and usually more like a few dozen. And it seems to be driven by hunches gleaned from examining people's behavior in a laboratory or their answers to questions. But a large trial, with hundreds of thousands of participants, testing the marathon qualities needed for marriage—now *that* is a modern study of midlife love.

Only one company has claimed its algorithms can find you lasting love. eHarmony launched its dating site in 2000, thirteen years earlier—not a long time, but time enough to see who made it through the seven-year hump, who didn't, and how to tweak their algorithms to increase the probability of love that would last.

Neil Clark Warren and I settled into two comfortable leather chairs in his spotless, airy office. As anyone knows from his ubiquitous television advertisements, the founder, who was then seventy-nine, looks like a grandfather, with a ruddy face, soft white hair, blue eyes behind his wire-rimmed glasses. He reminded me of Mr. Rogers, leaning forward to hear me in a pastoral way, speaking in a soft lilt, using small words. His demeanor deceives: It is easy to underestimate this man with a Ph.D. from the University of Chicago and a theology degree from Princeton Theological Seminary, this genteel man with 1950s manners who created an Internet juggernaut when he was past retirement age.

Just as I was turning on the tape recorder, he stopped me.

"Let's just chat a little while," he said. "I want to get to know you a little bit."

So we chatted for upward of two hours, and whenever I spoke, he watched me closely, like a psychiatrist, and with the earnestness of the evangelical Christian he is.

When we were bringing our informal chat to a close, Dr. Warren gazed into my eyes and said, "Barbara, I think every person should have five or six very close friends. I think I would like to have you as a friend."

"Dr. Warren, I'm so flattered. Thank you," I said, flustered. Then, feeling a little silly, I added, "I'd like to be your friend, too."

I suppose when you near eighty, you strip down to the bare essentials, the playground essentials. In the playground, Neil Clark Warren wasn't interested in running a company or sorting through other people's marital problems. He wanted a friend. Or else he was playing me. But my instinct says no.

Warren founded eHarmony to prevent the devastation he had seen during his forty years as a psychotherapist and marriage counselor, futilely trying to save troubled marriages and watching helplessly as countless engaged couples hurtled toward a cliff.

"I probably have presided over the funerals of more marriages than anybody in America," he said. "You just can't make a mismatched marriage work happily."

Warren realized that all the counseling in the world would fail if a couple was fundamentally incompatible. He concluded that the time to take action was before the marriage, before the engagement, even if possible before the first date, when chemistry can hijack one's better judgment. Warren believes the problem—and certainly one of the root causes of the gray divorce revolution playing out today—is that in today's culture, people make arguably the most important decision of their lives on a very narrow set of dimensions.

"For instance, if you like their looks and if you like their sense of humor and if you think they're bright and if you can kind of carry on a meaningful communication and if the two of you like to neck," he said, pausing to see if I understood the term, "if you have that kind of chemistry, then you ought to marry the person. And what I came to after a while was there are a lot more dimensions than that."

Warren realized the Internet would provide a perfect laboratory for reverse engineering from great long-term marriages. He and a small cohort of researchers surveyed five thousand married couples, asking them to fill out long questionnaires describing their values, interests, and characteristics, as well as their happiness with the relationship.

"We looked at a lot of people who had good marriages, a lot of people who had bad marriages, and we tried to get a handle on what are the differences," said Grant Langston, one of the original eHarmony cohort. "The people that have 'A' marriages, what do they have going for them? And what do we *not* see in the 'F' marriages, for lack of a better term?"

They found twenty-nine differences between happy and unhappy couples, giving rise to eHarmony's famous twenty-nine dimensions of compatibility.[11] Some rise to the top: You should be in the same ballpark of intelligence, energy level and sexual passion, ambition, sociability, and fighting style (two shouters are better than a shouter and calm, reasoned arguer). eHarmony's statistical analysis, Warren told me, meshed with decades of research suggesting that people who share similar personality traits and values find more happiness over the long term than those who don't.

eHarmony has been criticized for trying to match you with your identical twin, but that is not, actually, what they are doing. They don't care much about interests. They aren't worried about sending an opera lover on a date with a gangsta-rap aficionado. In fifty years— in the course of raising children, changing careers, coping with sickness or unemployment, taking care of elderly parents—differing tastes in music probably won't matter much. What will matter is whether they share fundamental values, traits, and style in approaching the world.

Early evidence suggests eHarmony is onto something. An article in the *Proceedings of the National Academy of Sciences* reported on a survey of nearly twenty thousand people married between 2005 and 2012 that found that couples who met on eHarmony had the lowest rate of divorce or separation of all couples—though not much lower than those who met online at other sites such as Match.com. eHarmony couples (and all couples meeting online) fared better than those who met offline, at church, work, sports bars, through friends, and the like. eHarmony couples also reported the greatest marital satisfaction of any dating site. The differences were small but significant.[12]

Eli Finkel at Northwestern University, who is one of eHarmony's biggest critics, stipulated that eHarmony may create slightly happier and longer-lasting marriages.

"But that's separate from whether their algorithm works," he told me. "Basically, what they are is a fancy country club. So if you're willing to pay your sixty bucks a month and you want to go to the place that says specifically that people interested in casual dating shouldn't come here, and we're a good place for traditionally minded people, I'm not surprised that you end up with a decent marriage rate. That's plausible to me, not because their algorithm works, but because of the way they've marketed themselves, and because of their expense."

"Well, sounds good to us!" Warren responded, when I relayed the criticism. "If people come to us who are serious about marriage, that delights us."

He also insists that their algorithms predict long-term marital happiness.

THE DISCONNECT
THAT LEADS TO DIVORCE

I thought eHarmony's core idea sounded pretty simple, and wondered: If all you have to do is find someone with whom you share fundamental values, why are so many marriages breaking up in midlife? Then I spent ninety minutes with Steve Carter, the company's vice president of matching and the brains behind the algorithms. I began to grasp the magnitude of the problem—not only for eHarmony, but for all those people who are looking for love, only to divorce years later.

Carter told me that many researchers and therapists agree about what makes a couple compatible for the long term: personality, values, and learned traits such as traditionalism.

"We built really powerful models for predicting which people, once they chose to get married, would end up being happy," he said. "But the compatibility algorithms really did a poor job of predicting *attraction*, of predicting who was going to want to talk to each other."

Why would that be?

"You don't choose who you're going to get into a relationship with based on compatibility," Carter said, in obvious frustration. "People basically marry at random."

People are not farsighted, he said. They enter relationships based on things like height or weight or the color of her eyes, on salary or profession or loyalty to the Red Sox, on whether the person lives in the same city or whether they feel an immediate spark. Not only are those things random, Carter said, but they pale in importance next to factors such as integrity or energy level or intelligence.

In the old days, Carter noted, before we were so independent, before we married for love, society had a way of zeroing in on a compatible long-term mate.

"It was up to your parents to choose: Is this suitor appropriate for you?" he said. "It had a lot to do with the parents making their decisions based on things that they know are important that you are not aware of yet. That you won't become aware of until it's too late."

Most people would not willingly return to arranged marriages or matchmakers, so eHarmony decided to fill the gap and offer the long view. It believed it had solved one side of the equation: selecting a match with the eye of a parent or a professional matchmaker. But it was stumped by the other half of the equation: How do you persuade people who would be compatible for decades to become interested in each other in the first place? Given that dating often leads to marriage, how do you take the randomness out of dating?

Carter tried to crack that nut for years. He tried inferential and statistical models. He worked with a famous mathematician from Italy and a computer scientist from Cambridge University. He tried big machine data learning, running through millions of cases to try to build a model that would predict attraction.

"Did it work?" I asked.

Carter shrugged helplessly. "It is still an unsolved science."

And it hit me: Could this be one clue as to why so many baby boomers are divorcing in record numbers? That they, like eHarmony, have not found the way to work backward from the future to the present, from long-term compatibility to short-term attraction? And who can blame us? Who can see the future? All we can see is that cute guy in front of us.

This is why, Grant Langston said, eHarmony wants people to trust them.

"One of our main jobs here at eHarmony is to help people keep an open mind," Langston confessed. I thought of Mary Lou hoping to find someone with her international background. "We tend to make the pool shallow by the prejudices that we bring to the process.

'Oh, I can't be with this, Oh, I can't be with that, I don't like this, I don't like that.' Well, the pool isn't as shallow as you think it is. So we help people entertain the idea of meeting somebody who's not their type."

What, I asked him, is the surprise ingredient that gives a relationship its staying power?

"The thing that is most important to a relationship's success above all the others is really adaptability," Langston instantly responded. "Because if you have adaptability, then the natural changes that happen in people—you're not the same as you were ten years ago, right?—you can ride through those changes. The terrible things that can happen in life, the mundane things that can happen in life—those don't destabilize the relationship because both of you are adaptable and can understand 'Hey, we need to morph a little bit this way so we can deal with this issue.' Two people who are highly adaptable are going to have a great relationship, all other things being equal."

I put the question to Dr. Warren: Is there any advice he would give people in midlife marriage?

"First of all, don't let yourself believe that myth that there are some marriages out there that are perfect," Warren said, slipping into a pastoral role.

No partner checks every box. If you abandon a pretty good marriage to find the missing boxes, he said, "oftentimes, you lose more than you gain."

"The biggest thing that makes a marriage work," Dr. Warren continued—and now I'm on the edge of my seat—"is to pick the right person in the first place."

EVERYTHING YOU NEED TO
KNOW WAS THERE AT THE ALTAR

After visiting eHarmony, I turned to Thomas Bradbury, a psychology professor and prominent marriage researcher at UCLA. "How critical is it," I asked, "that two people are similar?"

"The thing that matters most is just *your* personality," Bradbury assured me. "You might get a little bit of a bump from the similarity to your partner, but what really matters is: Are you an agreeable person? Are you an open person? Are you low on negative emotionality? That is going to get you really far."

Bradbury has tracked the course of couples' marriages from honeymoon to midlife. He believes you can trace marital bliss or destruction to the wedding day or even earlier. He calls this the "raw materials model."

"You look at your partner at the altar and you say, 'Everything that matters is true of us right now. Everything that is going to decide our fate is pretty much here right now.'"

Your personalities, your communication styles, and your personal histories—where you grew up, for example, whether you grew up in privilege or poverty, with education or not, whether your parents fought—will determine the success or failure of a relationship.[13]

Research supports this. Ted Huston at the University of Texas at Austin found that the seeds of divorce were planted by the first few months of marriage. The early patterns persisted over time: Those who treated each other kindly and affectionately usually enjoyed long and happy marriages. Turbulent courtships (including those that had the passion of a Hollywood film, and about the same length) foreshadowed unhappiness and divorce.[14]

The long and happy marriages were marked by a "warm amiability," Huston told me. "There was friendship coupled with a romantic and sexual relationship, and there was less urgency about the relationship. In some ways, the courtships, because they lacked drama, seem to an outsider to be very boring."[15]

But is the die cast on the wedding day? Can't a couple change and learn to accommodate each other?

"I think you can," Bradbury said. "But you are changing it within the constraints that are largely in place from the beginning."

The "old school" model of therapy argues that to be happy, each partner must change the way he or she relates to the other and, in particular, how the two fight. The therapy industry is built on that premise.

"But there is another model in ascendance right now," Bradbury said. "It says that actually what you need to do is accept your partner for who they are, and then they will change."

This was the conclusion reached by David Burns, a psychiatrist and cognitive therapist who persuaded twelve hundred adults, mainly in middle- to long-term marriages, to submit to interviews and a detailed questionnaire about married life.[16] He asked about finances, sex, recreational activities, raising children, household chores, and relationships with friends and relatives. He inquired about how much love they felt for their partners, how committed they were to their relationships, and how guilty, anxious, trapped, depressed, inferior, frustrated, or angry they felt. He poured all this data into the computer at the University of Pennsylvania, where he was then on the faculty. He was looking for the five or ten factors that would determine whether a couple would have a long and happy married life or a short, nasty, and brutish one. He found one factor: blame.

Burns calls blame "the atom bomb of intimacy." Don't blame your partner, he argues. Fix yourself. When you begin working on your own issues, then your partner will change, too.

WE, THE WIFE, AND DNA

Thursday, June 27

We had just pulled into Glen Maury RV park near Lexington, Virginia, when one of the other campers strolled over.

"Something's wrong with your truck," he said, squatting down and peering at our tires. "Sounds like the brake shoes. I'd get that looked at right away."

Here we were, on our third day, needing to find a repair shop. Which, it turns out, is not a simple process. You must have permission from Cruise America to take your RV to an approved mechanic. After waiting on hold for twenty-five minutes, I finally reached Jessica, who told me she'd call me back soon with the location of a repair shop.

"It's three-thirty now, and the service stations close soon," I told her. "Can't we just take it to the shop down the street?"

"No, ma'am, we need to find an authorized repair shop. Someone will call you within thirty minutes."

With nothing else to do but wait, we drove to Walmart for supplies. Walmart is the RVers' mecca—so many items, for so little money—but today I was anxious about the brakes. I began doing what I do best. I am a news reporter, and I had a deadline. Next to the deli section, I called our Cruise America sales representative and told her our plight, so that two people would be on the case. I hung up and called Directory Assistance for the names and numbers of the seven service stations within a hundred miles of Lexington. Devin appeared and gave me an inquisitive look.

"Just a sec," I said to him, dialing the first service station. No, the person told me, they don't service Cruise America RVs. Near the mayonnaise section, Devin tried to get my attention, but I was busy calling the next service station. Devin walked away, a frustrated click to his steps. At the cereal aisle, I received a call from Jessica. Rockbridge Ford in Lexington could fit us in at one p.m. tomorrow. Great! Problem solved. As I was selecting some tomatoes, I called Rockbridge Ford, just to confirm. Bob informed me they don't fix motor homes.

"You don't?" I said as Devin hovered nearby, trying to decipher the conversation.

"No, ma'am. I can tell you who does, though." He gave me some numbers. I thanked him and began to dial the first one.

Devin finally stepped in front of the shopping cart.

"Stop!" he said. "What's going on? What are you doing?"

"What's wrong?" I said, continuing to dial. "I'm doing the best I can."

"You're doing the best you can. That may be true," he said, a steely undercurrent to his voice. "But this is a 'we' thing. There are two of us in this situation. I just want to know what's happening."

In that moment, I realized that Devin was pointing at a major perspective problem, a shift I had never really made, even after more than a decade of marriage. I still think in terms of one. Maybe that is a little understandable for someone who was single until forty-three, who developed a career and bought a house on her own, who did not have children or build a family with her husband. But how long is the grace period on "I-ness"? *Oh well,* I thought, as I tapped in the next number, *I'll worry about that later. It can't be that big a deal. Can it?*

In fact, Robert Levenson, a professor of psychology at Berkeley, told me, "we-ness" is among the most important qualities of a happy marriage.

"If we-ness isn't there by the time you get to fifteen years," he said, "you're in trouble."

Levenson and several colleagues tracked 156 middle-aged and older couples as part of a longitudinal study that spanned more than twenty years. They were like photographers: Every five years they took snapshots of the marriages, inviting the couples into the laboratory, where they would videotape and code their conversations based on facial expression, body language, and tone of voice, as well as measure their physiological responses. They found that the couples who used "we" and "us" were far happier in their marriages than those who used singular pronouns.[17] Levenson says this is not just a matter of grammar.

"It would trivialize it to say, 'You need to say "we" a lot and you'll have a happy life together,'" he explains. It goes deeper than that: "It is that mind-set that you're in this together, that sense of pride that you've gotten through the tough times. It's a really good sign."[18]

That long-term study of thriving couples uncovered two other intriguing insights. The most controversial is that the wives are, as Levenson put it, "the emotional centers, the emotional historians, and the emotional thermostats of the marriage."[19]

The researchers found that regulating the woman's emotions during a conflict—not the man's—predicted happier marriages.[20] If a woman calmed down quickly during a fight (recorded in the laboratory)— if her heart rate and other physiological indicators lowered quickly— this predicted marital happiness in both the short and the long term.

"Women have a very complicated job description," Levenson said. "And one thing we found is that when wives are emotionally taken care of by their husbands, they will help their husbands in moments of conflict. They will invest in the relationship. But if the wives are distressed and not soothed or calmed, they will disinvest, and this is when the couples we studied did not do as well as others."[21]

Levenson reaped a whirlwind of trouble for this finding, but I decided to try to put this into practice. I tried not reacting when Devin and I would approach a quarrel, and I was amazed at how quickly arguments were defused. I regretted mentioning this tidbit to Devin, who would jokingly remind me that it was my job to keep an even keel, no matter what he said. Now I understand the backlash.

Even more intriguing is Levenson's finding that DNA can predict whether or not you will be happy in your marriage.[22] UCLA researchers Tom Bradbury and Benjamin Karney made the same surprising discovery: Namely, a certain gene variant, or allele, that regulates serotonin can influence the tenor of a marriage.[23] Everyone has two alleles of this gene, one from each parent, and people with two short alleles are far more sensitive to the emotional climate around them, whether in their family of origin or in their own marriage. These people are called "hothouse flowers," because they blossom when the climate is warm and they wilt when it is cold.

This strikes me as fatalistic and somewhat depressing information. You can't change your DNA or that of your spouse, so what do you do? Divorce the hothouse flower?

I put the question to Tom Bradbury, who said he initially had the same reaction. But after pondering it, he realized this finding could be useful. Say, for example, you know or suspect your partner is wired to respond to certain stressful circumstances in certain ways. You can do one of two things.

"You can try to change that," Bradbury said. "You can really bang your head against that wall and criticize your partner. Or you can embrace them. And you are just better off wrapping your arms around them and telling them that everything is going to be okay and that you are going to be standing by their side. That is the applied version of what is really an interesting set of phenomena involving our biology."

Wednesday, July 3

We were awakened this morning by *plink plink plink*, like dimes falling on the roof of the RV. They were distinct because they were close: just two feet above Devin's head and mine. Four days ago, our friends

Beth Wahl and Jack Kolpen joined us in Roanoke, Virginia. We offered them the "queen" bedroom at the back, and Devin and I moved to the crawl space above the driver's seat, since Jack, topping six feet, would have to fold like a Swiss Army knife to fit into that space. The rain gained in velocity until the skies started dropping not dimes but nickels, *thunk thunk thunk*, until, finally, it sounded as if the Treasury Department was dumping every coin at its disposal. We had chosen the rainiest summer on record for the southeastern United States to drive an RV down the Blue Ridge Parkway.

Beth and Jack are lawyers, as naive about RV operations as we (although Jack did bring bungee cords, which solved many a problem). We sold them on the idea that Jack and I, both avid cyclists, would bike thirty miles down the Blue Ridge Parkway each day, while Beth, Devin, and Sandra Day would pick us up afterward. Then, we promised, we would continue our dream vacation in unsullied campgrounds, hiking a little, and eating dinner under the stars. This idyllic dream almost instantly dissolved: The sun made an occasional appearance each day, but for the most part, it rained. Each day, Jack and I rode our bikes through a downpour as cars whizzed by, sending arcs of rainwater in their wake. Each night, we hunkered down in the increasingly damp RV and ate at the little RV "table."

Today, our fourth day of almost solid rain, we approached Happy Holiday RV park in Cherokee, North Carolina. The police were stopping traffic. Soon we saw why: Muddy water was cascading down a side street into our road in three-foot-high torrents, reminding me of my days as a camp counselor, when I took campers rafting down the rapids on the Colorado River. The entryway to the campsite was at a standstill, as some RVs were arriving and many more were leaving, getting the hell out of there, trying to find high ground, away from the water moccasins and who knew what else.

"Hotel?" Devin asked.

"Hotel!" we cheered, giddy at the prospect of a dry night's sleep.

Instantly, our resolve to be true RVers evaporated, with not a flicker of guilt that this might sully the purity of the experience. We headed for a restaurant before realizing the power was out all over town. This is how we ended up at Harrah's Cherokee Casino at four p.m. Of course the casino had a generator, and the place glowed with the light of a thousand slot machines as several hundred people with dilated pupils robotically fed them coins: an old man in a cowboy hat, a young woman covered with tattoos—what were all these people doing here in the middle of a Wednesday afternoon?

The food court looked like something from Dante's *Inferno*, people pushing and shoving to seize the last sandwiches from the dimly lit refrigerated case. By the grace of God, we found sandwiches and salads, and fell in line behind a score of other people, shuffling like the undead toward the cash registers.

We sat by the window, gazing out at the churning creek a hundred feet away, with a concerto of slot machine chimes and bells clanging just over our shoulders.

"My friend asked me if I really wanted to do this," Beth said. "And I said, 'Well, we will create memories.' And, well, we *are* creating memories."

I thought: *Remember this. This is a very good moment.* I was having the time of my life, in no small part because of the company.

Researchers would hardly be surprised. Friends, it turns out, are very good for marriage. Richard Slatcher, an associate professor of social psychology at Wayne State University, found that even friendships created in the laboratory seem to work some magic. He and colleagues put couples who had never met in a room and asked them to discuss personal questions such as: What is the most embarrassing moment of your life? The couples not only reported feeling closer to their partner but also reported more "passionate love" for each other.[24] The theory, which is based on Arthur Aron's premise that novelty triggers romance and passion, prompted the researchers to conclude that the most romantic thing you can do on Valentine's Day is go on a double date.

During our extended, weeklong double date in a thirty-foot RV, I remembered what Geoffrey Greif told me about couples. He and Kathleen Holtz Deal, both professors at the University of Maryland School of Social Work, interviewed scores of couples for their book *Two Plus Two*.[25] They found that couples who socialize with others say they are happier with their marriage. Greif said that being with others prompts you to stand back and look at your partner with new, appreciative eyes. For example, I became keenly aware of Devin's dry humor on our trip. You see how other couples treat each other: Does he hold her hand while walking into the restaurant? And maybe you'll do the same. Greif added that being with others gives you an excuse to make your spouse shine.

"I might say to the other couple, 'I don't want to brag but . . . ,' then you go ahead and brag about your spouse," he told me. "It can only make your spouse feel better."

He added that being with others can add chemistry.

"If my wife and I go out with a couple my wife really likes, it makes her very attractive because she is more alive, more fun, is enjoying herself, is excited," he says. "So you get a chance to see your partner in a new light, and hopefully it's an attractive light."[26]

All of this happened on our trip: I bragged about Devin's new Global Studies program at the university; I watched as Devin deftly navigated our way down the parkway and into RV parks while the rest of us read, talked, or napped. I was glad he was there. I was glad he was mine.[27]

NOT ROCKET SCIENCE

An enormous industry revolves around improving marriages, largely by tweaking the way couples communicate and fight. John Gottman, a professor emeritus of psychology at the University of Washington, has acutely diagnosed the cancers that can kill a marriage: the "four horsemen" of contempt, criticism, defensiveness, and stonewalling.[28] He claims he can watch a couple talking in his famous Love Lab for a few minutes and predict with 90 percent accuracy whether they will divorce or not.[29] He teaches couples how they can move from the "disasters" to the "masters" of marriage (his terms) by changing how they interact. Other psychologists suggest writing about a recent fight from the perspective of a neutral third party, which ideally shifts partners from their myopic perspectives.[30] Still others have found watching and discussing romantic movies just as effective as training sessions on acceptance or conflict management.[31] And several researchers have concluded that increasing the ratio of positive comments to negative comments will work wonders in a relationship.[32]

As insightful as these ideas may be, I will not cover them in this chapter. The subject matter is too massive; it would be like trying to stuff an elephant into a mitten. Beyond that, I am a little skeptical of therapies that try to fix communication skills while failing to address the root cause first; that's like applying topical ointment to a broken wrist. I am also leery of therapies that spend lots of time and money tracing back all problems, marital and otherwise, to one's childhood; that's like doing major surgery when you just need the bone set.

Marriage therapist Russell Collins has similar reservations about these prescriptions. Take, for example, the positivity ratio: Five good interactions for every negative interaction leads to a happy marriage.

"It is true," Collins says. "And one of the things that I sometimes say to people in therapy is, 'Look, I can save you a lot of time and a lot of money: For every negative interaction, take it upon yourselves as a couple to make sure that you have five positive interactions. And you're done.' You really will be." He paused. "But no one ever does that."

Collins says it is easy to say but complicated to execute, especially if the foundation of the marriage—the bedrock desire to be married to this person—is rickety.

Collins adds that the social science of relationships is squishy. Unlike, say, architects, who can rely on the principles of mathematics to build a bridge, marriage researchers cannot point to principles that are guaranteed to repair a marriage.

"What tends to happen is people come up with wonderful snippets of verifiable information, and then somebody else picks it up and makes a meal out of it," Collins says. "So there will be some tiny bit of information that applies to the public at large but may not have any relevance whatsoever to you, your life, and your situation."

Finally, I had found a practitioner who was not an evangelist, someone who would give me a clear-eyed answer to my nagging question. "Can people who are very different have a really good marriage?" I asked. "Not just survive but have a good marriage?"

"Absolutely," Collins said. "If they are similar in one thing: They are similar in their longing to be deeply connected, to feel loved, and to feel safe."

THERAPY ENTERS THE SCANNER

Dr. Sue Johnson is attempting to make a science out of bringing couples back from the brink. The clinical psychologist and founder of Emotionally Focused Therapy (EFT) cannot promise her method will work with every couple. But hers is the only type of marriage counseling that has submitted to rigorous scientific examination. If brain scans are any guide, she can claim that when you change the way you view your partner, you change not only your marriage but your brain as well.

"For the first time in human history, relationships aren't a mystery," the effusive Canadian told me. "We don't have to base our most important relationships on fairy tales and gossip. We have a map."

The map lies deep in our brains, and it was drawn millennia ago, in the earliest days of humankind. Humans have always needed other humans to survive, to hunt together and bring home dinner, to protect the tribe from outsiders, to help each other raise children. The most dangerous place was on the periphery of society. The most important connection, from a genetic standpoint, was the one that allowed our genes to survive to the next generation, providing a safe haven and a secure base. What was true thousands of years ago is true today.

"We're bonding animals," Johnson said. "Our need for safe emotional connection with a longtime partner is wired in. It's not sentiment or something we've created in our society. It's wired in and we are strongest and most adaptive and most functional when we can hold hands with a partner and face life together. We all know that deep in our hearts. We just haven't known how to put it all together."

Johnson believes she has an inkling: Emotionally Focused Therapy, a form of couples counseling that builds on attachment theory. This theory posits that a person forms a style of attachment as a child and imports that style into marriage. Someone who could count on a warm relationship with his parents usually forms a secure attachment, with them and his future partner. Someone who grew up with inattentive caregivers will worry about being abandoned and will later tend to cling to her partner, seeking reassurance. People who were abused or neglected as children tend to avoid deep connections in marriage to protect themselves from becoming dependent on someone else. The trick is to figure out one's attachment style and change the dynamics—which in fact rewires the brain.[33]

In 2011, Sue Johnson recruited twenty-four couples teetering on the verge of divorce and offered them a deal. They would receive EFT couples therapy, and in exchange, the wives would allow their brains to be scanned twice: once before twenty weeks of therapy and once after. For the study, Johnson teamed up with James Coan at the University of Virginia, whom I had met while researching the chapter on friendship and had administered a set of painful electric shocks. As you remember, Coan found that if his subjects were holding the hand of strangers or no one, their brains "lit up like a Christmas tree" in the areas of the brains that processed threat. When they held the hand of someone they trusted, those threat areas remained quiescent, as if their brains did not view the shock as a threat at all.

In Sue Johnson's experiment—before receiving twenty weeks of EFT—when the disaffected wives held their husband's hand, the threat areas of their brains became *more* active than when they held a stranger's hand or no one's hand at all.

Coan couldn't believe it. According to their brains, "it was very clear, they are much better off alone."

"One of the things we think is happening," Coan told me, "is if you are in a crappy relationship, it's not only that you're running out of money and that the kid is sick and you know you've taken all your sick days, so how are you going to deal with this? It's not only that. But now you've got this pain-in-the-butt spouse who's just adding another problem. And so your brain is having to work even harder because you've got this additional problem. When relationships are functioning well, your spouse takes a problem away. If the relationship is not functioning well, this adds an additional problem."

After twenty or so sessions of therapy, when the couples ostensibly learned to trust each other—as Johnson puts it, to become each other's safe harbor—the couples returned to the laboratory. One by one, Coan slid the wives (again, only wives for this study) into the brain scanner and found that these women whose brains had preferred to face a painful electrical shock alone than with their husbands were suddenly processing the threat as if they were happily married. In their minds, and in their brains, the husbands had been transformed from threat to ally.

"I was surprised by the magnitude" of the change, Coan said. "I was surprised that after twenty weeks of therapy with couples that were that bad, they looked a lot like our couples in our [previous] study who were very, very happy couples. Right down to which kinds of brain regions were impacted."[34]

Sue Johnson said that when you create trust, the other issues seem to resolve themselves.

"You can teach couples how to negotiate about the chores until you're purple," she observed. "Or do listening skills, or look to their past. You can do all those things. But it really is all about emotional connection and responsiveness."

Sunday, July 7

After learning that the forecast was for heavy rain to continue to hover over the Blue Ridge Parkway for the rest of our trip, Beth, Jack, Devin, Sandra, and I picked up stakes three days early and drove to our beloved Candy Hill Campground in Winchester, Virginia, out of the storm system and into the blessed sunshine.

Before Jack and Beth left for home, we toured the Museum of the Shenandoah Valley, dutifully walking through the Asian gardens and studying a fine art collection before gravitating toward the museum shop.

Devin showed me a small book, a biography of John Mosby, a Confederate battalion commander in the Civil War.

"Should we get this for Nancy?" he asked, since my eighty-seven-year-old stepmother named her dog Mosby, the latest in a string of golden retrievers named after Confederate war heroes.

"Maybe," I said, though in the end we decided against.

I would never have noticed that book, nor would I have made the connection between Mosby and Nancy. Which brings me to an embarrassingly corny but useful insight by Gary Chapman, a bestselling author and marriage counselor. You should speak your partner's love language: that is, how he expresses his affection.

Soon after Devin and I married, I realized that Devin wasn't fluent in my love language: Words of Affirmation. I live for words of affirmation. I love giving praise, which I do with abandon, whether merited or not. I love receiving praise, when I do a story for NPR, when I give a speech, when I cook a mediocre meal, when I take Sandra Day for an extra walk, when I dress up, when I dress down—it doesn't matter what the circumstance, I want you to praise me. Muted praise, which is to say ordinary praise, crushes me. I was raised on a high-calorie-praise diet, in which observations are ladled out in superlatives: That was the *best* speech (said to my brother, David, or me), or You are the smartest yet most honorable businessman (David), or You are a rising star at NPR (me), or You are the most tasteful decorator (Mom), or Your life is so remarkable it should be written up in *The Atlantic* (Dad). So you can see that a "Hey, good story" would send me into a tailspin.

Initially Devin did not know this, and once we had zoomed past the blush of infatuation, he did not seem inclined to develop this talent. He saw it as false. It took me quite some time to get over Devin's tendency toward honest assessment. I still don't much care for it, but I had never stopped to figure out Devin's "love language," and there, in the Museum of the Shenandoah Valley, I recognized it: Acts of Service. Devin is not showy; he quietly observes, he sees what needs to be done, and does it. He knows I hate balancing the checkbook, and even though he hates it, too, he does all the finances. As his father has lurched from one major health crisis to the next for the past three years, Devin has taken care of all of them: finding a great assisted-living home, selling the house, moving his father, meeting his father's daily needs, subtly persuading him not to marry the woman whose name he can't quite remember.

On this trip, Devin held steady when I wobbled. During a flash flood on July 4, after six days of rain, when Jack and Beth and I were ready to abandon the trip and return to D.C., Devin was the one to stay the course, to suggest we drive to Winchester instead of D.C., because, he said, I would never forgive myself for quitting. Devin has been the one who has upheld our marriage, who even in the darkest fights never threatened divorce, never took my bait. He has been a safe harbor that may not be marked with fluttering banners of praise, but he is a shelter from the storm.

THE FRUIT OF NOVELTY

Monday, July 29: Washington, D.C.

Your drawings were interesting," Art Aron mused.

Devin and I turned in the RV three weeks ago, declaring it truly The Best Vacation Ever. Aron, the psychologist at Stony Brook University whose research on novelty had sparked the idea in the first place, had analyzed the results of our test. If you remember, Devin and

I had each drawn a picture before the trip, and again upon our return. Each picture was supposed to include him and me, a car, a house, and a tree. Aron noted that this picture test is "new, not validated yet, but it has 'face validity,'" which means it makes sense.

I wondered what would be the clue to our marriage relationship: facial expressions, the sun shining, or some other measure?

"We look at how close the necks are."

"The necks?"

"Yes, we measure the distance between the necks of you and your husband before and after. In your first drawing, it was 10.1 centimeters—in the second, 7.4 centimeters."

"What about Devin's?"

"His went from 1.4 centimeters to 1.1 centimeters, which is about the same proportion," Aron noted.

"So novelty literally brought us closer?"

"It appears so," he said. Then he added, "There was a dog in all your pictures, which was interesting."

"Yeah," I said, "our dog is the center of our universe."

LEO TOLSTOY WAS WRONG

Middle-aged marriage is riding some pretty rough seas. Couples are abandoning ship so often that researchers have elevated the trend to a cultural phenomenon and assigned it a moniker: the gray divorce revolution. They cite boredom or differences in personality, they point to clashing conflict styles or DNA, they credit greater career opportunities and financial independence for women, they blame a generational focus on "my needs" that encourages people to walk out if those needs are not met. Then again, other researchers claim this is the best of times for the lucky few: These privileged couples enjoy a union of equals, allowing for self-fulfillment, partnership, and safe vulnerability as the old roles are tossed away.

After interviewing countless therapists, researchers, and couples, after reading way too many articles and books about marriage, I arrived at some conclusions. The first is: Leo Tolstoy was wrong. In *Anna Karenina*, the Russian author famously wrote: "All happy families are alike; each unhappy family is unhappy in its own way." But the research reveals countless ways for midlife couples to be happy, and just as many paths for unhappy midlife couples to navigate back to a vibrant partnership.

My second conclusion is related: There is no secret to solving the Rubik's Cube of midlife marriage, with its rotating demands of children, aging parents, and careers. There are more than enough ideas to keep researchers busy and therapists in business. In fact, every therapy and theory I encountered contained some penetrating insights about reviving marriages that are worn and damaged. Be adaptable, because everything changes. Think in terms of we, not I. Voice five positive comments for every negative one. Be the shelter from the storm for your partner, and he will likely do the same. Rent an RV, or if not, then inject some surprise into your routine. However, you never know whether a particular insight or therapy can restore your partnership, and it would be fraudulent for anyone to promise 100 percent satisfaction or your money back.

Still, I did notice some core ideas that bear repeating. While *young* marriages die amid crashing plates and angry words, *seasoned* marriages usually end with a whimper, when both sides stop trying, when they become disconnected and bored, when they quit investing domestically and look abroad. If this is true, as the research suggests, then one insight applies to marriage as well as all other ventures in midlife:

Engage with verve, because autopilot is death. Please don't misunderstand: I am not advocating living out one's years in a dead or abusive marriage. But if something internal murmurs that this is worth another try—and few decisions in life hold higher stakes for those we love, including children—then consider this: The marriages that beat the odds and escape the gray divorce revolution have been sculpted with intentional hands.

FINDING A LITTLE PURPOSE

Saturday, July 13

In the summer of 2001, two events washed over Mike Adsit's life: the Tour de France and chemotherapy. Mike was fifty-two then, the owner of a construction company in Milford, Pennsylvania, and recently diagnosed with small-cell non-Hodgkin's lymphoma. Queasy and weak from the chemotherapy toxins that he hoped would spare his life, Mike lay on his couch one afternoon, flipping through the channels until he happened on the famous bicycle race. Lance Armstrong, who had barely survived testicular cancer, was in the lead.

"I made an internal resolution that I was going to do something," Mike recalls, sitting at my dining room table on this humid summer day. He is a tall man with wiry white hair, trim and vigorous in his biking shorts and jersey, with the sculpted legs of a serious athlete. "I didn't like running, and I didn't like swimming, so I got out my bike, dusted it off, and started riding."

In 2001, Lance Armstrong had not yet fallen from grace and admitted to using performance-enhancing drugs. Back then, worried about his chances for survival, Mike Adsit knew only that Armstrong's story was a road map to a new life. At first, Mike could not ride his heavy mountain bike a quarter mile without walking. But slowly, he shed pounds and gained ambition. He hired a coach and began riding with other cyclists in the area. He entered his first race. He won his age division.

"I was hooked," he says, laughing as he confessed there were only five men in his division. But he trained harder and began entering more races with younger riders. "I got completely annihilated, but I was having the time of my life."

I am interviewing Mike because of an observation I have made: Midlife research is missing a crucial ingredient. It ignores a vital secret to thriving in middle age, during these long and dutiful years so full of responsibility. The research describes the challenges of keeping your marriage fresh and your career meaningful, the tools for sharpening your dulling brain, the rewards of investing outward and forward into the next generation. It is all good, it is all useful. But it is all so *Puritan*, this life of grimly paying our bills and sending in our taxes. It makes me want to jump out of a window.

I want to make a case for intentional frivolity. I argue that pursuing passions and hobbies is not incidental. It can hone your brain, it can boost your health, or, as in Mike Adsit's case, it can save your life.

In the two years after his cancer diagnosis, Mike lost eighty-five pounds, made new friends, and drove down his race times. His passion took him away from familiar territory, where he was competent in his job but a little bored. It took him to territory where he was a novice, where he had fresh, tangible goals, where he could not coast.

Thirty months later, the cancer returned. A new monoclonal therapy beat it into remission and Mike began to race with more than his own health in mind. Since he wore Livestrong jerseys, people discovered he was a cancer survivor. Friends and strangers he met at races would ask him to talk with their friend or family member who had just been diagnosed, who needed a guide through this perilous territory.

"I kind of viewed myself as their coach," Mike notes.

He encouraged them to take charge of their own research, to get second opinions, to keep moving forward.

"I'm saying, 'Come on! You got to get up tomorrow and you can't get behind, you got to get on top of this and you need to find answers. Here's a phone number, call them and talk to your doctor and talk to another doctor.' Some of them have gone on to do well. Some of them have lost their battle."

With his second bout of cancer in remission, Mike decided to try a national competition. In 2007, he qualified for and raced in the National Senior Games for athletes fifty and older. The event, which is known colloquially as the Senior Olympics because of its affiliation with the U.S. Olympic Committee, is attracting better athletes each year. Mike placed in the middle of the pack that year. He skipped the 2009 games (he was too busy saving his construction business during the recession), then placed seventh and tenth in two races in 2011.

"I thought, *Next time, I'm going to be on the podium.*" In the top five.

That aspiration, it turned out, would run into complications. In the summer of 2012, a few months after qualifying for the 2013 Games, Mike was looking in the mirror while shaving.

"And all of a sudden, I discovered these lumps on my neck," he recalled. "And lo and behold, my cancer came back after nine years of remission."

The disease had morphed into a different kind of cancer. His previous therapy no longer worked. The disease roared back: Every two or three days, another lump popped up, on his neck, his shoulder blade, his back. This time, his only recourse was a stem-cell transplant.

Mike began the treatment in August 2012, when he underwent a total of four multiday rounds of chemotherapy in the hospital. The first three pushed the cancer into remission before doctors could harvest and store his stem cells for the transplant. He needed to produce three to five million cells each time, which generally takes one to three days. Mike produced six million cells the first day.

"I don't know if it was a record, but it was close to it," Mike says, clearly pleased with his body's performance. "My body is just cranking out cells. I'm absolutely convinced it has to do with my fitness."

A final, six-day, grueling round of chemotherapy wiped out his immune system, before his doctors pumped his stored stem cells back into his body in November 2012. Mike recalls being almost too weak to walk, but he persuaded the nurses to move a stationary bicycle into the hallway, where he would spin as long as he could—sometimes just for five minutes, "more to say, *Damn it, I'm still here, and I'm not quitting.*" The day after Thanksgiving, the doctors sent him home with instructions to remain isolated for thirty days. He had no immune system and needed time to develop one.

Mike credits bicycling with his recovery, both physical and emotional.

"Sometimes you go up a hill and sometimes you go down a hill, and sometimes the hill is very steep," he says. "So you begin to look at these challenges of life and this cancer thing, and, much like you ride a bicycle, you say, 'Well, if I've got to climb the mountain, I've got to climb the mountain, and let's get the game face on and get it done.'"

He pauses.

"But I'm also sitting there, thinking, *I wanted to be on the podium in 2013 in Cleveland. Am I going to be able to do this?*"

Mike will know the answer in less than two weeks' time. I nod briefly, caught up in his suspense, before sitting back and thinking, *Wait a minute!* Eight months ago, this sixty-four-year-old man had been stripped down to a baby's immune system, barely able to walk, and now he's worried about whether he's one of the five fastest masters racers in the country? I suppose you can overlook a miracle when you're in the middle of it.

HOW TO BUILD A YOUNGER BRAIN

Kirk Erickson is not one to trash-talk intellectual stimulation. The researcher at the University of Pittsburgh began his career studying brain training and other mental exercises; he found these really do help people preserve their cognitive abilities. Then he conducted his first exercise studies. He realized that nothing will keep you as mentally acute as raising your heart rate a few times a week. Nothing.

"The effect [of exercise] was so much more consistent, so much more robust, so much more widespread in the brain," he says, that he shifted the focus of his research to exercise.

Exercise is a little like the Michael Jordan of cognition: well-rounded, versatile, dominating every game it plays. Does exercise preserve brain tissue as you age? *Yes.*[1] Does it increase the size of the prefrontal cortex, the area of our brains that allows us to plan, set goals, focus attention, and control our speech and fine motor skills—essentially, what makes us human? *Yes.* Exercise grew this region by as much as 10 percent in sedentary people.[2] Does exercise correlate with larger hippocampi, where memories are formed? *Yes.*[3] And does exercise improve one's memory, even physically change one's brain? Yes, yes, *yes!*[4] We have a new contender in the race to avert dementia.

I was particularly interested in Erickson's most recent study on the hippocampus of older adults. I had watched my father, as he moved into his eighties, lose his ability to encode new memories, to the point where he would lose the thread of any conversation that continued more than twenty seconds. And here Erickson found that older adults (fifty-five to eighty) who walked briskly for forty-five minutes three times a week scored better on cognitive tests in one year; those who did toning or stretching exercises saw no improvement. More astonishingly, those who did aerobic exercise saw the size of the hippocampus increase by 1 to 2 percent in one year, while those who did toning exercises saw this area shrink. At this age, the average hippocampus shrinks 1 to 2 percent a year, so this represented a difference for the exercisers of as much as 4 percent.

"Essentially, we turned back the clock by at least a year on these people," Erickson explains. "We reversed the brain aging. And as far as I know, there's no pharmaceutical treatment that's been able to show that same type of effect. Sometimes we spend a lot of money barking up the wrong tree. Sometimes, some of the simplest, most straightforward answers are right in front of us."[5]

Why would exercise make you smarter? Scientists are still figuring it out, but they have some clues. They do know that exercise creates new brain cells in the precise spot that handles new memories; it's called "neurogenesis." Ordinarily, cells in this area simply die off.[6] Scientists have also found that exercise greases the rails of white matter as it sends signals to various parts of the brain. It is like moving from a dial-up Internet connection to broadband.[7]

Until now, most researchers have recruited retirees for their exercise studies, because they have more time to participate. Erickson considers that a serious oversight. Midlife represents the fork in the road: One route leads to dementia, the other to healthy aging.

"This age range is a very critical time period for the development of risk factors for dementia," he says. "We often don't experience dementia until maybe our seventies or eighties, but a lot of the more basic biological pathways that often lead to cognitive decline are thought to occur several decades beforehand. If we can target a middle-aged population, we might have a more profound effect long-term down the road."

The few studies that have examined exercise in midlife are enough to launch me, at least, out of my chair and onto the treadmill.

Consider your brain. Regular exercise during midlife appears to prevent the formation of the plaques and tangles of Alzheimer's disease.[8] Middle-aged athletes may be one third as likely to develop dementia in their seventies as non-athletes. And it is never too late: People who began to exercise in their sixties reduced their risk of dementia by half.[9] Overall, longitudinal studies show, people who exercise—whether young, middle-aged, or older—score higher on cognitive tests than those who do not.[10]

Now consider your health: At least two studies have found that exercise may also be as effective as statins or other drugs in preventing heart disease and heart attacks.[11] Regular exercise performs as well as Zoloft in treating men with major depression, and it is just as good as antidepressants for mild to moderate depression.[12] And people who exercise have better sex lives.[13]

Given his own startling results with older people, Kirk Erickson has now turned his sights to the middle-aged group. In a new study, he is putting them through the same battery of cognitive tests and brain scans that the older adults received. But he is mixing things up a bit: Unlike his previous study, one group is exercising heavily, about 280 minutes per week. Another group (as in his previous studies with older adults) is exercising about 150 minutes per week. A third group diets— this is new—and a fourth group makes no changes to their routines.

Erickson's new study asks the kinds of questions that midlife people with jobs and children are asking themselves: What keeps cognitive decline at bay as you age? Is more exercise better, or is going to the gym three times a week just as good as seven? Must you hop on the treadmill, sweat and toil, even if you hate it? Or is it enough to choose the lean fish over the Big Mac? In other words, does your brain care more about exercise or diet?

My own opinion is that more exercise is better, but after meeting Ron Becker and Nancy Ley, I was less certain.

Ron Becker appears to be in the diet group.[14] Growing up in the Pittsburgh suburbs, with six sisters and five brothers, he was known as the "cleanup guy."

"If there was a little bit left over," the fifty-two-year-old construction worker told me, "I was the one that cleaned out the bowl of mashed potatoes or ate the last scraps of meat on the plate. I loved it."

But as an adult, that proclivity pushed him to close to 245 pounds. Ron could barely stand up after installing ceramic flooring all day. He worried about heart attacks. He heard about Erickson's study, in which researchers might put him on a diet or exercise plan and check out his heart: "I said, 'That's me.'" He was unaware at the time that they would be testing his cognitive abilities as well.

Over the past year, Ron has lost more than fifty pounds by eliminating meat, ice cream, and pasta from his diet. I try to imagine this trim, balding man with a gray goatee and gentle smile as lumbering and slow.

"I feel great," he said. "It's a moral victory. I've really impressed myself."

"Do you feel mentally sharper?" I asked.

"Quite possibly," he said. "My job does require a lot of measuring and thinking, adding and subtracting and this and that. And I feel I've been sharper at that, a little bit quicker and not having any problems, where maybe I did before, you know—just 'Hey, why isn't this working out?'"

A few moments later, I watched as Ron completed some standard cognitive tests on a computer, tests he felt quite sure he botched a year earlier. He raced through them, never missing more than one question. *Maybe diet is the secret,* I thought, remembering the pounds of Cheetos from NPR's vending machine that I have eaten in recent years. I dearly hope not.

The next day, I met Nancy Ley, a petite fifty-four-year-old systems analyst at a software company, who also volunteered for the study. For the past year, she has spent 280 minutes a week playing tennis, dancing to workout videos, bike riding, and, after she broke her collarbone, walking. She dropped thirty-five pounds, and from dress size twelve to size four.

"I feel sharper," she said. "I'm more alert, and I think that has to do with exercise. I do feel younger than I did a year ago."

"I wonder if your brain looks younger, too," I said.

"That's what I'm hoping."

That's what I'm hoping as well, although we will not know the answer for a few years. In the meantime, I've thrown out the tortilla chips and cookie dough ice cream. Just in case.

A CHAPTER WITHOUT PUNCTUATION

Saturday, July 13 (continued)

After Mike Adsit and I finished our interview, I wheeled my ten-year-old bike to the street. Mike lifted his sleek, light thoroughbred of a bicycle out of his SUV. He looked mine over, lifted it with a grunt, and with visible restraint, said, "Let's go."

I had agreed with some trepidation to ride with him around a twenty-mile loop. I attached a lavalier microphone to his shirt so I could record him for an NPR story while he rode up a hill, sprinted through intervals, and did whatever else he did to train for a race. Off we went. After about a mile, I said, "Okay, Mike, why don't you show me an interval. Just talk me through it."

"This is what we're going to do," he began.

"We?" I said, "I'm not doing the interval, you are."

"Naw, let's do it together. So, first, when we pass this sign, we're going to stand up for three strokes and get as much momentum as we can, then sit down and go as hard as you can for fifteen seconds."

I was still contemplating the "we" part.

He looked over. "Only fifteen seconds," he said, then suddenly, *"Now! Go go go!"*

I pedaled my little heart out, ever the obedient girl, but also curious to see what I could do.

We shaved four minutes off my best time for the twenty-mile ride.

"You're a good rider," he said afterward. "You've got a very good foundation. That's usually the hardest part."

"If I wanted to consider going for the trials next year—" I began.

He cut me off. "What's this 'if'?"

"Okay, what would it take?"

"It would take a coach, and a lot of training," Mike said, adding, "I coach several women."

I was intrigued. I adore biking. A year ago, after running almost every single day for thirty-five years, I could barely walk up the stairs. The orthopedic surgeon who replaced my mother's hip studied my X-rays and told me I had arthritis, and while it was too early to consider a knee replacement, it would not get better. I was fifty-three.

"So no more running?" I asked.

"No running," he said, unaware that he was stripping me of my identity.

"How about biking?"

"Sure," he agreed. "Arthritis doesn't like pounding, but it does love exercise."

I began to bike, and then take spinning classes when the weather grew cold, and I realized one day that all my knee pain had vanished. The muscles around my knee had grown so strong that I could sprint up the stairs without a thought. And biking temporarily vanquished another, more debilitating problem: When I am peddling, I never think about the chronic pain in my throat. This was a revelation. Those moments on the bike, I thought, might suggest a path to healing.

The physical relief was only part of it. You can get that with Percocet. Rather, there is something quickening about athletic competition, a psychological shot of adrenaline that Catharine Utzschneider described to me in an interview. Utzschneider is the author of *Move!*, a book and a training program for adults who want to compete at an elite level. A Ph.D. who teaches at Boston College, she is well known for coaching masters runners (middle-aged and older) and helping them compete nationally. Most of her clients, however, had never taken up a sport before meeting her. Most of them showed up at her office in the middle of, if not midlife crisis, then midlife malaise.

"Middle age can be a very disorienting time," Utzschneider observed.

Childhood and early adulthood have an externally imposed framework: graduating from school, building a career, marrying, and raising children. But at midlife, when the children are leaving and the career is set, the chapters lose their beginning and end points.

"There are no periods, no paragraphs, there's no punctuation," Utzschneider said. "There's no structure to give us a sense of order. So having an athletic goal provides an anchor, a structure to look at the years ahead, because adulthood has always gone on and on. And now it goes on and on and *on and on!*"

Her words hit their mark. After our conversation, I reflected on the quiet, seamless task of writing a book. I realized that as much as I loathed the unpredictability of the news business, I also missed the small victories that hitting those deadlines delivered. I recognized that I craved short-term goals, something to work toward. I wanted to stretch my physical abilities and prove to myself that midlife will not catapult me down the hill. Not yet.

I think I'd like to qualify for the Senior Games. I'd like to try to win them.

MUSIC FOR THE HEART AND BRAIN

Step inside Middle C Music and you vault back to 1965. Guitars hang by the dozens from the ceiling, drums crouch next to the amplifiers, just down from the keyboard pianos and several shelves of vinyl records. Here, on a bustling street in Washington, D.C., people dip a toe into their pent-up dreams.

Myrna Sislen, a compact woman with a direct gaze and authoritative touch—she persuaded me to try out a guitar even though I had come for an interview—saved the store from bankruptcy twelve years earlier. As we navigate to one of the practice rooms, I scoot sideways down an aisle crowded with instruments, children, and adults. Middle C teaches more than four hundred students a week, and almost half of them are adults. Sislen can pinpoint when middle-aged people began to arrive at the store for themselves, without their children.

"It was about four years ago, and a middle-aged man walked in," she recalls. "He came over and he said, 'Is it okay if I play the trumpet?' And I said, 'Excuse me?' I mean, he was whispering. He was not even speaking. And he whispered again, 'Is it okay if I play the trumpet?' I said, 'Of course it's okay if you play the trumpet.' And he started taking lessons."

Around that time, she says, more people between forty and eighty years old began picking up instruments.

"I think it's the baby boomers saying, 'I'm going to do what I want to do, when I want to do it. And now is the time.'"

Sislen, who taught classical guitar and played professionally for years before buying Middle C, says it feels almost magical to watch a middle-aged adult take up the saxophone and, little by little, progress from no sound or random sounds to playing a tune. He may never achieve greatness, but it doesn't matter.

"I think it is satisfying something in each person's soul," she says. "Sure, it helps with your dexterity. It helps with your memory. But if it's not going to feed your soul, you're not going to do it, because no instrument is easy. At any stage of life, that's important, and as you get older, it's even more important."

A few moments later, I slip into the tiny practice room where Dana Sebren Cooper and her instructor are warming up. When she was a girl, Dana played flute with a passion: Since her dad was in the military, her family moved often, and her flute was the only constant.

"I used to withdraw into my music. It was the one thing I could count on that was always going to be there."

In high school and college, Dana regularly performed as a soloist in concert orchestras. But then came law school, marriage, and children, a career in the U.S. Senate and the Clinton White House. She dropped her former love for twenty-seven years. Her children began taking music lessons at Middle C, and she would think, *I should do this, I should begin playing.* But then she'd think, *I've got asthma. I've got arthritis in my fingers. Not now. Not yet.*

"And the reason I picked it back up was, I had a very close friend who died of brain cancer suddenly at fifty," Dana says quietly. "And it made me realize: Life is short. I've been talking about this for a decade. If I'm going to do this, I have to do it now."

She cringes at the memory of her first few lessons.

"It was just awful. I was forty-eight years old, and I couldn't puff a single note. And these rooms are not soundproof, *let me tell you*," Dana adds, laughing. "You had to swallow your pride and you had to be willing to go back to baby steps. It was a long, hard slog."

Three years later, her fingering is back, as is her breathing. And while Dana's concert solo days are behind her, her music, as imperfect as it is, is something she owns. It is hers, hers alone.

"I've worked very hard in my very noisy life to have any personal peace. That's not a bad thing. I love my life. But this—it makes my soul soar," she says.

Dana pauses, and in her words I heard my own thoughts, maybe the thoughts of anyone in the middle years.

"It's maybe a little bit of Peter Pan, but I want to go back to that feeling I had when I was seventeen and I could, you know, belt out a solo with our orchestra. I wanted to have that little bit of youth still in me before it's just too late."

Ed Angel carried around the symbol of his youth for decades.

"I actually bought my guitar in the 1970s," he tells me, a few minutes before his lesson. "I tried to teach myself, and that didn't go so well, but as I moved around, I always kept the guitar with me."

The guitar represented the volcanic and unbounded promise of the sixties, a time when music and antiwar protests wove together to create something singular, unrepeatable. Ed has a photo of himself marching with folk singer Pete Seeger. And one day, about a year and a half ago, he was reflecting on how disappointed he was that his kids were practicing so little for their lessons at Middle C.

"Then I thought, *Well, I can't really be disappointed with them if*

I've been carrying this guitar around for forty years and haven't picked it up," he says. "So I brought it in here one day when I took the kids to a lesson. They said that it was in very good shape. I let them go ahead and fix it and started taking lessons."

Ed founded a firm that conducts historical research for attorneys, government agencies, and documentary filmmakers. Over the past thirty years, his firm has opened offices around the country. Ed did not take up the guitar to add to his list of achievements. He took it up because this is one area where, no matter how clumsily he plays, it simply doesn't matter.

"Everybody has to perform daily. Everybody has to perform before clients, coworkers, employers," he says. "This is something you can do for yourself. You can close the door, pull the guitar from the case, and just wail away. If it's not perfect, you still get enjoyment."

I turn to his tutor, John Linn, and ask if teaching adults requires more patience.

"In some ways, they're easier," Linn says. "Music is a language, so they already understand the concept of language really well. Some of my students are six. They barely read English. To teach them another language is really something."

When Gary Marcus took up guitar at age thirty-eight, he held out some hope that this might be true, that adults might bring something to their lessons other than clumsy fingers, duller memories, and slower processing speed. His was a gossamer thread of hope, given the "critical period" theory, which states that complex skills, such as playing the guitar, must be learned within a particular window of time—and if you delay past, say, age six, you can forget it. Marcus was also haunted by his own musical abilities as a child.

"I had a rhythm deficit," Marcus confesses, one that thwarted his fervent attempt to learn the beloved guitar as a child and throughout his life.

Then Marcus, who is now a cognitive psychologist at New York University, decided to spend his sabbatical year giving guitar one more concerted effort. He immersed himself in his music, practicing for hours a day, taking lessons, and finally attending a week-long music camp for kids called DayJams. Marcus was the only adult student. He quickly saw that his preadolescent bandmates had some advantages: They could concentrate for hours on the same musical section, and their finger-work outshone his.

"But I knew more about music just as a lifelong active listener," he said. "I had a knowledge base that they didn't that was really very helpful."

For his band's final performance—playing a number they had created in front of all the other campers, their parents, and his—Marcus shaped and structured their song.

"I would be like, 'What if we repeat this part?' and they would be like, 'Great!' 'And how about if we have this guy who knows how to do the classical piano stuff, put that at the beginning of our rock song, and then you over there, you'll smash on the drums.' And they would be like, 'Great!'"

Marcus's obsession with guitar extended beyond the personal. As a researcher interested in developmental learning, he wanted to test the critical-period theory, using himself as a guinea pig. That theory has strangled the dreams of many an adult who wanted to learn to play the piano or speak French, learn chess or take up tennis. But Marcus suspected that the theory was overrated. He plunged not only into guitar but the research on learning, writing up his journey in his popular book *Guitar Zero*.[15]

True, Marcus found, children do pick up everything more quickly and better. Children can develop perfect pitch in a year; adults rarely can. Children are better at rote memorization, partly because their brains have more synapses, or connections between brain cells, and partly because they have a clean slate. But Marcus concluded that children get their edge less from raw ability than from "time on task."

"If they're interested, which is a big if, kids have much more stick-to-itiveness," he says. "I've seen kids at this camp who play the same thing over and over. And I'm like, you know, 'I've got bills to pay. I can't keep playing this thing.'"

Marcus found his greatest encouragement, and a road map for his own guitar playing, from barn owls. Barn owls are not quite as blind as bats, but they do rely heavily on sound. When they are born, they calibrate their eyes with their ears, which allows them to use sound cues to navigate their world. In 1990, Stanford biologist Eric Knudsen, curious to see if their brains were "plastic," put prisms over the eyes of barn owls, which shifted their world by twenty-three degrees. The young barn owls quickly adapted. Unfortunately, the adult barn owls had a tough time in their new world. Bad news for the middle-aged team.[16]

"If that were the only paper I had read, I would have given up guitar right there."[17]

Then he stumbled upon Knudsen's follow-up study, where the biologist gave the older barn owls a second chance.[18]

"It turned out that if you gave them prisms that were smaller—you deal with the smaller problem, then a medium-sized problem, and then a hard problem, do it incrementally—adults do it almost as well as the young barn owls," he says. "And so what that said to me is that this critical-period theory stuff is not etched in stone."

Some barriers can be overcome: by the way you train, the number of hours you spend working specifically on your weaknesses, and your willingness to take each step incrementally.

"So I decided I was going to take baby steps, like those barn owls."

By the time he went on book tour, Marcus was good enough to play live on the BBC, a "terrifying" experience.

I asked him what advice he would give to a middle-aged adult who wants to take up a new pursuit.

"If you're thinking about doing something like this, do it," Marcus says. "If you can accept that I'm doing this so that I can see how well I can do it—so that I can enjoy it rather than so that I can play in a big band or be the world's greatest golfer, but you're just doing it for your own enrichment—I think it can be really satisfying."

"What do you think happened to your brain?"

"I clearly got a lot better at rhythm, and that may have involved some rewiring in my cerebellum, perhaps," Marcus speculates, but he did not have his brain scanned before and after, so he does not know for certain.

"Do you think you're sharper?"

"As a human being?"

"Yep."

"I think I'm happier as a human being."

TEACHING ADULTS TO LEARN A DIFFERENT WAY

Fear of dementia, it turns out, sells a lot of foreign-language training courses. When fifty-something adults began signing up for Rosetta Stone's language courses in surprising numbers, the company queried its customers about why. People mentioned travel and business, but as often as not, they spoke of a dull dread: They looked at the future and saw dementia. They thought that learning Turkish could save their brains. Company officials heard this so often, in fact, that they bought a brain-training company, Fit Brains, to attract more baby boomers to their programs and see how they might meld neuroscience with language.

Learning a second language does not prevent dementia, but researchers believe it does help people cope with the symptoms, perhaps by creating alternate neural routes and greater cognitive reserve. In one of the only studies on adults and bilingualism, British researchers found that people who learned a second language as adults raised their IQ levels and slowed the aging of their brains.[19] Other researchers speculate that the cognitive tasks involved, such as working memory, sound discrimination, and task switching, are precisely the brain areas linked to declines in old age.[20] The earlier you start, the easier it is, but no matter when you tackle the new language, you will create new pathways and sense the difference.

Jane Gantz was only vaguely aware of this evidence when she walked into Spanish 100 at Indiana University at the age of fifty-nine. True, she had watched her mother suffer the intellectual indignities of Alzheimer's disease and hoped to avoid the same fate. But dementia did not drive her into that classroom: Like virtually every person I interviewed who seriously pursued midlife hobbies, Jane saw her new passion as renewing her spirit, springing her out of her rut, ushering her into a new world with new mores and new friends. The brain stuff—that was a bonus.

"I don't know if my brain is sharper, I just know that I'm happier," she tells me, echoing Gary Marcus.

Jane had wanted to learn Spanish ever since her family hosted an exchange student when her children were in high school. She had been waiting and waiting, and when she retired early from her post as senior associate director of admissions at Indiana University, she leapt.

Without knowing it, she employed the very principle that, according to Gary Marcus, allows children to excel at everything from cello to Chinese: sustained and focused attention. She learned like a child.

"As a mature person, I was not going to do this in a haphazard way," Jane recalls. "I was going to learn it right and I was going to learn the grammar and I was going to nail it every class. So here I am in classes with freshmen, and I had this routine. I'd go to class every morning—I always took early classes—and I'd go to the library and I'd study for three hours."

After moving through the 300-level classes, Jane decided to step onto the high wire without a net: She booked a trip to Costa Rica for an immersion course.

"The night before I left, I cried and cried, I was so afraid," she says.

Jane worried about traveling alone, worried that she would fall functionally deaf and mute as Costa Ricans rattled away at her for three solid weeks.

"And it changed my life," she laughs, delighted by her own temerity. "Spanish has changed my life. I think about this almost every day because of the connections that I have made, not only in Costa Rica, but people I meet at my school, Latinos in my community who are now my friends, the conversation groups that I go to. And I pursue this very vigorously even now because I'm terrified that when I'm not in Costa Rica, I'm going to lose it and I'm going to sound like Tarzan."

The language has seeped into every corner of her life: She watches Spanish television, she meets with Spanish-speaking friends five times a week, she works with a tutor. She returns to Costa Rica for six weeks every winter. It infuses adventure into what could be the blandest of years. It has turned back time.

"I love to get out of my comfort zone," she notes. "I don't do risky things. I don't climb mountains, I don't jump out of planes, I don't ride motorcycles. But *traveling!* I've learned that I love traveling by myself."

You may be thinking, Who in midlife has the time for this? To which I say: Maybe you don't now, but you probably will at some point. And how will you spend it? Frittering away the time? Or in full-throated pursuit of a passion? Even if you have full-time work and children at home, as many people in midlife do, you still can take small steps to punctuate the days and weeks with a hobby that gives you a little zing every time you think of it.

Jane's story offers some key insights for pursuing a new passion as an adult. True, the critical-period theory—that learning a new language is easier for children than for adults—is well established. But it is not the only relevant fact. A six-year-old American can acquire a native French accent; the average thirty-year-old almost certainly cannot. A study of more than two million people found that the older you are, the harder it is to learn a new language: It is harder at fifty than at forty, harder at thirty than at twenty. But no one has ever identified an age when a healthy person cannot add Chinese to his repertoire, if he is willing to put in the time.[21]

Learning *anything* new past the age of thirty is an upward climb: Researchers find that your cognitive abilities (and in particular, processing speed) begin to decline in your twenties and thirties.[22] In midlife, you are slower at memorizing new foreign words, and much slower at retrieving them when you need to say something. This parallels the middle-aged brain's retrieval problem with proper names: Just as there is no semantic reason Angelina Jolie should be called Angelina Jolie—which creates a big problem for the brain—there is no obvious reason that a mouse should be called *souris* in French.[23]

In a cruel act of betrayal, the middle-aged brain even turns its singular advantage—our experience—against us. "Interference" occurs whenever we accumulate expertise in one area.[24] It explains why changing from a PC to a Mac makes people homicidal: You have to learn a new operating and key-command system, something your brain and fingers resist.

"If you have a lot of expertise in one language and then you're trying to learn a new one, you have to say, 'No, two is not *dos* anymore, it's *zwei*,'" says Sherry Willis at the University of Washington. "Interference actually increases from midlife through old age because your store of knowledge—the number of file drawers you have to go through to get to the relevant information and refile the information—increases with age."

And yet even at midlife, "the more languages you know, the easier it is to learn more," insists Lisa Frumkes, who heads the language-learning-product group at Rosetta Stone. Adults have an edge over young children because they not only understand the structure of language but also understand concepts.

"So when you're somebody like me who likes to collect languages—I'm about to start on my twelfth language—you have a lot more concepts," she notes. "You didn't know when you first started studying Chinese, for example, that every time you talk about 'sticks,' you have to use a special word like 'chopstick' or 'baton.' But once you come across that kind of concept again in another language, like Indonesian, you think, *Well heck, I already know what this is. I can relate it to something.*"

I guess she's right. I'm still fixated on the twelfth-language part.

Adults have another advantage over children: desire. Adults are not required to learn a new language, as schoolchildren are, but they will if they want to travel to Italy, or read *War and Peace* in the original Russian, or sell iPhones in China. Jane Gantz did not sit in Indiana University's library each day because she was dying to conjugate Spanish verbs. She sat there because she wanted to travel, to make new friends, to embark on new adventures, and the conjugation—well, that was a means to an end. And she did it methodically, carefully, religiously, just as children study if they like the subject—which is the key to becoming proficient at any age.

Let's say you want to take up a new hobby. Let's agree that your experience can give you a leg up. But you still face another enemy: your own mental habits.

"We like our routines," neuroscientist Paul Nussbaum explains. "It's hard to change routine. Why? Because you don't have any neural circuits set up yet to make that new thing easy."

Nussbaum cofounded Fit Brains, the brain-training company bought by Rosetta Stone. He says by middle age we run our lives on autopilot. He says most of our day involves "procedural memory." What learning a new language or new musical instrument does is shift you toward new, directed learning.

Nussbaum tells me the story of a man whose hippocampus was removed because he had a history of seizures. He could not remember what happened seconds before. A famous neuroscientist, one of Nussbaum's dissertation advisors, played golf with the man one day.

"They come up to hole number one," Nussbaum says. "They stop the cart, he gets out, he goes around the back, picks up a club, tees up, hits the ball really beautifully down the fairway, at which point he picks up his tee, goes back, puts his club in the golf cart, sits down in the golf cart. And immediately, he stands up, goes to the back of the golf cart, takes out his club as if he had never hit the ball."

This illustrates the difference between what is called "episodic" (or "explicit" or "declarative") memory—that is, remembering details of one's life, what you had for breakfast, whether you already hit the golf ball—and "procedural" memory, that is, relying on skills we know by heart, such as driving or walking or hitting a beautiful drive down the fairway.

"So if you do something you are really good at, it's procedural," Nussbaum says, adding that routine is not very helpful to the aging brain. "But if you're going to try to learn the guitar or Spanish, that's not going to be procedural at all. That's going to be a whole different memory system, a whole different learning system."

"So, if I read *The New York Times* every day, I'm *using* my brain but not *challenging* it?" I ask, hoping Nussbaum will say reading *The New York Times* is good enough to keep my brain sharp.

It isn't.

"My question to you is: Is reading *The New York Times* novel and complex for you?" Nussbaum asks. "No? Okay, let's get you something that is novel and complex. Another way of saying that is: Tell me what you are *not* good at. Tell me what you *don't* want to do. *That's* where we want you to be."

I do not have to give up my talents, he reassures me. But my talents are overly learned. They have a very short span of time between one neuron firing information and the other receiving it.

"Doing something novel and complex is going to take some time, it's going to be painful, it's going to hurt, you're going to cry," Nussbaum says, a little tongue in cheek. "But as we clear out that brush, we develop new neuron connections, and you'll say, 'This isn't so hard.' Those are words that are literally describing what is going on in the brain: I'm actually building some neural circuitry, speeding up the amount of time it takes for me to fire and receive. As a result, I am feeling a little better about myself."

Mercifully, for I have no desire to put myself through the misery of learning a foreign language, not everyone agrees with every part of what Nussbaum says.

"There's one caveat to that, and this is what I call the 'crossword puzzle problem,'" Benjamin Mast says. Mast is an associate professor of psychology and brain sciences and a clinical psychologist at the University of Louisville.

"Many people have heard that crossword puzzles are good for maintaining brain health and therefore, regardless of whether they enjoy them or not, they continue to do crossword puzzles daily. I don't enjoy crossword puzzles, and so for me the question is: Are they helpful enough that you should do them even if they're unpleasant? You should pick something else that stimulates you."

He says there is little evidence at this point that learning Spanish helps your brain more than, say, dancing, or listening to lectures, or (happily) writing a book.

"In terms of science, the bottom line so far seems to be that staying mentally active and engaged is key."

In the end, you need to find that magic combination: a hobby that stretches your brain and gives you something to look forward to each day or week. Not a grand endeavor, but a little purpose in life. That, Jane Gantz believes, is the secret of midlife.

"It's pursuing my passions. It's finding something that I enjoy, and doing it well," she says. "You know, I don't want to just sit around and drink wine. I want to be doing something and planning, and I feel with Spanish I have found the perfect project for me because it will never end."

WALTER MITTY MEETS
DELIBERATE PRACTICE

I think of myself as a Division III type of gal, good but not a standout. For example, I won the Illinois Division III state track championships in the 5,000- and 10,000-meter races in the late 1970s (before transferring to Williams). But when I entered a Division I race in Chicago, I felt certain that someone poured cement into my racing flats. At least, that is what I told myself after the gun went off and the other women disappeared around the first curve as I was barely out of the starting blocks. I was a Shetland pony in a field of thoroughbreds. I don't think they lapped me, but they came close.

But in my early fifties, I yearned to recapture a piece of my youth. I wondered: If I trained hard, could I become a competitive athlete again? I called K. Anders Ericsson at Florida State University, probably the best-known researcher on expertise. For those of us with moderate talent, Ericsson offers a glorious message: It's not about talent.

For four decades, Ericsson has studied internationally ranked chess players, world-class athletes, musicians, writers, scientists, foreign-language interpreters, and even typists, to see why some rose to the top while others remained good but unremarkable.[25] His theory has been incorrectly abbreviated to suggest that genius springs not from genes or innate abilities but from practicing for ten thousand hours or ten years.[26] He believes many more factors, such as family support and mental discipline, contribute to exceptional performance. People who begin training earlier (as children) are more likely to reach the elite level, suggesting that Ericsson is not a critical-period denier. Equally important is whether the student works with an exacting trainer or coach who can identify his weaknesses. And most important of all: Does he engage in "deliberate practice"—that is, focusing on his weaknesses until he masters them? These controllable factors make for exceptional performance. He says with one exception—body size—genes matter little.[27]

"What is surprising with all the work done on mapping out the DNA," Ericsson says, "is that people have been unsuccessful in finding individual genes that somehow would explain why some people get very good, whereas other people don't."

Obviously, plenty of researchers argue that IQ or natural talent determines who will become a singular cellist like Yo-Yo Ma or a tennis champion like Serena Williams.[28] I do not want to wade into that debate here. My more pressing question involves midlife pursuits. Can a middle-aged person have any hope of excelling at a hobby, whether guitar or cycling—or is it too late?

Ericsson believes that the drop-off in performance of adults has nothing to do with age and everything to do with shifting priorities. An eighteen-year-old elite pianist can spend hours each day at the keyboard, while a thirty-six-year-old is pulled away by his job, his family, his daughter's travel soccer team. Even if he does practice each day, he is unlikely to do focused, deliberate training. If he does, he will not lose his edge. Ericsson has found that when older pianists keep up deliberate practice, they perform almost as well as younger ones, even though their fingers are less nimble and their brains a little slower.[29]

The same principle applies to athletes. "I have looked at masters athletes who are competing in their fifties, sixties, and seventies," he says. "I found once you equate the intensity of training that they engage in, little [of the decline] can be attributed to age directly."

When he compared the performance of young athletes with that of older ones in 5,000-meter races and marathons, "we could not find physical declines that were not related to practice," he says.

The difference boils down to one thing. "Younger people train harder," Ericsson notes. "I think it's almost an excuse for some people: 'Okay, I'm old. I don't really need to be held responsible here for being able to perform at a higher level.'"[30]

This pleased me but did not persuade me. What about the role of talent? Specifically, what about my friend Mary Breed? Mary began competitive cycling when she was thirty-six, and after two years of racing, she captured the national championship title for her age bracket.

She can ride more than thirty miles an hour for nearly a mile. Many people, including her coach, consider her the best natural athlete they have ever seen. I am not. I am a plow horse. True, Mary is eighteen years my junior, but the yawning chasm in our performances cannot be blamed on age or training; natural talent must account for some of the reason she leaves me, and many professional cyclists, watching awestruck as she bolts away into the horizon.

I mentioned this to Neil Charness, who is Ericsson's colleague at Florida State and also an authority on the science of expertise. Charness asked if Mary and I train the same way: Do we put in the same miles, and practice with the same intensity?

"I'm not sure that I find talent a very helpful construct," Charness said, "in part because of the way it's so poorly defined. Usually it's: *I know it when I see it*. But you have no idea how much training, or the type of training, that person engaged in, which I think is probably far more important."

I told Charness about my Walter Mitty dream of competing in the National Senior Games. He suggested I try to do the same training regimen as Mary. With the idealism of one whose goal is more than a year away, I vowed that I would ride the same number of miles (two hundred to three hundred a week) and punish myself with the same speed workouts. In fact, I told Charness, I was thinking of hiring Mary's coach, Pete Lindeman, who seemed to turn every cyclist into a champion.

"I bet you do a lot better than you did a year ago," Charness said. "It's an empirical question."

Later, I reported my bold plan to Anders Ericsson, who likes these sorts of real-world experiments. He cautioned me against overreaching: Go slow, build up gradually, because as much as my head denies my chronological age, my body is dealing with biological reality.

"Everything I've seen when it comes to older runners and other athletes is that nobody goes [quickly] from twenty percent to ninety-five percent training without bad things happening."

I would soon learn what he meant.

IGNORING THE WISDOM
OF A CHAMPION

Saturday, July 20

The National Senior Games opened today in Cleveland. My first stop was the Cleveland State University swimming pool, where Liz Hogan is competing. I interviewed Liz a few weeks ago. She is fifty-six years old, with approving, mischievous eyes, a broad face, high cheekbones, and dark hair and bangs. As a child, Liz swam six hours a day and qualified for the U.S. Olympic trials when she was fifteen and nineteen. As a senior in high school, she was ranked number one in the United States and number two in the world for her age. A few weeks later, she was in a movie theater watching *Butch Cassidy and the Sundance Kid* when she collapsed from a bleeding ulcer caused by a birth defect. A few months later, while she was still recuperating, her brother died. She never regained the lost ground, and after swimming one year on UCLA's team, she quit—for twenty-seven years.

What ended the long hiatus initially almost ended her life. A car accident left her with a broken femur, pelvis, and hip, two broken ankles, and two broken wrists. After she had been in the hospital for three months, the physical therapist suggested she rehabilitate in a pool. She began swimming again. A few weeks later, she approached the coach of the masters swim team in Annapolis, Maryland.

"I was on a cane," she recalled, laughing. "I said, 'I'd like to join your team,' and he kind of looked at me. So he had me go in, and I swam down a length, and I swam back. And he goes, 'You've swum before, haven't you?'"

Liz joined the team, and the first time she competed in the Senior Games, she won all six races she entered. That was 2007. Competition stiffened in 2009, and more still in 2011. Now, just before her first race in the 2013 Games, Liz sat quietly on a bench, gathering her thoughts, while other competitors chatted nearby. She seemed nervous; she told me she had been traveling constantly for work and had barely trained. She placed fourth in her first race, the 200-yard individual medley: a clear disappointment. But she won her second race, the 100-yard butterfly. I asked her how she felt about swimming now, when she had once been the fastest young woman in the country.

"If you decide to go back to something that you haven't touched for a long time, just take it as ground zero," she told me. "Whatever you do as you improve, you're getting better. I'll say, 'Oh, my time's a little bit slower than six months ago,' and people will say, 'Well, you are getting older.' I say, 'No, not until I put myself really out there am I going to use that as an excuse.' I'm looking forward to retirement to see how fast I can get. I don't ever expect to be what I was when I was young, but I don't really care. I just want to enjoy it."

In that instant, I realized Liz had revealed wisdom that I desperately needed, an insight about relinquishing youth and enjoying the moment. I scanned these competitors in the Senior Games. I did see a few lean men and women. Indeed, some of the fastest men and women were swimming at the level of college students. But mostly, I saw way, way too much white flesh. What did I expect? The sinewy bodies of

Michael Phelps or Missy Franklin? These people were more than a half century old, for Pete's sake.

I left feeling sober. In that pool, I had seen my future and it was not appealing, or skilled, or (aside from a few people like Liz) particularly inspiring.

I grabbed my bike. I found Cleveland's famous towpath, which runs all the way to Akron. I rode furiously for two hours, without slacking, eighteen, nineteen, twenty miles an hour, pedaling to prove I was not old, trying to outrun the future. I am not ready to be old. I am not even ready to be middle-aged.

I wonder if this is because I do not have children of my own, where I can gaze at them and recognize that my DNA is essential to the future. My DNA means nothing to the future. So I pedaled a little harder. I know this yearning, this ambition, should have settled by now. I should be more mature. But I am not. Instead, I want to be—for a little while longer—young.

NOT OVER UNTIL IT'S OVER

Thursday, July 25

Hundreds of cyclists are warming up in this wooded park outside Cleveland. It is perfect weather for eight minutes of sheer pain. At least, that is how quickly Mike Adsit expects to cover five thousand meters in today's race. Mike rides up to me looking happy and confident. We chat. I want him to win so badly. We all love Hollywood endings, but this is more, this is about cancer and survival, death and victory.

"You don't seem nervous," I observe.

"No, I'm not nervous at all," Mike responds.

"Because I'm nervous as hell," I laugh.

"I'll tell you why I'm really loose," Mike says. "I'm so thankful to be here. I've lost a lot of friends along the way, fighting this same battle. November thirteenth, I had zero immunity, and here I am, walking and talking."

"What's your goal for today?" I ask.

"I'm here. So I met my goal. Whatever happens is kind of academic to me."

A few moments later, Mary Emmett and I are standing near the finish line, waiting for Mike to barrel around the last turn and streak across the line. Mary, I suspect, is Mike's "next chapter." A slim, vibrant sixty-seven-year-old, Mary is the mother of Mike's cycling coach. When Mary's husband of forty years died suddenly a few years ago, she felt set adrift, purposeless. She decided, at age fifty-eight, to bicycle across the country, from Oregon to North Carolina, averaging ninety miles a day, exhausted, furious at fate, sometimes screaming at the wind.

"My body was killing me, and I just had nowhere to go," she told me. "I didn't want to go home. I had no direction in my life. So I just stayed on the bike," stayed on until she reached the Atlantic Ocean.

"And you are never the same after that," she said. "There is a well that you draw from that you don't even know that you have. You just know you can pretty much do anything if you want to do it."

Mary found her new passion: She is turning the apple orchard she owned with her husband into a sustainable farm, using organic practices.

"I just think it's the key when you're aging to not allow yourself to settle. You have to just push yourself, whether it's on an intellectual level or physical level. You set a date. You set a time and let's just see if you can make it."

Mike comes flying down the hill. It was a good, swift ride for someone who could barely walk eight months earlier, but not fast enough for the top five. Not on the podium this year.

We sit at a picnic table while Mike recovers his breath.

"So what's your new goal?" I ask Mary, turning on my digital recorder.

"Well, these senior races intrigue me," she says. "And if you're in, I'm in. You're on the spot, Barbara."

"I really wish you hadn't said that on tape," I observe.

I turn to Mike. "Will you be coaching her?"

"Oh, yes," he says. "I'll be coaching you, too."

8.

WHEN BAD STUFF HAPPENS

Thursday, August 15

Two weeks ago, at Mike Adsit's urging, I purchased a new bicycle, just in case I try to qualify for the Senior Games. My new Giant Envie, black with red lettering, is so light I can lift it with one hand. Too light, perhaps: It skitters around like a foal on a blustery fall day, a little unsteady, darting about with a mind of its own.

At a little after seven this morning, I was clipping along at eighteen miles an hour down MacArthur Boulevard in Bethesda, Maryland, just past the one-lane bridge, when I apparently hit something—a pothole? a rock?—and felt myself launch into the air. I remember I saw trees whizzing by, giving me the sensation of flying laterally, my arms outstretched like Superman's. I don't remember hitting the ground and cracking my bike helmet in six places. I don't remember how long I was unconscious, but when I came to in my fetal position, I could see a man's calves and biking shorts.

"I'm Scott," he said. "Do you know your name?"

"Barbara Bradley Hagerty," I whispered, reciting my NPR signoff.

"Do you know what day it is?" he asked.

This seemed like a trick question. I thought for a long time.

"Wednesday?" I said tentatively.

"Okay, do you know where you are?"

"MacArthur Boulevard?" I ventured, adding, "I'm about to ride up the big hill, and then I have two interviews this morning."

"I'm a doctor," he said (who happened to be out on his morning ride), "and I don't think you'll make your interviews. Who should we try to reach?"

I gave him Devin's number, and moments later an ambulance arrived. I asked to go to the hospital near my home, but the medics demurred.

"Suburban Hospital has a much better trauma unit," Scott explained.

It was then that it dawned on me that I might have a problem. It was then, when they strapped me to the gurney and lifted me into the ambulance, that I realized I really would have to miss my interviews. It was then, as the medics peppered me with routine questions that seemed simultaneously simple and impossible, that I began to worry that I might not be driving to Pittsburgh tomorrow for a reporting trip. It was then, when I awakened in the CT scanner, that I realized I might blow right through my book deadline.

Damn it, I thought later as I gazed at the ceiling tiles in the emergency room, *now I have to be resilient.*

One week earlier, I had spent the day in Philadelphia observing researchers from the University of Pennsylvania train 150 soldiers in the art and science of resilience. The Army wanted these sergeants to learn techniques that would buffer them from the stresses of the long wars in Iraq and Afghanistan, principles that would help them cope with the trauma of seeing their buddies killed by a bomb or their marriages collapsing under the weight of multiple deployments. I was intrigued by the research, in a theoretical way. Until now. Now this training seemed acutely relevant.

Middle age makes no exclusive claim to stress, trauma, and the need for resilience. People break bones, lose their jobs, develop cancer at all points in their lives. But it seems that for many of us, troubles start to cluster in midlife: You are more likely to lose a parent or spouse after forty, more likely to be diagnosed with cancer after forty-five, and much more likely to be replaced by a younger, cheaper, more tech-savvy employee after fifty. I never gave much thought to rebounding from setbacks in my twenties or thirties, because life was ascendant and setbacks were rare. Now I feel as if I spend half my time trying to plug leaks in the dam. Happily, the research indicates, I may be better equipped than ever, because I have lived for five and a half decades.

"As you age, there is some evidence to suggest that there is a natural increase in resilience," Richard Davidson, a neuroscientist and professor of psychology at the University of Wisconsin, Madison, told me. "As people get older, they have more experience under their belts. They learn through their experience to better regulate their emotions. They also learn that the challenges that they confront are not the end of the world, and that life will go on."

Davidson has been studying the neuroscience of resilience for the better part of twenty years. He believes you can change your set point—how quickly or easily you fall into a funk, how quickly or easily you bounce back—by changing your thinking. Which got me to wondering: What is resilience, anyway? Are some people more resilient than others, and if so, why? Is it immutable, or is it something that you can build, like a muscle?

These were questions that Dennis Charney and Steven Southwick pondered in the 1990s, when they were psychiatrists at Yale University School of Medicine. Charney remembers a pivotal moment in their research. They were trying to figure out the biology of posttraumatic stress disorder, and possible treatments for it, when they began to work with a group of veterans who had been prisoners of war in Vietnam. The POWs had been tortured and isolated for up to eight years, and yet they displayed no signs of depression or PTSD. How could that be?

"We said, 'You know, maybe we could learn how to better treat PTSD and depression by studying people who had been traumatized and did *not* develop those problems,'" recalls Charney, who is now dean of Mount Sinai's medical school. "It was somewhat analogous to the people who get the AIDS virus but never develop AIDS. They have a really strong immune system. We felt we could learn from people who were resilient."

They began interviewing people who had suffered all manner of stresses and traumas: Gulf War veterans; people living in abject poverty and violence; victims of earthquakes, sexual abuse, physical abuse; people suffering with debilitating diseases like spina bifida. They found common themes, including optimism and a network of friends and family, and then devised a list of ten critical ingredients.[1]

Resilience, they concluded, is a mixture of personality traits, biology, and life experience, each part shaping the others. Resilience looks an awful lot like Bob Stifel.

THE BIOLOGY OF RESILIENCE

Friday, February 2, 2007, capped a decidedly unpleasant week for Bob Stifel. For several days, the forty-nine-year-old IT manager had felt weak and miserable with a sore throat and a piercing pain in his left leg. Finally, just after midnight on Friday night, he drove himself to the hospital and described his symptoms to the doctors.

"They took my vitals and then they coded me. *Boop, boop, boop,*

boop, boop!" he recalls. "They basically call everyone down into the emergency room because somebody's not doing too good, and that was me. I said, 'Is that me?' They said, 'Yeah.'"

And then Bob flatlined.

Six years later, Bob, his wife, Theresa, and I are talking in a sunny room filled with paintings and handmade jewelry. Their store, Stifel & Capra, sells artwork by local artists in Falls Church, Virginia. Bob is a large man, physically and temperamentally: His gregarious manner, his frequent and deep laugh, fill the room. If you were to look for a "resilient personality," Bob Stifel would be on your short list.

After they revived him on that Super Bowl weekend in 2007, the doctors tried to halt Bob's runaway infection and stabilize him, with intermittent success. They were mystified until Monday morning, when Theresa noticed his leg was swollen and blotchy. The doctors realized he had developed an infection, necrotizing fasciitis, and it was eating his leg.

"They said, 'We will take his leg and we will try to save his life,'" Theresa says. "You know: 'Stay tuned.'"

"I remember getting up Monday morning and being mad that I was still in the hospital and that I probably had missed out on the football pool," Bob recalls, laughing. "That's when my main doctor—I had about thirty-six of them—said, 'Mr. Stifel, you don't understand how incredibly sick you are.'"

"Were you afraid?"

Bob shakes his head slowly.

"It's like you just come up against that door: What do you believe? And I believed that I was going to see my Maker, or I was going to wake up and kiss my wife. And either one was going to be okay, because I felt safe and comfortable in my faith. So I wrote some terrible scratchy notes to my children—and I still don't remember what exactly I said—but then off we went."

Bob's comment reflects the most basic biological quality of resilience: Resilience is the ability to regulate one's response to fear. For Bob, his religious outlook had this calming influence. For others, it could be natural optimism, trust in one's own resourcefulness and ability to thrive, the support of friends, or even past experiences and training that reduce a towering mountain to a scalable hill.

How resilient you are is based in large part on your brain and, specifically, how the reasoning part of the brain, the prefrontal cortex, and the fear center of the brain, the amygdala, talk to each other. We need the amygdala for survival; we want it to (briefly) go berserk when we see a sticklike object on the path, because it could be a snake. But we also need the prefrontal cortex to (quickly) calm down the amygdala, once the immediate danger has passed.

"It looks like the prefrontal cortex, which modulates the activity of fear centers in the brain, like the amygdala, seems to be particularly active in patients who are resilient," says Dennis Charney. Charney, who has studied the brains of resilient people in the brain scanner as they respond to fearful thoughts, realized that they possessed a neurological advantage. "They have a capacity under stress to suppress the fear, the fight-or-flight reaction, to the point that they can handle things."

Even, or especially, if the threat is real. You do not want a flustered person whose amygdala is running wild next to you as you patrol the streets of Baghdad. You want someone with the cool thinking of an active prefrontal cortex.[2]

Of course, we have no idea how Bob Stifel's brain behaved when he was told he might lose his life or his limb. We do not know whether his prefrontal cortex automatically soothed his amygdala when faced with this threat. But given that behavior and feelings reflect the internal activity of the brain, I suspect that Bob had a wellspring of natural resilience, one that would serve him well as his ordeal unfolded.

When Bob emerged from surgery, his left leg had been amputated above the knee. He was shocked at first, and he cried (once). His next, and lasting, response was gratitude.

"I was full of love, like George Bailey in the last fifteen minutes of *It's a Wonderful Life*," he recalls. "Everything was great. I spoke to everyone who walked into the room. 'Hey, how ya doing? You mopping up? Hey, what's your name? Sarah? How long you been at the hospital?' I had orderlies sitting on the edge of my bed, chatting with me until they got in trouble for hanging out in my room too long. Everybody would come and visit."

Hospital staff were not his only well-wishers. When he awakened from his medically induced coma, more than five hundred "Get well soon" cards covered every square inch of his hospital room walls. Theresa almost needed a spreadsheet to schedule visits from a constant stream of visitors.

"There's this idea that resilience researchers talk about," I note. "They say OPM—*other people matter*. Resilient people rely on other people to help them."

Bob nods. "You know, there was a young man, only twenty-six years old, in one of the many hospital rooms I was in, who had a terrible car accident," he says. "He was all alone. He had no girlfriend, no wife, no nearby family, and he was going to be discharged into a nursing facility. It struck me how important it is to have someone— and I'm not saying to be married and have the two-point-one children—to just have that someone in your life that is there for you. And my wife is the Rock of Gibraltar. She coped for me. I mean, she held me up, and our friends, our church, held us up. I hate to say it, but it wasn't that hard."

"I'm glad he's still vertical," Theresa says. "I'm glad my kids have a father, I'm glad we just celebrated our twentieth wedding anniversary (yay!) a couple of weeks ago. And I know it sounds really simplistic but to me that's just it. It's black-and-white, you're alive or you're not alive, so live."

Many people think that resilience depends on internal resources, a pulling-up-by-the-bootstraps mentality. In fact, the opposite is true, says Steve Southwick at Yale Medical School.

"The really highly resilient people tend to have very good social networks," Southwick says.

They seem to instinctively know that their bodies demand friends, a biological fact that loneliness experts are chronicling.

"When I am in the company of people that I trust and I face a stressful or traumatic situation, my neurobiological stress response is considerably better modulated than when I am alone," Southwick says. "It doesn't overrespond. It comes back to baseline more readily. My blood pressure doesn't shoot up as much. My heart rate doesn't go up as much. When I have more social support, because I know there's a net to catch me, I will be an active coper."

This does not mean coping will be easy, especially when the friends return to their normal activities and one is left with the aftermath of trauma. In Bob Stifel's case, the disability—the limitations, the inconvenience of fatiguing more easily and walking more slowly—is background noise next to the ceaseless clamor of pain. Bob's brain believes his leg is still attached, and so he suffers from "phantom pain" every minute of every day in the limb that was removed. On a good day, it feels like a severe sunburn. Other times he experiences intense and painful tingling. The "stabbers" are the worst, as if a knife has been thrust into his ankle.

"It never goes away completely, but even in that, there's a bright side to it," Bob says. Because the pain gives him the impression that his natural leg is still there, he walks more confidently on his prosthetic leg.

"Let's be real. I mean, I'd be much happier to have both my legs, but there are a lot of good things that have come of it. We probably wouldn't have this business that we're sitting in right now," he says, gesturing to include the paintings and artwork in their store, "because Theresa decided life is short and things happen and she's always had this dream to do something like this."

Finding meaning in adversity[3] tracks closely with the quality most associated with resilience: optimism, that is, a realistic buoyancy that acknowledges the bad facts in front of you and is not consumed by them.[4] The studies on the mental and physical benefits of optimism would fill a library. For example, faced with daily missile attacks, optimistic civilians are far less likely to develop PTSD or depression.[5] Optimists seem to enjoy better health if diagnosed with breast cancer, and recover more quickly and robustly after heart surgery, a heart transplant, or coronary bypass surgery.[6] Elderly optimists are far less likely to die over fifteen years than pessimists.[7] They seem more immune to infectious diseases; they are even less likely to get colds.[8]

Optimism is rooted in the brain. Richard Davidson at the University of Wisconsin credits the prefrontal cortex with helping people take trauma or stress in stride. Not only does this reasoning part of the brain tamp down the fear center (amygdala), but it also keeps the ventral striatum, a region that is important for positive emotions, merrily engaged for longer periods of time. After a happy experience—a compliment from your editor (please) or a laughing jag with a friend— "the resilient person maintains that kind of positive glow for a much longer period of time," Davidson says.

Years after he lost his leg, Bob Stifel admits that life is not anything close to normal. Yet he has returned to work, he continues to handle the finances for Theresa's store, and he is selling his own line of barbecue rubs. Bob keeps in his center vision all that he has done, and lived, and loved, because he did not die on the operating table: shepherding his son through Boy Scouts and watching him perform in high school plays, cheering his daughter as she competed as a nationally ranked high school rower, looking forward to one day walking her down the aisle. Daily, Bob reminds himself that he can perform all these small feats without a left leg.

"I'll have down days and I'm just like, 'Ugh, it stinks to be me.' And that's part of the cycle," he says. "How do you cope with it? You get over it."

He finds ordinary things to do—going to a ball game, mowing the lawn, walking up and down a flight of stairs—to remind himself of how rich his ordinary life is.

"You just reboot and remind yourself you've got all this," Bob says, sweeping his arms to include his wife, the paintings on the walls of their store, his children, his friends, his church—all things vibrant. "You haven't got that"—he points to his missing left leg—"but you've got all this."

THE GOLDILOCKS OF TRAUMA

You may be wondering: Am I blessed with the genes and the personality to bounce back from the midlife traumas certain to come, whether the death of parents, partner, or friends, the scary diagnosis, the strain of retirement when the stock market has coldly stolen half my savings? Would I react as Bob Stifel did, with humor, gratitude, perspective?

One of the clues lies in your history—and not in the way you might expect.

Roxane Cohen Silver began to think about the cost of a lucky life when she was a young professor studying stress and coping. Silver, now a social psychologist at the University of California, Irvine, had a friend who was a uniquely gifted athlete. He never lost a competition into his twenties. After ending his athletic career, he applied for a job, confident he would land it easily, as he had everything else in life.

"He didn't get the job and became seriously depressed," Silver recalls. "And his mother said to me, 'When he was a little boy, he used to win every race that he competed in. Sometimes I used to just hope that he would come in second.'

"And it was the most amazing comment to me, because what she was saying was: He never learned to lose. And I thought about that comment for twenty years, trying to think how I could study that issue. How could I explore the benefits of adversity?"

Silver found her chance after the terrorist attacks on September 11, 2001. Beginning a few days after the attacks, she tracked more than two thousand people, surveying them seven times over several years. She measured the amount of adversity they had experienced in their lives, asking them to select from a list of thirty-seven possible negative events, ranging from divorce to the death of a relative, from violent attack to natural disasters. She also queried them about their mental health, their well-being, and their reactions to traumatic events, including the terrorist attacks.[9]

Nearly two hundred people said they had never experienced a single traumatic event. *"Who are these people?"* she wondered. "Did they ever get out of the house? But in fact, they were not demographically that different. They were just lucky. They had lived charmed lives."

When Silver and her colleagues analyzed the data, she realized that a charmed life can come at a high price. The people without trauma "were more reactive to 9/11 and they were more reactive to events that had occurred in the prior six months. Their levels of well-being were lower than [for] people who had had a few [negative] life experiences, and their baseline levels of distress were higher than [for] people who had experienced a few [negative] events."

The happiest, most resilient, and most mentally healthy people had suffered two to three stressful events in their lives. Silver—whose work fits into a body of research variously called "hardiness," "steeling," "stress inoculation," or "toughening"—found that *no* stress was almost as damaging as multiple traumas.[10]

Silver adds that she did not compare the types of negative events people suffered with their resilience levels. She suspects that major violations, such as childhood abuse or rape, could overwhelm a person and weaken her ability to cope. But adverse experiences such as a divorce or the death of a parent may help inoculate one to future stressors.

"I think it suggests that a few events teach people how to cope and people learn from these experiences," Silver says. "They learn their own strengths and weaknesses, and they come out stronger for the next event."[11]

Even animals can use a little challenge. Karen Parker, a behavioral scientist at Stanford University, showed that young squirrel monkeys who were exposed to stress—that is, they were removed from their mothers and siblings for one hour every week for ten weeks—became braver, less anxious overall, and less rattled by stressful events than the coddled squirrel monkeys. Their cortisol levels were lower and, in a startling parallel to humans, brain scans showed that they were better at controlling their fear center, the amygdala.[12]

Even in the case of monkeys, it seems, whatever doesn't kill you makes you stronger.

WHY NO ONE WANTS POSTTRAUMATIC GROWTH

I had kind of a turbulent childhood," Maya Thompson recalled. "So I learned to let it make me stronger. I wasn't going to be a victim to my pain."

Even with her childhood "steeling," nothing could have prepared Maya for her present pain. When I first met her, Maya was in her mid-thirties, a beautiful woman who has witnessed her worst nightmare. Her voice wavered slightly, thinly, not just when we were talking but when she answered the telephone, when she herded her boys into the minivan, when she talked to the neighbors. She lived on the verge of tears. From my position at her dining room table, I could see a photo of her family, blown up to four feet by three feet, hanging in the hall-way. They are standing in the ocean, waist or knee high, depending: her husband, Woody, her twin boys Liam and Quinn, and three-year-old Ronan, a striking boy with blond hair and extraordinary blue eyes. Ronan was the boy who died three days before his fourth birthday, on May 9, 2011, the day Maya's world collapsed.

When she first spotted Ronan's drooping eye and received the diagnosis of neuroblastoma, a common and commonly fatal strain of child-hood cancer, Maya coped by chronicling the journey. "We have our plan in place and the Thompson family combat boots are on," read her first blog entry. But over the next nine months, her words lurched from hopeful to angry to grimly resolved. There was an inevitability to it, as Maya and Woody desperately tried one more doctor, one more clinical trial, anything to find a way out of this maze of death.[13]

After her son's death, Maya prayed she would die. She noticed nothing but her grief—not her family, not herself. A few months later, she met her grief counselor in Sedona, Arizona, and together they climbed Mount Wilson. The day, so hot and sunny on the way up, turned threatening at the summit. The temperature dropped thirty degrees, the heavens opened with hail and rain, thunder and lightning. Maya sprinted down the mountain, splashing in every mud puddle she could, splashing for Ronan because he could not. And for the first time in forever, she laughed.

"I just had a moment of, you know, 'This is the life I've been handed now and he doesn't get this anymore and I do and I can't just throw it away,'" she recalled. "You let this pain kill you, or you let it make you stronger. I mean, it's a choice. I have to make a choice every single day to get out of bed and be somebody that Ronan would be so proud of."

From that moment, Maya turned her pain into her passion, as she put it, raising money to find a cure for neuroblastoma.

"I promised Ronan that I would fix him and obviously that didn't work out," Maya told me. "I have a lot of guilt around not being able to get my baby better. But I also promised him that I would try and fix this world, the world of childhood cancer."

Within two years, Maya had funded one clinical trial in Philadelphia and was about to spend $500,000 on two other trials at children's hospitals in Houston and Boston. A year after my visit, when I was thinking about resilience, I called Maya up. Her voice trembled a little less.

"Has it gotten any easier?" I asked.

She paused.

"That's such a hard question," she responded. "I feel like maybe the day-to-day stuff is a little easier. My pain is always there. I don't get to take a vacation from it. But it's not as sharp as it used to be. It's not so suffocating and it's just not as sharp."

Maya is happily distracted, too, by her baby girl, who was born nearly two years after Ronan's death in 2011. But, she told me, her emotional life no longer revolves around playdates or soccer games or lunch with friends. Her emotional life plays out in the oncology ward of the hospital.

"I will be forever changed because of this," Maya said. "The world that I used to belong in won't ever exist for me again. So this new life is completely different, and I find it extremely beautiful and heartwarming and inspiring. And hopeful, in a way.

"This is what I will do for the rest of my life," she added. "I made Ronan a promise and I do not intend to break it. Ever. So this is all I'm doing for the rest of my life."

Maya Thompson's story has all the hallmarks of "posttraumatic growth." PTG is a cousin to resilience, but more of a thug: meaner, more brutal, more devastating—and more transformative. Rich Tedeschi and Lawrence Calhoun, psychologists at the University of North Carolina, Charlotte, coined the term in 1995, when they noticed that some people did not recover from their traumatic experiences in a typically resilient fashion.[14] Rather than return to their set point, everything about them radically changed: their worldviews, their goals in life, their friendships.

"It's not just bouncing back," Tedeschi explains. "Most people talk about that as resilience. We distinguish this from resilience because this is transformative."

"The one thing that overwhelmingly predicts it is the extent to which you say, 'My core beliefs were shaken,'" Calhoun adds.

What kind of core beliefs? "The degree to which the world is just," Tedeschi says, "or that people are benevolent or that the future is something that you can control. Beliefs about, basically, how life works."

For the past couple of decades, the two researchers have worked with many people who have suffered horrific traumas: the death of a child, a rape, a car accident that left the victim quadriplegic, the loss of almost everything to a tsunami. You never know what will trigger posttraumatic growth. For example, one of their patients breezed through his cancer treatments but came undone by his divorce, because it shattered his confidence about the future. Many of their patients have plunged to the depths only to emerge with a wholly new purpose in life. One woman became an oncology nurse after her son died of leukemia. One man, a drifter and drug addict, earned his master's degree in rehabilitation counseling after a car accident paralyzed his legs. But one major difference with resilience, which seems to return you to the emotional set point you had before the trauma, is that the sadness never goes away.

"So just because you're a more compassionate counselor and a better husband and a better rabbi doesn't mean that you quit grieving for your lost child," Calhoun says. "Those positive changes don't nullify the tragedy you have experienced."[15]

Posttraumatic growth, I realize, is terrible for the person, good for the world. It has, for Maya, no redeeming element; but it may redeem the world, or a piece of it. Because Maya's main purpose in life has veered from raising children to attacking cancer, it is possible that a four-year-old in the future will live. It is possible. Not worth the price of Ronan's life, but she will take any coinage she can.

BATTLE-READY RESILIENCE?

Wednesday, August 7

It seems to me that three questions determine how one will respond when tragedy strikes. First: How are you wired? Second: What were your experiences before the stressful event or the trauma? And third:

What are you going to do about it? Put another way, can a person develop resilience?

The Army is betting more than $140 million that the answer to the last question is affirmative. In unquestionably the largest resilience study in history, the Army is requiring more than a million soldiers of all ages to participate in resilience training, hoping to head off PTSD and depression before a traumatic event occurs, *before* the IED (improvised explosive device) detonates, *before* the debilitating mental chaos can take root in a soldier's mind. This has sparked a major dustup among psychologists—more on that later—and it is why I find myself in a low-ceilinged conference room in a Sheraton Hotel in downtown Philadelphia.

It is eight-thirty in the morning, and I am bobbing in a sea of camouflage. One hundred fifty sergeants, dressed in their Army uniforms, hunch over long tables, scribbling notes and watching Karen Reivich with rapt attention. Reivich is the only other civilian here, and for ten days she will train these soldiers to prepare for the worst; they will then train the soldiers under them. What I did not know at that moment is that she would soon be training me.

Reivich is a psychology professor at the University of Pennsylvania. She helped Martin Seligman, who is considered the father of positive psychology, develop the Penn Resiliency Program.[16] In 2007, Seligman had a fortuitous and ultimately lucrative conversation with General George Casey, Jr.

"General Casey came on board as chief of staff of the Army at a time when he saw the stress and strain of continual, long-duration conflicts and the impact it was having on the force psychologically," explained Lieutenant Colonel Sharon McBride during a break, "not just the soldiers, but the family members and the civilians. It's the right time for this."

Casey wanted resilience, not just physical fitness but also emotional fitness, "to be incorporated into the fabric of the Army," she said, and so he launched the Comprehensive Soldier and Family Fitness program, in which thousands of sergeants are absorbing Penn's principles of resilience, and then training the soldiers under them.

"At first, I didn't think it was going to work," Karen Reivich told me, because it was developed for civilians. "But then I realized what we're talking about in this program is life skills," how to cope with trauma, in a war zone or in the family, how to reframe your perspective, rely on character strengths, and improve your relationships. Of course, no one program can prevent the psychological shrapnel of seeing your friend killed by a bomb, she said: That's what PTSD treatment is for.

"I think of this as inoculation," she said. "If we know how to prevent something, we don't wait for the person to get sick and then treat them. We try to prevent it from happening in the first place. That's what we're talking about here. Let's see what we can prevent by increasing overall psychological health to deal with everyday stressors. And then when treatment is required, let's get treatment."

On this particular morning, Reivich opens by asking the 150 soldiers to "hunt the good stuff": listing a few good things they experienced each day. Reivich then moved on to handling thinking traps (patterns of negative thinking) and recognizing icebergs (small problems that have much larger causes). She talked about problem solving and catastrophic thinking, when your thoughts spiral out of control and you imagine the worst case as the only case.[17]

Meanwhile, I was beginning to do a little spiraling of my own. I was scheduled to interview Reivich and, impossibly, nine soldiers during lunch. As the clock ticked closer to noon, I noticed Reivich was not wrapping the session up. *What if she's late?* I thought. *Will I have to cut her interview short? She's my most important interview. Or should I try to interview nine people—nine people!—in thirty minutes?*

Just then, Reivich told the soldiers, and me, how to conquer catastrophic thinking. "Put it in perspective," she explained, in five easy steps: First, describe the event; second, capture the worst-case scenario; third, generate the best-case scenario; fourth, identify the most likely outcome; and finally, develop a plan.

As my stress level climbed from a simmer to a boil, I decided to try Karen Reivich's approach. The worst-case scenario: Reivich runs over by fifteen minutes and I have to choose between her and the soldiers. Best-case scenario: Reivich ends her presentation this instant and I have all the time I need. Most likely scenario: Reivich ends in five minutes, we begin the interview ten minutes late. So I made a plan, crossing out questions, and then I sat back and . . . *relaxed!* As it happened, we began the interviews late, but I had plenty of time, and astonishingly, the stress melted away, probably the first time I have ever relaxed on assignment. Given the deep grooves of anxiety in my psyche, especially regarding deadlines, I considered this a major victory.

Maybe this resilience training works after all, I mused. *I just hope I never have to use it.*

ORDINARY MAGIC

I'm not aware of any study that's ever made people more resilient," George Bonanno, a psychologist at Columbia University, tells me.

Nor does Bonanno believe resilience training is necessary. While people like Maya Thompson and Bob Stifel are truly admirable, he says, they are neither superhuman nor rare. You don't need to train people to become resilient, because they already are.

"We're naturally resilient because we have this great stress response system," he says, which sweeps in with a wave of brain responses and chemical reactions when we are in danger, and quickly releases soothing signals and neurochemicals once the acute danger has passed.

"And so I think the question we need to be asking is not 'Why are we resilient?' but 'Why isn't everybody resilient?'"

Because the research usually zeros in on pathology, Bonanno says, psychologists consider chronic grief and depression to be the *normal* response to loss or trauma. Sigmund Freud and Elisabeth Kübler-Ross insisted that grief needs to be worked through methodically, in stages, and then fixed. Any less fraught response suggests that one has an emotional chip missing.

But these theories clash with observed reality for researchers such as Ann Masten, a professor of child development at the University of Minnesota, who investigated the inner lives of children who grew up in poverty and adversity: Instead of unearthing psychological frailty, she discovered natural resilience, what she called "ordinary magic." Bonanno discovered the same magic among adults. In the 1990s, when he began videotaping and coding interviews with widows, he realized their facial expressions and body language told a different story—not one of crippling grief, but sadness mixed with laughter. He wondered if Freud and his intellectual progeny had gone astray: Maybe this sort of natural coping was not psychotic; maybe it was normal.[18]

Bonanno then examined all sorts of traumas: spinal cord injuries, breast cancer, unemployment, divorce, death of a child, even the upheaval of witnessing a terrorist attack. Generally, only about 10 percent of people suffered psychopathology, that is, chronic depression or PTSD that hampered their everyday functioning. On average, 60 to 65 percent of people functioned normally after they lost a spouse, a job, or the use of their legs.[19] He found that two thirds of New York residents returned to normal functioning after the September 11, 2001, terrorist attack that destroyed the World Trade Center towers.[20] People may grieve, they may feel frustrated or sad, but within a few days or months they reset to their previous emotional temperature. The rest (25 percent or so) settle somewhere in between, not back to their old selves, but neither depressed nor traumatized.

Recently Bonanno scrutinized PTSD in the military, analyzing data involving 77,000 soldiers who had been deployed at least once.[21] Of those, he says "eighty-three percent of the soldiers had just no symptoms at all. They were just zero PTSD," he says. "What happens when you take that group of people and say, 'We're going to make you more resilient'? Some of those eighty-three percent become less resilient."

Bonanno is *not* saying that learning to reframe your thinking is deleterious. It could ease the immediate pain, just as taking ibuprofen can dull a headache, even though it would resolve on its own. He merely believes that we should conduct some smaller studies before thrusting resiliency training on a million soldiers.

Yet, in a pinch, give me that Advil. And I'll take some resilience training on the side.

Monday, August 19

I came home from the hospital four days ago with my left arm strapped to my torso like a broken wing. It turns out that a collarbone is quite delicate; it can snap easily when you put your arms out to break a fall, as I did when I catapulted off my bicycle. It doesn't hurt particularly—Percocet helps with that—but it is inconvenient.

For example, I can't really wash my hair, or dry it, since I need two hands for the blow-dryer. I can't dress myself, not yet, because I can't maneuver my arm through the sleeve. I can't type—bad news for a writer—I can't drive and I can't travel, which means I have had to cancel three reporting trips over the next two months because I can't rent a car.

So far, I have put on a chirpy front—Percocet helps with that as well—but today, as Devin washes my hair, I begin to cry. I feel overwhelmed by the certainty that I cannot finish my reporting by the time I return to NPR in January, when my book leave ends. I feel bereft because I have only one sleeveless button-down shirt—the only kind I can get into—and I've worn it the past three days. I am terrified that I will miss my book deadline and lose my book contract. I am desolate because it is such a beautiful day and I can't go for a ride. I begin to sniffle.

"What's wrong?" Devin asks. He's in a hurry. The last thing he needs is to have to clean and dress me every morning before he leaves for work.

"I can't believe what I've done to myself," I say, letting loose the first good wail since my accident. "How am I ever going to finish my book?"

"You'll finish," Devin says, as an impish glint comes into his eye. He squirts more soap in his hands and creates a lather that grows larger until the suds look like a generous helping of cotton candy and, before I can object, he scrubs my face, cutting off my complaints and making me forget, for a second, that my life is going off the rails. I begin to laugh through the suds and realize how lucky I am.

But I recognize the signs. What did Karen Reivich at the Penn Resiliency Program call it? Catastrophizing? And I think, *Well, let's take this resilience training out for a spin.* True, my broken bone hardly rises to the level of war-zone trauma, but perhaps learning how to master a small-scale setback would be useful to someone reading this book. I e-mail Reivich and make a phone date.

Tuesday, August 27

Karen Reivich and I spoke for an hour this morning. She is witty and insightful and seemed to be intrigued by my challenge.

The first order of business, she said, is to halt the catastrophic thinking, the imaginary downward spiral that begins with a broken collarbone and ends with my having no job, book contract, or status. This seems a Herculean task. After all, over the past five decades, I have allowed my thinking to plunge into catastrophic spirals at small setbacks, or even imaginary ones, which is useful when I am on deadline, since I always have a backup plan. The antidote to catastrophic thinking, Reivich said, is purposeful action.

"One of the ways people can take purposeful action is through their thinking," Reivich added. "So ask yourself, 'Is there anything good that can come out of this?' Even that—taking the reins of my thinking—is purposeful action because I'm changing my mood and I'm changing everything else that comes downstream from my thoughts."

Next, she said, assume "mastery" over the situation by focusing on what I can control rather than what I can't. In this case, she prompted, I could say, "'Okay, my domain of control just got a lot smaller, but I'm still able to . . .' and then name some of the things I do have control over."

Then Reivich extolled the virtues of what is a foreign state of mind for me, a person who is loath to let anyone help her: OPM, *other people matter.* "That willingness to see the power of your connections and how they matter so much is, I think, the untold story of resilience," she said.

It struck me that she is correct: Gone is my independence, but oddly, people don't appear to mind stepping into the breach. Devin actually enjoys blow-drying my hair, even though when he's done I look a little like Bill the Cat from the comic strip *Bloom County*. Caroline took me shopping for sleeveless shirts (I now have seven), and my next-door neighbor, Susanne, brought me along grocery shopping.

Reivich's final question was the most intriguing and, ultimately, the most helpful.

"What are your top character strengths?" she asked. "Who's Barb in your essence, at your best? How can you pull on those strengths even more during this time of struggle, and what would change, what burden would be lessened, if you did that?"

She suggested that I fill out the online survey at the University of Pennsylvania's Authentic Happiness website, which has helped millions of people identify their strengths.[22] Once I discover my top five strengths (out of a total of twenty-four), I should fall back on them to overcome the daily challenges. Around eight p.m., I logged on and plowed through the 240 questions. I pushed Enter. I waited. Then I blanched. The algorithm gods had looked into my soul and found it crushingly drab.

My top strength, they proclaimed, is: Industry.

Second: Gratitude.

Third: Spirituality, sense of purpose, and faith.

Fourth: Fairness, equity, and justice.

Fifth: Humor and playfulness.[23]

I immediately wrote Reivich, with the subject heading: "Can I take the questionnaire over if I don't like my strengths?

"Look at the first one," I wrote. "Industry. Does anyone truly want *industry* as their top strength?! *Oh, my wife* . . . I can imagine Devin murmuring as he points me out at a party . . . *isn't she . . . industrious?* And, by the way, I really want to be brave."

"*Breathe, Barbara, breathe,*" Reivich responded thirty minutes later. "At least your number one [strength] wasn't Prudence. Think of the teasing you would have endured in middle school."

She went on to say that my strengths, particularly industry, didn't surprise her. "You could have used your collarbone as an opportunity to watch all the episodes of *Chopped* or *Breaking Bad*, but you got yourself a transcription device and are still working your butt off."

I felt a little better.

"So from a resilience perspective," she continued, "the question is this: How can you use your signature strengths (the top bunch) to cope with this setback, even to transform it into a growth experience?"

Then she signed off, parenthetically noting her signature strengths: Authenticity, Humor/Playfulness, Bravery ("Sorry, I don't mean to gloat"), Fairness, Social Intelligence.

I am stricken by character-strength envy. Reivich's virtues are the stuff of biopics and adventure movies. Mine are the subject of Sunday school class. Other than Industry, I could not conceive of how Gratitude or Spirituality/Purpose would help me write a book with a broken collarbone.

But over time I came to appreciate my strengths. As for industry, I realized I can still do interviews, thanks to my tape recorder. I hired a graduate student who needed part-time work to help me with research, drive me to interviews, and transcribe them later. I derive enormous solace—and distraction—from my work, which feeds into my second strength, gratitude.

Sometimes—and this is *not* the Percocet—my eyes well up with tears of gratitude. I'm grateful that this happened in the summer, when I can wear short-sleeved shirts and don't need to put on sweaters. I'm grateful for Devin, and his confidence in me, and for Sandra Day (dog not Justice), my constant companion. I'm grateful for Vivian, how much she loves her dad, how much she loves me. I'm grateful that

I can walk to physical therapy and that we can afford the thirty-dollar deductible. I'm grateful we have a recumbent bike so I get my daily endorphins. The list goes on and on, and that is only one journal entry. Gratitude may not have written a single paragraph in my book (although, actually, it just did) but it cheered me up and, I suspect, made me more bearable to be around.

I even found some meaning and purpose in the accident, or as Reivich put it: Is there anything good that can come out of this? Immediately I thought of one person who could benefit: my ninety-one-year-old mother, who had stopped her physical therapy soon after shattering her thighbone in March. I arranged for us to do our physical therapy together, at the same clinic. This had the triple benefit of letting me see her, getting her out of the apartment, and giving her something to look forward to three times a week.

I survived. Six weeks later I was driving, seven weeks later I was in California on a reporting trip, eight weeks later I was on a spinning bike. Would I have survived without intentionally using the principles of resilience? Of course. George Bonanno is correct: Most people are naturally resilient. Would I have thrived; would I have as easily reframed my thinking? Of that I am less certain.

BETTER LIVING THROUGH MEDITATION

In all likelihood, I sculpted my brain a little bit during this process. Imaging studies have shown that when people intentionally reappraise an event, they alter their brain activity. In my case, when I recognized that the event (collarbone break) was not the end of my world, and that something positive or meaningful could come out of it, the reasoning part of the brain may have tamped down my fear center—at least temporarily.

What makes this possible is neuroplasticity, says Sharon Begley, a science writer who has authored several books on the subject. Neuroplasticity involves the relatively recent discovery that your brain continues to change through your lifetime, shaped not only by your experiences but also by your thoughts and intentions.

"You can cultivate greater resilience by tinkering with these connections and patterns of activity," says Begley, coauthor with Richard Davidson of *The Emotional Life of Your Brain*.[24] "It's almost like a stew—a little less curry, a little more turmeric"—a little more prefrontal cortex activity, a little less amygdala activity, and voilà! You've created a more resilient person.

How to do this? In their book, Davidson and Begley suggest specific practices to shape the resilient brain. One approach involves "cognitive reappraisal," favored by the Army and the majority of Western psychologists. The other method is "mindfulness meditation," which entails sitting quietly, focusing on your breathing, and whenever your thoughts stray to, say, this IED or deadline or cancer diagnosis, you pull them back nonjudgmentally to your breathing. It's far more elaborate than this, of course. But Davidson has found in his neuroscience laboratory at the University of Wisconsin that mindfulness strengthens the connections between the prefrontal cortex and the amygdala, giving the reasoning part of the brain the upper hand over the emotional part.

"It is very much like going to the gym," Davidson says.

If you look at the research, you get the feeling that the answer to every problem—pain, depression, sleep disorders, terrorism, the disappearing ozone layer, an audit by the IRS—is mindfulness meditation. This perplexes me a little, because I have tried meditation for thirty days, on the strength of countless meditation studies suggesting I would become a calmer, less anxious, and happier person. It backfired: I became impatient, surly, and my husband was relieved when the experiment ended.

"Have you tried any of those mindfulness practices?" I asked Begley, a fellow journalist.

"People ask me that all the time," she said. "They ask, 'Do you meditate?' I say, A, I don't have time, and B, I'm just, you know, one of these impatient, self-satisfied, oblivious people who think that basically she's okay. It works for me. I mean, you can't be a journalist and be happy, content, and mellow. It's not going to happen."

Maybe journalists are not cut out for mindfulness—Dan Harris at ABC News being the exception. But let's see what it is about meditation that makes neuroscientists and resilience researchers swoon.

THINKING AWAY YOUR PAIN

Can a meditative practice or just a disciplined mind conquer not merely psychological but also physical pain? I will admit this question has colonized much of my own emotional life ever since I developed chronic pain in my vocal cords. But if statistics are any guide, I have plenty of company: Some seventy million other Americans suffer from chronic pain. Researchers have found that older adults (sixty and older) naturally develop strategies for living with unremitting pain, particularly using "coping self-statements," that is, intentionally thinking positive or affirming thoughts about pain and their ability to handle it. By contrast, younger and middle-aged adults wage an emotional fight against the pain, and lose.[25]

Could meditation teach those coping mechanisms to the young and

middle-aged, offering a sort of Advanced Placement course in controlling your mind to help you control your pain? Could it be that your
thinking soothes both soul and body?

"The mind is a powerful organ," Madhav Goyal told me, "and the
beliefs and expectations that it forms have effects on the body."

I visited Goyal, a doctor and researcher at Johns Hopkins University, a few days before he moved to India. Goyal's family had already
decamped, and he met me at the door of his near-empty house, be-
spectacled, with an open face and appealing smile, the kind of smile
that apparently springs from two hours a day of meditation. In fact,
it was his early, painful experiences with meditation that eventually
led to his writing the definitive journal article about the benefits of
meditation.

A few years ago, Goyal attended a ten-day Vipassana meditation
retreat, which involves sitting cross-legged for more than ten hours a
day. He arrived with some trepidation. During a previous retreat, he
had been a little overzealous with the lotus position and had aggra-
vated a bad knee. It had plagued him ever since. Goyal decided that
if his knee started to act up, he would ask for a chair. On the third
day, he said, his knee began to throb uncontrollably and he asked the
teacher for a chair.

"The teacher was this old-fashioned guy who said, 'You know, I
understand you're a doctor and all that, but you've been doing very
well sitting down there. I've been watching you. I think you should just
go back and sit down on that cushion again.'"

Goyal debated: argue or accede, chair or cushion? He eventually
returned to his cushion.

"That next hour, I was watching my pain with a great degree of
concentration and I was seeing that it was about a nine out of ten. It
was just unbearable," he remembered, unconsciously rubbing his knee.
"And then I noticed that the pain was not there constantly, that it

was coming and going rapidly, kind of like the way electricity goes through a light bulb. It was a nine out of ten one second, and then a zero out of ten.

"It had just completely disappeared," he said, amazed at the memory.

Goyal was free of pain for the rest of the retreat, and although the pain has returned a little, it does not bother him nearly as much.

"This experience taught me quite a bit about what I thought was a pathologic problem for which I had seen numerous orthopedists and had numerous MRIs," he said. "A lot of it [the pain] was also something deep inside me, whether you call it psychological or something else. And this experience in particular got me interested in looking at the effects of meditation on symptoms of pain."

Goyal analyzed every study he could find on meditation, including those that claimed that mindfulness meditation reduces pain, anxiety, depression, weight problems, substance abuse, sleep disorders, and a host of other ills.[26] Of the twenty thousand studies he examined, only forty-seven had been conducted in a scientifically rigorous manner. Some studies suggested that meditation eased psychological stress (anxiety and depression), but I was interested (as was Goyal) in physical pain: Four studies found that meditation eased discomfort, including irritable bowel syndrome, muscular-skeletal pain, and pain after an organ transplant.[27]

Goyal says no one knows why mindfulness meditation relieves long-lasting pain, but he says there are clues from his own experience, when he was able to look at his pain "in a nonjudgmental, nonreactive way." Chronic pain in particular is exacerbated by the emotion and anxiety surrounding it. When he meditated, Goyal removed the emotional element, and he believes that stripped off a layer of pain.

Pain has two components: When you throw out your back or put your hand on a hot stove, that originating pain moves from your back or hand to your brain. That acute pain ebbs quickly or slowly. But there's a second component—the emotional side of it—and this brain process is what turns pain, especially lasting pain, into a negative experience.

"Let's say I have a migraine coming on," Goyal said. "I may have an internal emotional reaction to the migraine symptoms where I'm thinking, *Oh no! It's going to get worse. I'm going to be in bed all day. It's going to be a lot of pain I have to deal with.* All of these are things that one does that catastrophizes what we're about to go through or what we're already going through. You can imagine that the symptoms just get worse and they snowball. And it could be that mindfulness meditation helps to stop that snowball from getting bigger."[28]

Happily for those of us who cannot serenely focus our scattered thoughts, researchers are looking beyond mindfulness meditation and into the brain, to see how *thinking* affects chronic pain. Here we arrive at the so-called placebo effect, the idea that one's beliefs can have a significant impact on one's body, including reducing pain.[29]

Placebos, or beliefs, perform poorly on some conditions that have objective measures: For example, they will not reduce the size of a tumor or overall mortality.[30] But beliefs excel at treating symptom-driven conditions like chronic pain and mood disorders, when what matters is a person's own conviction. In the past few years, researchers at Harvard and elsewhere have demonstrated that a person's beliefs can be as powerful in reducing pain as drugs or surgery. Placebo pills are just as good at relieving migraine headaches as rizatriptan, a widely used migraine drug.[31] Sham acupuncture cures persistent abdominal pain in nearly two thirds of the subjects.[32] Sham knee surgery relieves arthritic pain as much as removing cartilage.[33] These and a towering pile of other studies make the same point: Your thinking dramatically affects your pain.

Tor Wager at the University of Colorado is pioneering the research into the effect of thinking and beliefs on pain. Ironically, Wager was raised in the Christian Science religion, whose adherents believe in the power of prayer and thinking to heal the body of all sorts of ailments. Wager, like me, left Christian Science but retains a healthy respect for the power of belief, and he says his religious background influenced the direction of his research.

In a series of studies, Wager has found that people report less pain when they believe they are putting on an analgesic cream after being burned or physically shocked, even though the cream is really Vaseline. He then put subjects in a brain scanner and watched the pain centers of their brains become quieter when they put on the Vaseline, even though it has no analgesic properties. In another study, he discovered that believing you are receiving treatment releases natural pain-killing chemicals in the brain.[34]

"A lot of what creates the disability with pain, and even supports the pain itself, is the significance you attach to it—the 'badness,'" Wager told me. "When we experience something that's painful, we activate a lot of brain regions that have functions beyond the pain itself. We activate the prefrontal cortex, and I think what we do is elaborate on the significance and the badness of that experience."

Wager's research dovetails with that of Vania Apkarian at Northwestern University, who notes that "chronic pain is the inability to turn off the memory of pain."[35] In fact, Apkarian can predict with 85 percent accuracy whether or not a person will develop chronic back pain after an injury.[36] It boils down to a brain abnormality. The more connected two regions of the brain involved with processing pain and processing emotion are, the more likely a person is to develop chronic pain. That abnormality heightens the emotional memory of the pain and makes it more difficult to turn it off later.

In other words, meditation researchers (relying on people's own reports of pain) and placebo researchers (relying on self-reports and brain scans) have arrived at the same conclusion: Emotion puts an ex-clamation point on pain, and if you can lessen the emotion, you relieve the pain.

Okay, I am persuaded. My vocal cord pain—and my brother's, which is much worse—is exacerbated because we fear it: Every time I am crashing on deadline to get a radio story on the air, every time David has to give a speech, the stress and anxiety turn up the intensity. *Will it hurt? Will my voice hold out for an hour?* If you have any sort of chronic pain, you know what I'm talking about.

The trick is to turn down the volume. But how do you do that, other than with drugs and meditation? One proven method is distrac-tion, but you can't distract yourself forever.[37] Then Tor Wager raised an intriguing possibility, one rooted in brain science but nonetheless speculative: Strip the pain of its personal intimacy.

"One of the aspects of persistent pain," Wager said, "is you start to identify it as you. It's very possible if you dis-identify with the pain, you could essentially stop the miswiring in the [brain]. It could stop the process. It could block it."

This appealed to my formerly Christian Science heart. What if I saw my pain as *not* intrinsic to me? I wondered. What if it's a brain-wiring problem?

Which, it turns out, it is.

IT'S NOT ME, IT'S MY OCD

When I began having voice problems in the spring of 2012, my brother recommended I contact Dr. Diane Bless, a top voice specialist at the University of Wisconsin. Diane became the bright sil-ver lining to my voice problems. For several months we talked each week by Skype. The exercises she guided me through strengthened my voice so I could work, and her friendship provides a raucous dose of laughter to this day.

Diane suggested that I visit the hospital in Madison in December for a week-long medical boot camp with specialists who would put my vocal cords through every sort of test. We were all surprised at the resulting diagnosis. Despite the continuing pain, my vocal cords looked and operated normally. The paralysis and neurological damage caused by a virus had been for the most part healed, but my traumatized vocal cords never stopped firing, even when I was not talking. They never rested from their nervous activity; they were Mini-Me. Therefore, my pain was the result of a signal from my brain, telling me something was terribly wrong, when, in fact, there was nothing really wrong. As one doctor told me, "The pain could last a lifetime, or it could go away."

Initially his prognosis depressed me. It meant I was chained to Neurontin six times a day. It's a miracle drug: It dulls the pain and allows me to survive. But it also makes me feel as if I am trying to sprint in a swimming pool. I feel sluggish, mentally uncoordinated, and unfocused, hardly banner traits for a news reporter.

But when I began to look at the resilience research, I wondered if I could test some of these insights on my vocal cord pain. Placebo pills were out, of course, because I would know they were inert. I considered acupuncture, but I wanted to find something I could practice on myself, every day. I tried biofeedback once, but after I broke my collarbone a few days later, I could not drive to the appointments. And then I remembered a conversation six years earlier with a researcher at UCLA named Jeffrey Schwartz.

You may have heard of Schwartz. Leonardo DiCaprio has. The actor had just landed the lead in *The Aviator*, the 2004 movie that portrayed the life of Howard Hughes, a billionaire turned recluse plagued with obsessive-compulsive disorder. DiCaprio's business manager sent the script to Jeffrey Schwartz, who was famous for his innovative treatment of OCD. Over the following weeks, the neuropsychiatrist taught the actor how to think like, and even become, a person with the disorder.[38]

Schwartz explained that OCD is a neurological quirk that hyper-connects two parts of the brain: the error detection circuit and the habit center. When a person with OCD worries that there are germs on her hands, even though she knows she recently washed them, the error detection circuit bombards her with warnings—*germs, germs germs!*—and the only way to calm the fear is to repeat the habitual response. The mental peace is short-lived. Only minutes pass before she feels she needs to wash her hands again. Sometimes the habit involves checking doors or counting stop signs. Or, in DiCaprio's portrayal of Howard Hughes, it was verbal: The actor said a variation of "Show me the blueprints" forty-six times in one scene.

Before Schwartz came along, people with OCD had little hope of breaking free of this "worry circuit" without a lot of drugs and their side effects. In the 1980s, Schwartz began doing PET scans on his patients, injecting a tracer and watching how the blood flowed in their brains. Schwartz then showed his patients how their brains behaved, pointing out that their worry circuits lit up, even at rest, compared with people who did not have the disorder. It was a watershed for them.

"People learned to re-identify the inner experience as—to use one of our most important, famous lines—*It's not me, it's my OCD!*" Schwartz told me.

There, on their brain scan, they saw in vivid color what they knew rationally to be true: Their fears were not based in reality. They did not need to wash their hands or count the stop signs. Their brains had faulty wiring.

"As soon as one realizes that these intrusive, unwanted thoughts are basically just the residue, the symptom, of a brain-wiring problem, then one pays a different kind of attention to them," he said. "One realizes that literally 'my brain is sending me a false message.' And then when one uses that insight to focus one's attention differently, one changes that brain circuitry."

Schwartz taught his patients to relabel their fear as rubbish, to dismiss it, and then to distract themselves by going for a walk or gardening. Within ten weeks, their symptoms largely dissipated; this mental treatment was as effective as drugs.

"You are not the slave of your brain," Schwartz said. "You can change how your brain works by the way you direct your attention."

"When you say, 'change your brain,'" I clarified, "you mean literally the OCD circuit calms down?"

"Yes! That's a good layperson's way of putting it. We saw the error detection circuitry in the brain become less activated. And even more clearly, we saw this hyperconnection between the error detection area and the brain's automatic transmission, the caudate nucleus area, decrease. So you had a brain that was in 'brain lock,' and you could literally see this brain lock loosen, decrease, and be released from brain lock!"

In other words, the patients' thoughts—how they focused their attention—changed the physical activity in their brains.

Schwartz, who began publishing his research in the 1980s, offered some of the first tangible evidence of "neuroplasticity": Our brains can change through our lifetime, even at midlife, even after years of destructive thought patterns. What's more, our brains do not need experiences or medicine or surgery to start functioning differently; they change in response to our thoughts and intentions.

As I pondered this some six years later, I saw some sunlight. Research shows that distraction alleviates pain. Moreover, according to the meditation and placebo studies, so does looking at the pain clinically, by stripping it of its emotional layer. And here were Jeffrey Schwartz and his patients, calling the worry circuit's bluff: *It's not me, it's my OCD.*

Suddenly, I spotted the parallel with my vocal cord pain. My problem, I realized, is not based in reality. The vocal cords had healed. This is a brain-wiring problem. Even I—with decades of stress that my doctors believe eventually triggered the nonstop firing of my vocal cords, with the attendant chronic pain—could change my brain. So I thought, *Why don't I tackle my brain-generated pain as Schwartz's patients had tackled OCD?*

I decided that every time I felt pain, which was often, I would shout silently to myself: *"False alarm!* This isn't based in reality. This is a brain-wiring problem." Then I would distract myself—interviews helped; so did a bike ride—and I would see what would happen.

I described my plan to my brother one day. David looked at me for a long moment.

"You are going to be a very, very strange old lady," he said.

9.

GIVING IT AWAY

SEPTEMBER

Saturday, September 28

Sandra Day and I arrived at the Armed Forces Retirement Home in Washington, D.C., just before nine on this bright, crisp morning. As if on cue, five dogs and their owners hopped out of their cars, and the pack of us threaded our way, with the assistance of two men in wheelchairs, to the basement. Happy chaos greeted us: dogs darting here and there, smelling one backside after another, an occasional outraged bark but nothing serious. We twenty-four humans fidgeted nervously in our seats, each of us wondering whether our dog would pass the test.

Jack, the head of People Animals Love (PAL), recited a brief history of the group, which dispatches dog-therapy teams to schools, retirement homes, and hospitals around the Washington area. We split into three groups to test each dog's obedience. I had read about the stringent standards for therapy pets, and worried that my eighty-pound dog, who flunked out of puppy school, would not make the grade.

"No dog has ever failed," Jack assured me. "We just want to see the relationship between you and your dog."

Moments later, all the dogs had passed. I swelled with pride and amazement as Sandra sat, lay down, stayed, and came on command. Perhaps the dog treats I slipped her retrieved those long-buried commands she had learned before her untimely departure from obedience school.

After Jack congratulated us all, the newly minted teams marched up to the third floor, the dementia unit, where a dozen men and women sat in chairs, silently staring into the middle distance. Sandra ignored them, dragging me toward a kitchenette, where she vacuumed up some food on the floor. She could not have been less interested in the people—this, a glimpse into our future as a therapy team—and pulled me toward the exit after finishing the last crumb. After a few minutes, Doris rolled up to us in her wheelchair and began stroking Sandra's silky ears.

"I'm planning to get out of here soon, get my own place, and get a dog," Doris told me.

"That's great," I said. "What kind of dog?"

She paused. I thought she was contemplating the question. Then she looked me in the eye.

"I'm ninety-seven. I'm shooting for a hundred."

"I think you'll make it," I laughed. At that, Sandra leapt up, tugging me toward the door. *I hope Sandra grows to like pet therapy,* I thought, *because this is my shot at generativity.*

PLATINUM GENERATIVITY

I desperately want to be generative. Erik Erikson said I should be. The groundbreaking psychologist believed there were eight stages in a person's development. The seventh stage, "generativity," is the hallmark of a healthy middle age, when we stop focusing on acquiring—family, home, career, and financial assets—and begin to invest outward, into the next generation, or the community, or a cause.[1]

"Erikson has a great phrase," Marc Freedman told me. "'I am what survives me.' Humans are part of a generational project, passing on to the next generation what you've learned from life."

By this standard, generativity defines Marc Freedman's career. He worked with underprivileged young people when he was in his twenties, before casting his net in the opposite direction. He founded Encore.org, a nonprofit that taps the talents and experience of middle-aged and older adults to solve social problems by, for example, placing them in nonprofit organizations.

Freedman says Erikson's ideas have even more traction today, fifty years after the psychologist coined the term. With people living longer and healthier lives, they have the time and energy to not just leave a legacy but live one.

"It's not a deathbed thought," he said. "You might have twenty legacy years where you really are actively fulfilling and passing on important wisdom and experience."

If you fail in this altruistic stage, Erikson warned, you risk "self-absorption and stagnation," a spiral into isolation, physical and mental decline, and bitterness. That got my attention. Since I have no children of my own, and my stepdaughter was raised beautifully by her mother nearly halfway across the country, I missed the off-ramp to the most natural route to generativity: raising children.[2] As I worked obsessively at my job in my forties and early fifties, this inward focus began to trouble me. I wrestled with an emptiness in my ambitions, a misallocation of resources, as I plowed all of my efforts and talents into my seasoned career instead of letting them roll downhill, to the next generation and beyond. At fifty-four, I decided to build my generative muscles. Of course, taking Sandra to retirement homes is not exactly investing in the next generation, but even Erikson is flexible on that point. It is enough to invest outward.

I confess some skepticism that generativity is the signature trait of midlife. It seems to overstate the impulse in middle age, and understate it for surrounding ages. On the one hand, most of my midlife friends are madly raising children, putting them through college, taking care of parents, all while juggling greater responsibilities in their work. They are not scanning the horizon for causes to invest in. Alternatively, I do not believe people live self-involved lives until a biological switch flips at forty, flooding the system with generative hormones.

Marc Freedman offered a new frame on Erikson's idea. Of course, he said, generativity is a lifelong impulse, expressed in various ways at different times. But there is a "particular character" to generativity at midlife: a robust, urgent altruism that occurs, he said, paraphrasing psychologist G. Stanley Hall, "when the shadows begin to slant eastward."[3]

"It is that moment where the sun is still up, but you can start to see the intersection of the beginning and the end," Freedman said. "At midlife, people feel a sense of mastery. They have been around the block, they have learned a few things, and they realize they don't have an endless period of time to put that wisdom into action. I think it's motivating."

This suggests a smarter way to define generativity, one I will freely appropriate: It is altruism in a specific phase of life, one that can put more runs on the board than the altruism of youth or old age. And here I want to offer a distinction and a plea. True, *volunteering* is generative, but anyone can volunteer at any point in life. Simple volunteering is my second choice for people at midlife. The type of generativity I favor draws on skills, passions, and character honed over four, five, six decades, which make each of us a unique individual with distinctive assets and ideas to pass along. I will call this "platinum generativity," a potent altruism—the kind possessed by Judy Cockerton.

By the time she was forty-eight, Judy had navigated two careers, first as a teacher, then as the owner of two toy stores near Boston. "I loved what I did," she told me. "My children were flourishing. It was a lovely, lovely life."

One night her husband handed her an article about a baby boy who had been kidnapped from his foster care parents in the middle of the day. A little like the "butterfly effect" of chaos theory—in which minor perturbations, such as the flapping of the wings of a distant butterfly, can alter the path of a hurricane weeks later—that newspaper article would change the lives of the Cockertons and countless others. The article spurred her to research foster care, and what she discovered horrified her: Some twenty-five thousand children in Massachusetts alone lived in foster homes, sometimes abused, sometimes neglected, if they were lucky enough to find a foster home at all. For many, the foster care system was a pipeline straight to poverty and misery.

"On your eighteenth birthday, your social worker came to you and said, 'Here's two hundred dollars. I will drive you to the nearest homeless shelter and wish you well,'" she said. "I stumbled on this reality I couldn't ignore. It grabbed me by the ankle and it really wouldn't let go."

The Cockertons decided to adopt two sisters, five months and seventeen months old, from foster care, a generous act by any standard, but as it happened, this was only the warm-up act. Judy sold her toy stores and established a nonprofit called Treehouse Foundation, aimed at creating a family environment for children who have no families: those in foster care. Working with a housing group and a welfare organization, she built Treehouse Circle in Easthampton, Massachusetts, a neighborhood where the children live with their adoptive families in houses next door to the equivalent of grandparents—elders who want to invest in the children's lives and help lift them from a future of poverty. There is a community center with a kitchen, library, and café. Grandparents teach kids to bake, kids shovel snow for the grandparents. The community could be in an episode of *Leave It to Beaver*. Fifty percent of foster kids drop out of school. Treehouse children have almost perfect attendance, and the oldest of them are going to college.

This is classic generativity on steroids. But let's look at it through the lens of my platinum generativity. Judy took her teaching and entrepreneurial skills, and wove them together with her passion for children and her experience with foster care. Her generative efforts have radically altered the lives of underprivileged children, airlifting them from their unstable homes and an impoverished future to a secure family life and a future with promise.

Judy Cockerton was sixty-one when we spoke. She admits to having a frenetic life as a social entrepreneur, child advocate, and mother of two adopted girls, now teenagers.

"It's not a job," she said. "I am living out my purpose."

A purpose beyond oneself. *It sounds so appealing*, I thought. It also sounds so *complicated*. As if she read my mind, Judy leaned forward and lowered her voice.

"Find a way to give something of yourself, a piece of your talent, a piece of your goodness," she said. "Give it back to your world. Give it back to your community. It really makes you feel so wonderful inside. It makes you a better person."

WHY HAROLD GAVE HIS KIDNEY AWAY

When I began to explore generativity, I quickly realized that there is virtually no scientific research on the subject. Bad news for me. But scientists are looking at generativity's cousins, altruism and empathy, by studying the psychology and biology of extreme altruists. Studying people like Harold Mintz.

Harold Mintz and Gennet Belay sit side by side on Gennet's couch, engaging in animated debate about the existence of God. His wife and her husband flank them, but they stay out of this friendly dispute; they've heard it many times before. Harold, a secular Jew and filmmaker from Hollywood who is on the fence about God, is six-foot-four, lanky, with an impressive white mustache, white hair, and a craggy face. Gennet, a devout Ethiopian Christian, is soft-spoken, a hundred pounds at most, with high cheekbones, and skin that is both beautiful and tortured: Her bouts with cancer and kidney failure have etched scars from skin grafts up and down her arms.

Harold and Gennet are connected by a kidney. She has one of his. Theirs is a story that has puzzled scientists for some time: Why do some people make sacrifices for perfect strangers? What is it about Harold Mintz's brain that drives him to extreme altruism?

Gennet has suffered kidney infections and poor health since she was a child living in Ethiopia. She fell in love and married Tsegaye Wolde, an economist, and moved to the United States in 1987.

"Ten months after we get here, I went to the doctor," she recalled. "He told me that my kidney works only ten percent. When it is five percent, we will start the dialysis."

Over the next twelve years, Gennet endured forty-five surgeries and dialysis three times a week, sometimes too sick to eat for weeks on end. Gennet, her husband, and two children lived in permanent dusk, between hope and despair, life and death.

"My concern was every day, What will happen?" Tsegaye said. "What's going to be the next morning?"

During this time, Harold Mintz was trying to give away his kidney. His impulse, he insists, sprang not from extraordinary goodness, but from the accumulation of small moments.

"Nobody wakes up one day and says, 'You know what I'm going to do today? I'm going to start giving out body parts to people I don't know,'" Harold said, laughing. "So for me, it was certainly a series of events that put me on that path to donating."

He started donating blood in high school to impress a cheerleader. He read a newspaper article in college about a teacher who gave her kidney to save a student's life. Later, flying cross-country on a business trip, he wept at a Debbie Reynolds film about a boy who donated his kidney to his grandmother. When he landed, Harold sent away for information, only to find that it was illegal to donate a kidney to a stranger. But in 2000, he discovered that Washington, D.C., had launched a pilot program that allowed so-called altruistic donors to give their kidneys to strangers. He was thrilled. His wife, Susan, was not. Initially she balked, but then she relented.

"I figured that he probably would not pass the physical or mental evaluations," she told me, laughing. "When those evaluations came back positive, I figured, it's basically his body and if he wanted to save somebody's life, who was I to say no?"

In December 2000, Harold arrived at Georgetown University Medical Center, where a team of transplant surgeons cut him open, removed his left kidney, and put it in a beer cooler full of ice, which was then driven to a hospital in Fairfax, Virginia. Moments later, the Fairfax surgeons implanted Harold's very large kidney into Gennet's small body, and waited.

"The phone rings, seven o'clock maybe," Harold recalled. "It's the lady in charge of the experimental program. She says, 'Look, I'm not supposed to tell you anything about the recipient. Would you like to know a little bit about the recipient?' I'm like, 'Yeah.' 'Well, it's a woman. She's a wife and a mother. Two kids. She's an accountant. She lives in Springfield, Virginia.' And this is a quote. She said, 'As soon as they put your kidney in her, it started peeing up a storm.' And I went, 'Uh, is that good or bad?' And she said, 'That's *fantastic*. It started functioning immediately when they put it inside of her. It started working instantly.'"

"He saved my life," Gennet said, looking up into his face. "He is a gift from God for me."

"I was always thinking, What type of man is this guy?" Tsegaye said. "What type of heart does he have? Does he have a family? Children? How's his health? Why did he risk? So I was eager to meet him. And we became a family."

Harold contends that his sacrifice was nothing special. Anyway, he says, he received as much as Gennet did.

"Not a day goes by where I don't think about it," Harold said. "Every day. I'll never be a rock star who hears his songs on the radio. I'm not a lifeguard who saved somebody's life at the pool or the beach. But I wake up and I know that I'm part of a group or a team or a family that helped save a person's life. She wouldn't be alive if all of us didn't do what we did that day twelve years ago. Psychologically, I'm much better for it. And when I share the story, that rush of endorphins comes right back."

"You don't think you're a little heroic?" I asked.

"Absolutely not!" he said. "I feel strongly that if Barb had been through exactly the same series of events that I did, you'd have been on that surgeon's table."

"I haven't given a kidney," I replied. "So, aren't we different?"

"Well, we're different in that I've already done it."

Only Harold believed this argument. It was as if his wildly altruistic instincts made him blind to everyone else's mediocrity.

"Harold, you must understand, in this family, you are a hero," Tsegaye insisted. "You gave Gennet her life. You gave me my wife, and you gave her children their mother. You may argue, but in this house, you are a hero."

THE BRAIN OF AN ALTRUIST

While Harold Mintz was giving away his kidney, Abigail Marsh was pondering these questions as a Ph.D. student at Harvard University: From where do our cruelest and most generous instincts arise? Why would some altruists risk their lives to save yours, while some psychopaths would take your life for no reason, without a twitch of emotion? Can the difference be traced to biology or life experience, nature or nurture?

The questions had dogged Marsh, who is now an associate professor of psychology at Georgetown University, ever since one summer night nearly two decades ago. She was twenty years old, driving over a bridge on her way home to Tacoma, Washington. She swerved to avoid a dog, sending her car into doughnuts across the freeway. Suddenly the car stalled, and she found herself on the bridge, facing oncoming traffic. Cars and semitrailer trucks were flying toward her.

"I couldn't get the car to turn back on," she recalled. "I don't know how long I sat there, when this man appeared at the passenger's-side window, and he said, 'You look like you could use a little help.' And I said, 'Yeah, I don't know what to do.' And he said, 'Move into the passenger's seat and I'll get in.'

"And so he waited for a break in traffic, ran around the car, got in, figured out that the car was still in drive, which is why I couldn't turn it on. He got it turned back on, waited for another break in traffic, gunned it across the freeway, and then parked it back behind his car on the off-ramp. And I don't even think I said thank you. I just remember being sweaty and shaking, and he offered to follow me for a little while. I said, 'No, no. I'll be okay.' And then off he went. So I don't know who he was. I don't know why he stopped and ran across the freeway in the middle of the night to save a stranger, but I'll always be grateful."

She began to wonder: What kind of a person would do something like that?

Since graduate school, Marsh had studied the brains of psychopaths. She and colleagues put children and adults in the brain scanner, flashed photos of people with fearful, angry, or neutral expressions, and observed how their brains processed the different emotions. Later, outside the brain scanner, they showed them more faces—anger, disgust, fear, happiness, sadness, surprise—and asked them to identify the emotions. Two differences with normal people caught her attention. First, the psychopaths failed miserably at recognizing fearful expressions. The second distinction involved the amygdala, a part of the brain highly sensitive to emotions, particularly fear. In normal people, the amygdala lit up when they saw fearful expressions; in psychopaths, the amygdala showed no change and, in some cases, grew a little quieter, as if seeing others' fear was calming, not upsetting.

She thought psychopaths might offer a clue to what makes altruists tick. If people are on a continuum from psychopathic to extremely altruistic, "who are the anti-psychopaths?" she wondered. After some thought, she realized, "Altruistic kidney donors fit the bill."

Marsh found nineteen donors, including Harold Mintz, who were eager to participate in her brain-scanning study, some of them flying across the country at their own expense. Almost all of the volunteers were in their forties and fifties, the sweet spot for generativity and the center of midlife. By contrast, she had far more trouble finding twenty "normal" people to participate, even though they lived in the area. And as she predicted, the results showed that extremely altruistic people are wired differently from the rest of us. Not only are they much better at recognizing fear and distress, but their amygdala fired more actively and was physically larger than the amygdala of the average participant.[4] Their brain reflected their outsized compassion.

"What do you make of this?" I asked.

"One possibility is that in giving you the ability to experience fear, the amygdala is also enabling you to simulate or reproduce that same experience when you're looking at somebody else's expression," Marsh said. "That's what enables you to identify what they're experiencing. Maybe you're putting yourself in somebody else's emotional shoes, and that helps drive your compassionate response to them."

Harold Mintz rejected her interpretation. He pointed out that the very act of donating a kidney, something he had thought about every day long before the donation, inevitably changed his brain.

"My brain looked just like yours before I did this," he told her. "So anything you find out that's postsurgery doesn't mean pooh!"

Marsh agrees that everything we do changes our brains, but the research on psychopaths strongly suggests they were born with a neurological quirk that drove their insensitivity to fear. She believes people like Harold Mintz have a neurological quirk as well. She says they are not saints, but they're not like the rest of us, either.

"Have you thought about donating a kidney?" I asked.

"I've never been tempted at all," she said.

I laughed. "Neither have I."

WIRED FOR THE GOLDEN RULE

A fierce debate rages among scientists: Does pure altruism really exist? Does anyone ever perform a wholly unselfish act?

On the face of it, we are clearly an altruistic species, and grow more so as we age. We volunteer, donate to charity, give blood, give our resources away, not only to our family and friends but to people we may never meet, those who lost their homes in a tsunami in Thailand, for example, or during earthquakes in Haiti and Nepal.

But *why* we do these things—the psychology of it—now, that gets sticky. Many psychologists think that, deep down, we believe we will receive payback: If I help you, you—or someone else—will help me in the future. That is "direct reciprocity." Others argue that when you give to charity, or help a friend move furniture, you receive an indirect benefit: a rise in status, a reputation for being a mensch. Sometimes social pressure makes altruism a de facto requirement: When was the last time you did *not* leave a tip for a waiter?

Psychologists Jamil Zaki at Stanford and Jason Mitchell at Harvard do not dispute that social pressure and reputation are powerful forces. But they believe something else is at play. Doing good actually feels good.

"In economics, it's called 'warm glow,' the fuzzy feeling that you get when you do something nice for someone else," Zaki says. "The whole idea of empathy, the idea that we share other people's emotions—that we feel good when they feel good, we feel bad when they feel bad—suggests we might want to help people because in helping them we feel good. Emotions are contagious, and we might catch some of that ourselves. And that might be the motive that drives us to act altruistically."

They tested their hypothesis by scanning a person's brain while he played the "dictator game." In that game, one person has a sum of money that he can split up any way he wants: keep it for himself, or give the other player a little money or a lot. When the dictator acted fairly, a part of the brain associated with a reward lit up.[5]

"We can say that acting altruistically seems to engage some of the same processes or brain systems as getting money or a good meal," Zaki says.

Zaki did not mention sex, but he and a number of other researchers at the National Institutes of Health and elsewhere have found that giving away money activates the same reward systems as food, water, sex, and social attachment—our most basic needs.[6] Perhaps not surprisingly, generous brains behave differently from selfish ones. Researchers at Duke University could actually predict which participants would give money to a charity and which would keep it for themselves. In a brain scanner, when generous people give away money, the parts of the brain that allow them to tune in to the actions and intentions of others glowed brightly.[7] This is the brain's rendition of the Golden Rule: I want to treat them the way I want to be treated.

Other researchers pointed to the temporoparietal junction, where the temporal and parietal lobes meet, as the sweet spot for self-sacrifice. This area is involved in understanding other people's feelings, walking in their shoes. Generous people had more gray matter at that junction.[8] And those who chose (in a brain-scanner-friendly game) to save another person from physical harm, even if it meant harm to oneself, had more activity in that area as well.[9] There are even unselfish genes: A person with a specific gene variation will give you the shirt off his back, while that other guy with a slightly different variation will happily take it from you.[10]

The bottom line is this: Altruism is not an evolutionary option, it is deeply wired in us and essential for survival. We wouldn't be the people we are today without it.

It is so deeply wired, in fact, that empathy, which is sort of rudi-

mentary altruism, preceded us. I already suspected this, as has probably every other dog owner. I remember the day after I broke my
collarbone, when I (briefly) tried to resist taking Percocet for the considerable pain. I was leaning with my back to the kitchen wall, exhausted by the pain that had kept me up all night; slowly I slid down
until I was sitting on the floor. Sandra Day watched me closely, a concerned look on her face (not that I anthropomorphize), and raced over
to fetch Devin in the living room. He petted her, unaware of her signals as he read the newspaper, and soon she sprawled on her back for
a tummy rub. Lassie she is not. But I swear that she had every intention
of soliciting help, until she was diverted by her own comfort.[11]

I was happy to see my suspicions about animal empathy confirmed.
A researcher at the National Institute of Mental Health, for example, visited homes to observe how young children respond to family
members' emotions. She instructed people to pretend to cry, sob, or
choke. The children responded—and so did the pets: They hovered
nearby and put their heads in their owners' laps.[12] When some researchers in London yawned in front of dogs, the dogs yawned back
nearly three quarters of the time—much more than humans. (The dogs
were not fooled by fake yawning when the researchers merely open
their mouths wide.) Researchers believe that contagious yawning, previously seen in chimps, is a rudimentary form of empathy.[13]

Rhesus monkeys refused to pull a chain that delivered food to
themselves, if doing so delivered a shock to a companion. One empathetic monkey went without food for twelve days after witnessing
another monkey being shocked. More recently, a rhesus monkey saved
a companion that had been electrocuted by high-voltage wires at a
train station in India. In a video that went viral on YouTube, we see the
monkey scoop up his friend, bite him, shake him hard, and then dunk
his limp body in water until he revives twenty minutes later.[14] Vampire
bats, despite their dark reputation, share food with other vampire

bats, even if they are not related.[15] And in one experiment, scientists put one rat in a closed cage, a piece of chocolate in another cage, and allowed a second rat to roam free. The loose rat taught himself how to open the cages, but instead of hogging the chocolate for himself, he freed the caged rat first and then opened the cage with the chocolate, which they proceeded to share.[16]

No one thinks that the generosity of a vampire bat is in the same class as Harold Mintz's kidney donation to a stranger. Still, these nascent forms of empathy and altruism convince many scientists that the impulse to help others is both primal and imperative.

One ancient chemical that is found in both man and beast seems to lie behind altruistic behavior. To observe that chemical in action, I needed my dog, myself, and Paul Zak.

THE MORAL MOLECULE

Oxytocin is a shy molecule," Paul Zak tells me, as he searches for a vein in my arm and slides the needle in. "It's got a half-life of three and a half minutes, and degrades rapidly at room temperature, so we have to grab it fast and keep it cold."

Zak, an economist and director of the Center for Neuroeconomics Studies at Claremont Graduate University, draws a vial of my blood and places the tube in his portable centrifuge. He turns on the machine, which separates the heavy red blood cells from the lighter plasma, where my hormones live. This is my baseline blood draw. In a few hours, he will extract more blood for comparison—to see whether, and how much, my oxytocin levels surge after a morning of altruistic behavior.

Zak traces his fascination with this happy molecule back to his mother, who was a nun before she left her order and married.

"She had a direct pipeline to God, and if you had any questions, she would let you know exactly what the answer was, in black-and-white."

Although Zak rejected that view—"If God exists, God's going to live in the gray zones"—his upbringing set him on a quest to understand the nature and biology of morality. The more he studied trust, then compassion, generosity, and altruism, the more he bumped into this moral molecule, oxytocin.

Zak has built his research around oxytocin, which has been variously called the "cuddle hormone," the "connection chemical," the "trust hormone," the "moral molecule," even the "goody-goody hormone."[17] Initially, scientists spotted it in childbirth and breast-feeding, but upon further investigation, oxytocin seems to show up wherever warm and fuzzy feelings do.[18] In various studies, Zak and others have discovered that the hormone makes people more trusting, more generous, more willing to trade and cooperate, happier, and more loving. It has even been shown to help fighting couples reach a happy solution. Oxytocin does have a dark side: It can make some people more suspicious, jealous, and prone to gloat; it can also intensify bad memories.[19] But in general, it beats alcohol as a social lubricant.

"Isn't it an amazing thing that we have this deep innate sense that if you play nice, I'll play nice?" Zak asks me, as he places a test tube of my blood in a cooler of dry ice. "Because oxytocin is so evolutionarily old, it suggests that this reciprocal behavior, this Golden Rule kind of behavior, is also a deep part of our human nature."

Oxytocin is subtle: When it spikes, you may feel slightly more relaxed, but often you sense no physical change at all. It reduces stress levels and boosts your immune system. Over the long term, it changes one's life for the better. Studies have found that people who release more oxytocin than others are happier, Zak says, "because they have better relationships of all types—romantic, friendships, better with strangers, better with family."[20]

Zak has measured oxytocin in a variety of ways: He has drawn blood from people playing economic games (to measure cooperation and generosity), from people watching a sad video (to measure empathy), from psychopaths (lack of empathy), from a bridal party at a wedding (love), from people jumping out of an airplane (trust). He has shown that the hormone does not simply reflect generous emotions. It sparks them. When Zak and others sprayed the hormone up people's noses, they watched as most of them became more cooperative and gave more to charity.[21]

In short, oxytocin infuses generosity—that is, unless you are stressed (a state that numbs you to the feelings of others) or you are a psychopath. This latter category concerned me. Just a week earlier, when I traveled to Los Angeles, Zak invited me to watch a heart-wrenching video of a father playing with his son, who was dying from brain cancer. Zak has tested hundreds of people with this video. Oxytocin spikes in about 90 percent of the people.[22]

"Of the ten percent who don't," he told me, "half of those are really stressed-out. Or they have many of the attributes of psychopaths."

Uh-oh. I knew, when I was watching the video, that I felt nothing, nothing except jet lag from the previous day's cross-country flight, and exhaustion from driving two hours in the Los Angeles traffic to arrive at Claremont by nine a.m. And sure enough, when the results came in, I showed virtually no spike in oxytocin, no biological evidence of compassion or empathy.

But today I may redeem myself. I know I am an empathetic person. Really. I just need proof. Zak happened to be in Washington for a conference, and he offered to accompany my dog and me to a rehabilitation facility in Virginia. This is why we find ourselves an hour later in the

Woodbine Rehabilitation and Healthcare Center, Sandra Day ready to
bring joy to the patients, and me secretly hoping for redemption.

We wander in and out of patient rooms, chatting with people recov-
ering from a fall, illness, or surgery. Eventually we stroll into the common room. A dozen people sit around tables eating cherry pie, a little
dazed as the television blares CNN. I spot an African-American
woman who looks much too young to be here, sitting quietly in a
wheelchair by the window. We approach. She greets me formally. Her
name is Claudia. She reaches down to stroke Sandra's ears, and my
dog, who has not sat still for anyone so far, leans in.

"Hi, precious," Claudia coos to Sandra. "My girls would love to
have you. You're a good dog, Sandra," and to me: "Is she the only
one?" Yes, I tell her, but we're thinking about getting a puppy. "Would
you like to have a little brother or sister?" she asks Sandra. "That
would be nice, wouldn't it?" And we chat quietly for ten minutes, about
her children, about the upcoming holidays, but always circling back to
Sandra, who leans against Claudia, transported, barely able to keep
her eyes open.

Finally I stand up.

"You're going to leave me?" Claudia asks, but she's smiling.

"We are," I say, "but we will come back."

Claudia nods, and then takes my right hand gently in hers. She
strokes it once, then lifts it to her lips and gives it a butterfly kiss.

Zak, who has been watching us, takes me by the elbow and steers
us to the hall.

"You had the world's best interaction," he whispers. "Let's do
this now."

We rush to the car, where he draws two vials of blood and spins
them in his centrifuge. Then he seals the test tube in the Styrofoam
cooler. I ask him if he thinks my oxytocin levels rose during my conversation with Claudia. He nods. But he cannot be certain. It strikes

me that his uncertainty is fitting for a hormone that is so other-centered, so involved with empathy and self-sacrifice.

"In general, you can't make your own brain release oxytocin," Zak says. "You can just give that gift to somebody else. So, you are giving the gift of Sandra Day, interacting with these people, and if I took their blood, I have no doubt that many of them would have released oxytocin and been less stressed."

I would not automatically experience a surge as well, although in all likelihood, Claudia handed the gift of oxytocin back to me during our gentle conversation. We would not know for several weeks.

I ask Zak: Is there any way to increase oxytocin? Can I ramp up my biological altruism? Is that what happens when people think about investing outward, into the next generation?

Zak says there is no evidence that oxytocin levels naturally rise as one ages, which rules out a simple biological explanation for midlife generativity. However, animal studies strongly suggest that it can be increased with use.

"The more one releases oxytocin," he says, "the easier it becomes to release it. The threshold for release becomes lower."

In other words, if I help you, you are happier, and we both get a ping of dopamine reward, which then reinforces this behavior. A virtuous circle begins.

Zak's own experience with hugs, which has transformed him from an introvert to a man with many rich relationships, suggests that practice makes perfect. If I keep volunteering, or empathetically engage with other people, if I give a hug every now and again, I will ratchet up my oxytocin levels. And in turn, I would nurture my generous instincts with this biologic Miracle-Gro.

I glance over at Zak as we leave. Why would he spend his day in Washington driving to a rehabilitation center, then roaming around with me until we could find a FedEx office that would ship a container of blood in dry ice? His generosity, his enthusiasm for my one-person experiment, has changed the relationship and made me feel expansive. What's that I feel? A surge of oxytocin? A ping of dopamine? Whatever it is, it speaks to a virtuous circle. If I can help Paul Zak in the future, you bet I will.

A few weeks later, Zak e-mailed me the results. My oxytocin levels had increased 62 percent at the rehabilitation center.

"This is *enormous!*" he declared, noting that the average increase in oxytocin levels for the people who watched the video about the boy with cancer was 47 percent. "And some of these people cry! A sixty-two percent increase indicates that you really cared about the people you were interacting with—you connected to them emotionally. What could be more generative than that? Huge!"

I feel redeemed. I even feel altruistic.

PAGING MARCUS WELBY

Paul Zak's research gave me a road map. The way to increase altruism, maybe even generativity, is to exercise it like a muscle. Help people out, which creates more happy interactions, which makes you feel good about life and yourself, which prompts you to more acts of altruism, and so on in this virtuous circle. As long as you don't burn out—and studies show that two hours a week of volunteering is the perfect number—your altruistic impulse will glide along on a glassy sea of oxytocin and dopamine.[23]

Still I wondered: Can you *train* yourself to be more empathetic, that step that starts the virtuous circle in the first place?

So far, scientists have tackled the empathy problem in two ways. One involves "perspective taking." In a famous experiment in 1991, psychologist Dan Batson found that putting oneself in another's shoes triggers empathy and an altruistic act. In that experiment, a woman named Elaine (secretly working with the experimenters) was assigned a task in which she would receive an electric shock at random intervals. When the (unknowing) assistant learned that Elaine was terrified of electric shocks, she offered to take her place.[24] In trial after trial, most of the unsuspecting assistants volunteered to take the shocks.

The other approach is meditation. Scientists have found that people who were trained for eight weeks in mindfulness meditation were three times as likely as those in a control group to give up their seats when a person on crutches walked into the waiting room. Half of the meditators jumped up, while only 16 percent of the control group (people who had been wait-listed for meditation training) offered their seats.[25] To which I say: *Really?* The vast majority flip through *People* while some poor woman on crutches leans against the wall wincing? (Yes, they had her wince.)

In another study, people who engaged in seven hours of compassion-meditation training gave twice as much money to a stranger in need as those who were not trained. Moreover, their brains reflected that compassion: The networks involved with understanding others' suffering and with regulating emotions became more active.[26] In another study, people who practiced cognitively based compassion training for eight weeks became much better at recognizing emotions than those who learned about mind-body topics. Once again, the brain regions associated with empathy lit up more.[27] Training people to recognize emotions is a key to empathy: As you recall, one of the signature findings about altruistic kidney donors (and, on the other end, psychopaths) is the acute ability (or failure) to identify emotions on a face, particularly fear.

"There is promising evidence that you can get people to engage altruistically a lot more," said Stanford's Jamil Zaki. "There are lots of things that will get people to be more altruistic in the context of an experiment. The question is: For how long? We don't know. Probably not very long."

Helen Riess is banking on a long-term solution. She is hoping that she can help those who were once empathetic regain their humanity: doctors.

Riess is a psychiatrist at Massachusetts General Hospital and an associate professor at Harvard Medical School. About ten years before I met her, she participated in a study with twenty pairs of patients and psychiatrists. The researchers had a hunch that if a doctor and patient were emotionally in sync—if the doctors were empathetic and elicited trust—then their physiology would be in sync with the patient as well, and the healing process would go better. Riess selected one of her young patients, a college student who had been trying to lose weight for years. The researchers put sensors on their fingers; the sensors measured skin conductance, or tiny bits of perspiration on their fingers. They videotaped the session. That videotape, Riess said, was "career changing."

"When I saw the physiological tracers, I was completely blown away," she told me. "What had appeared to be a very self-contained, self-confident woman turned out to be someone who was massively anxious."

The physiological lines reflecting their stress levels moved up and down at the same time, Riess said, "except that her tracings were wiggling at a furious rate while mine were much smoother. And so we were in sync but her level of anxiety was about five times greater than mine."

When Riess showed her patient the graphic, the patient nodded and said, "I feel like I'm looking at an X-ray of my psyche."

Riess studied the tape as if she were an "emotion detective," noting when the patient's stress spiked, and whether that stress leaked out in her actions. Riess realized that whenever the patient was uncomfortable, she flipped her hair back, lowered her voice, or looked away. From then on, whenever Riess keyed in on these cues, she would stop the conversation, go deeper, and empathize with her. Within a year, the patient had lost forty pounds.

Riess has no shortage of empathy—she is a psychiatrist, after all—but she recognized that the medical community had a crisis on its hands. Some of the thorniest problems in medicine, in fact, could be traced back to an empathy deficit: Studies show that if a patient does not consider his doctor to be empathetic, he will ignore the doctor's advice and fail to take the prescribed medicine.[28] Patients are much more likely to sue a doctor who is rushed or indifferent, the one who does not look you in the eye, the one who has his hand on the doorknob during the visit. Riess said the doctors weren't having much fun, either, with rampant burnout and suicide rates about 50 percent higher than that of the general population.

"We were interested in knowing whether empathy could be taught," Riess said.

She learned everything she could about the neurobiology and physiology of emotions and empathy. She learned about mirror neurons, how we map on our brains the actions of others. She found research that showed that when you see a loved one in pain, the parts of the brain involved with emotional pain light up.[29] Other research showed that when doctors distanced themselves, patients responded at a molecular level.[30]

Her conclusion: Empathy heals, lack of it harms.

Riess designed a training program based on how our brains perceive and respond to the suffering of others. When I met her, six specialties at Mass General had included empathy training for their residents. Residency is the time that empathy takes a nose dive: This is when young doctors begin to have more contact with patients. Often they become overwhelmed and create an emotional distance to protect themselves from being sucked into their patients' pain and suffering. The results of the randomized controlled trial were significant: Doctors who completed the three-hour training course scored much higher on patient ratings than those who did not.[31] And, Riess said, they reported feeling "more joy in their work."

I asked Riess what her chief insights about empathy training were.

"Recognize that the human face is a road map of their emotions," Riess said, "and take the time to meet people's gaze, to look them in the face to see what emotion is being expressed."

Okay, eye contact. The others include commonsense tips that would smooth almost any social situation: Introduce yourself, sit down so that you are at eye level. Call the person by name, early and often, because "people love the sound of their own name." Ask them about their concerns and worries. Ask them about themselves and remember that they are more than "high blood pressure with a father who died of a heart attack." Listen. Riess has timed it: Empathetic interactions require only a minute or two longer; they will be much happier for both people, not to mention less litigious.

"We're not claiming that if you are on the really low side of the spectrum that you could become Marcus Welby, M.D.," Riess said. "But maybe you could move somewhere toward the middle."

I watched two groups of doctors absorb Riess's insights. One afternoon, I saw her train five residents. Two of them listened closely. The other three slouched, looked bored, and barely participated. When Riess turned off the lights and led them through guided meditation, two of these future doctors began to laugh. I thought, *Sheesh, remind me not to look for empathy from a young doctor.* But on another morning, I saw Riess make her presentation to a roomful of middle-aged doctors. They listened attentively, taking notes and nodding as she made her points. Maybe they were less frantic. Maybe they had the wisdom of years. Maybe they saw the shadows slanting eastward, and had reached a point in their lives when their own frailties drove them to alleviate the frailties of others.

I left Boston with two conclusions: First, it really is better to give than receive, both biologically and psychologically. And second, we are in the Stone Age when it comes to understanding our altruistic impulses.

SSN 111-11-1111

Sandra Day and I finally received our badges for George Washington University Hospital. Sandra's ID photo is a close-up of her white face with SANDRA DAY HAGERTY typed underneath. The security guard filled in her Social Security number as 111-11-1111. At least she won't forget it. Now my beloved dog and I can roam around the hospital and visit patients, the emergency room staff, and (most in need) the nurses in the intensive care unit.

Every other Wednesday night, Sandra and I drive downtown to the hospital. We arrive around dinnertime, which has served Sandra well, since pieces of food fall freely from plates. One man tossed her an entire hamburger when my back was turned. She wolfed it down in less than five seconds and looked up for another.

Over the months, Sandra and I have visited scores of people with, by turns, tragic stories and remarkable gumption: a pregnant woman on bed rest for four months, a man who was allowed no solid food for seven weeks, a teenager with multiple sclerosis whose arms gyrated wildly, quieting down only when she petted Sandra. There was the woman who looked great until she told me she had pancreatic cancer.

Stroke victims, men with heart conditions, amputees waiting for rehabilitation. For all of them, my retriever, and sometimes the ensuing
conversation, offered their only refuge from thoughts of disease or
death.

At 6:45 one night, I met Kathy (person) and Madden (dog) in the
hospital lobby. As Kathy and I were discussing how to split up the patient list of thirty dog requests, a young man and woman in their early
twenties approached us.

"Are these therapy dogs?" the young woman asked us, twisting
back her long black hair into a makeshift bun.

"Yes, they are," I said.

"Would you go visit our friend in room 451?" the tall young man
asked. "She's been wanting to see her dog all day, she keeps crying
about it."

"Of course . . ." Kathy looked at the sheet of paper. "She's already
on our list."

Kathy and I kept our dogs on a tight leash as we tiptoed into room
451. In the dim lighting lay a young woman, twenty-four years old,
splayed unnaturally across the bed. Julie (not her real name) made a
noise when she spotted the dogs, and struggled to push herself up in
bed, but her left arm and leg were useless. Her friends hoisted her up
gently, and she reached out her right hand to Sandra. Sandra moved
forward, not at all reluctant, and stood quietly as Julie gently caressed
her silky left ear. Tears began to roll down Julie's cheeks.

"Oh, it's good crying," the girlfriend assured us. "She's been asking
for a dog all day."

I looked more closely at the young patient. Her blond hair had
been shaved off the right side of her head, revealing what looked like
an eight-inch zipper from the crown of her head to right above her
forehead, an angry red scar.

"What happened?" I asked Julie, sensing she could understand and wanting to give her the dignity of acknowledgment.

"She had a stroke," the young man said. "She's been unconscious for eight days. This is her first day awake."

At that moment, I noticed the nurse on the other side of the bed, tending to the monitoring machine. She turned to look at the dogs, then at Kathy and me.

"I've been working all day to get her blood pressure below 140," she said. She pointed at the monitor. In less than a minute, it had dropped to 131.

"Are you all from around here?" I asked.

The black-haired young woman shook her head. "Julie and I moved here from California. We were looking for a place to live, staying with my boyfriend," she said, gesturing to the young man.

"And nine days ago," he said, picking up the story, "we were home and Julie went into the bathroom and locked the door. And no one noticed until her dog went berserk. He was running back and forth in front of the bathroom, and finally he broke the door handle. That's how we found her."

Julie was watching him talk. She nodded slowly.

"Do you want Sandra to come up on your bed?" I asked.

"Yes," she said quietly.

I patted the space on her right side, and Sandra leapt up, then settled down right on top of her legs.

"Oh, I'm sorry, is that okay?" I said.

Julie beamed, stroking Sandra's back.

"Perfect," she said, so quietly I could barely hear her.

I could hardly wait another week before seeing how Julie was. When we arrived, her friend was there, reading; the boyfriend was asleep in the La-Z-Boy chair.

Julie cried out, "You're back! You came back!"

She moved her legs to create a space. Sandra jumped on the bed.

"Wow, you look better," I observed.

"Yeah, it's been a hard day because I was supposed to go to rehab today, but then I found out it's going to be tomorrow, and I was really bummed about it all day." She turned her gaze to Sandra. "But now you're here."

"Rehab already?" I said. "That's fast."

"Yeah, look at this!" she said, raising her left arm slowly until it was parallel to the bed. Last week she couldn't move a muscle.

"And she walks to the bathroom by herself," the friend said proudly. "It's kind of a miracle."

"So they think you'll make a full recovery?"

"Yep, a full recovery. I can't wait to get out and see my dog. Thank you," she said, and she was smiling broadly. "This is the best part of my day." She paused. "When will you come back?"

"We're not scheduled to come back for another two weeks," I said, "but I'll try to get here next week, too."

"Oh, thank you! I miss my dog. Please bring Sandra back. I'll be in rehab," she said, adding, with a hint of pride, "but not for long."

We never saw her again; she was released within the week.

I know I would build more lasting relationships if I took Sandra to an assisted living home each week, or if I took her to schools where children with learning disabilities could read to her. But somehow, visiting GW Hospital feels important to do. I will probably never see these people again, but Sandra was there in their urgent need. Few people remember the name of the ambulance medic or the ER doctor, but he or she is a bridge from death to life. And in some ways, Sandra is, too.

THE SELFLESSNESS DILEMMA

I f you want a healthy glow and a happy midlife, here's a secret. Give it away: your time, your money, whatever is at your disposal, give it to someone else.[32] Especially your time. Volunteering prolongs your life.[33] It makes you happier and spares you depression.[34] And heart attacks.[35] It helps you stay sober,[36] and boosts your immune system.[37] It cures burnout.[38] It fires up your dopamine system, giving you chemical rewards. It lowers your stress level and reduces chronic pain.[39] It gives you purpose in life.

"If you could put this stuff in a bottle and sell it at Rite Aid, you'd be a billionaire," observed Dr. Stephen Post, the author of *Why Good Things Happen to Good People* and director of the Center for Medical Humanities, Compassionate Care, and Bioethics at Stony Brook University.

As it happens, not all volunteering is equal. *Why* you volunteer and *how* you volunteer actually matter: Those two words could determine whether you reap any benefits from service or whether you continue to volunteer past the first couple of tries.

The *why* first. Studies suggest that if you volunteer for truly selfless reasons ("It's important to help others"), you will live a longer and happier life. But if you help others for self-referential reasons ("Volunteering is a good escape from my own troubles" or "Volunteering makes me feel good about myself"), you are just as likely to die early as the person who didn't lift a finger.[40]

The *how* seems particularly relevant to people at midlife, who have both less free time and more finely honed skills at their disposal. I am referring here to a distinction I never considered before volunteering at GW: between volunteering and working pro bono. This is somewhat analogous to the difference between regular generativity and "platinum generativity."

I began musing on this distinction while roaming the halls of the hospital with Sandra Day. After a few months of our biweekly visits, I watched Sandra's excitement turn to reluctance. Her gait would slow as we approached the hospital. She found the flower bed near the hospital entrance endlessly fascinating, and by that I mean *endlessly*; she would have sniffed around for hours. One evening, after we had spent several minutes loitering around the flowers, I pulled her toward the hospital, and she sat down in front of the automatic doors. I could not blame her. She reflected my own sentiments. Each time we visited, we received a long list of patients, sometimes thirty of them, sending Sandra and me on a three-hour odyssey through illness and trauma, leaving us parched and exhausted.

One memory is revelatory. We were making the rounds with Kay and her dog, Molly Malone. Kay, a hardy seventy-nine-year-old who has a gift with patients, had taught Molly to sneeze on command. Kay says, *"Achoo!"* After the dog sneezes, she says, *"Bless you!"* And the dog sneezes again. I watched in amazement while they were entertaining one patient, completing the *Achoo-sneeze-bless-you-sneeze* loop six times (twelve sneezes in all). *This dog is a natural performer,* I thought, as I felt Sandra tugging me toward the door.

After this display, we visited Mr. Martin, who had recently suffered a stroke. He was literally gray, his face drawn and sunken, nearly absent a spark of life.

"Hi, Mr. Martin," I said cheerily, striding in with Sandra as a nurse fiddled with the lines going from machine to body. "This is Sandra Day."

I saw his mouth twitch as he looked at her. The nurse was watching him.

"Named for the Supreme Court Justice."

His mouth was slowly curving into a smile.

"We wanted a smart blond, but 'Hillary' was too divisive."

Now he was smiling broadly, looking from Sandra, to me, and back to Sandra.

"That's the first smile I've seen since he arrived," the nurse whispered to me.

I stepped aside. Kay scooped up Molly Malone and suspended the dog by her chest over Mr. Martin's stomach. The white dog peered down at Mr. Martin's face, her legs dangling, slowly paddling the air as if she were swimming. Man and dog gazed at each other, entranced. I looked down at Sandra, who was sprawled on her side, panting. When she met my eye, my old dog scrambled up, barely getting purchase on the tile floors, and pulled me toward the door. She was done. So was I. I looked over my shoulder and called goodbye to Kay and Mr. Martin as Sandra dragged me down the hall to the elevator and waited as I pushed the Down button.

For some reason, this was a pivotal moment for me, when I saw that my earnest enthusiasm had run its course and that Sandra and I were not "called" to pet therapy. *Why are we here?* I wondered. Visiting patients in a hospital does not play to my gifts or my passions, nor to Sandra's.

About the time I was reconsidering pet therapy, I spoke with a friend who founded the Tahirih Justice Center, a nonprofit legal organization in Falls Church, Virginia, that helps immigrant women and children escape violence. Layli Miller-Muro asked me to conduct a live interview with one of their clients at their annual fund-raising gala. When I first met the client, "Mercy," she took more than two hours to tell me her painful and complicated ordeal. Over the next few weeks, we shaped her story into a tight, fifteen-minute interview. At the gala, Mercy held the audience in the palm of her hand, making them laugh at times and, at others, gasp at the brutality she described. The interview was flawless. It sounded like something you would hear on NPR. Although the preparation required hours of work, I loved every minute. This fell into my area of passion (legal issues) and this—shaping stories, performing in public—was something I was trained to do.

This reminded me of an insight by Aaron Hurst. Hurst served as president of the Taproot Foundation, which links professionals with pro bono service. He said that when LinkedIn asked its members whether they wanted to volunteer, more than a million people responded. But only a thousand organizations on LinkedIn were seeking volunteers. As one nonprofit leader told Hurst, "If I get any more volunteers, I'm going out of business."[41]

Hurst suggests that professionals fill their hunger for greater meaning by strategically using their skills, not just their time, for the greater good. Marc Freedman, the founder of Encore.org, believes much the same thing.

"People are going to have much more impact and satisfaction by doing things that they have honed and developed over time," Freedman told me. "And in a counterintuitive way, it allows for more growth, because people are building from a foundation of knowledge."

Please understand: I am not bashing volunteering. But I would argue that people still active in their careers should take a strategic approach, offering their skills and experience, rather than a scattershot approach, as I took at GW Hospital. Would a homeless shelter prefer to have an accountant keep its books or serve breakfast? Would Habitat for Humanity rather have an experienced lawyer handle its legal questions or hammer nails into wood?

Would the family of a hostage rather have David Bradley write a check for the protection of journalists or secure his release?

HOSTAGES AND A TWIST
ON GENERATIVITY

My brother does not consider himself altruistic or generative, even though he has started charities and operates a foundation. After founding a research company in my parents' living room with nothing more than a good idea, David became wildly successful and wealthy, and famous for his generosity. He gives away not just his money but also his time, particularly when people are in crisis over their careers or their health. After selling his (by that point) two companies, the Advisory Board Company and Corporate Executive Board, he bought *The Atlantic* and transformed it from a stodgy, struggling magazine to a provocative and profitable bastion of ideas, both online and in print. I think that preserving an icon of American journalism counts as generative.

But in 2011, Dave entered a new sort of generative phrase, one that accords with the definition I am advocating for people in midlife: targeting a problem using one's unique talents and resources.

The story begins in early April 2011, a few weeks into the Arab Spring. On that Friday afternoon, David was meeting with several editors of *The Atlantic*. Before they sat down, they told him that a freelance journalist, Clare Gillis, had been captured in Libya. She had written for the magazine's website five or six times.

"I said, 'What are we doing about it?'" David recalled, as we sat in his office one Sunday afternoon in November 2014. "We weren't doing anything about it. I said, 'We've got to do something.'"

Over the weekend, David gathered eight or ten staff members and two Georgetown University students who spoke Arabic.

"Since I'd run a research company, and have a load of experience in dividing up research, I went right at it," he said. "Maybe four or five minutes into it, it was already clear to everybody else, and then it became clear to me, that I had no idea what I was talking about. I just stopped and said, 'Actually, I have no idea what we should do. Anyone have any ideas?'"

They pulled out an easel with a large flip-chart pad and began drawing concentric circles on the paper: At the center was Clare, then the people who held her, then the people who knew the guards, and on and on. They drew a line vertically down the center of the circles. On the left, they said, let's assume she is being held by the Islamists. Media reports recounted which factions were fighting in the area where she was captured, and who their leaders were. On the right, they hypothesized, let's say the government of Mu'ammar Gadhafi is holding her. Finding paths to Gadhafi was more straightforward: He had bought an Italian soccer team and given money to Harvard, he went to parties with friends and business associates who were named in the press. By the end of the first day, David's team had fifty leads, which would quickly grow to ninety. They began to make calls.

David habitually works on a problem until he understands everything "out to the corners of the map," as he puts it. The breakthrough hailed from a far corner. A woman named Jackie Frazier had befriended Gadhafi's son Saadi, who hired her to work for him in Tripoli. After the bombings started, the Gadhafis moved Jackie to Malta, where she was sitting in a hotel doing nothing.

"I said, 'Well, let me do this call,'" Dave said, who has a gift for putting people at ease. "I got on the phone, she's suspicious, but within a couple of minutes, she was joking around. Really, really quick sense of humor. She said, 'Okay, if I get to go back in, then I'll help you.'"

Two days later, Jackie had returned and located not only Clare Gillis but also three other foreign journalists. Jackie arranged for all four of them to be transferred to a villa in Tripoli.

A few nights later, David received a call from Mu'ammar Gadhafi's chief of staff.

"He said, 'We have your journalist and she came in illegally,'" Dave recalled. "I said, 'I know she did.' He said, 'She had no visa and we've got to put her before a court.' My heart sank when he said that. Then he said, 'I should be able to do that by Tuesday and she'll be out by the end of the week.'"

He kept his word, and all four journalists came home. But one of them, James Foley, returned to the Middle East and was captured in Syria on Thanksgiving Day, 2012. When David heard about Jim Foley, he called his mother and offered to put together a group to help find him again.

"It had taken six weeks from start to finish with Clare, and I just assumed Syria was going to be the same."

It was not. Libya had the feeling of a comic opera at times, with bumbling and foolishness and cruelty all in the mix.

"Syria never had a happy moment," he said. "It was just astonishingly dark."

Unlike in Libya, this time the Islamists, not the government, had captured the American journalist. This would be much harder.

Dave continued to collect hostage assignments. A few weeks after agreeing to work on Jim Foley's case, he was sitting next to a woman at a dinner party in New York.

"She said, 'My cousin is being held, Peter Theo Curtis. His mother is seventy-six years old and there's nobody. He was a freelancer, he has no employer, nobody working for him. It's a couple of cousins and the seventy-six-year-old mom. Would you be willing to help us?' I said, 'Sure.' I fell in love with the family."

Soon Dave had assumed the cases of Jim Foley and Peter Theo Curtis, and three other young Americans who had been taken hostage: Steve Sotloff, Peter Kassig, and Kayla Mueller. *The Atlantic* had employed none of them; but once they heard about Clare Gillis, all the families approached David. By their own account, the families sought help from the U.S. government, but the FBI shared little information with them.[42] The White House's overriding principle at the time—it has since been changed—was summed up in two words: No ransom.[43] The families turned to David, as did sources in and around Syria, who fed him information.

Eventually David met with Ali Soufan, a former FBI agent who owned a security consulting firm with offices in Qatar. Soufan arranged for a meeting with Qatar's security chief in Doha. He and David arrived in Doha on a Friday afternoon, during Ramadan, planning to meet the Qatari official after sunset. They waited from six p.m. to one a.m., but the man did not show. The next night, they waited from seven p.m. to three a.m. Again, no luck.

At one a.m. on the third night, the official finally arrived. David showed him the fliers for the five hostages he was trying to help: Jim Foley, Steve Sotloff, Peter Kassig, and Kayla Mueller, who were being held by the so-called Islamic State (or ISIS), and Peter Theo Curtis, who was captured by Al Nusra, an offshoot of Al Qaeda.

The Qatari official stopped at the photo of Peter Theo Curtis.

"He said, 'Oh, I know this name. I've been working on this one. I can get this one out. The ones held by ISIS, I don't know, because we don't have any relations with ISIS.'"

"I asked, 'Will you do it?'" Dave said. "He said, 'Yeah, yeah, I'll do this.'"

The Qataris persuaded Al Nusra to release Curtis, without a ransom payment. On the night of his release, David said, an FBI agent was sent to receive Curtis at the Jordanian border—the wrong border, according to David's sources. David let the FBI know Curtis would be crossing into Israel. Two days later, Dave received a text from his Qatari contact: "Done."

"It was such a happy moment," he recalled, leaning back in his chair and laughing. A brief respite from a much darker moment: A week earlier, Jim Foley had been beheaded on video.

"There's a scene in the musical *Mame*," Dave said, "where everyone's depressed, and so they break into song: 'We need a little Christmas, right this very minute.' I had that song with me that whole day. I knew it was about to happen. We really need this, we need this. We've just lost Jim. Even though it's going to go grim again, which it did, with Steve Sotloff. Give us this minute, we need this."

All the other hostages have died: The men were beheaded on video, and Kayla Mueller died while a prisoner of ISIS.

Since he first learned of Clare Gillis's capture nearly three years earlier, my brother has spent at least four hours a week trying to save hostages. Plus trips: three to Qatar, one to Belgium, one to London, and one to Istanbul.

"The trips add up," he said, referring to time, but so does the money. He has paid for his own travel, and has hosted all the families in Washington three times, helping to cover the travel expenses for some of the families as well.

"Why would you do this?" I asked. Other media owners had the money, the research capabilities, and the connections to look for the hostages, but they didn't. Dave said he felt compelled to help after meeting the families.

"If you lose a child to cancer, maybe it goes on for a year, two years, but you have good days as well as bad days, and you're with the child," he said. "Here you hear nothing about the child except that you learn that your child has been waterboarded and is still being beaten and electrocuted, and then one day you see your child being killed on video. It's really hard not to put yourself in the position of these family members."

I suggested that this sort of empathy is one of the crucial ingredients of altruism. Yet David insists he is not altruistic, because he found the whole process—investigating, tracking down the hostages, meeting with agents and spies, hunting for a way to free the young Americans without contravening U.S. law—so compelling. That, he believes, cancels out the purer motives.

"If you said, 'Is it good?' I'd say, 'It's good,'" Dave said. "If you said, 'Is it self-sacrificing?' I'd say no."

"You're not looking for credit," I said.

"No, I'm not looking for credit."

"You're not getting money. You're giving money."

"I mean, I'm wealthy," Dave said. "You couldn't pay me in a way that would give me satisfaction. Things that are appealing for me now are what's really interesting. It's sort of being part of a cause, somebody else's cause. It's really interesting to me. And that's rewarding."

I told him I don't buy it.[44] Neither did Marc Freedman.

Recall that Freedman thinks of generativity as altruism expressed at a specific period of time: during midlife or a little later, when you are still very much in the game. Freedman noted that David saved the lives of two young American hostages, a feat he could accomplish only now, after years of building up his achievements, reputation, and wealth.

"He might have wanted to do that when he was a junior at Swarthmore taking his honors exam, but he wouldn't have known anything," observed Freedman, who was five years behind Dave at the college. "But here he is, in a position to integrate the various strands of his life—the research expertise he developed, the connections he has, the financial resources—and bring them together in a way that may ultimately involve some of his most significant contributions. Even if they're not nearly as well known as the Advisory Board and The Atlantic."

Of course, we cannot all be generative on a grand scale. But we can console ourselves that whether the result is large or small, whether it is freeing hostages or teaching children to read, it arises from the same impulse. And the related impulse—to lift up your eyes from the minutiae of your daily work and wonder if there might be something more—that restlessness comes at midlife, too.

At least, it did for me.

10.

THE MEANING OF WORK

A few years ago, my brother and I were helping Dad clean out his apartment before he moved out. As I sorted through his file cabinet, I spotted a folder labeled "Barbie." Inside, yellowed but still legible, was my kindergarten report card.

"Barbie always listens very carefully to the stories we read, and asks questions about why people do the things they do," the teacher wrote, adding: "She's very dexterous with the scissors."

Scissors aside, here were the makings of what I would eventually become: a journalist whose lifeblood is to ask questions and tell stories. In fact, many of my journalist friends say they had the same childhood inclinations. Clearly, when I became a low-level "copy kid" at *The Christian Science Monitor* after college, I landed in the right professional zip code. These interests and talents were a core part of my identity, and they are my central gifts decades later.

Yet just as you can change your address within the same zip code—you marry, you have kids, you need more space—it is natural to reconsider your career address as your needs, priorities, and interests unfold. That is the beauty and the terror of midlife. Early in my career at NPR, I found that the demands of broadcast news—reporting live, responding instantly to breaking events, dropping everything to chase after the story—while hugely exciting, took an enormous emotional and physical toll on me. For more than a decade, as I worked to establish myself on a national level, I staved off my nagging questions and threw myself into my job with all the vigor I could muster. But one day in the not-too-distant past, I began to wonder: Can I tweak my script? Is it possible to play up the core elements of my identity in my own life that I glimpsed as early as kindergarten—curiosity and listening, telling stories and using those skills to entice people into caring about big ideas—and eliminate the parts I no longer had the desire or the energy to do? And how on earth do I do that?

These questions would reach a critical mass in October 2013.

Millions of people find themselves with the same unsettling questions. Part of midlife's challenge is to closely examine the old script—the one that family and society writes for you, the one in which you are meeting everyone else's expectations—and see if it needs revision. The new script is tailored to your core identity—your own talents, passions, and personality—and these should shape your goals. For some, this means a major revision, bringing in a new cast of characters and an entirely new location. For others, it means rechanneling one's energies just a few degrees into something that gives them meaning and verve.

Altering a career course at fifty can be a perilous thing, and many people, if not most, do not traipse merrily down that path. The luckiest among us find their work fulfilling, and cannot imagine why they would leave. Others would follow their passions if they could, but college tuition, the mortgage, and the care of parents or children or both buckle them into their present work, at least for now. Still others are simply scared—with good reason, because the job market does not necessarily embrace mid-career transitions.

But many others have re-envisioned their work and find that the sacrifices are well worth the new vitality and joy. For a year, I interviewed or corresponded with dozens of people who managed to bushwhack through the thicket of fears and obstacles and make it to the clearing. As you might expect, this shift in life's purpose is more art than science, more psychology than neurology. Allow me, then, to take a page from Harvard Business School and present some case studies of change.

PROGRESSIVE FINE-TUNING:
THE DISRUPTION

As Beverly Jones arranges the tea, milk, and sugar before us, I wonder how many lives have taken a sharp and unexpected turn at this dining room table. It is for this reason that Nancy Augustine and I have arrived at this elegant home in a residential corner of Washington, D.C., on a brisk October day. Nancy's pen is poised over a notebook, my tape recorder is rolling. We are here to experience a transformation.

Beverly Jones, owner of Clearways Consulting, has coached hundreds of people through their career transitions. Her new client is Nancy Augustine, a forty-eight-year-old visiting professor at George Washington University. Nancy's contract runs out at the end of the school year. She is not on the tenure track, and she has no idea what comes next. Over the next six months, Nancy and Bev will re-envision Nancy's future, exploring paths the college professor never considered.

"I don't want to coast through the rest of my life," Nancy says. "I could work for another thirty years, and I want to take an active role in deciding what that could be."

Bev begins by taking Nancy's history: She queries her about high school and college, her parents' values ("I was taught that there is no higher calling than public service"), the jobs she has held, the twists and turns in her personal and professional life. Nancy is fortunate on two scores. First, she has a long exit ramp, nine months, before her work disappears. Second, and this is key, she is married to someone with a job. Both these facts give her breathing room.

Nancy spent much of her career in urban planning before earning her Ph.D. at age forty. Today, the professor of public policy and public administration is remarkably candid about her anxieties. "I feel time slipping away," she says at one point.

Bev regards Nancy closely, her face and body language, looking for clues. By reading the psychological themes of a person's past, Bev believes, you can navigate to a more fulfilling future. Bev herself has crossed this emotional bridge. A little more than a decade before, the energy company where she was a senior executive merged with another. Rather than finding another job as an attorney in the energy business, she asked herself: *What is the theme of my career? What brings me energy and joy when I go to work every day?*

"To my surprise, I liked being a lawyer, but it was not about the law for me," Bev recalls. It was about mentoring younger professionals and helping them develop their leadership skills. Bev became a career coach.

"I took the thing that I've always loved to do, and found a way to turn it into a career," she explains. She plans to help Nancy do the same.

Slowly, subtly, Bev quizzes Nancy about how she defines a successful career and how she defines herself. She jots down a note when Nancy's face lights up as she describes her forays into local policy making, or crafting a syllabus for her classes at GW, or mentoring students. But at other times, Nancy's voice flattens; she seems weary, burdened by uncertainty.

"I was brought up to think that I have to move through the ranks and rise to the top," Nancy says. "I'm capable of rising to the top, I should rise to the top, I should work as hard as I possibly can, I should be a good role model for other women. On the other hand, I wonder if I really have the energy for it. Do I still have it in me to pursue that, or is there some other path that's less arduous that I can take that would be meaningful for me?"

"Let's declare that you are at the top," Bev says. And here we get the first glimpse of what the business world calls "disruption": challenging Nancy's hierarchical view of success. "If working to the top were no longer relevant, what would you want to work for?"

"What an amazing question," Nancy says. "I've never thought about that before."

I nod. Bev gave voice to a question that had dogged me for more than a decade. When I was forty, it occurred to me that I would never write at the caliber of David Brooks or Steve Coll, that I would never craft an audio story as well as Ira Glass or Edward R. Murrow. I know that I possess talent. I know I can claim my share of NPR "driveway moments," making people late for work or dinner as they sit in their cars to hear how my story ends. But these writers, the Brookses and the Colls, the Glasses and the Murrows—their talents inhabit a different country. They reside in the land of genius, and their words not only entertain and inform but also shape (or challenge) the worldview of almost everyone who reads them.

For more than a decade, I thought if I pedaled a little harder,

I might, just might, achieve that sort of genius, or at least beauty. I strove with dogged determination, but under a shadow of futility. I was defining myself by my failure to match those journalists, and I realized that therein lies a long, sad decline. Bev Jones's advice for Nancy applied to me and, I suspect, to others in midlife: I must shift my eyes from the next step on the ladder, the one just outside of my reach, and scan the horizon for my unique contribution, that combination of storytelling and voice that I am tailor-made for—something, perhaps, that no one can do quite the way I can.

Bev then turns to the problem of energy. When you have been on the same kind of career path for a while, it's easy to look at the next opportunity or step on the ladder and feel uninspired.

"It's not unusual to think, 'Oh, I just can't get up the energy to do that one more time. I'm getting old, what's the matter with me?'" Bev explains. "But what may feel like a lack of energy may be something that's more akin to boredom, or lack of excitement, or this sense that there's nothing new here. I'm not learning."

"That really resonates with me," Nancy says, nodding. She says teaching at GW is a "breath of fresh air," but since her teaching contract is nonrenewable, she assumes that she would be heading back to her former career track in government or nonprofit work. Just thinking about this prospect saps her energy.

"I think what I'm dealing with is some boredom. I'm in a rut."

Nancy had been scaling a mountain called "academic research and urban planning" for so long, thinking it was the only mountain in the range. But just over there might be another mountain better suited for her life at forty-eight.[1] Bev was urging Nancy to lift her eyes from this particular mountain, this particular career trajectory, and take in the neighboring peak. That one may be just what her life needs. Bev suggests that, before the next meeting, Nancy should brainstorm about the kinds of jobs or organizations she could be interested in. She should go wild, open the aperture, toy with possibilities she never dreamed of before.

Then Bev lets drop the second "disruption." Nancy has long thought of herself as a member of a government or academic entity. Bev suggests that she mentally recast herself as an independent entity.

"Start thinking of yourself as a business, as an entrepreneur with certain product offerings," Bev says. "What's your brand? What do you have to offer? Who are your potential customers? How are we going to market them?"

Nancy looks slightly stricken, and my mirror neurons are firing: I, too, recoil at envisioning myself as a brand to be marketed.

"That's a little overwhelming," Nancy says. "But I need to understand how I am different. When I described my strengths to you, I said leadership, management, and research, and that's kind of generic. Well, I feel a little generic. I know I'm not generic. I just need to pinpoint it."

"Exactly," Bev said. "It's scary, and it's really, really hard."

Finding one's "brand" is a marketing term for something much more psychologically penetrating. It is about identifying one's signature qualities, talents, personality traits, proclivities, and experiences—all the ingredients that define one's essence, particularly in midlife. But that insight would come later.

I am keenly interested in Nancy's story because it parallels my own. I sense that my own heretofore linear path is about to take a turn. Some reporters thrive on the drama of news: They run to the fire or the earthquake's epicenter. I wish I were that way, but after thirty years of trying to rewire myself, I must admit I am not. I am sure my chronic vocal cord pain springs directly from years of chronic deadlines.

Yet NPR has become my identity, my calling card; it's the first detail I mention when I meet someone new. I am fiercely proud of NPR. How can I contemplate casting off the comfort of my work life and the identity that has served me so well? No, I am not a spectator in this exploration. I am scared to death.

THE TRIGGERS FOR CHANGE

Not everyone would paint the desire for change so floridly. But this feeling among people at midlife is, I suspect, nearly universal. At least, almost everyone I know yearns for renewal at some point on the road from young to old. Marci Alboher has thought deeply about what pushes people to make what is arguably one of the scariest decisions in life: to begin a new career. Alboher, author of *The Encore Career Handbook*, calls herself a "serial career reinventer."[2] She began reinventing early on, as a young attorney practicing advertising law in New York.

"I was the person who said [to the client], 'Well, that's completely unethical. Why do you want to do that? You're fleecing customers,'" she recalled. "It wasn't a good fit for me."

Still, Alboher stayed the course because she had not reached what she calls her "early encore moment." That occurred as she lay sunning herself on a beach in Rio de Janeiro, enjoying her first vacation in two years. Her phone rang. Things have heated up for one of their clients, her boss told her. Could she catch the next plane back?

"I knew right then and there that I wouldn't go home," she said. "It was so clear to me. I also knew that when I did go home, I would leave that work and figure out a way to do work that felt like more of a matchup with my values and that I could feel proud about."

Here we see one trigger for leaving one's job: "crisis of conscience." Alboher left the company, scaled back her lifestyle, and began writing about career reinvention. She eventually wrote her first book and then landed a blog in *The New York Times*. She enjoyed her dream gig for several years, until she faced a second kind of trigger, what she calls "the end of the line." This is when you have reached the top of your career path and you are no longer growing. Or, at the other extreme, the career has left you behind—literally, by ending your job, or metaphorically, by changing so much that you cannot, or choose not to, retrain and keep up. In Alboher's case, the 2008 recession prompted the scariest and most humbling option: The *Times* discontinued her column.

"For the first time, I was really dealing with what so many Americans were going through," she said. "I had now hit the end of the line. So I went back and read all the columns and blogs I had written about what you're supposed to do in this situation, and I tried to take my own advice."

Tell people you are looking for work, for example, and take a bridge job while you are finding something permanent. Then she got a lucky break: The *Times* let her write two final pieces about her experience around the canceling of her column and blog. That led to freelance projects, and eventually her position as a vice president at Encore.org, a nonprofit that is building a movement to tap the skills and experience of those in midlife and beyond to improve communities and the world.

Alboher has identified other triggers, and they tend to overlap. These triggers can happen at any time, but they tend to frequent middle age. Aside from the "crisis of conscience" and "end of the line," she finds people leave because of burnout; "that nagging feeling" that has you wondering, *Is this all there is?*; a loss or crisis (a death, divorce, illness) that suddenly shifts your perspective; and "a dream deferred." I see myself in five of them, everything except "crisis of conscience."

If you are over forty, I would wager that you see yourself in at least one of these. If you are sixty and claim you relate to none of them, you are very, very lucky. How a person processes these triggers ranges from total overhaul to minor but meaningful tweak.

THE REINVENTOR

Burl seems transported, peaceful, squeezing every ounce of pleasure out of this moment. Swathed in a yellow life jacket, he paddles mightily, trying to swim against the current, trying to reach the bag of treats. He is an old dog, a black Labrador with white around his muzzle, but for an hour, he does not limp with arthritis. For an hour, he is a puppy again. His owner, Mary, sits by the side of the dog-therapy pool, beaming at Burl like a proud and happy mother. In the pool with Burl, cradling him so that he always keeps his nose above water, sometimes pulling him back so he must work for those treats, is one of the most successful female attorneys in the country. Or used to be. Before she left the law for dogs.

Laurie Plessala Duperier spends up to thirty-five hours a week in this small, eight-by-twenty-foot pool, catering to a parade of dogs and their adoring owners. The sun streams through the floor-to-ceiling windows, reflecting off the ceramic tiling that lends Italian elegance to this little room. Laurie, fifty years old, has an expressive face that always seems on the verge of a laugh. Perhaps because I know how successful she was, I see in her smile a keen intelligence: She's counted the cost and couldn't care less if her career move looks crazy. It is this defiant, tensile spirit that I like most of all.

Laurie grew up in Port Arthur, Texas, and knew early on that law was her destiny. Her father was a lawyer, her brother was a lawyer, her cousin was a lawyer. It was "lack of imagination" that led her down that route. But she excelled, eventually joining Philip Morris, which posted her in Hong Kong and Switzerland and later brought her back to the United States to head up a group of lawyers who, among other things, supported the tobacco company's lobbying efforts. She was one of the few female senior executives in the company.

Around forty, Laurie was burned out and tired of "being shot out of the cannon" every day.

"I'd say to myself in the morning, *I think I can do this for another couple of years*," she told me, in between dog-therapy sessions. "But I'd stay in bed to the last moment. I had lost my passion. I'd tell you objectively it was a really good job, but I could never get to my happy place. I could go higher, but not be happy inside."

When she was forty-two, Laurie knew she would leave. But what would she leave *for*? She had no hobbies, no burning passions: All she did was work. Then one day she realized that what brought her happiness, aside from her husband, was taking care of her beloved but very sick black Labrador retriever, Gunny. As she contemplated this radical leap, her intellect rebelled. She was, after all, just coming into her peak earning years. The money and the influence were seductive. That is, until the hammock broke.

It was a Sunday, a beautiful September day, a perfect afternoon for lounging in the hammock and reading *The Washington Post*. As she sat down, the hammock stand cracked.

"The arm of the hammock catapulted into my head and knocked me out of the hammock and onto the ground," Laurie said. "I have no idea how long I was unconscious. When I woke up, there were tremendous amounts of blood, because head wounds just bleed terribly."

A fraction of an inch one way, she could have lost an eye; an inch the other way, she could have died or suffered brain damage. The crisis—Laurie's trigger—eviscerated her doubts about leaving her job.

"I thought I had time to figure this out, and it never occurred to me that I might die in my backyard reading *The Washington Post*," she said. "So the question that formed in my mind was: How long am I going to wait to start living my life? And the answer seemed to be: not very long, because apparently you can die in your backyard while reading *The Washington Post*."

Laurie realized her passion, more than litigation, more than crafting legislation, lay in caring for dogs. She knew from her countless hours with veterinarians that there was great need for water therapy for dogs, but there were few dog swimming pools in the area. She knew from conversations with friends that many couples with grown children or none at all (like her) would gladly pay to give their old dogs a respite from their aches and pains. Laurie and her husband sold their home and bought a new one with enough room to build a pool house. That was the easy part. Convincing her friends and colleagues that she had not lost her mind was more difficult. Many of them did not see the point of her new career.

"This is ironic to me, right?" she says, laughing. "I'm a tobacco lawyer. Seriously. They saw value in that, but they didn't see value in making an old dog feel better and giving their mom peace of mind that they were having happy days at the end of their life?"

On the theory that if you build it, they will come, Laurie started her therapy business in the middle of the recession with no clients. By the time we talked five years later, she was seeing twenty-five to thirty-five dogs a week. She earns about a fifteenth of what she earned as an attorney.

"It's pretty weird to get a paycheck for your whole life and then nobody pays you anymore," she says. "And that was a very difficult adjustment, and that caused a new kind of stress in my life that hadn't been there."

But she has not regretted her decision for "one second of one minute of one hour of one day." As she looks back, she says the hardest part about her midlife career shift was getting the gumption to stop.

"Once you start doing something else, you have forward motion," Laurie says. "Once you walk through that door, more and more doors just keep opening. And it's like I can't turn my brain off. I could tell you three different things that I would like to do."

She smiles then.

"This is not close to the last chapter."

UNCONVENTIONAL ADVICE AT HARVARD

I would define midlife to be when you start measuring time future and stop measuring time passed," Howard Stevenson observed. "It's when you are starting to say: 'How am I going to use these glorious days for the best purpose?'"

Stevenson is one of the most beloved, now retired, professors at Harvard Business School. He addressed the Class of 1977 during its thirty-fifth reunion on a windy October day in 2012. Stevenson's message on that day, and always, is that no matter how successful you are, you need to regularly pause and cast a cool, analytical eye on your career. At midlife, especially, it may be time to recalibrate.[3]

"I'm amazed at how many talented people don't accomplish that much," he said.

This may have come as a startling message to the Class of '77. By all standards, this was a highly successful tribe of investment bankers, entrepreneurs, senior executives, and CEOs from a range of companies. Stevenson, however, does not measure success by money or title. He measures it by courage, chutzpah, the willingness to start afresh rather than guard one's spoils.

"There's a difference between twenty years of experience and one year of experience twenty times," he told me. "People do the same thing and they don't grow. They don't face new challenges."

Stevenson noted that he upended his career repeatedly, moving from Harvard to corporations to nonprofit organizations and back to academia. He even gave up tenure at the business school, because he looked at the future and blanched at what he saw.

"I interviewed a whole bunch of tenured faculty," he recalled. "They were my colleagues and friends, and I asked them, 'What's it like?' And I discovered most of them were unhappy, because they felt trapped. They were very good at what they did, but they were doing the same things that they had been doing for twenty-five years. In some cases, teaching the same course. And I thought, *That's not me.*"

Stevenson's words triggered an almost physical reaction in me. They gave voice to a suspicion I had never dared to acknowledge, at least not out loud. Journalism, and particularly NPR, will always be my first great love. The *stuff* of news—the twists and turns of a presidential race, the investigative stories, the evocative features—can hold you in its riveting orbit for a lifetime. And yet, the *structure* of newswriting—how we put together a story—can become formulaic. Indeed, following a formula is practically the only way you can regularly bang out a four-minute radio piece or 800-word print story on a tight deadline. But Stevenson made me wonder: After three decades of reporting, do I have thirty years of experience, or one year of experience thirty times? Is there another way to channel my curiosity and the thrill of the story? These are deeply personal questions, ones that my colleagues or competitors might not entertain, but I began to ask myself: Is there a different sort of hill to climb? Am I just too scared to look?

FACING THE EXISTENTIAL
NECESSITY OF CHANGE

Carlo Strenger believes that for most people, changing course in midlife is not a luxury but an "existential necessity."

Strenger, a psychoanalyst in Israel, has written, to my mind, some of the most perceptive articles on midlife career shifts.[4] He says the shift may be prompted by internal forces, such as a desire for more meaning in life. It can be driven by external forces, such as losing your job, or recognizing that you are at a professional dead end. It looks different for every person. For one person, the change may be dramatic, such as leaving a secure job for a new profession; for another, it may be barely perceptible, such as dropping to a four-day workweek and volunteering on the fifth. But eventually, he believes, people who thrive rather than merely survive in midlife must make the change. If they fail to do so, the inaction exacts a price.[5]

"In some cases it's regret, in other cases it's that people begin to develop symptoms," Strenger told me. "From psychosomatic symptoms, to depression, to symptoms that can be actual physical illnesses generated by psychological distress."

Strenger said many of his clients showed physical symptoms, particularly chest pains. Personally, I have little doubt that the chronic pain in my vocal cords was exacerbated, if not created, by remaining in the daily news business so long.

"If people don't take a hard look at what kind of changes they want to make, in the end those changes are going to be forced on them," Strenger said. "The basic idea is: Don't wait until the changes are forced on you. Be proactive."

Strenger does not advocate just any change at all. It should be carefully considered and grounded in reality.

"We all have fantasies of total transformation," he told me, "you know, those hyperdramatic changes that the popular press likes a lot, like the lawyer who becomes a chef, and a doctor who turns into an organic farmer. They're really very rare cases."[6]

Strenger believes there are two powerful myths that assault people in mid-career, and people need to steer between them. On one side lurks the monster Scylla—that is, resigning ourselves to our growing limitations and throwing in the towel at sixty-five. On the other side skulks Charybdis, the illusion that, in midlife, we can enjoy "boundless change," which requires a ground-up radical transformation.

If you accept the first, more desultory myth, then you are likely to keep trudging on until retirement. This is something that almost no one can afford to do, Strenger says, since people are living twenty or thirty years past retirement age. The second myth, which he calls "magical transformation," is more seductive, and more likely to flame out. Strenger says the best course is navigating between the two.

"One of the things I very much emphasize in my work with clients is: 'Let's look at the empirical evidence for what kind of assets and abilities you have built over the last forty, fifty, sixty years,'" Strenger says. "Let's see how these can be reconfigured in a way that would be more appropriate to your needs today, that will be more satisfactory to you."

A mid-career professional has lived enough years and created enough of a biography to know herself—where she excels and where she flails, what she enjoys and what she dreads—and those innate and learned abilities should guide her into the next phase. Here we come to what, for me, is his most helpful concept of all: *Sosein*, which in German means "essence," or as Strenger translates it, "thus and no other."

There is something inborn in each of us that is "recalcitrant to change," Strenger says. "To become the author of our own lives, we need to accept that we have not chosen the base materials of who we are. We can only choose to shape them with a clear view of our strengths and weaknesses."[7]

This was a revolutionary idea: change within the boundaries of your natural talents, proclivities, personality traits, and skills.

"How does it work?" I asked him. He cited the case of "Albert," a bank manager who desperately wanted to leave his job. Albert's dream was to make movies, which Strenger considered "a fantasy." But when they explored what drew Albert to the movie business, what they uncovered was not a deep longing to act in or direct a movie, but a desire to surround himself with creative people and to devise strategies for bringing artistic ideas to fruition. Albert eventually met a group of actors and producers who wanted to form their own media company. They had the creative skills but not the management or fund-raising skills. Albert had the latter and was able to make that happy connection between his skills and his aspirations. He did not throw out his abilities: He repurposed them.

RETURNING TO ESSENCE

If I were to guess at what Marti Trunnell's *Sosein* is—what she is at the core—I would say: healer. Her father had been a doctor, the type we remember from black-and-white television shows, who would spend hours with patients at their bedside, listening to their stories. After Marti became a physician's assistant, she was able to practice that sort of healing, listening to patients, using her heart as well as her mind.

Over the course of two and a half decades, though, Marti's primary care work descended into a "literal hell." Her job revolved around numbers: in particular, the number of patients she could squeeze in during a workday. At twenty patients a day, she always scored highest in patient satisfaction but lowest in productivity.

"I didn't feel like you could fit people's stories into little data bites, you know," Marti said. "And it was just sort of killing my spirit. I just had to do something else because I just felt like I was sort of drowning. I was having to be someone I wasn't."

After her three children left home—she had divorced and raised them on her own—Marti had the luxury to pause and consider how she could recapture her first love: an old-fashioned approach to healing. She accepted a job to run a clinic on Northstar Island in the Arctic Ocean off the coast of Alaska.

"When I stepped off the plane, it was forty below with forty-mile-per-hour winds," she recalled, laughing. "I thought, *What planet have I landed on? What have I done?* But at the same time, it was exhilarating because it was such an adventure."

Her clinic caters to sixty workers and their families at the Prudhoe Bay oil fields, and she works three weeks on, three weeks off, when she flies back to Utah. She has returned to the essence of her career, where patients are more important than numbers.

"If people need to talk, we can talk," she said. "If they need to be really checked out, I can have them lie down and start an IV. I have a full clinic and I can spend time one-on-one, and that is just such a blessing. Such a difference. I call it a godsend."

Like many people, Marti Trunnell experienced several triggers in her decision to leave her work in Utah: burnout and crisis of conscience, surely, but also, she had reached the end of the line in her career. Medical technology had so dramatically changed her daily tasks that she chose to find a way off the treadmill. Indeed, galloping technology is assaulting every sort of profession.

Marti is fortunate: She has trained in an industry that will always welcome her. The throngs of aging baby boomers guarantee that the health care industry (from nurses to surgeons to psychologists) will need all hands on deck. Other industries may also be a promising bet for people seeking to change or pivot their careers: Counseling, law, editing, teaching, career coaching, and the whole nonprofit world—anything that requires wisdom, experience, and pattern recognition is worth a look.[8]

AN IDEA TAKES ROOT

Quietly, over the course of many conversations—with Carlo Strenger and Howard Stevenson, with people who had reinvented and renewed themselves, who had punched through their boredom or fear to a larger purpose—a tiny thought insinuated itself into the back of my mind: *Maybe you could do that too.*

It sounded like a whisper at first, but once I acknowledged it, my hopes and concerns grew louder, they became a chorus, they sang incessantly, in stereo. They wouldn't shut up.

From the left speaker boomed the negative reasons, pushing me out the door at NPR. While I adore NPR and all it does, I was reaching a threshold there: My chronic pain (which is exacerbated by deadline stress), the certainty that I was miscast as a hard-news reporter, the fear that I would forever be NPR's religion correspondent—these concerns haunted me.

From the right speaker trilled the higher, more pleasing notes, the happy possibilities that were drawing me toward new adventures. I *loved* writing my first book, *Fingerprints of God.* I loved the freedom to write about my own and others' spiritual journeys in my own voice, without worrying about sounding objective. I knew I had not mastered the long narrative form in that one book, and the challenge thrilled me. Mainly, I wanted to try something outrageously hard, original, something only I could pull off. I didn't know what it was, precisely, though I knew the zip code. But I was quite certain I would not find it on my present course.

Everyone I interviewed seemed to be finding true work passion. I dared to wonder: *Why not me?* I was being seduced by my own reporting. I realized I had no appetite for total reinvention. I love asking questions and telling stories way too much. But I was intrigued by people who, like Marti Trunnell, pivot on their core strengths and turn them in a different direction. In the process, they find not only freedom but meaning.

MEANINGFUL WORK IN THE SECOND HALF

I trace my first glimpse of the "encore career" to a sparkling February day in Sausalito, California. The annual meeting of the Encore movement (hosted by Encore.org) came as blessed relief: I was one of the youngest people there (an increasingly rare event), and I was surrounded by scores of cheerful, purposeful, optimistic people— adjectives not typically associated with those over sixty.

The man in charge was Marc Freedman, the CEO and founder of Encore.org. Freedman is seen as the creator of the Encore movement, which, at its essence, tries to connect middle-aged and older people with meaningful work that promotes the social good. Or, as Freedman puts it, "passion, purpose, and a paycheck."

Freedman, who at fifty-four was younger than most of the people involved, seems to be revered with the kind of affection reserved for the Dalai Lama. With his curly gray hair, wire-rimmed glasses, and aw-shucks smile, you would not single him out in a room. In fact, he darts away from the spotlight, hunching over a little and appearing shorter than he is.

He is throwing a restless, nearly retired, discarded, and bewildered generation of baby boomers a lifeline, with the message that we have not passed our expiration date.

"A lot of people have identity very much tied up in their working lives beforehand and then they find themselves in an identity free fall," he told me. Society treats them as if they are "a step away from being the walking dead."

This is a ridiculously wasteful way to look at the baby boomer generation, he argues. For one thing, unlike previous generations, which could be counted on to die within a few years of retirement, many baby boomers will live thirty years past retirement age. That is almost the length of a traditional career. Second, they are healthy and energetic and not ready to be shipped down to Florida. Finally—and I have noticed this in myself—they measure the years differently from their younger and ascendant colleagues. The role of people in their second half of life is not to build up for themselves (family, career, home), but to begin to give away their time, energy, and talents.

"People realize that there are fewer years ahead than there are behind," Freedman noted. "Their priorities shift, they're more focused on the legacy that they'll leave, [the legacy] they'll actually *live*. And there's also the realization that there's probably enough time ahead to do something significant, and in many cases, it's an imperative."

There are two ways to look at the math. Baby boomers are deadweight, the villains who run up the nation's health care bills and siphon off their grandchildren's futures. Or, people upward of fifty-five offer a priceless resource of experience and perspective. Rather than squander all that wisdom, Freedman reasons, why not use them to further the greater good?[9]

If Freedman were arguing his case in court, Tom Cox would be exhibit A. When I met Cox at the conference, he was sixty-three years old, with a craggy face that has seen many a Maine winter. He landed in the state in the 1970s, a young banking lawyer who specialized in debt collection and foreclosures. When the savings-and-loan crisis washed over the country in the 1980s and 1990s, Cox found himself dragging companies and even neighbors into court, forcing them into foreclosure or bankruptcy.

"I ended up getting depressed, and I mean really depressed," he told me. "Ended up leaving the profession."

His marriage collapsed, he lost all contact with his children, and he began building houses with a friend, until that work dried up in the 2008 recession. He was fifty-five.

With nothing but free time, Cox walked into the Maine Volunteer Lawyers Project, where he had worked on pro bono cases over the years. He offered to advise them on a program they were launching to help people who were about to lose their homes in foreclosure. It was a fortuitous offer: Cox had written a book about how to conduct foreclosures in Maine. They handed him the case of a family about to lose their home.

"I was just stunned by the abuses of the legal system that I saw coming out of the nation's largest banks," he recalled. "I was seeing a series of affidavits from one company, GMAC Mortgage, and one individual in that company, that I knew were false. You wouldn't know they were false, but I knew they were false because I'd done the work on the other side."

In short: Tom Cox uncovered the robo-signing scandal. Banks hired people to swear they had reviewed the documents supporting a foreclosure, even though they had not, creating a fraudulent foreclosure machinery that was throwing thousands out of their homes. After Cox won his case, the top home lenders, including GMAC, JPMorgan Chase, and Citigroup, halted their foreclosures.

Tom Cox was never a high-flying litigator. He did not come from privilege or with a great pedigree. The man who changed the fates of thousands of people was not young and TV-ready, he was not at the peak of his career. He was a sixty-three-year-old bank lawyer in Maine.

"A lot of people think once you hit your sixties, it's kind of over," I observed.

"Yeah, that's the myth." He laughed. "I may not be able to work quite as intensely as a thirty-year-old, but boy, I know a whole lot more than that guy does. I've had so much more experience in the system."

He paused.

"It's hard to describe the delight of being able to take that knowledge and that skill and use it so effectively for such good purposes," Cox said quietly. "It's difficult to put words to it. It's just extraordinary."

While Cox made an accidental leap into his encore career, Marc Freedman believes people should start plotting their later life work in their fifties or even their forties. This would give them time to make the transition and still enjoy twenty years of meaningful work. He insists this is the smart move. After all, except for the wealthy or lucky few, most of us will need to work at *something* well into retirement.

"It's not so much a choice between work and playing thirty years of golf," Freedman said. "Working longer is an imperative. So, if you are going to work longer, the question is: What kind of work are you going to do? Is it something that's going to provide a sense of purpose and identity, a feeling that your life is worthwhile?"

Or will you fight tooth and nail—against the gravity of declining energy, against the swell of younger colleagues and new technology—to continue treading the same path?

THE MEANING SEEKER

arc Freedman has built an organization around the signature question of midlife: How will I use these glorious days remaining to me? The question had nagged at Erika Shell Castro for some years. It was a remote voice she could largely ignore. Until she couldn't. Two upheavals—one happy, one terrifying—brought the question center stage.

By the time she was forty-five, Erika had raised two children and built a fast-paced career. She created a program for a large hospital system in the Midwest that provided language services for those who were deaf or spoke limited English. Erika's program became a model for other hospitals, and she found herself speaking at conferences and eventually being hired away by a technology company that wanted to provide those services to hospitals by video.

Then, in the span of a few months, Erika's internal world took her career off cruise control. She became pregnant at forty-four—a surprise and delight—and six months after she gave birth, she was diagnosed with multiple sclerosis. Erika realized she may not have many good years ahead of her: the crisis trigger. She did not want to spend them in a frenzy of travel and away from the core of her life, her family.

"Frankly, I don't even remember much about my first son's childhood because I was working all the time," Erika recalled. "I was starting up these programs in these hospitals. I was building a career. I close my eyes and I can picture maybe one or two instances when he was little, but I hardly remember. I thought, *You know what? I need to totally reevaluate everything that I'm doing and realign my life, my spirit, whatever, with the things that are most meaningful to me.*"

She began surfing Craigslist for nonprofit postings, and one caught her eye. Montaña de Luz, a Honduran orphanage for HIV-positive children, needed an executive director. Most of the children had been born with the disease. For some, their families could not afford the expensive treatment. For others, it was a sadder story: After the parents died, their children's relatives put them in the orphanage, fearing that they could become infected by eating from the same plates or using the same sink.

"I was like, 'Hmm, I've always wanted to be the director of an orphanage,'" she recalled. "I applied, and I got a second interview. I came home and said to my husband, 'I'm interviewing for this job, and I think I really want it, but I'll probably have to take a twenty-five-thousand-dollar cut in pay.' He said, 'You know what? If it's what you want, we'll make it happen. We'll get rid of cable, sell a car, whatever it takes.'"

As it happened, she needed to make none of these drastic cutbacks. The CEO of the technology company offered to pay the difference in salary, and all her health benefits—so critical for someone living with MS—if she would consult for his company one day a week.

Now she uses some of those skills honed in her corporate years—project development, mentoring, strategic planning, leadership—to give children who had been rejected by their relatives a place to live, medicine, a future. The orphanage began as a hospice. But with new medicines and treatments, the children, now young adults, are moving out and into the world.

"I wake up every day grateful that I get to take this journey the way that I'm taking it," Erika told me. "I don't know why I got so lucky and all the stars aligned for me. I think part of it is about being grateful and being open to new possibilities and having the courage to take them. I embrace change. I mean, I don't want it all the time. I don't want chaos, but I enjoy the new challenge."

She notes that her MS gives her zero problems, which leaves her awestruck. To my mind, there is no luck, not even a puzzle, here. Like Tom Cox, like the older people ("escapees") who showed no signs of the Alzheimer's disease that riddled their brains, having a purpose larger than yourself can heal.

PROGRESSIVE FINE-TUNING:
FROM THEORETICAL TO CONCRETE

Nancy Augustine has galloped along, under the guidance of her career coach, Bev Jones. In the past two months, Nancy and Bev have brainstormed about Nancy's starting her own consulting firm, about making college education accessible for veterans, about coaching and mentoring, about doing community relations for hospitals or universities, about figuring out a way to remain at George Washington University. Nancy has been active, too, taking people out to lunch, working her network, looking for jobs, and designing an online course for the summer.

Nancy has also started to notice what excites her, because that passion could signal a direction for her career. She says every time she sees an article about the transformation of higher education, "I read every single word and I take notes and I circle things. I'm fascinated by it." This would turn out to be a critical clue.

On this, their third meeting, Nancy and Bev begin what feels like a new phase: switching the lens from wide angle to telephoto.

"Now we want to rein it in a bit," Bev says. She suggests dividing Nancy's tasks into categories: immediate job search, research about veterans' education or online learning, talking to people about setting up a business, reaching out to GW colleagues about opportunities there.

"The trick here is when you've reached that natural stopping point, when you've done the obvious, you need to push yourself beyond that," Bev says. "When you go beyond the obvious, that's when the break-throughs tend to occur."

People tend to pluck the low-hanging fruit first, talking to people they are comfortable with about their job hunt.

"A lot of people are shy about calling a stranger or pushing them-selves on somebody they don't know very well," Bev says. "There's a tendency for people to say, 'Ugh,' to get discouraged, to give up, and maybe try something else. In each of these areas, when it gets hard, that's when you say, 'Okay, this has just been a platform. Now I've got to do the hard stuff,' and the hard stuff is thinking harder, looking broader, thinking more widely, getting out of your silo."

"And making the difficult phone call?" I offer.

"Making the difficult phone call," Bev says. "I think that very often the exciting opportunities start coming when people start playing long shots. It's the long shots that break you out of your normal channels where you come up with new ideas and new opportunities. We almost have to trick ourselves because sometimes the long shots sound silly."

Bev says she once applied to a law firm that was looking for a tax specialist. She was not qualified, but she sent off a letter anyway. She heard back from the headhunter, who told her she was not the right fit for that job but put her in touch with another firm. In a week, Bev had a partnership offer.

I nod. I note that nearly two decades earlier, before I came to NPR, the radio network advertised for a managing editor. The job was laughably above my experience level, but I applied. The vice president for news called me in and almost instantly rejected me, because he could see I still wanted to be out reporting, not managing other report-ers. He was right, of course. Six weeks later I received a call from the editor of the foreign desk.

"She said, 'Why don't you come in to be a temporary editor during the holidays?'" I recall happily. "And that was eighteen years ago. That's how I got to NPR. I just applied for something that was so out of my league, but I knew I wanted to be there."

"The trick is to stretch in an unlikely direction when you don't particularly feel like it," Bev says. "Surprising things develop. And then all of a sudden it becomes obvious and you look back and think, *Why did it take me so long? This is so obvious.* But I think it doesn't become obvious in the abstract."

Bev and Nancy discuss their goals for the coming month: Nancy needs to think about her "brand," ramp up the networking, reach out to people on LinkedIn, make the hard phone calls, start tweeting, blogging, or contributing to other people's blogs in her area of expertise. If Nancy pushes each category forward every day or two, eventually, in the fashion of the tortoise crossing the finish line, she will figure out her new career. That's the theory. It makes my head spin.

WHY YOUR BRAIN WANTS YOU TO STAY PUT

Twelve women and three men wait quietly in a small conference room at the Harvard Faculty Club. Just before nine a.m., Srini Pillay strides into the room. He is a study in contrasts, with his Harvard tie, black cowboy boots, and mop of black hair, unruly as if he was unexpectedly roused from bed. Pillay teaches at Harvard Medical School and Harvard Business School, and he has identified a lucrative niche straddling the two: As founder of NeuroBusiness Group, he tries to use discoveries about the brain to help business leaders understand why they resist change, and how to push through the resistance.

"The expectation, I think, is really within each of you," he says to the group. "If you want to actually bring yourself to a point of transformation, I think you will be transformed."

With that, we are off to the races. Pillay talks almost too quickly to compute, he is funny, and his demeanor lands somewhere between hustling entrepreneur and sage counselor. He speaks in metaphors when describing the brain: the fear center, the thinking center, the action center, the navigation center, the accountant, the conflict detector. He talks about "habit hell," "memory magnets," and "context cages." The concepts rush by like a mountain stream during the spring thaw. Still, he is so likable, so enthusiastic, that he sweeps you into his wake.

Pillay says the brain likes its habits—*cells that fire together, wire together*—and hates change. The brain despises conflict: It reasons that I may be happier over there, but I am earning a good paycheck here, and in general it resolves this cognitive dissonance in favor of the familiar. At the bottom of every dilemma, he says, is fear, and the brain always prefers the bird in the hand to venturing into the bush, even if you are clutching a scrawny black crow. When that amygdala fires, as it tends to do when you consider embarking on a professional adventure, you run to safety.

To leave a dead-end job for a potentially exciting one, Pillay says, you need to move your mind-set from "On your mark" to "Get set"— that is, from thinking wishfully without serious commitment, to being poised in the starting blocks and ready to burst forward. Until you are committed to leaving, the brain will always find reasons to stay put.

"Your brain comes back and says, 'Well, how are you going to pay the mortgage? And the kids just went off to college, how are you going to pay for that?' The brain tends to want to resolve this dissonance by pulling you back. It says, 'You know what? Don't go forward, go back.'"

The way to prod the skittish brain from paralysis to forward motion, he says, is to face the questions head-on and work toward solutions.

"You've got to say, 'Well, let me take a look at this,'" Pillay says. "I've got to take a look at how I can figure out a way to manage my expenses, because there is a way. If I say to my brain, 'I want to get to this goal,' the more data I feed my brain about where I want to go, the more likely the brain is to come up with the way to get me there."

The brain, Pillay claims, is not crazy about risk, but it *hates* ambiguity. The more information you can feed your brain about how you will handle the risk—"We can move to a smaller house, I will do some consulting on the side"—the more comfortable the brain feels with change.

In looking at Pillay's work, his ideas seem sound in theory but have not been road-tested much. Scientists have plumbed the effects of fear in the brain and how to overcome fear through training. But most of those studies involve people with phobias or anxiety disorders, not someone considering, say, switching jobs or launching a nonprofit.[10] Pillay seems to be one of the first to try to apply the findings of neuroscience to career choices. At this point, real-life dilemmas seem to fall more into the realm of psychiatry than neuroscience.

Which was good news for me. Because Srini Pillay is a very good psychiatrist.

I discovered this halfway through the afternoon session. Pillay had requested that each person write a "change commitment contract," that is, a habit or lifestyle or job that he or she wanted to change. They split up in pairs, one acting as coach, the other acting as client.

I walked up to Pillay, seeking some clarifications from the morning's lecture. What I got instead was a revelation. It was like sprinting up and down the emotional Rockies, psychiatry at 78 rpm. Pillay asked me if I wanted to try the change exercise everyone else was doing. Why not? What follows are the highlights of the conversation.

SRINI PILLAY: So, can you identify one change that you would like in your life?

BARB BRADLEY HAGERTY: Yeah, I can. I'd like to have a life that is more controlled than the one I have now.

SP: When would you like it to occur?

BBH: Immediately. Today.

SP: Is there anything stopping you from doing it today?

BBH: Yeah. My identity as an NPR reporter . . . It's an identity issue for me.

SP: And so, it sounds like we're talking about long-term memory and we're talking about the fact that your identity has been shaped by the notion that you're a reporter. Is there any other way that you can reframe that identity?

BBH: Yeah. I'm a storyteller, primarily. That's what I do in my work. I tell stories. What I care about is having people care about ideas, and the way I make them care about ideas is to tell a good story. So, reframing it that way, it doesn't have to be a deadline-driven life.

(Now I pause, because I had never admitted this to anyone but my family before.)

I actually don't care about the breaking news. What I care about is that people hear ideas from NPR, from me, before anyone else.

SP: So, what's the actual conflict for you right now?

BBH: I think the conflict is I'm afraid they'll say no. So, if I go in there and say, "You know, I'd like to see if I can craft my job differently," I'm afraid they'll say no, partly because of the economy, and partly because they can get someone less expensive. So there's this economic conflict.

SP: Is that the conflict right now?

BBH: Well, not really, because my husband is encouraging me to stake out new territory and try to create a new identity in my work. So there's something else going on. I think it is fear of not being able to say: "Hi, I'm Barb Bradley Hagerty with NPR." It gives me instant approval.

SP: So, what would be the reward for you if you changed to this new life?

(Here, I reach up and touch my throat.)

BBH: It'd be physical and emotional health. I currently have chronic pain in my vocal cords. The doctors think that it was partially caused by the stress. So there's a physical reward for not being under that kind of stress.

SP: So, I notice that when you talked about your health, your level of emotion rose because you recognize something about it. What are your fears if you do not make this change today or in the next week? What could happen?

BBH: If I don't, eventually I think I'd have a physical breakdown. I don't think, physically, that I can do it with my throat hurting like this. I just don't think I can do it. So there's a real consequence.

What Pillay did, in less than six minutes, was have me confront my conflicts and envision a new life without the pain. I was a little shaken, a little relieved. Here was a Harvard psychiatrist seeing me as distinct from my role as a news reporter at NPR. Few other people view me that way. Is it possible that I could tell stories without the frantic deadlines of broadcast news? Maybe I do not have to die on that sword. Maybe there is another way to live.

For those making a change, Srini Pillay recommends mindfulness meditation, so you can observe your fears clinically. He also suggests visual imagery: imagining yourself in the new position, just as a competitive diver imagines the triple back somersault before he executes it.

I did neither, but I soon met other people who figured out a way around the fear, without the meditation or mental calisthenics.

TESTING THE WATERS

Every expert I spoke with offered this advice: Dip your toe in the water before leaping to a new career.[11] The quickest and least expensive way to test the waters is volunteering. Serve on the board of that environmental nonprofit, or offer to do the accounting for the local Habitat for Humanity chapter, before you give notice. If you love it, great, but if you don't, you have burned no bridges with your current employer.[12]

A more expensive route to trying an industry on for size is to go back to school. Some people plunge right into school, because they recognize they cannot begin to follow their passion without a new degree.[13] If you have considered the options and know where you want to go, it is always better to make the transition sooner rather than later. At midlife, you may have time for one more major career change.

Others follow a more cautious route. After college, where he majored in economics, Al Bunis became a banker in New York, eventually settling down at Goldman Sachs, where he was in the capital markets and money management business.

"I was never that enamored of what I was doing," he told me. "I was just never that passionate, never that instinctively interested in it."

Al married, and he and his wife, Lynn, had two children and bought an apartment in Brooklyn Heights. He could not up and leave banking. He considered many other careers: teaching, advertising, politics, the toy industry, real estate, the nonprofit world. Nothing excited him, until his family began attending a nearby church in the 1990s.

"My interest in my relationship with God just jumped off the page," he said. "It became a consuming interest. I found what I was looking for."

Lynn, the practical one, wondered how he could follow a divine call and they could pay the bills on her salary alone. So Al took the slow boat to his passion, to her great relief.

"It wasn't like he came home and said, 'I'm going to be a minister tomorrow,' you know?" Lynn said. "He came home and said, 'Well, I'm going to go to divinity school.'"

Al found himself, in his mid-forties, with two young children, learning about hermeneutics and parish ministry by night, scheduling classes and papers around his business trips. For him, divinity school made his banking job more bearable.

"I wasn't really trudging anymore," he said. "I felt like there was a light at the end of the tunnel."

Al continued in this way, keeping his options open for close to ten years, until he had a conversation with a fellow seminarian. As she described her internship at a church, Al had "a V8 moment. It was like, 'What am I doing? What am I waiting for?'" he recalled. "And the moment I started lining up a church to be a seminary intern at, I knew it was going to be great."

After Al worked as an interim senior minister, he and Lynn moved to Miami, where he is senior minister at Plymouth Congregational Church.

"It's the first time in my life I ever felt like I was doing anything inspired."

As I listened to stories about dipping one's toe in the water, I realized that I knew someone very well who had done just that. Me.

When I realized about a decade ago that I was not suited for daily news, I decided to try my hand at book writing. I love long-form narratives, and I thought I had a personality suited to it: I am more tortoise than hare, but I am a driven tortoise. Happily, I found an agent who was willing to work with me, and an editor willing to take a risk.

That year writing my first book was among the happiest of my career. I had found a new outlet for storytelling, one that used my years of journalism experience and allowed me to control my time and focus on the stories I cared about. Every interview I did felt crucial, because it led me to insights that I considered important.

By the time I returned to NPR from my book leave, I had built an off-ramp, one that looked more and more appealing after I developed voice problems. I was a little nervous by the option I had created; far safer to stay the course in journalism, with its weekly paychecks, than to hope for royalties that might never arrive. I chafe when people tell authors, *Don't quit your day job.* I chafe because it rings so true. And yet, one fact kept calling to me. I knew I loved writing books. I had paddled around in that pool and could not wait to dive back in.[14]

LET THE ANGUISH BEGIN

Tuesday, September 17

This week, NPR announced it wants to cut 10 percent of its workforce. It would offer buyouts that turned out to be quite generous. You would think this would put a song in my heart, but instead I feel as if I am wearing a ticking time bomb. The theoretical is suddenly real and needs to be decided by this time next month. I think about "loss aversion," in which people strongly prefer to *avoid losing* something than to *gain* something of equal or greater value. Suddenly, the prospect of losing my job at NPR, even if it is my choice, looms far larger than all the freedom and new challenges I have been fantasizing about. I have entered Srini Pillay's territory.

I mentioned the buyout to Devin, trying to sound casual.

"Are you thinking about it?" he asked.

"Sort of," I said in a small voice.

He was quiet for a moment.

"You know, I want you to start your next stage."

"But I don't want you to feel trapped," I half protested, "while I go off and follow my dream."

"It's your turn," he said, noting that I had long supported his relationship with his daughter, and helped save for her college tuition. (Which in my opinion was a bargain, since I get to have Vivian as a stepdaughter.)

"We will be fine," he said. "I want you to do this."

I felt like crying.

In the course of my reporting, I would notice time and again that the people who struggled the most in their career transitions were navigating them alone. A partner who provides financial support, as I have, as Nancy Augustine has, gives you breathing room and emboldens you to take more risks. But I noticed that even psychological support alone provides a buffer. I heard story after story of women who were raising their children alone, and those children gave them love and an impetus to find another job (if they had lost theirs) or move to a sustainable career.

What counts is having someone in your corner.

REALITY CHECK

There's nothing like a large dose of reality to throw cold water on one's dreams. During these crucial few weeks of decision making, I began reading e-mails from NPR listeners. If you recall, I had sent out a query on NPR's Facebook page with the question: "How's midlife treating you?" My inbox exploded with more than seven hundred e-mails in twelve hours. Of course there were scores of inspiring, hopeful stories, but as I worked my way through the pile, I began to see the dark side.

If this is a snapshot of America, I thought after reading one particularly distressing e-mail, *I want to shoot myself.* Remember, these respondents are, demographically, the most educated and informed slice of America. And some of them are desperate.

A real estate developer reported living out of his car. A Ph.D. is living on food stamps, unable to find a job teaching anything but flamenco. A longtime sales representative answers phones as a temp at a law firm.

One fifty-five-year-old woman, a former bank executive, lost her job in 2009. She earned a master's degree in sustainability management (a "green" MBA) at Columbia University. Her first year out was dismal: She lost her home and sold off everything she could to pay the bills. The next year brought some hope: She landed a couple of internships and small contracts from nonprofits and green businesses. She survived because her mother allowed her to stay in her apartment and rent out the extra bedroom. When I last contacted her, the woman had no job prospects, despite sending out hundreds of résumés and working with a career counselor at Columbia. Her mother was suing to evict her, and only because of the kindness of a friend was she able to sublet an affordable apartment.

She didn't mind the downsizing. "What is much harder to do," she said, "is to give up my hope and expectation that I could work for the last (productive) twenty years of my life in a way that allowed me to have meaningful work that paid enough for me to cover expenses, pay down debt, and save enough for retirement. That dream is fast disappearing."

But, she added, "I will keep fighting until I can't fight anymore."

Indeed, I saw astonishing resilience in those e-mails and follow-up interviews. One fifty-year-old man left his job as a technology director at a Santa Fe newspaper to pursue a master's degree in writing, only to leave the program early because of money. He returned to Santa Fe, where he worked as a barista at the coffee shop across from the newspaper, serving former colleagues skinny lattes and double espressos. It took him four years to regain his footing, but he had a marketable expertise. He developed online skills that few people in Santa Fe media possessed, and is now the publisher of an alternative weekly magazine, just down the street from the coffee shop where he worked.

Perhaps my favorite story was Robert Bidney's. At age fifty-two, when the recession was just gaining traction, Rob was laid off from his advertising agency in Florida. Jobs in his industry vanished in the recession, since advertising budgets are often the first thing to go. He took any freelance project he could find, but those dried up as well, and he found himself working at a couple of pawnshops, seven days a week. His wife, a freelance journalist, took a job at a call center. They lost both cars, and the bank started foreclosure proceedings on their home. Life was pretty bleak, although not entirely: Once or twice a week, he brought his guitar and played music at an adult training center for mentally and physically disabled adults.

"It gave me a sense of worth that helped me out immensely," Rob said. "Immensely."

He also wrote and performed a song called "Pill for Poverty" that struck me dumb as I listened.[15] Here was this white middle-class guy, stripped of hope and, worse, dignity. But Rob, who did not have a coach to tell him to network, to tweet and blog, to go on LinkedIn, did possess one thing: a twenty-five-year reputation for generosity and integrity.

"I made a lot of wonderful friendships and relationships through-out my career," he said, and when a job in the advertising department of Office Depot opened up, "it was a perfect storm."

Four people independently recommended him for the job. He was hired at a significantly lower salary than what he was accustomed to, but he was "very, very grateful." He loves the work, he loves his colleagues, and he has worked his way up to close to his previous salary.

Rob's last comment echoed in my mind as I pondered my own next move. Every day, he said, he rides the elevator with his fellow employees.

"On Monday morning, they groan, 'Oh, it's Monday.' And then you go down the elevator on Wednesday and they say, "Oh, it's Wednesday! I'm halfway through the week!' And then you go up in the elevator Friday morning and they say, 'It's Friday! I'm so glad I got through the week!'

"And every time I hear these comments, I say to myself, 'I'm so glad that I have a job, and you're complaining about getting through the freakin' week!'"

PROGRESSIVE FINE-TUNING: *LAUNCHED*

Oh!" Bev Jones says as we settle in for this, our last session. "The journey is reaching the finish—are you ready to launch?"

"I think I've pretty much launched," Nancy Augustine says, laughing. "I've been trying to think how this has worked out so well, and I think a lot of it is just being clear about what I'm good at and what I want to see happen."

"Yes, that's it," Bev says. "As soon as you get clarity about what you want—I've seen it again and again—it's almost like magic. Things start falling into place."

This is the update since we last met three months ago. A consulting project with the federal government, which had been on the back burner, came through. Nancy's university has offered her one of the few part-time permanent positions. She will keep her title, her office, and teach half-time.

"In addition to this—this is another of the cool things that happened as a result of networking—this coming year I'm also going to be the director of graduate studies for a small program," Nancy says. "So there's a small stipend for it but it lets me move into a leadership position."

"Fabulous," Bev says, beaming. "This is wonderful. The pieces are click, click, clicking."

It doesn't always click along. Nancy has advantages others might not enjoy. She has a husband with a job, she is highly educated and professional, she is healthy and still on the near side of fifty. But she has also toiled at this, and she has a spreadsheet to prove it, tallying the minutes she spent networking, creating her brand for a consulting company, researching the future of education, taking people to lunch, looking at job listings, tweeting and doing every single painful thing that Bev has suggested. Most of all, she has acted strategically at the university, volunteering to craft the mission statement for the department and see where there were gaps, "which so happened to be things I wanted to do." In other words, she began to tailor her interests to the university's needs. It worked.

I admit, I am surprised. Anecdotes in the media are often this neat, but life rarely is. As I reflect on Nancy's trajectory, I remember something my dad told me about how to fire a torpedo. He served during World War II, so the technology was pretty crude. When the torpedo is fired, the engineer watches its path on sonar, and ninety-nine times out of a hundred, its path is overshooting to one side of the target or the other. So he executes minute adjustments: first, two degrees to the left, now one degree to the right, half a degree to the left, little tiny calibrations until—*bam!*—the torpedo hits its target.

I think this is how Nancy and Bev charted Nancy's future. No dramatic swings; Nancy is not leaping from law to dog therapy. She is just making tiny adjustments within the areas she excels at and loves—education, research, management, the environment, consulting—and bit by bit, she nears her mark. When she arrives at their final session, I am struck by how these tweaks have guided her to this place.

"Nancy, I'm trying to remember what you wanted to do when you first came in," I venture. "What were the ideas?"

"I remember feeling lost," she says. "Boy, did I even have particular ideas?"

Bev looks back at her notes from the first session.

"You didn't know if you wanted another job. You didn't know if you wanted to teach. You didn't know if you wanted to look at another university. You were still looking very much at other universities, possibly different kinds of roles," Bev says. She looks up. "Really, you've come a long way."[16]

COLD FEET AND WARM

Sunday, October 13

Yesterday Devin and I were at L.L. Bean, looking for blue jeans. We wanted the classic cut. I saw a salesman, a fifty-something guy, wearing an L.L. Bean name tag, aimlessly straightening out pants on a shelf.

"Do you work here?" I asked, because, despite the name tag, he didn't seem very invested in the merchandise.

"I guess I do," he replied.

"Where are the classic-cut jeans?" I asked.

"Over there," he said, pointing vaguely over my shoulder.

I waited a beat, to see if he would lead us there, but he turned back to his task of straightening the shelves.

Devin and I walked away.

"I think he's a white-collar guy who lost his job," Devin whispered sympathetically, "maybe a banker, or some other professional. But I don't think he aspired to work at L.L. Bean."

In two days, I plan on telling NPR that I will take the buyout, and the sales guy at L.L. Bean is not helping. What am I doing, leaving a company I love just because I don't have the perfect job? Leaving a job without a job? Leaving one of the few journalism companies that is solvent and has a bright future? Leaving a medium that is so creative, has so much impact, where my voice is known—for *what*? The hope that I can make a living writing books and being creative?

What am I doing?

To which I reply, What else can I do? If not now, when? This fear right now is the flip side of freedom; it's like the sound barrier, turbulent and loud until I can push through it and find a measure of quiet. Of course I'm scared; that's utterly predictable. But one thing I am not is bored.

THREE PATHS IN THE FOREST

Now that we have bushwhacked through the dense forest of midlife career advice, I can spot a few thematic paths to help navigate through the thicket. It seems to me there are three essential questions for anyone contemplating a mid-career course correction.

First, what will you do with these glorious years? Our longevity is both a blessing and a responsibility. Almost no one can afford to retire at sixty-five and play golf. And even if you could, would you want to? So the question is: What will be the texture of those additional years? Investing inward (more stuff)—or outward (more meaning)? We're given a chance to leave a legacy: What will it be?

Second, what is your *Sosein*, your essence, and how will that guide you? A fifty-year-old may lack the energy of a twenty-five-year-old, but she makes up for it in self-knowledge. She knows where she excels and what floods her with energy and life. People who make this transition rarely reinvent themselves from the ground up. Rather, they build on their considerable skills, experience, and passion. Their venue may change, the industry may change, but they do not. It looks radical from the outside, but on the inside, it feels familiar.

Third, what are you really afraid of? You can expect to be anxious: Our brains resist change, they rail against it, our amygdala will always want the safe bet. But are the obstacles truly insurmountable? Is it a brick wall? Or is it a sliding door, which, once you decide to approach it, begins to swish open? Because even though our brains prefer safety in the short run, in the long run they crave meaning, challenge, and novelty.

***

It is just after five on a Saturday morning. I have been awake for hours, struggling to find a satisfying end for this chapter. A neat conclusion, a victory assured. But lying in bed, staring at the clock, feeling the weight of my still husband and softly snoring dog, I realize I cannot deliver a tidy conclusion. How can I? This story isn't over. Will I flop? Not if I can help it. Anyway, that is yesterday's question. Asking it now, looking over my shoulder, begs paralysis. It is too late to fret and mull.

More pressing is today's glorious work. I have an epilogue to write.

EPILOGUE

Midlife is a time to pause and take stock. So is an epilogue. As I review my decade experiencing midlife and two-plus years studying it, I realize that I have changed on the surface—witness the wrinkles—and at the core: I am more intentional about my relationships and the individual moments of the day; I am more equipped to bounce back from setbacks, more likely to spring out of bed in the morning because this day holds the possibility of something good, a new lesson, a surprise. My evolution springs from the insights of researchers, surely, but also from the stories of others who have hit snags, endured tragedies, reappraised the landscape, and carved out new paths through their middle years. Ultimately, I have tried to bake the academic research and lived wisdom into my own story. Please indulge me while I tie up some of my own narrative threads.

Friday, April 4, 2014

Devin called this morning. He has been traveling, and without access to his favorite channels, he's found himself grudgingly watching network news in the morning and evening. During the commercials, something clicked. The morning-time commercials, he observed, are aimed at middle-aged women: They peddle facial creams and miracle technologies to take away wrinkles. The commercials during the evening news seem geared to both men and women past their prime, with their Cialis ads and medication for arthritis pain.

"It's all about surface solutions, trying to hang on to youth through topical creams," Devin said. "That's the easy way. What you're finding is: The solution is from the inside. It's all about how you think, how you engage your mind, your marriage, your career. It's harder, but it works."

As I mulled over this observation, I realized that Devin had identified an unspoken theme of the research on midlife. Yes, autopilot is death, yes, you need to engage life with verve, but please note the fine print. It's arduous. Flipping the switch from autopilot to engagement demands intention, energy, and effort every single day.

Every idea in this book runs against our natural tendency to want to relax, take it easy, reward ourselves for decades of work and child rearing. Our default mode at midlife is entropy. But default is not destiny, and on this, the research is unequivocal: For every fork in the road, you are almost invariably better off making the harder choice. Harder in the moment, that is, but easier over the years, as your body and mind remain strong. By resisting entropy, by pushing through the inertia that beckons us to rest a little longer, to slow down just a notch, until your life has narrowed to a pinprick—by resisting those forces, you dramatically up the odds that your life will be rich to your final breath, deeply entwined with family and friends, engaged in intellectual pursuits, and infused with a purpose that extends beyond yourself. Yes, it's hard.

Yes, it's worth it.

MIDLIFE IS NOT FUN. IT'S FUNNY

Thursday, July 3, 2014

I can fight it no longer. I am surrendering to hearing aids. I am weary of being in a world of Seinfeldian "low talkers," straining to hear the words, working to fill in the blanks, finally losing the energy to follow the conversation. And that, research shows, is death, or at least dementia.

Once I crossed the psychological Rubicon, I discovered that twenty-first-century hearing aids are kind of nifty. They are practically invisible to the unpracticed eye, small, sleek, with a tiny speaker that fits snugly into the mouth of the ear tunnel. Since our insurance covers most of the cost, I ordered the deluxe model with sixteen channels and the ability to sift out ambient noise, to figure out whether I want to hear the voice in front of or behind me, and to teach itself what my preferred settings are. I wondered if it could make dinner as well. Or write a book about midlife.

"And it comes with the choice of two accessories," Danielle, the audiologist, said, holding open the brochure.

"I get two? Like, a salad and a dessert?" I asked.

Danielle laughed. "Just like that."

I ordered the remote volume control and a device that connects your hearing aids wirelessly to your iPhone. With those decisions, I arrived in the land of the hearing-impaired. In truth, I have lived here a long time but only now admit it.

Friday, August 1, 2014

Last night, we invited some friends to dinner. I could not wait to try out my new hearing aids in a real-world setting, sitting on the patio on a balmy summer evening. Eager to actually hear conversation, I threw out the question: "Twenty fourteen is the year that . . . what? . . . What insight, what extraordinarily good thing, what major lesson, have you had? How will you remember 2014?"

Our friend Jerry began to talk, and here is where things went south. As he bared his soul, I found I could zero in on every third word. But I had spectacular fidelity when it came to nonhuman noises. Dinner sounded like a construction site. I heard him say "watershed," before his next words were obliterated by piercing clinks and sharp clattering as people passed around the hamburger platters or set down their wine-glasses on the wrought-iron table. Jerry talked about "crisis," followed by a breathtaking screech as Mark's patio chair scraped on the flag-stones. I thought I heard the phrase "doors closing," but I couldn't quite hear through the racket as Jennifer scooped some more pasta onto her plate. I just nodded at Jerry, inwardly wincing at the cacophony, not let-ting on that I had no idea what he was saying, except to know that I was missing something really interesting. Next time I will sit next to Jerry and ask him to speak up. And I'll leave the hearing aids next to the bed.

I later traded in my hearing aids for a simpler model. I can hear human voices now, along with nonverbal bumps and screeches. The car air conditioner still sounds like Niagara Falls. They say it takes a couple of months for the brain to rewire itself to differentiate the nonhuman noises from the human voice. I fervently hope so. For now, I must muddle through, until the clattering in my head gives way to lilting speech. It doesn't even have to be lilting. Any intelligible speech will do.

FINDING A LITTLE PASSION

Saturday, May 17, 2014

Nine months after I soared off my bike and broke my collarbone, this is the day that I qualify (or not) for the National Senior Games, for athletes fifty and older. Mike Adsit and I have traveled to Newport News, Virginia, for the state races. The top three finishers can compete in the national competition in July 2015.

"I'll be glad when it's over," Mike said grimly.

"Me too," I agreed, a little alarmed at his ebbing bravado. He has raced many times before. I have competed in a cycling race exactly twice, and been soundly beaten by women twenty years my junior. I hoped to fare better today.

We arrived early and rode the course three times, Mike instructing me at each turn.

"Shortest distance around a turn is a straight line," he yelled, swinging wide into the lane before cutting diagonally toward the curb and missing it by an inch. I followed, mimicking him, and suddenly I felt a swell of affection for this man who introduced me to my new passion, this new friend who cares more about my races than his own. Mike swung around a turn, looking over his shoulder to watch me, and I thought, *He has pedaled through so much,* through the cancer, through the bone marrow transplant, through the trauma of helping others with cancer who ultimately died.

A few minutes later, they called the twenty-kilometer race. A dozen women lined up, but after the starting gun, I shot away with one other woman. I was not confident that I could keep up with Margie, but once I was drafting, I relaxed. She led for the first half of the five-kilometer loop, occasionally shaking her head as if trying to dodge the wind.

"You want me to lead?" I gasped, and she motioned with her hand. I spun ahead, and the wind hit me like a wave. We clipped along in goodwilled teamwork, alternatively leading and drafting so we could both ride faster against our mutual enemies, the wind and the road. We barreled down the straightaways, took care not to fall at the ninety-degree turns, but when we saw the finish line, the comity vanished. Margie swung around and sped past me. I chased her, I was gaining on her, but I didn't have enough time to spin past. Margie beat me by one second. I will be going to the national Senior Games in July 2015.

Almost immediately after the race, I began berating myself. *Where is my competitive spirit?* I thought. This was not a difficult field: Was I a quitter?

But in the next instant, I realized my journey to Newport News had little to do with a bike race. It is about creating a new challenge for the first time in two decades, aiming for a goal with the very real possibility that I will fail. To ride faster, to stay upright and not crash, to surmount my fear and sidle my bike up to the starting line, pushes me beyond my comfortable midlife boundaries. That so rarely happens to us in our busy middle years. We watch our bodies and our brains slow down as younger bodies and brains zip past us, and we just accept it, not realizing there is a whole world offering to sharpen and improve us. We simply need to look for it.

Sunday, May 3, 2015

A year later, and two months before the National Senior Games, reality has settled on me like a lead apron. The past year has not transformed me from a happy rider to a fierce competitor. Midlife responsibilities—among other things, visiting my homebound mother and writing this book—have dominated my hours and eviscerated my Walter Mitty dreams. I will not dash away in Secretariat fashion from the other fifty-somethings I will meet in Minneapolis. Whatever illusions I held were shattered today at the Bunny Hop.

The Bunny Hop Criterium in Suitland, Maryland, is a terrifying event in which cyclists tear around a one-kilometer loop of (potholed) road, circling again and again for forty minutes. The cyclists draft so that each rider is three inches behind the wheel of the cyclist in front of her; the tight pack moves like a school of fish in perfect synchrony. Or not. Sometimes they jostle each other when they try to break from the pack, sometimes they bump as they careen down the hill and around the curve. Sometimes they crash. Sometimes an ambulance is needed.

What have I gotten myself into? I thought, feeling slightly nauseated as I warmed up. I am fifty-five. I have no experience riding in a pack. I've already broken my collarbone once: Am I courting a second break?

I was never in the slightest danger. There is zero jostling when you ride alone, at the back. I stayed with the other cyclists for three loops, then they pulled away, and once that happens, you are toast. You save about 30 percent of your energy by drafting behind the person in front of you. If you are riding alone, you battle the wind by yourself. It's a grind, it's dispiriting, and, it turns out, it's a little humiliating. Every time I rode in front of the grandstand (alone), the announcer yelled, "There's Barbara Hagerty!" and I would just laugh and shake my head. The fifth time he announced my name, he said, "There's Hagerty! She's thinking, *Will he quit announcing my name?!*"

When I came in second to last, my first emotion was gratitude: *Thank God it's over.* Despite my poor ranking, I rode hard, a twenty-mile-an-hour pace for thirteen miles. Obviously I was not competitive with the young racers—the winner finished nearly four minutes ahead of me—but it was not a terrible showing for a fifty-five-year-old novice cyclist.

Driving home from the race, I called Devin.

"I came in second to last."

"Oh," he said, sounding genuinely stricken. He always thinks I'm better than I am. "I'm sorry."

I told him a little about the race. Then I blurted out, "I *hate* racing. I hate it hate it hate it. I love riding my bike, but does that mean I have to compete in the Senior Games? Maybe I should just ride for enjoyment, forget this Senior Games stuff."

Devin paused, weighing his words. "Isn't one of the points of midlife that you don't have to do all the things you hate to do? Shouldn't you do what you enjoy doing?"

He was right. One of the upsides of midlife is letting go. Maybe, in my fifties, I need to grow up and stop following orders from my inner Mussolini, who barks commands that make no sense. I don't have to listen. I can tell the little dictator to shut up. I'm a middle-aged American now. I'm free.

Free, that is, after I compete in the Senior Games.

Wednesday, July 8, 2015

I inch up to the starting line, numb with fear. In two minutes, I will launch myself into a furious sprint on my bicycle for the most terrifying, and probably painful, hour of my life. The dreaded hour has arrived, the first race in the Senior Games, my first national cycling competition. I am pitted against two dozen women ages fifty-five to fifty-nine, some of the fastest masters cyclists in the country.

I glance at my competitors in the forty-kilometer (twenty-five-mile) road race, hoping to see Pillsbury dough-girls: soft, friendly, motherly. Instead, I see women with long, ropy muscles and the cool expressions of elite fighters: a Delta Force detachment, only female.

Then, all too soon, we are off, twenty women shot out of a cannon trying to be the first to reach the turn. I dread corners—racers sometimes cut them too close and knock you over—and I was horrified to find that this course on the Minnesota State Fairgrounds contained 112 sharp turns. It looked like a toddler had gone wild with an Etch A Sketch. "A pro racer would have a tough time with this course," Mike Adsit muttered, which didn't help. Compounding my corner phobia was my inexperience riding in a pack, with the jostling, drafting, and sudden breakaways. Many times before this moment, I have envisioned my crumpled body, a Humpty Dumpty in cycling gear on the side of the road, complete with broken collarbone or worse.

But a strange thing happened in that first turn. I felt eerily comfortable, casually warning the woman next to me, "On your right, by the way," so she would give me a wide berth. *That wasn't so bad,* I thought, as I prepared for the next turn. We rode politely, warning each other of cracks in the pavement, and we rode fast (for me), between twenty and twenty-seven miles an hour; soon I realized the only way to stay with the leaders was to draft, to snuggle up to a "good wheel" (a rider who handled her bike well) and have her shield me from the wind. *I'm drafting!* I sang to myself. *I am in the game!* My fears evaporated; this was not *fun,* exactly, but I didn't consider swallowing cyanide a preferable alternative. After twenty miles, the leaders made a break, creating a yawning gap between two others and me. But when I crossed the finish line in ninth place, I was pleased with my performance: I stuck with the leaders for a good long time, I cornered with aplomb, I drafted confidently, and most important of all, I conquered a deep fear—a rare event in midlife, when we hum along with familiar proficiency.

Saturday, July 11, 2015

Mike Adsit arrived two days ago, a man on a mission. I am to leave every ounce of energy on the road, he announced. During the time-trial race, one cyclist leaves the starting line every thirty seconds; there is no drafting, no strategy, just an all-out sprint for ten kilometers. I move to the starting line and an official holds my bike upright while I clip into the pedals. It is a minor miracle I am here, counting down the seconds. Less than three years ago, I could barely climb a flight of stairs, so debilitating was the arthritis in my right knee. But then I met Mike, a cancer survivor and elite cyclist, who encouraged me to buy a bike and coached me through qualifying for the Senior Games.

"Your mind will play tricks with you," Mike says, offering last-minute advice. "It will lull you into thinking you can't go any harder. So you break it down. You look at a telephone pole, and go as hard as you can until you reach it, and then pick another telephone pole, and another, and when you see the finish line, you give it every ounce you have. I'll carry you back to the car if necessary. But you need to focus every second."

I nod—three, two, one, *GO!*—and I shoot off, the wind behind me, over the small hill and down past the lake. I feel my breathing and legs fall into a comfortable cadence. Suddenly I remember Mike's warning: *Your mind will lull you,* and I realize this is true, true of this race, true of midlife. *Autopilot is death,* I tell myself, and I focus on a telephone pole a hundred yards away, aware only of my breathing, suddenly so loud, the terrible ache in my legs, and that pole.

Halfway through, the wind shifts, hitting me with blunt force. This is so much harder. I start to feel sorry for myself. Then I think of my mother after her stroke, unable to form sentences, until one day she whispered to herself, *Push through, push through, push through to the other side*—and looked up and finished her sentence, the one that would presage her complete recovery. I recall the nearly unbearable pain in my vocal cords, and how I would think: *Can I endure this for an hour? No. How about thirty seconds? Yes, I can endure this for thirty seconds.* Can I ride this hard until the next telephone pole? Yes, I can. And the next. And the next. And suddenly, I spot Mike on the side of the road, roaring, *"Go, go, go, GO!"* And I sprint faster, my lungs burning, I sprint for my life and yours, I sprint for my friend.

I won seventh place, a respectable showing for a novice racer. But for me, this race represented an emotional rebirth. In my early fifties, I had hopped on a bicycle, set a goal to qualify for a national race, and exceeded my realistic hopes. This race tells of new beginnings at midlife, of making new friends, of putting punctuation back in this endless paragraph that stretches through our middle years. My legs feel like lead. My spirit feels like breath.

A photographer snapped a picture after the race. I am stretching up to kiss Mike on the cheek. My face is flushed, there are little drops of sweat poised at the tip of my hair. Mike is grinning, his eyes closed. Mike—who like so many people here was spurred to compete to combat his cancer—found a new passion at, and for, midlife, and passed on that gift to me.

THE POWER OF THOUGHT

Friday, June 13, 2014

I have been weaning myself off my pain medicine. I do note the irony here: Two decades ago, I left the religion of my youth, Christian Science, once I had discovered the joys and immediate relief of Tylenol.

Now I want out of the relationship with medicine—not a complete breakup, but maybe we could see each other a little less often. A year ago, I was taking pills every three hours, after which time the vocal cord pain came roaring back. But on Sunday, after cutting back a pill a day every few weeks, I managed to go all day without any pain pills, and took some medication only at night to help me sleep. For the first time in two years, I feel as if my mind can sprint from one thought to another, unencumbered by medicinal sludge.

This has been my study of one, my secret mental experiment that I have kept under wraps until I compiled some results. Now I have them. I couldn't wait to tell my voice doctor, Diane Bless, during our monthly conversation on Skype.

"This is a very big deal," Diane marveled. I think she, like me, thought I might suffer from chronic pain for the rest of my life. "How did you do it?"

"Well, when I feel the pain in my throat, the first thing I do is say, *False alarm!*" I said, laughing self-consciously. "I tell myself I don't have paralyzed vocal cords. There is no reason for this pain. It's a brain-wiring problem. Then I do some trills to loosen my throat. And finally I do an interview, or something else to distract me. And it goes away. I hope one day I can get off the medicine altogether."

"I think that's possible," Diane said, and we beamed at each other in happiness and wonder.

That was Monday. It's been five days now, and I have kept it up. I feel twinges of pain now and again, especially when I am stressed-out about the talk I have to write, or my mountain of tape to be transcribed. Still, I can't believe this is happening. My throat has been the dominant fact of my life for more than two years. It was my thundercloud. And now, it is dissipating. Slowly, through either the normal course of waning neuropathy or the miracle that my thinking is rewiring my brain—I don't know which—I feel as if the leg irons have been removed, and I am bound to this wall of pain by only one loose hand-cuff. I am almost free.

DOING GOOD WORK

Thursday, February 26, 2015

My friend and I braved the ice storm to meet at our favorite hole-in-the-wall sushi place. Tonight she needed some bucking up. My friend, who asked that I not identify her, has prospered in her career. She has a great job—for someone else. It does not play to her unique gifts, interests, and personality. She dreams of carving out a second act with her core passions occupying center stage, but that is scary.

I detect a wholly familiar problem: a mismatch between what she loves and what she does. With five decades behind her, my friend knows the contours of her passions and talents, but for most of her working life, she has been jammed into the ready-made requirements of a large institution.

"You know, the day I took the buyout, Jeff Goldberg called me up," I told her. Jeff is a friend and a writer for *The Atlantic*. "He said, 'Let me tell you how it's going to play out. After this book, you're going to step away from your subject area, and your thoughts are going to drift to your areas of interest. They're going to obsess you, and you'll realize, "Oh, what I'm really interested in exploring is . . . X." And you'll write a book about a story you covered fifteen years ago. You'll be able to engage ideas at the limit of your talent, the limit of your acuity. You're going to follow your obsession.'"

"Jeff Goldberg," she observed, "is a very good friend."

"Yeah, he is," I agreed, feeling a rush of fondness for him. "And here's the thing I've learned after all my research. When you're at midlife, you don't have an infinite amount of time. You have maybe one good spin at the wheel left. So make it Plan A. Make it what you really want to do. What you have passion for. If you fail, fine, then you can go back to the safer Plan B. But not yet. For now, forget Plan B. Shoot for Plan A."

I sat back, a little surprised. I had blurted out an insight that had been marinating for two years as I listened to people who found meaningful work in their forties or fifties or sixties. None of them regretted shooting for their passion, even if they failed and returned to prior work. Failure only sharpened their appreciation for their previous trade. The *only* people who voiced regret, I realized, were those who never tried.

In that moment, I had no idea how seminal that insight would prove to be, as I considered the next stage of my career.

CHOOSING WHAT MATTERS MOST

Saturday, August 2, 2014

This week we occupy a little corner of paradise: my brother's home on the Eastern Shore, with a pool, bikes, Jet Skis, and, best of all, a motorboat that drags along a giant raft for tubing. On the theory that parents of preteen children don't have lives, we invite families with young children to visit for a weekend in the summer, letting the kids play until they drop, and allowing the parents to enjoy a civilized glass of wine at dinner. This morning, all the parents disappeared on bikes, so I served as Captain John's "spotter" while three of the boys went tubing. I watched them for an hour as they gamely tried to stand up on the wobbly inflatable raft and inevitably bounced off into the water. I laughed, I took videos for their parents, and I wondered why I had made such a colossal mistake by not having children. How could I have let the most important part of life slip through my fingers?

A few hours later, I watched a TED talk by Clayton Christensen, a Harvard Business School professor who made his name by developing the theory of "disruptive innovation." He argues that successful companies fail not because they make poor products but because they make tiny, shortsighted decisions. For example, he said, Toyota did not enter the U.S. market with the Lexus; Toyota arrived with a piece of tin called the Corona. Rather than protect that downscale part of their business, U.S. companies simply ceded it. Just a little decision, and then another, all to maintain their profit margins. But the Japanese carmaker kept moving upmarket, and eventually, Christensen said, those initially inconsequential decisions to follow the path of least resistance helped push GM into bankruptcy.

Christensen believes this explains what happened to his classmates at Harvard Business School—and, I thought, to many marriages that seem so promising at first and dissolve by midlife. At his fifth class reunion, he said, everyone was happy. Most were married and flourishing in their careers. But at the tenth, fifteenth, twentieth reunions, many of his classmates were divorced, living apart from their children, and miserable.

"I guarantee that none of my classmates ever planned to go out and get divorced, and have children who hate their guts," Christensen said.

From the outside, these people possessed everything—financial success, career accomplishments, large homes, and fast cars—but as their lives unfolded, the bill on their short-term decisions came due. They implemented a strategy that brought them to a point of emotional bankruptcy, like GM ceding market share to Toyota rather than bat-tling to keep those lower-end customers, even if it meant a loss. What his classmates protected was not profit margins but achievement.

"Everybody here is driven to achieve," Christensen told the TED audience, "and when you have an extra ounce of energy or thirty minutes of time, instinctively and unconsciously, you'll allocate it to whatever activities in your life give you the most immediate evidence of achievement."

We close the sale. We ship the product. We pull the all-nighter to put a story on the radio. We get promoted. We are praised for a job well done.

"In contrast, investments in our families don't pay off for a very long time," Christensen continued. "And as a consequence, people like you and me who plan to have a happy life—because our families truly are the deepest source of happiness in our lives—find that although that's what we want, the way we invest our time and energy and tal-ents causes us to implement a strategy that we wouldn't at all plan to pursue."

As I listened, I felt myself go numb. *This is me,* I thought. All those tiny decisions that made me feel affirmed in the short run. Working on my story on Saturday as a cub reporter at *The Christian Science Monitor,* rather going out with my friends. As a twenty-nine-year-old single woman, following my career to Japan, where mar-riage prospects were slim. Toiling away in NPR's tiny edit booths hour after hour, night after night. Every story, every beat, seemed so urgent, so crucial, and they gave me instant gratification. Then I looked around and I was single and forty. NPR was the only love of my life.

I defied the odds and married at forty-three. Now I have Devin, and I have Vivian, the Best Stepdaughter Ever. But I will never quite know that visceral, biological drive to love and protect someone else above my own life, to live through the daily dramas of childhood with him or her, to cry because someone bullied him a little at school, to lie awake at night stricken with worry for her safety, to be utterly exhausted and wrung dry with love for my own gene pool.

And yet, midlife invites second chances, particularly with love. Harvard psychiatrist George Vaillant discovered this happy insight as he tracked the lives of Harvard men for six decades. Many of these men failed at their marriages several times before finding a love that persisted; and these men flourished as much as any who found great love early in life.

This gives me hope, and a responsibility. I am lucky to have found Devin and Vivian when I did. Now I must make the small, quotidian decisions in favor of family, the ones that seem impractical in the moment: putting off an interview in favor of a (long, hot) baseball game, or visiting Devin's ailing father when I would rather run errands. Mainly, paying attention, being engaged with the stuff that enlivens my family, micro decisions that may not bring the instant gratification of achievement, but that will be the wise investment in the end.

It was Vivian, in fact, who breathed life into this theoretical distinction between the short-term zing of achievement and the deep-rooted love of family. It was few days before I traveled to Newport News to try to qualify for the Senior Games. Viv, then nineteen, dropped by the house as I was rolling my bike toward the door for a training ride.

"I'm so proud of you, Barbie," she said.

"But why?" I asked. "I haven't qualified yet."

"Because you broke your collarbone and got back on your bike."

I looked at her, truly puzzled. The insight penetrated my brain at a glacial pace, so foreign was the thought. Viv didn't admire me for my performance; she admired me for my persistence. Viv cared little about whether I won a race five days hence, but she cared greatly that I was robust, and fulfilled, and a little brave. The world discards; family gathers, family provides a shelter in the storm. I have much to learn from Vivian, and happily for me, I have many years to do so.

ONE FINAL STORY

Thursday, June 19, 2014

Let me end by looking beyond midlife, to the future years, to the secret of living with purpose and contentment right through our final days. This brings me to my mother. After all my research, I have concluded that a middle-aged person like me can find no better road map for the second half of life than my mother's daily routines.

True, her physical world has narrowed mainly to a 2,000-square-foot apartment. But her family and social worlds thrive. She traveled to New Jersey to watch her grandson graduate from college, and plans to be at the youngest grandson's graduation when she is ninety-six. She invites friends one and two generations younger to her home for lunch, insisting on hearing every detail of their lives, offering compliments or, when asked, thoughtful advice. Her intellectual world knows no boundaries. Sustained by her voracious appetite for news, she roams widely through debates and catastrophes here and abroad. She will be passionate, engaged, and open to ideas that fly in the face of her worldview to her last day. I hope to do the same.

Today, when I walked into Mom's living room and sat down in my usual chair, she pointed to *The New York Times*. The lead story described how the Republicans in Congress planned to sue President Obama for using his executive powers to push through his agenda, since he could not persuade Congress to pass his legislation.

"Honey, the Republicans are unrecognizable," announced my

mother, who is a lifelong Republican. "I think I'm going to change my party affiliation."

My first thought was: *You're ninety-two. You will be ninety-five when the next presidential election comes around.*

My second thought was: *Bully for you, Mom.*

"I think you should," I said. "I can help you with that."

"Oh, thank you, honey," Mom said, and then we switched to her favorite subject: Ajax, the dog.

As I half listened to the adventures of her Cavalier King Charles spaniel, which largely entailed sleeping on the couch or barking furiously at airplanes, my mind wandered back to election day, 2008. Mom was eighty-seven. She had not yet had her hip replaced; she walked painfully, and sparingly. But I knew that my mother, who had never voted for a Democrat, admired Barack Obama. On the morning of the election, I offered to take her to the polls.

"Oh, honey, thank you," she said, "but I think I'll just stay tucked in today."

"Mom, this is a pretty historic day," I countered. "Obama might become the first African-American president. Do you really want to miss taking part in it?"

She paused a few seconds, and I could imagine her steeling herself for the pain.

"You're absolutely right, honey," she said. "Thank you."

The line at the polling station snaked out of the building and down the block for at least a half-mile. Under our big umbrella, we were dry and garrulous, chatting with strangers, impervious to the downpour. We finally arrived at a cavernous room with a dozen curtained booths. Mom limped into one of them, cane in hand. Moments later, she emerged, and I could see on her face the gravity and the elation of the moment.

My mother glanced around. A few feet away stood an elderly

African-American woman, a poll watcher, directing traffic. They looked at each other, and these two octogenarians, one white, one black, walked to each other and hugged. They embraced for several seconds, in a silent acknowledgment that they—that we—had crossed over to a place where skin color was no longer a barrier to the most powerful job in the world. Then they drew apart, looked each other in the eye, and smiled.

This explains, in part, why Mom flourishes into her nineties. For as long as I have been an adult and conscious of such things, she has swum against the stream of habituated opinion. She possesses the humility of intellect to consider new ideas, yet the confidence of intellect to allow her to settle on a conclusion. She never takes the judgments of other people as gospel, much less that of political parties. She is always learning, reading, listening, evaluating. She is never on autopilot, which is why this white woman, who grew up in a wealthy Boston suburb where black people came in the back door, could vote for Barack Obama. It is why, at ninety-two, she was toying with changing her party affiliation. It is why she—with the help of Ajax the dog—will live to be one hundred.

AFTERWORD:
SIXTEEN SUGGESTIONS
FOR MIDLIFE

As I review the research and the stories in this book, some insights bear repeating. I started with more than a hundred of them, but that seemed a bit ambitious. Allow me to submit these sixteen suggestions for a meaningful midlife.

On Aging Well

If you feel the midlife blues, remember that everyone else does, too—and your most joyous years are ahead of you.

Aim for meaning and not happiness, and you will find both.[1]

Ask yourself regularly: How will I use these glorious days for the best purpose?

The middle-aged brain is a thing of wonder. It can learn any new trick—if you challenge it.

On Living Exuberantly

At every stage of life, you should be a rookie at something.[2]
Midlife can be like Kansas, long and flat. Creating a goal will
    energize your days.

On the Power of Thought

It's harder to hurt when you're laughing.
Take trouble in stride: A few setbacks are just what the doctor
    ordered.
Watch your thoughts: Your thinking shapes your experience.

On Doing Good Work

If possible, go for Plan A. And it's possible more often than not.
Pivoting on your strengths beats starting from scratch.
Redefine success according to your values, not those of the rest
    of the world.

On Choosing What Matters Most

Pay attention: The biggest threat to seasoned marriages is mu-
    tual neglect.
Do you value that relationship? Then cut him some slack.
It's dangerous at the periphery.
As George Vaillant noted, happiness is love. Full stop.

ACKNOWLEDGMENTS

Jake Morrissey, my editor at Penguin/Riverhead, is a man of courage. Faced with a project that could easily have filled a dozen volumes, he took a risk and pushed forward. Jake exhibited superhuman patience when midlife complications upended my schedule, and he brought fresh insight to every carefully edited page. I should know by now just to accept all of Jake's suggestions. He is always right. Add to that his wicked sense of humor, and I am one lucky author. Kevin Murphy has answered every administrative question with cheer and alacrity. Dorian Hastings cleaned up every sentence in the copyedit, no small feat. Finally, Katie Freeman and Liz Hohenadel crafted a publicity campaign with smarts and enthusiasm, and gamely tried to work around my (social media) shortcomings.

My determined and farsighted agent, Raphael Sagalyn, saw merit in this project even when I had my doubts. He talked me down from the ledge when broken bones and family responsibilities wreaked havoc. I am grateful to have so respected an agent as Rafe in my court.

The central question of this book—*How does one thrive at midlife?*—set me adrift on an ocean of research that had no discernible boundaries. Fortunately for me, I found two talented young journalists to work alongside me. Breann Schossow plunged into the studies, conducted interviews, and tried to teach me social media; by the time she moved on, Bre could finish my sentences. Desiré Moses rode to my rescue after I broke my collarbone, driving me to interviews, creating spreadsheets to keep track of a thousand stories, and turning up research I never would have found on my own. Sarah Knight, a research librarian at NPR, routinely saved the day with her creative searches. Finally, I am not sure when this project would have been finished without the aid of Sarah Mason, who transcribed dozens of interviews as fast as I could upload the audio.

Journalism, whether a four-minute radio story or a 400-page book, rests on an odd social contract. The journalist asks people to carve out time to explain their research or tell their personal stories. In return they receive a few paragraphs or a quote. Some people do not even receive that, a sad but inevitable fact in a book that involved more than four hundred interviews. I want to thank some of these unnamed sources who shaped this book, knowing that, once again, I will miss many others.

My appreciation goes to those who gave me insight into the midlife condition through their personal journeys. Kathleen Sellers gathered a focus group of friends in Virginia; Molly Molpus did the same in Cleveland. My NPR colleagues Jennifer Ludden and Gerry Holmes introduced me to happy couples (Chris Connolly and Tony Hake; Carl Bergeron and Courtney Dunakin; Susan and Jimmy Kemp; and Michael and Sarah). I learned much from Marta Satin Smith and David Smith, as well as from Jen MacLeod and Daryl LeBlanc, and Emma Sellers's friends Lucille and William Randolph. Helen White is an inspiration as a sixty-something senior athlete. Colonel Gregory Gadson, India Penney, Sarah Glatz, and Maria Montoya showed me what resilience looks like, in both attitude and career, as did Chris Dionigi, Bob Paterno, Jeff Norris, Sue Burton, Leslie Nickel, and John Guislin.

Many researchers also molded this book selflessly and without much credit. On aging well: Karl Pillimer at Cornell University and author Bronnie Ware. On the midlife brain: David Balota and Kathleen McDermott at Washington University, Sandra Bond Chapman at the University of Texas at Dallas, Erin Costanzo at the University of Wisconsin, Kateri McRae at the University of Denver, and Robert Wilson at Rush University Medical Center.

On training the midlife brain: Sharan Merriam at the University of Georgia, Sylvain Moreno at Simon Fraser University, Carol Hoare at George Washington University, and Victoria Marsick at Columbia University's Teachers College. On midlife friendship and marriage: author Carlin Flora, James Fowler at the University of California at San Diego, Alexis Seubert and Rene Morrissette at Little Brothers Friends of the Elderly, and research psychologists Bianca Acevedo and Galen Buckwalter. On resilience: David Spiegel at Stanford University School of Medicine, Keith Bellizzi at the University of Connecticut, Alicia Crum at Stanford University, and trauma experts Lynda and Daniel King. On career: Doug Dickson was one of many career experts who imparted wisdom, along with Teri-E Belf, Mary Radu, David Corbett, Nick Lore, Sandra Mobley, Jay Bloom, Lester Strong, and Nancy Morrow Howell.

On a personal note, my friends rooted me on at the starting line, during the long middle, and right through to the finish line. Diane Bless gave me back my voice, through her friendship and voice therapy sessions. Frank Sesno offered me a perch at George Washington University; he and I commiserated, and supported each other, through our book-writing journeys. NPR was exceedingly generous when I asked for a second book leave in six years; for their support, encouragement, and friendship, I want to thank Margaret Low Smith (now at *The Atlantic*), Chris Turpin, Steve Drummond, and Cindy Johnston, to name just a few in my NPR family. I received prayers and encouragement from friends at church, beginning with my pastor, David Hanke, and including Elizabeth and Wray Fitch, Mary and Logan Breed, Rachael and Griffin Foster, Libby Boulter, and Jan and Gary Haugen. My spiritual directors, Susan Bowers Baker at the Jesuit Center in Wernersville, Pennsylvania, and Martina O'Shea in Washington, D.C., also provided spiritual guidance, as did Father Tom Reese, who, besides being winsome, funny, and a bestselling author, is unembarrassed about his love for God. George Sanchez improved my appearance considerably during and after taking my photo. Steve Levin deserves a mention for his creative attempts at titling this book and, more fundamentally, for his constant and hilarious friendship.

Mike Adsit has received considerable space in these pages, but not enough thanks. Without Mike, there would be no Senior Games for me, no broken collarbone (!), no need to overcome acute adversity. I might have found my midlife passion for cycling without him, but maybe not; plus, he drove to Minneapolis just to coach me through my races. My life is much richer because of Mike.

Obviously this book would be far drabber without the vibrant presence of my mother, Mary Ann Bradley, who reminds me daily that one's nineties can be vigorous and engaged; her vitality is a thing of wonder. As for my brother and his wife, David and Katherine Bradley: It is true, they leave a large public wake, whether in journalism or education reform, but their success runs deeper, in character, generosity, insight, and humor. I am lucky indeed to have them in my corner.

Aside from Sandra Day, our thirteen-year-old retriever, who padded after me every morning at five a.m. and kept constant, if dozing, vigil during the long hours of writing, two others carried me through this project. Vivian Grace Hagerty, my twenty-one-year-old stepdaughter, has taught me much about unconditional love. Her quick intelligence, classic beauty, and deep kindness make her the most remarkable young person I know. I feel like Maria in *The Sound of Music*: I must have done something good.

And what can I say about Devin, who believed in this book, and in my abilities, from the start? You lived through the research, from listening to my daily findings to driving an RV. You spotted themes when I was drowning in details, you protected me from distractions when I needed to write, you gave me perspective when I despaired of ever finishing, you spent days carefully editing every page of this book: Talk about an act of generosity. You are my reward for waiting for love. You are my shelter in the storm.

NOTES

CHAPTER 2. PLEASE DON'T HAVE A MIDLIFE CRISIS

1. Elliott Jaques, "Death and the Mid-life Crisis," in Gabriele Junkers, ed., *Is It Too Late? Key Papers on Psychoanalysis and Ageing* (London: H. Karnac Books, 2006), 1–26; originally published in *International Journal of Psychoanalysis* 46 (1965): 502–14.
2. Ibid., 12.
3. Daniel Levinson, with C. N. Darrow, E. B. Klein, and M. Levinson, *The Seasons of a Man's Life* (New York: Alfred A. Knopf, 1978).
4. Ibid., preface, x.
5. Ibid., 199.
6. Gail Sheehy, *Passages: Predictable Crises of Adult Life* (New York: Bantam Books, 1974).
7. Susan K. Whitbourne, *The Search for Fulfillment: Revolutionary New Research That Reveals the Secret to Long-term Happiness* (New York: Ballantine Books, 2010).
8. Susan K. Whitbourne, *The Me I Know: A Study of Adult Identity* (New York: Springer-Verlag, 1986).
9. Orville Brim, who was then the director of the MacArthur Foundation Research Network on Successful Midlife Development, led the posse. See O. J. Brim, *Ambition* (New York: Basic Books, 1992).
10. Elaine Wethington, "Expecting Stress: Americans and the 'Midlife Crisis,'" *Motivation and Emotion* 24 (2000): 85–103.
11. Wethington says there is evidence that certain personalities are more likely to claim a midlife crisis: namely, people who see the world through the lens of crisis and catastrophe. They could develop a crisis-prone personality because of a trauma, for example, or a history of depression or alcoholism. "You are just more likely to react to adversity in life by calling it a crisis."
12. Susan Krauss Whitbourne said she found only one group of people to suffer from malaise: what she called the "Downward Slope" group, the people who looked successful in

college and even afterward, but throughout their lives made poor choices that left them unfulfilled. I asked how common such malaise was, noting that I see a sort of ennui among my journalist friends who look around and say, *Is this it? For the rest of my life?*

"I don't really think it's typical," Whitbourne said.

"Really?" I asked, surprised.

"No, I don't. I think the average person really just doesn't think that deeply about aging or their lives or their happiness or anything. I mean, the successful agers hardly ever do. They just minimize, deny, minimize, deny—just focus on the positive." She paused and looked at me, perched in front of her holding my microphone in one hand, taking notes with the other, earphones capping my head like earmuffs. "It may be the kind of job that people are in," she said. "If you're constantly faced with news that's depressing—you know, off in some rural area in Africa—it is really tough. You're preoccupied, and how can you not be? So I think the more you open yourself up to the full range of experiences, the harder it is to find a balance."

"So, I just picked a depressing career?"

"Apparently you did," Whitbourne agreed, laughing. "Journalism—so uplifting. That's why they have animal stories, right? I think it's for the journalists, not for the audience."

13. See M. E. Lachman, "Development in Midlife," *Annual Review of Psychology* 55 (2004): 305–31; and M. E. Lachman, S. Teshale, and S. Agrigoroaei, "Midlife as a Pivotal Period in the Life Course: Balancing Growth and Decline at the Crossroads of Youth and Old Age," *International Journal of Behavioral Development* 39, no. 1 (2015): 20–31.

14. Recently, Andrew Oswald began having doubts about the explanations for the midlife dip in happiness. The theories about angst, failure, self-forgiveness, and then, finally, appreciating the smaller joys of life—all those theories are fine when you are talking about humans.

But what if apes have midlife crises?

"In principle," he observed, "that would put a lot of theories into the dustbin."

A few years ago, Oswald heard that Alexander Weiss, a young lecturer in psychology at the University of Edinburgh, had gathered data on the happiness of apes. With Weiss's contacts in the worldwide zoo community, and Oswald's expertise on quadratic equations and happiness, they decided to ask this question: Do middle-aged apes suffer midlife crises? They recruited zookeepers in the United States, Australia, Canada, Japan, and Singapore who cared for a total of 508 chimpanzees and orangutans. The zookeepers, who had been tending to these apes for at least two years, knew their charges well enough to recognize their moods and know when they were off their feed.

The zookeepers were given a four-item questionnaire, which was, we are assured, "a well-established method for assessing positive affect in captive nonhuman primates." The zookeepers were first asked to rate how good (or bad) each ape's mood was. Then they were to assess "how much pleasure the subject derives from social situations." The third question queried how "successful the subject is in achieving its goals." And the fourth question (my personal favorite) asked the zookeeper to walk in the ape's shoes: How happy would the zookeeper be if he or she were that particular ape for a week?

Obviously, Oswald said, they cannot ask the apes what is going on in their heads.

"I don't know whether they want to have sex with younger apes, or want to jump up on the bars more, or want to have the equivalent of a sports car, but I do believe the keepers can tell their mood," Oswald said.

As it turned out, the zookeepers reported that apes between the ages of twenty-seven and thirty—which is the equivalent of the late forties in human years—seemed to fall into a midlife funk.

Obviously, apes do not have stressors such as mortgages, corporate downsizing, divorce, or concern about male-pattern baldness. So is it possible, I asked, that there is an evolutionary purpose for this U-shaped dip in happiness for midlife apes as well as humans?

"God, I don't know, Barbara! How would I know?" Oswald said, laughing. "It might be inefficient in midlife after the babies are born for nature to have us sitting around with our feet up, drinking English beer. Maybe it's best to make us discontented and then we go out and find new pastures to conquer—new lands like the United States, even though they eventually throw us out. And that might be good for the species. So maybe some discontent in the middle of life after you have the offspring might be a spur to the species."

But, he said, at this point it's all conjecture.

"It's probably more plausible than thinking that the apes look ahead on the time horizon, see that they're going to die, and think, 'Oh, I haven't accomplished all that I want to accomplish,'" I proposed.

"Yes, exactly," he said. "Although it's not impossible. Obviously the more that science goes on, the more we're discovering that apes are like us. So it's not impossible that one day we will discover that apes know they're going to die."

And maybe they will fret about forgetting why they came into the room. See A. Weiss, J. E. King, M. Inoue-Murayama, T. Matsuzawa, and A. J. Oswald, "Evidence for a Midlife Crisis in Great Apes Consistent with the U-Shape in Human Well-being," *Proceedings of the National Academy of Sciences* 109, no. 49 (2012): 19949–52.

15. D. G. Blanchflower and A. J. Oswald, "Is Well-being U-Shaped over the Life Cycle?" *Social Science & Medicine* 66, no. 8 (2008): 1733–49.

16. Osborne noted that "undoubtedly," some people will have no U-curve and others will have an extended or extreme U. "What we know is that that is the pattern on average. Just like some people can smoke until they're a hundred and twenty and still pull it off. But not very many." But Susan Krauss Whitbourne at the University of Massachusetts at Amherst believes the U-curve, particularly the upward swing in happiness after midlife, is a statistical artifact: "Who are the people who are still around at the end of the U?" she asks. "They're the ones that didn't die. . . . A lot of the risk-takers are gone, the unhappy people are gone, the people they can't get to, [such as] criminals." All this, she suggests, creates an illusion of midlife dip.

17. A. A. Stone, J. E. Schwartz, J. E. Broderick, and A. Deaton, "A Snapshot of the Age Distribution of Psychological Well-being in the United States," *Proceedings of the National Academy of Sciences* 107, no. 22 (2010): 9985–90.

18. One major exception may be the Russians. Carol Graham of the Brookings Institution scrutinized answers from the Gallup World Poll from 2011 to 2013, and found that happiness in Russia peaks at age fifteen and rolls inexorably downhill from then on—until

age ninety-one, when, presumably, sweet sleep awaits. See Christopher Ingraham, "The Data Are In: Life Under Putin Is a Continuous Downward Spiral into Despair," *Washington Post,* April 1, 2014.

19. This all raises the question: Why? With the exception of the Russians, why are people most miserable when they are at the top of their careers (and presumably, earning power), when their health is still good and their brains have not yet (really) atrophied? Why is being older, creakier, more forgetful, more aware that death is breathing down your neck or the necks of your loved ones cause for celebration? Arthur Stone admits this is "the big puzzle." One theory, he told NPR, is that "when you're younger, you're making decisions with a forward-looking, aspirational head about you. That is, you're looking to achieve things in life. And that may mean that you're not really focusing on your current well-being. When you get older, you sort of know where you are in life. You stop looking forward quite so much, and you start focusing on smaller things in life, like being with friends and families or hobbies or volunteering, that bring you immediate satisfaction." See interview with Guy Raz on NPR's *Weekend All Things Considered,* May 30, 2010, http://www.npr.org/templates/story/story.php?storyId=127279055.

20. This is what his next act looked like when I checked back a year later: Cliff's leukemia had gone into remission and he had landed a job. After Cliff was out of the woods, Gene moved to China for a year, where he was learning Mandarin and teaching English to kindergartners. He loved his work and hoped to parlay the experience and language into a new career in San Francisco. "I am not sure what will come of this when I get back next June, but after everything, this is where I landed," he wrote. "Some guys in their late forties buy a Porsche. I came to China."

21. Howard S. Friedman and Leslie R. Martin, *The Longevity Project* (New York: Hudson Street Press, 2011). Among these gems about how to live a long life: It is a bad idea to enroll your child in first grade before the age of six, because he or she is less likely to learn to play well with other children. Another tidbit that falls into the schadenfreude category for me and others with an average IQ: The smartest Terman kids did no better, or worse, than their less gifted peers, having landed in professions such as policeman, seaman, typist, and filing clerk. This result forced Lewis Terman to conclude, "We have seen that intellect and achievement are far from perfectly correlated." See Lewis Terman and Melita Oden, *The Gifted Child Grows Up: Twenty-five Years' Follow-up of a Superior Group,* Genetic Studies of Genius, vol. 4 (Stanford, CA: Stanford University Press, 1947), 352.

22. The extroverts in the Terman study tended to do risky things—getting drunk, driving too fast—and died younger. The optimists tended to gloss over warning signs—*Oh, I won't worry about that cough,* or *I don't need to back up my computer*—which often resulted in calamity. But the conscientious men and women saw their doctors, took their medicines, wore seat belts, and—this is key—were drawn to other conscientious people. For those of us who were shy and less than glamorous as children (and adults), this was happy news indeed.

23. Terman and Oden, *Longevity Project,* 147.

24. Leslie Martin, interview by Jennifer Ludden, *Talk of the Nation,* National Public Radio, March 24, 2011.

25. George E. Vaillant, *Triumphs of Experience: The Men of the Harvard Grant Study* (Cambridge, MA: Belknap Press, 2012), 52.

26. Initially, Vaillant pushed back. "I said, 'Pooh-pooh,' and for the first ten years as I followed the men from forty to fifty, second marriages didn't look that terrific," he said. "I wasn't impressed. But by the time the men were eighty, many of the happiest marriages were fifty-year marriages, and many of them were second, third, and in one case, even a fifth marriage."

For example, a man the researchers called John Adams married three times in the first half of his life; he met his fourth wife at age forty-five and lived happily with her for more than forty years. He was still alive when *Triumphs of Experience* went to press.

"What you're suggesting," I said, "is that, done right, you can have a good second and third marriage. You can still get a divorce and pull it off."

"Absolutely," Vaillant said. Which is precisely what he has done.

27. Vaillant, *Triumphs of Experience,* 352.

28. Ibid., 234.

29. Later, Waldinger's secret came out in an offhand remark about his meditation group. As it happens, at Robert Waldinger's core was a yawning spiritual hunger. When he was fifty-four—eight years earlier—he began to practice Buddhist meditation. In a few days, he would shave his head and be ordained as a Zen Buddhist priest. It was not his newfound peace that he found so appealing. It was the new sense of meaning, and a connection that transcends the particular person and the specific moment.

CHAPTER 3. CAN A MIDLIFE BRAIN REMEMBER NEW TRICKS?

1. Dellis claims that anyone can do what he does—and that his feats of memory have nothing to do with IQ and everything to do with imagination. When he sees the king of clubs, he imagines Tiger Woods. The queen of clubs is Paris Hilton. He has an image for every card, and with each one he sees, he builds a little narrative. "You're creating these stories that are very vivid and colorful. That is, essentially, just paying an extreme amount of attention to something, and that's why it works." Like the middle-aged contestants, Nelson Dellis is also driven by fear of losing his memory. His grandmother, who died in 2009, had Alzheimer's disease. He promised himself that he would never succumb to the same fate if he could help it; he started training to build up "cognitive reserve," a neural cushion to protect against dementia. Dellis became "obsessed" with training, he says, and within two years he had won the USA Memory Championship. I would later learn that whether or not he can build up cognitive reserve through brain training is a matter of fierce scientific debate.

2. K. Anders Ericsson does not believe Mental Athletes, or MAs as they are called, are born with unique brains. The psychology professor at Florida State University is one of the people most credited with changing our view of human memory, at least in modern times. In 1981, as a Ph.D. student at Carnegie Mellon University, Ericsson and psychology professor Bill Chase challenged the academic wisdom about short-term memory. Specifically, they tackled the theory proposed by Harvard psychologist George Miller in his 1956 paper that argued that the human brain could not remember more than seven, or at best nine, numbers at a time. See G. A. Miller, "The Magical Number Seven, Plus or Minus Two: Some Limits on Our Capacity for Processing Information," *Psychological Review* 101, no. 2 (1994): 343.

Their secret weapon in this bold frontal assault was an undergraduate identified as "SF," who worked for them in exchange for reduced tuition.

"Was he extraordinarily bright?" I asked Ericsson.

"No," Ericsson said carefully. "In fact, he was very average in terms of his SAT and other types of measures that we had."

In an experiment surely unrivaled for both its monotony and its difficulty, SF listened as someone read out numbers at a rate of one per second, and then tried to repeat back as many as he could remember. At first, true to Miller's theory, SF struggled to recall eight digits. But as he practiced hour after hour—250 hours over two years—he began to make breakthroughs. SF, a runner, began turning numbers into something meaningful for him. For example, the number 359 became 3 minutes, 59 seconds, for the time Roger Bannister broke the four-minute mile. By grouping numbers into "chunks" and imbuing them with personal meaning, this average student was able to store the numbers in long-term memory, which has an unlimited capacity. Eventually SF could remember eighty numbers in a row. See K. A. Ericsson and W. G. Chase, "Exceptional Memory: Extraordinary Feats of Memory Can Be Matched or Surpassed by People with Average Memories That Have Been Improved by Training," *American Scientist* 70 (1982): 607–15.

"Were you surprised he did as well as he did?" I asked Ericsson.

"I think it was a magical process when he started to improve well beyond what these early investigators had found," he said. "But that is the key idea behind expert performance—that what you're developing is not expanding your general capacities, or your IQ, or whatever. You're really building up this new structure that allows you to perform at a vastly better level than other people."

In the case of most Mental Athletes, the structure that allows them to memorize not just numbers but names, faces, and decks of cards is an imaginary building called a "memory palace." Alternatively known as the method of *loci* ("locations" in Latin), this method traces back to 477 B.C. and a Greek poet, Simonides of Ceos. After reciting his poetry before a large audience, he left the banquet hall. Moments later, the building collapsed, killing everyone inside. Simonides was able to identify every person in the room, moving from table to table in his mind's eye. Twenty-five hundred years later, those intent on remembering grocery lists do likewise, turning familiar places into memory palaces, placing one grocery item after another in strategic spots: broken eggs oozing down the front door, orange juice tipped over onto the front hall table, rib-eye steaks being wolfed down by your dog standing on the coffee table. And on and on.

I mentioned to Ericsson that this seems beyond the ken of a normal person.

"I don't see a lot of evidence suggesting that their brains are different," he replied.

"Could anyone do this?" I asked.

"The question is: Do we know the reason why people would *not* be able to do it if they were motivated enough to do the practice?" he asked rhetorically. "I would say no to that question."

3. Happily, the next set was easier, a testament to the vagaries of intelligence. Stegman tested me on how many numbers I could recite back—first forward (nine), then backward (eight). She gave me series of numbers and letters and told me to rearrange them in my head, putting the numbers first, in ascending order, then the letters, in alphabetical order. It was easy up to five or six; after that I became muddled. But it turns out my auditory memory is quite good, something of an advantage for a radio reporter.

4. S. M. Jaeggi, M. Buschkuehl, J. Jonides, and W. J. Perrig, "Improving Fluid Intelligence with Training on Working Memory," *Proceedings of the National Academy of Sciences* 105, no. 19 (2008): 6829–33.

5. H. Stepankova, J. Lukavsky, M. Buschkuehl, et al., "The Malleability of Working Memory and Visuospatial Skills: A Randomized Controlled Study in Older Adults," *Developmental Psychology* 50, no. 4 (2014): 1049.

6. More recently, two meta-analyses—which summarize the effect of brain training across different training studies—found that brain training that improves working memory also affects fluid intelligence. "Which does not mean that the field is not controversial anymore," Jaeggi wrote me. See J. Au, E. Sheehan, N. Tsai, et al., "Improving Fluid Intelligence with Training on Working Memory: A Meta-analysis," *Psychonomic Bulletin & Review* 22, no. 2 (2014): 366–77; and J. Karbach and P. Verhaeghen, "Making Working Memory Work: A Meta-analysis of Executive-Control and Working Memory Training in Older Adults," *Psychological Science* 25, no. 11 (2014): 2027–37.

7. Peter Brown, Henry L. Roediger III, and Mark A. McDaniel, *Make It Stick: The Science of Successful Learning* (Cambridge, MA: Belknap Press, 2014).

8. D. M. Burke, D. G. MacKay, J. S. Worthley, and E. Wade, "On the Tip of the Tongue: What Causes Word Finding Failures in Young and Older Adults?" *Journal of Memory and Language* 30, no. 5 (1991): 542–79.

9. C. L. Grady, M. V. Springer, D. Hongwanishkul, A. R. McIntosh, and G. Winocur, "Age-Related Changes in Brain Activity Across the Adult Lifespan," *Journal of Cognitive Neuroscience* 18, no. 2 (2006): 227–41.

10. Grady believes something may be going wrong in the switch that controls which brain networks come online and which ones dim. She and others suspect that the frontal parietal control network—which has connections with most other brain networks—may grow feeble and less decisive as the brain ages. For example, Grady says, if she is working at her computer, her motor network and her visual network are active, because she is typing and looking at the words. "Then if some noise happens off in the corridor while I'm working in my office, that might distract me because now the *auditory* network has come online," she says. "Maybe I'm not so good at suppressing my *default* network, so while I'm sitting here working on my computer, I find myself thinking about my book club meeting last night."

11. Oh, one more piece of bad news, this one exclusively for the ladies. When you have reached, say, fifty-three (to pick an age out of the hat), tomorrow is often not a better day, at least for the brain. Especially for the brains of menopausal women. Apparently the "brain fog" of menopause is a scientifically proven phenomenon. Researchers at the University of Vermont College of Medicine scanned the brains of twenty-three women, twelve of them (uncharitably) labeled "cognitive complainers," and thirteen classified as "noncomplainers." When given a working–memory test, the brains of the complainers had to recruit more brain resources and work harder to achieve the same performance. This may, or may not, hint at pathology and dementia down the road. See J. A. Dumas, A. M. Kutz, B. C. McDonald, et al., "Increased Working Memory–Related Brain Activity in Middle-aged Women with Cognitive Complaints," *Neurobiology of Aging* 34, no. 4 (2013): 1145–47.

    Adding to the misery, researchers at the University of Rochester Medical Center found that those who complained of memory problems not only worked harder to remember, but also remembered less. They performed worse on working-memory tests—the ability to manipulate new information, which could explain why it is suddenly more difficult to calculate a tip or adjust one's itinerary on the fly when a flight is canceled. The menopausal "complainers" (really, isn't this piling on?) had more trouble focusing their attention as well, which may explain why an author might find it difficult to finish her book on deadline. See M. T. Weber, M. Mapstone, J. Staskiewicz, and P. M. Maki, "Reconciling Subjective Memory Complaints with Objective Memory Performance in the Menopausal Transition," *Menopause* 19, no. 7 (2012): 735.

"If a woman approaching menopause feels she is having memory problems, no one should brush it off or attribute it to a jam-packed schedule," said Miriam Weber, neuropsychologist at University of Rochester Medical Center, who led the study. "She can find comfort in knowing that there are new research findings that support her experience. She can view her experience as normal."

Well, I'm comforted. But I'm not sure about her fix: When someone gives you a new piece of information, she advised, "it might be helpful to repeat it out loud." See "'Brain Fog' of Menopause Confirmed," *ScienceDaily,* March 14, 2012.

12. "Hearing Loss in Older Adults May Compromise Cognitive Resources for Memory," *ScienceDaily*, August 16, 2005, citing A. Wingfield, P. A. Tun, and S. L. McCoy, "Hearing Loss in Adulthood: What It Is and How It Interacts with Cognitive Performance," *Current Directions in Psychological Science* 14, no. 3 (2005): 144–48.

Subsequent studies brought worse news. Dr. Frank Lin at Johns Hopkins University School of Medicine followed some two thousand older adults for nearly eight years. He and his colleagues discovered that people with mild hearing problems saw their cognition decline *41 percent more every year* than those who had no hearing problems. In another study, in which he tracked more than six hundred people over twelve years, he found that for every ten-decibel loss in hearing, the risk of dementia rose 20 percent. See F. R. Lin, E. J. Metter, R. J. O'Brien, et al., "Hearing Loss and Incident Dementia," *Archives of Neurology* 68, no. 2 (2011): 214–20.

13. For an excellent (and readable) summary of their findings, see K. W. Schaie and S. L. Willis, "Mind Alert: Intellectual Functioning in Adulthood," Special Lecture, Joint Conference of the American Society on Aging and the National Council on the Aging, March 2005, sharepoint.washington.edu/uwsom/sls/Documents/MindAlert.pdf.

14. One explanation is the so-called Flynn effect, named after Professor James R. Flynn, who documented how the general IQ scores of a population changed over time. See J. R. Flynn, "IQ Gains over Time," in R. J. Sternberg, ed., *Encyclopedia of Human Intelligence* (New York: Macmillan, 1994), 617–23. Researchers have noticed that the IQ scores of people around the world have been steadily rising since the 1930s—about three points per decade in the United States. They say that the rise in IQ, which measures both fluid and crystallized intelligence, has been too rapid for genetic selection, and is probably the result of better education and nutrition, smaller families, and greater (technological) complexity. Another explanation: Maybe we got better at taking IQ tests.

15. Sherry Willis proved that with a little training, older people could regain their processing speed, memory, and reasoning abilities. She and colleagues worked with 2,832 cognitively intact elderly adults who participated in a clinical trial called ACTIVE (Advanced Cognitive Training for Independent and Vital Elderly). They visited them in their homes and conducted ten one-hour training sessions over several weeks. The train-

ers helped some brush up in memory skills, some in processing speed, some in reasoning skills. The people who had declined significantly in inductive reasoning and memory scored as high on tests as they had fourteen years earlier. Others performed better than their younger selves. The groups who learned strategies for reasoning and processing speed held on to those improvements for ten years. Just for fun, one researcher culled through Seattle driving accident records and found that these two groups had 50 percent fewer accidents than those who received no training.

But as pleased as Willis is with these results, she says midlifers need to start protecting their brains as early as possible. The brain begins to have significant changes in its forties—just when we're busiest, just when we're reaching peak performance. That can lull us into a dangerous trap. "Sometimes we're so busy that we defer things," she says, such as exercise, or a healthy diet, or cognitively challenging hobbies. "But I think people really need to seriously ask themselves: 'How am I preparing for the second half of life?' And the importance of developing habits or patterns of living is certainly a lot easier then than it's going to be later. And you need time to develop those. You need a good five to . . . fifteen years to hone those important lifestyle [habits] before you hit older ages." See George W. Rebok, Karlene Ball, Lin T. Guey, et al., "Ten-Year Effects of the Advanced Cognitive Training for Independent and Vital Elderly Cognitive Training Trial on Cognition and Everyday Functioning in Older Adults," *Journal of the American Geriatrics Society* 62, no. 1 (2014): 16–24.

Also (for accident records) see K. Ball, J. D. Edward, L. A. Ross, and G. McGwin Jr., "Cognitive Training Decreases Motor Vehicle Collision Involvement of Older Drivers," *Journal of the American Geriatrics Society* 58, no. 11 (2010): 2107–13.

16. J. L. Taylor, Q. Kennedy, A. Noda, and J. A. Yesavage, "Pilot Age and Expertise Predict Flight Simulator Performance: A 3-Year Longitudinal Study," *Neurology* 68, no. 9 (2007): 648–54.

17. Even in a job that requires quick decision-making with little margin for error, such as directing air traffic, older employees kept up. Arthur Kramer at the University of Illinois compared two groups of air traffic controllers, one with an average age of fifty-seven, the other group on average twenty-four years old. (He traveled to Canada for the study, since the retirement age for air traffic controllers in the United States is fifty-five.) Kramer put them through hours of cognitive testing and then asked them to simulate their daily work. He found the senior controllers performed as well as the younger controllers. Their processing speed was slower, but they used their experience to head off (simulated) midair collisions. In two key tests—imagining three-dimensional planes from two-dimensional images on the screen, and sorting through complex, sometimes conflicting information—the air traffic controllers performed equally well. Experience, if not trumped, then at least equaled fast thinking. See Ashley Nunes and Arthur F. Kramer, "Experience-Based Mitigation of Age-Related Performance Declines: Evidence from Air Traffic Control," *Journal of Experimental Psychology: Applied* 15, no. 1 (2009): 12–24.

18. D. Park and P. Reuter-Lorenz, "The Adaptive Brain: Aging and Neurocognitive Scaffolding," *Annual Reviews of Psychology* 60, no. 1 (2009): 21–24.

19. Yaakov Stern says you can try to understand brain reserve as hardware or as software. When you look at the physical brain, some people are born with larger brains and more neural connections. Their brains are New York City, with more acreage for the streets

and tunnels, which makes them more vibrant and resilient than, say, Peoria, Illinois (sorry, Peoria). Recently, scientists have discovered that brain reserve can be increased, just as people keep developing new property in the suburbs of New York.

What fascinates Stern is the brain's software, a process by which your brain somehow moves information—such as the name of a friend—out of long-term storage to the language area of the brain, without getting bogged down in the mud of dementia or the plaques and tangles of Alzheimer's disease. He doesn't know how the software works. Maybe people blessed with cognitive reserve have more neural connections. Or maybe those people have more efficient brains, "so that even if they're impaired by the pathology of it, they can still maintain performance," Stern says. "You know, like a car with more horsepower, you can pull out a cylinder and it can still keep going."

Or, he suggests, perhaps some brains have many different pathways to send the information, and if the Lincoln Tunnel is congested, they take the Holland Tunnel.

"Like when my daughter was learning seven plus six and she had to remember that it's thirteen," Stern says. "She was working very hard to remember that fact. I said, 'Here's a good way to do it. Why don't you do seven plus three plus three?' You have various approaches so it gives you more ways to solve this problem, sort of a flexibility of problem solving."

20. See D. A. Bennett, J. A. Schneider, A. S. Buchman, et al., "Overview and Findings from the Rush Memory and Aging Project," *Current Alzheimer Research* 9, no. 6 (2012): 646. We will delve deeper into this happy finding in chapter 5.

21. Y. Stern, B. Gurland, T. K. Tatemichi, et al., "Influence of Education and Occupation on the Incidence of Alzheimer's Disease," *JAMA* 271, no. 13 (1994): 1004–10.

22. In one study, for example, Brandeis researchers Margie Lachman and Patricia Tun found that college-educated seventy-year-olds performed as well on memory tests as high school–educated sixty-year-olds. See P. A. Tun and M. E. Lachman, "Age Differences in Reaction Time and Attention in a National Telephone Sample of Adults: Education, Sex, and Task Complexity Matter," *Developmental Psychology* 44, no. 5 (2008): 1421.

23. N. Scarmeas, G. Levy, M. X. Tang, and Y. Stern, "Influence of Leisure Activity on the Incidence of Alzheimer's Disease," *Neurology* 57, no. 12 (2001): 2236–42.

24. Tun and Lachman, "Age Differences in Reaction Time and Attention." In a study two years later, researchers looked at all sorts of activities and once again found that three cognitive activities per week put high school–educated older people on a par, memory-wise, with college graduates. See S. Agrigoroaei and M. E. Lachman, "Cognitive Functioning in Midlife and Old Age: Combined Effects of Psychosocial and Behavioral Factors," *Journals of Gerontology, Series B: Psychological Sciences and Social Sciences,* 66B.Supp 1 (2011): i130–40.

25. Engagement becomes a must for those with the APO e4 allele, considered the most significant risk factor in late-onset Alzheimer's. The most intellectually active people across their lifetime suffered cognitive problems nine years later than those who were least engaged. See P. Vemuri, T. G. Lesnick, S. A. Przybelski, et al., "Association of Lifetime Intellectual Enrichment with Cognitive Decline in the Older Population," *JAMA Neurology* 71, no. 8 (2014): 1017–24.

26. D. C. Park, J. Lodi-Smith, L. M. Drew, et al., "The Impact of Sustained Engagement on Cognitive Function in Older Adults: The Synapse Project," *Psychological Science* 25, no. 1 (2014): 103–12.

27. At this point, Denise Park paused, reflecting on her own life. "I've changed jobs a few times in my life, maybe four or five times, which for a college professor is a lot," she said. One year, she moved from the University of Georgia to the University of Michigan in Ann Arbor. She was a single mother with two children and suddenly had to negotiate a completely new world. "I had this intuition that I felt so much smarter. I just seemed more alive and mentally active than I'd ever been in my life."

At first she dismissed it as ridiculous. But now she believes, based on brain science, that the move honed her mind. "I mean, you have to think about: Well, where did you park your car? Where's the drinking fountain? How do you get to the bank? And all of the simple tasks of everyday living are a small to large mental challenge, depending on your situation. And so I've come to believe that there's a lot of stimulation that comes from moving to a new environment."

28. And the most exciting news about neurogenesis comes from rats. The word on the street, Rutgers University neuroscientist Tracey Shors tells me, is that mice are smarter than rats. And yet, even with their lesser IQs, Shors has been able to elevate the game of generations of rats.

It all began with neurogenesis, a relatively new discovery that we humans, along with other species, create thousands of new brain cells every single day. Happily, they are born in the best of all possible places: the hippocampus, which is key to making and keeping memories, as well as learning new things. But Shors says that in a "nonstimulated environment"—that is, a boring environment—more than half of the cells die.

Back in the early 1990s, Shors began to wonder: How can we keep those brain cells alive? Scientists are barred from experimenting on human brains, so she turned to her beloved rats. She injected them with the drug BrdU (bromodeoxyuridine), which would label a "cohort" of cells born within a couple of hours. Then she could watch the life, or death, of those new brain cells. Shors could observe what Denise Park and so many others had deduced: To keep new brain cells alive, you have to challenge them.

"It has to be difficult," Shors told me, "meaning either the task itself must be difficult, or it must be difficult for the individual to learn. It has to be engaging. If something's really simple to learn, it's not enough to rescue these cells from death."

In her early studies, she found that nearly all the new brain cells survived if the rats were challenged. If not, all of them died. Her latest studies involve a "rotorod," a specially designed metal rod to test a rat's motor skills. It starts out rotating slowly, as in an easy log-rolling contest, then speeds up.

"It takes a little more skill than running on a treadmill," she said, and I began to laugh, imagining the scene. "You have to kind of hang on and put your whole body into it in order to stay on the rod, because the rod is turning faster and faster."

The rats that master this terrifying challenge preserve more brain cells.

"Sure enough, there are lots more cells," Shors exclaimed. "I think it may be because they're more encouraged or motivated."

Whether you are talking about the brains of rats or the brains of humans, she says, the way to preserve new brain cells is to impose novelty and a little pain.

"If we train animals on something they already know, it doesn't keep the cells alive. So to me, that's one of the pitfalls that sometimes happens when we get older. We tend to want to do the same things over and over."

People often ask her if doing crossword puzzles or playing guitar will preserve their brains. Those are fine activities, she says, but it would be better to tackle something more demanding, such as learning to speak Chinese or to play the ukulele. Even a variation on a theme would help.

"Say you did learn how to play guitar when you were in high school," Shors said. "Now you decide, I'm going to play the violin. You could take some of that information that you learned when you were young and apply it to this new situation. And by virtue of that information, you're going to be better. You can keep more cells alive. So even though it's good to go out of your comfort zone and pick something new, it doesn't have to be entirely new."

She sighed. "And, actually, at our age, nothing is entirely new."

29. Jaeggi and Buschkuehl emphasize that since I represent a single case study, they cannot determine whether any improvements I experienced were due to my improvement in working memory skills (that is, my training), my belief that the training actually helped (an expectancy or placebo effect), or both. In order to find out, they would need more participants, and a control group that trains on something other than working memory. In other words, they would have to compare my (and my group's) improvement against the improvement of a control group in order to really determine whether the training made me better. Still, Jaeggi maintains that the amount of improvement I showed is impressive and is likely to be more than a retest and expectancy effect.

CHAPTER 4. THE SHIFTING SANDS OF FRIENDSHIP

1. J. A. Coan, H. S. Schaefer, and R. J. Davidson, "Lending a Hand: Social Regulation of the Neural Response to Threat," *Psychological Science* 17, no. 12 (2006): 1032–39.

2. Coan realized he was thinking too much like a psychologist. Perhaps, he says, he should think like a behavioral ecologist. Ecologists think about habitats: A salamander likes a cool, dark, damp place to live. A bear likes a cave.

"But humans live everywhere," Coan says, in cold climates and warm, in tropical rain forests and deserts. "What if the human habitat is anything that includes another human? We create our own habitat and take it with us. What we see with animals, if they are in their habitat, [is that] they show less stress. So with humans, if we are with supportive people, we show less stress."

3. When you are in the company of a good friend or a trusted romantic partner ("trusted" being the operative word—more on that in the chapter on marriage), you are using the other person's mental resources. You are essentially expanding your mental territory.

"Your self literally gets larger and it expands to include not only the resources in your body, but the resources in *her* body," Coan says. "Your perception of the world changes and becomes less challenging. You have fewer things that you have to do by yourself and so you can either relax or do something other than deal with that threat."

It gets even more "mind-blowing," Coan says. Coan's scans show that we not only depend on our friends and partners, but our brains consider them part of us. Coan conducted a variation in the test. One person (in this case, Barb) is still in the brain scanner, but the electric shock is given to either a stranger or a trusted friend / romantic partner (in this case, Cherie). In study after study, when Coan threatened to shock the stranger, the threat regions of the test subject's brain showed virtually no activity. *Why do I care?* the brain seemed to say. *He's a stranger.* But when the test subject knew that a friend or romantic partner might receive a shock, then the test subject's brain lit up in almost the same way as it did when he worried about getting a shock himself. As far as the brain is concerned, Coan says, people close to us become part of ourselves.

Maybe Bill Clinton didn't really feel your pain. But your best friend did.

4. One of Coan's colleagues, Dennis Proffitt, found that a hill does not appear as steep when you are about to climb it with a friend. Friendship alters your visual perception, making the task look easier because you are tackling it with someone else. See S. Schnall, K. D. Harber, J. K. Stefanucci, and D. R. Proffitt, "Social Support and the Perception of Geographical Slant," *Journal of Experimental Social Psychology* 44, no. 5 (2008): 1246–55.

5. People sacrificed in pedestrian and operatic ways. Karen Scott, for example, donated her kidney to her best friend of thirty-three years. They met in second grade and shared the good moments. They were in each other's weddings. They live down the street from each other. They are godmothers to each other's children. Then came the harder stuff— kidney failure, and soon thereafter, her friend's mother was diagnosed with late-stage cancer. This theme recurred over and over: Long friendships rode the transition from (young) lives whose milestones bring joy and advancement, to middle years, when the milestones often carry loss and complication. "We used to talk about puberty and boys, then marriage and kids," Karen told me. "Now we're dealing with the death of our parents. This is midlife, and we're going to deal with everything together."

6. L. F. Berkman and S. L. Syme, "Social Networks, Host Resistance, and Mortality: A Nine-Year Follow-up Study of Alameda County Residents," *American Journal of Epidemiology* 109, no. 2 (1979): 186–204.

7. L. C. Giles, G. F. Glonek, M. A. Luszcz, and G. R. Andrews, "Effect of Social Networks on 10-Year Survival in Very Old Australians: The Australian Longitudinal Study of Aging," *Journal of Epidemiology and Community Health* 59, no. 7 (2005): 574–79.

8. C. H. Kroenke, L. D. Kubzansky, E. S. Schernhammer, M. D. Holmes, and I. Kawachi, "Social Networks, Social Support, and Survival After Breast Cancer Diagnosis," *Journal of Clinical Oncology* 24, no. 7 (2006): 1105–11.

9. K. Orth-Gomer, A. Rosengren, and L. Wilhelmsen, "Lack of Social Support and Incidence of Coronary Heart Disease in Middle-aged Swedish Men," *Psychosomatic Medicine* 55, no. 1 (1993): 37–43.

10. W. Ruberman, E. Weinblatt, J. D. Goldberg, and B. S. Chaudhary, "Psychosocial Influences on Mortality After Myocardial Infarction," *New England Journal of Medicine* 311, no. 9 (1984): 552–59.

11. As Nicholas Christakis and James Fowler have shown in a series of studies and in the book *Connected: The Surprising Power of Our Social Networks and How They Shape Our Lives* (New York: Little, Brown, 2009), few things chart your health and happiness as powerfully as friendship networks—for good or ill. On the ill side, if your friend becomes obese, you have a 57 percent higher chance of gaining weight yourself. Back pain spreads among friends, as do suicide and heavy drinking. On the good side, if your friend stops drinking or smoking, you are more likely to quit as well. And if your friend is happy, that will boost your happiness: The researchers calculated that a happy friend is worth more than a $10,000 raise.

12. N. Cable, M. Bartley, T. Chandola, and A. Sacker, "Friends Are Equally Important to Men and Women, but Family Matters More for Men's Well-being," *Journal of Epidemiology and Community Health* 67, no. 2 (2013): 166–77.

13. K. A. Ertel, M. M. Glymour, and L. F. Berkman, "Effects of Social Integration on Preserving Memory Function in a Nationally Representative U.S. Elderly Population," *American Journal of Public Health* 98, no. 7 (2008): 1215–20.

14. Teresa Seeman at UCLA added a twist on the friendship idea and arrived at the same place. She thought the studies might be overlooking a critical question—not just whether you have friends or not, but whether the relationships you have are good ones. She followed more than 3,500 adults, aged thirty-two and older, testing them on memory and executive function ten years apart. The people with a larger number of social contacts and warm relationships performed better at every age than those with fewer friends and more strained relationships.

    "If you have hundreds of Facebook friends," I asked Seeman, "are you all set? Or does the quality of those friendships matter more?"

    "It's not just having a bunch of relationships. It's the quality of those relationships that's really the driving force here," she said. "Which makes sense if you think about it. If you had a ton of relationships and fifty percent of them are really negative, that's not going to have a good outcome."

    The stress of bad relationships—spiking your cortisol (stress hormone) levels, raising blood pressure, inflaming the tissues, and weakening the immune system—will wear down your brain as well as your body. After all, Seeman says, the brain is just a muscle, albeit the one you can't do without. See T. E. Seeman, D. M. Miller-Martinez, S. S. Merkin, et al., "Histories of Social Engagement and Adult Cognition: Midlife in the U.S. Study," *Journals of Gerontology Series B: Psychological Sciences and Social Sciences* (2010): gbq091.

15. According to the U.S. Census Bureau, the percentage of unmarried people forty-five to sixty-five (that is, divorced, never married, separated, or widowed) has grown five percentage points in twenty years, from 31 percent to 36 percent (between March 1994 and 2013). See U.S. Census Bureau 2013 household survey (Current Population Survey Annual Social and Economic Supplement). For a superb article on the Gray Revolution, see I. F. Lin and S. L. Brown, "Unmarried Boomers Confront Old Age: A National Portrait," *Gerontologist* 52, no. 2 (2012): 153–65.

16. This group of women represents one slice in the sociology of singleness. It was summed up by a brutal but accurate tagline of a documentary I heard about, which described single Christian men and women in their thirties and forties: *"Cream of the crop meets bottom of the barrel."* The idea is that talented, ambitious, highly educated Christian men marry in their twenties. Talented, ambitious, highly educated Christian women defer marriage in favor of their careers. When the women look up at, say, age thirty-five, they find that all the suitably successful men are gone. Obviously this is a gross overstatement, but I must say, this rings true for me, and for many of my friends, particularly my Bible study group.

17. Tim Kreider, *We Learn Nothing* (New York: Simon & Schuster, 2012), 96.

18. The math mapped nicely onto ancient and modern history: From hunter-gatherer societies to Amish communities, from eighteenth-century English villages to modern Christmas card lists, the sweet spot for a typical community is about 150 people. As for the layers, ranging from 500 to 1,500 people, Dunbar says, "It turns out that these layers mirror almost exactly the structure of modern armies. Americans always like to do

things a little bigger than everybody else, so their numbers are a little on the bigger side. The British are more retiring and shy, so they have slightly smaller ones. They all benchmark these particular layers. Interestingly, of course, the smallest layer of five turns out to be the standard unit size for Special Forces—as well as terrorist cells." Dunbar suspects you can increase capacity for juggling friendships—but only when you're younger, before your brain is fully developed. Adults are stuck with their capacity for friendship. See R. I. Dunbar, "The Social Brain Hypothesis," *Evolutionary Anthropology* 6 (1998): 178–90.

19. Dunbar and others have also corroborated the patently obvious: Men and women approach friendships differently. The (scant) sociological research on the gender differences seems to confirm stereotypes. For example, women center their relationships around conversation, preferably face-to-face, and they know the tiniest details of their friends' lives. Men want to do something physical, like play basketball. They generally avoid face-to-face, intimate conversation. Does your buddy know the names of your children, or even if you have children? Hence the popularity of going to football games or sports bars, where men can sit side by side and avoid eye contact.

   Men also possess fewer friends: Dunbar says men average four friends in their inner circle, while women average six. Men spend less time maintaining them. In one TED talk (TedXObserver, March 21, 2012), Dunbar explained that "[women's] phone calls last one hour on average, and [men's] calls last 7.3 seconds on average: *'I'll see you down at the pub.'*" People in the audience laughed and nodded to each other knowingly. When I asked him about it later, he said it is a joke, not a real statistic—but the fact that most people believe him suggests it reflects life experience. Perhaps this correlates with another finding by Geoffrey Greif, author of *Buddy System*, a book on (male) friendships: Women turn to other women to discuss their problems; men turn to their wives.

   Dunbar says that female friendships, particularly the closest ones, require more care and feeding; but there is a dark side to that intensity.

   "Those relationships are very fragile," Dunbar said. "This seems to be a big difference between male and female friendships. Female friendships tend to break catastrophically. Guys just seem to smack each other, and then they go and have a beer. It seems to be that they don't have these kinds of intense relationships with other guys, or girlfriends in the generic sense of girlfriends, as opposed to a romantic partner. They're much more *Here today, gone tomorrow.*"

   Some of these stereotypes vanish as men and women reach their fifties and sixties, Greif told me. Greif, a professor at the University of Maryland School of Social Work, interviewed nearly four hundred men and more than a hundred women for his book on friendship.

   "There's a general shift across time. . . . Men and women—men, especially—become androgynous with age," he said. "So we [men] become less driven by testosterone, less competitive. We mellow with time. If I'm on a cruise and happen to meet another guy, I'm not as interested at sixty-five in proving I'm a bigger success than he is."

   Even the shoulder-to-shoulder, don't-look-me-in-the-eye approach softens.

   "It's not as easy to go out and do shoulder-to-shoulder stuff as it is when you're young," Greif says. "And the fear of appearing to be gay goes down with age, too, even though it still exists in men. So men don't mind sitting and talking to each other, because they feel more comfortable." See Geoffrey L. Greif, *Buddy System: Understanding Male Friendships* (New York: Oxford University Press, 2009).

Rebecca Adams at UNC Greensboro wonders if women will begin to adopt the style of masculine friendships, not because of age but because of career. "I think one of the reasons that men have never seen friendship as important is that they couldn't really engage in it. They were in competition with most of the people they spent time with," she says. "Now that women are also being put in competition with the people they spend most of their time with, we're going to become more like men."

20. As a reporter, I always search for anecdotal evidence for the assertions I make. But it's no easy matter finding isolated people. The usual places I plumb to find my "anecdotal leads"—churches, nonprofit organizations, advocacy groups—are useless, because isolated people don't belong to groups. I did find one group that caters to lonely people, but they are older, not middle-aged. Still, Teresa Santos Taylor's story is illustrative of how isolation affects one's body and emotions.

Alexis Seubert introduced me to Teresa Taylor. Seubert, a winning twenty-something brunette with hip eyeglasses, is one of four staff members at the Boston chapter of Little Brothers–Friends of the Elderly, a national nonprofit group that organizes visits and parties for older lonely people. I first glimpsed Teresa as Alexis and I were strolling down the corridor of Teresa's apartment building. Teresa stood in the doorway, a large smile on her face. She happily waved us in. She had been waiting. Our visit loomed large in her small, quiet world, a world that had shrunk to a pinprick until two years earlier. Back then, before Seubert had received a tip and phoned her, the eighty-five-year-old woman entertained no visitors: Friends had died or moved away; her estranged daughter rarely visited. The loneliness was killing her.

On this brittle Boston afternoon, Teresa gave us a tour of her tiny apartment. We stopped at a wall of pictures. "This one here is when Herbie saw me for the first time," she said, gesturing to a young man in a Marine uniform. They married in 1968, four years after she emigrated from Brazil to the United States. They were married twenty-two years, until he died from diabetes. "It wasn't a very good marriage. But you try."

Teresa's white hair fell to her shoulders; it seemed candescent next to her olive skin. She wore bright red nail polish on her fingers and toes, a purple-and-white polka-dotted shirt, black pants, and sandals. She had taken care for this visit. After she retired from housecleaning, Teresa said, she had virtually no contact with the outside world.

"I started to go to bed late and get up late. I wanted my days to be short."

She stopped taking her medicine. She often skipped meals.

"It was the worst time of my life. I just wanted to die. I just wanted to disappear. Every night, I thought, *Okay, that's the last night*. And the next morning I was still here! And on and on, until I got a call from Alexis. Little Brothers. It was just like a prayer: I was lost, and now I'm found."

Little Brothers organizes four to five hundred volunteers a year to visit elderly people who would otherwise face every Christmas and Thanksgiving, every birthday and holiday, alone. They throw parties every month, they drop by for a chat, they bring groceries. They give these older people what they need almost as much as food and water: companionship.

The monthly parties and frequent visits provided blessed relief from loneliness that seemed to pervade this apartment house for the elderly. Teresa had an existential fear, a common one, that she would die and no one would know. Recently, a man down the hall barricaded himself behind his door. No one found him for days. It's easy to wall off the old, she said.

"Let's not bring him for Thanksgiving," she said. "Let's not invite him or her. It's not convenient. He's got the walker. He's got the cane. The last thing is a wheelchair. That's the last step. And many times the family rejects us because there's a lot of inconvenience. We are no longer attractive. We're no longer sexy or glamorous or interesting. Just an old bag."

"I think you're pretty glamorous," Seubert protested.

"Alexis, she's great," Teresa said, turning to me. "Many times I call her because I just want to talk to somebody, I'm just getting bored, and I call her for some little reason or something. And last year, they were beside me the whole year. I was very sick, and they did grocery shopping for me, they sent flowers, she took me out for lunch. Alexis does a lot of stuff. They changed my life. They gave me a reason to live. It's not just about the lunch once a month or the free ride. It's to know that there is something there for us."

After three hours, Seubert and I began to leave, which turned out to be a lengthy process, with a barrage of logistical questions from Teresa, stalling like a child at bedtime. Walking down the stairwell, Seubert said that while it was "heartbreaking" that an extrovert like Teresa was isolated for so long, she was one of their easiest cases.

"A lot of people become more isolated and more paranoid and wary of people the longer they've been isolated," she said. "It's sort of like a self-fulfilling prophecy."

I would later learn that lonely people lash out and retreat because their bodies and their brains are telling them to.

"Sometimes it's circumstance and sometimes it's personality, but they become isolated," Alexis continued. "And then someone comes into their life who is trying to make a difference, and this person becomes suspicious, or angry, and acts out, and they cut off that source of socialization or help or whatever it is. As this happens over and over, you develop this reputation, and no one wants to come visit you because you're rude, you're mean, you're ungrateful. And that person becomes even more suspicious, and even more spiteful, and it keeps building, and you can just see how it has spiraled."

"And how do *you* deal with that?"

"You laugh!" Seubert said. "That's what you do. You laugh. We are these people who just keep going back. You're rude to us today and you call tomorrow and we will still answer the phone and will still talk to you." She shook her head and laughed softly. "I guess we just don't learn."

21. "Loneliness Among Older Adults: A National Survey of Adults 45+," *AARP The Magazine,* September 2010.

22. M. McPherson, L. Smith-Lovin, and M. E. Brashears, "Social Isolation in America: Changes in Core Discussion Networks over Two Decades," *American Sociological Review* 71, no. 3 (2006): 353–75.

23. The researchers analyzed 148 studies tracking 300,000 people across an average 7.5 years. While some studies have found lower rates of mortality and disability and others

have found higher rates, this study is the most comprehensive to date. See J. Holt-Lunstad, T. B. Smith, and J. B. Layton, "Social Relationships and Mortality Risk: A Meta-analytic Review," *PLOS Medicine* 7, no. 7 (2010): 1–20.

24. J. T. Cacioppo, L. C. Hawkley, G. J. Norman, and G. G. Berntson, "Social Isolation," *Annals of the New York Academy of Sciences* 1231, no. 1 (2011): 17–22.

25. S. W. Cole, L. C. Hawkley, J. M. Arevalo, et al., "Social Regulation of Gene Expression in Human Leukocytes," *Genome Biology* 8, no. 9 (2007): R189.

26. R. S. Wilson, K. R. Krueger, S. E. Arnold, et al., "Loneliness and Risk of Alzheimer Disease," *Archives of General Psychiatry* 64, no. 2 (2007): 234–40. For an excellent overview, see J. T. Cacioppo and L. C. Hawkley, "Perceived Social Isolation and Cognition," *Trends in Cognitive Sciences* 13, no. 10 (2009): 447–54.

27. In this study, Scottish researchers tracked the mental ability of 488 Scots from the Lothian Birth Cohort study, testing them at age eleven and seventy-nine. After controlling for age, gender, years of education, and social class, only loneliness was associated significantly with changes in IQ. See A. J. Gow, A. Pattie, M. C. Whiteman, L. J. Whalley, and I. J. Deary, "Social Support and Successful Aging," *Journal of Individual Differences* 28, no. 3 (2007): 103–15.

28. L. C. Hawkley, K. J. Preacher, and J. T. Cacioppo, "Loneliness Impairs Daytime Functioning but Not Sleep Duration," *Health Psychology* 29, no. 2 (2010): 124.

29. Researchers at the University of California–San Francisco studied 1,604 people over the age of sixty from 2002 to 2008, following up every two years. Those who identified as lonely or isolated at the beginning of the study had a 45 percent higher risk of dying and were 59 percent more likely to have problems with basic tasks, such as housekeeping. See C. M. Perissinotto, I. Stijacic Cenzer, and K. E. Covinsky, "Loneliness in Older Persons: A Predictor of Functional Decline and Death," *Archives of Internal Medicine* 172, no. 14 (2012): 1078–84.

30. Lonely people don't realize it, but their bodies never relax. Cacioppo recognized this during one of his first studies at Ohio State. He surveyed several thousand students, selected a few of them, and divided them into three groups: lonely, sort of lonely, and not lonely. They wore mobile blood pressure cuffs, they chewed on cotton balls to measure cortisol in saliva, and they slept in the sleep lab and in their dorm rooms with electrodes pasted to their heads to monitor their sleep. Cacioppo put them through stressful situations—giving a speech on short notice, for example—and measured their physiologic reactions. Whenever he beeped them, nine times a day for seven days, they filled out questionnaires about how they were feeling, took their blood pressure, and saved a sample of saliva. At the end, Cacioppo found that the students who were distressed about not making friends had higher blood pressure and higher cortisol levels, which is great if you need to outrun a lion but not so great over the long term.

"That's because the brain is already sitting there—whether you're aware of it or not—knowing that it's on the edge of a social perimeter and therefore it's surveilling for threats."

These lonely students could not even get a decent night's sleep.

"They break out of deep sleep more quickly," Cacioppo said. "And we now think that is because the brain is still sitting there on alert for threats. So it's very dangerous to go into a deep sleep and remain there."

31. But how did this work? To find out, Cole put some infected T cells in a test tube. Then

he took some of the stress hormone norepinephrine. Norepinephrine is hugely sensitive to threat: It underlies the fight-or-flight response by making your heart pound faster, releasing blood sugar (energy) into the bloodstream, and sending blood to your muscles so you can fight like a man or run like the wind. Cole dumped the norepinephrine on the infected cells, stood back, and watched. "When I put norepinephrine on them," he said, "the virus replicates *three to ten times as fast*. So it seems that the fight-or-flight stress response is most likely to be responsible for these kinds of dynamics."

32. Cacioppo and Cole analyzed the genes of fourteen people in Chicago. Six scored in the top of the UCLA Loneliness Scale (where you don't want to be), a widely used method to measure feelings of isolation. The rest did not suffer from loneliness, according to the tests. When the researchers reported that loneliness reprogrammed people's genes, making them more vulnerable to diseases and viruses, the study became a national sensation. "I do studies all the time. People ignore them, nobody cares, that's the rule of my life," Cole said, laughing. "And suddenly people are writing me e-mails saying, 'It is so wonderful you're doing this work. I have to tell you this story of my aunt . . .' Or, 'How much I believe my loneliness has contributed to this cancer I got.' Or, 'Finding the right relationship helped my autoimmune disease go away.' I mean, people responded to this thing with an intensity of interest and encouragement that I had never experienced at all." See S. W. Cole, L. C. Hawkley, J. M. Arevalo, et al., "Social Regulation of Gene Expression in Human Leukocytes," *Genome Biology* 8, no. 9 (2007): R189.

33. Dan's phrase inspired a limerick. One evening, I was telling my friend Libby Lewis about his book. "One of my favorite lines in Dan's book is: *The voice in my head . . . is kind of an asshole.*"

Libby laughed. "That's poetic."

"It does sound poetic, doesn't it?" I said. "Is it iambic pentameter?"

"I'm not sure," Libby said, metering it out. "The voice in my head is kind of an asshole. No, it's not quite right."

The next morning, Libby and I had this text exchange:

Barb: *By the way . . . I figured out the iambic pentameter: The voice in my head is a bit of a jerk.*

Libby (instantly): *It sometimes will drive me a little berserk.*

Barb: *It's where my anxieties all seem to lurk.*

Libby: *Well, everyone else I know has their own quirks.*

Barb: *My self-aggrandizement is one of the perks.*

This may not win the Nobel Prize in Literature, but it certainly captured my mind-set.

34. J. Tooby and L. Cosmides, "Friendship and the Banker's Paradox: Other Pathways to the Evolution of Adaptations for Altruism," *Proceedings of the British Academy* 88 (1996): 119–43.

35. P. DeScioli and R. Kurzban, "The Alliance Hypothesis for Human Friendship," *PLOS ONE* 4, no. 6 (2009): e5802.

CHAPTER 5. IT'S THE THOUGHT THAT COUNTS

1. D. A. Bennett, J. A. Schneider, A. S. Buchman, et al., "Overview and Findings from the Rush Memory and Aging Project," *Current Alzheimer Research* 9, no. 6 (2012): 646.

2. Beginning in 1991, David Snowden, then a young assistant professor at the University of

Minnesota, persuaded the Sisters of Notre Dame to help him with a unique cognitive exploration. See David Snowden, *Aging with Grace: What the Nun Study Teaches Us About Leading Longer, Healthier, and More Meaningful Lives* (New York: Bantam Books, 2001). The 678 Catholic sisters, who were between ages seventy-five and a hundred two when the study began, would submit to cognitive tests each year and allow their brains to be autopsied after they died. Then Snowden stumbled on a priceless piece of evidence. In some dusty green filing cabinets in the basement of one of the convents, he found the nuns' autobiographies, written some six decades earlier. In 1930, the Mother Superior of the order in North America required every sister to write a short sketch of her life, including her family life, "edifying events of childhood," education, influences that led her to the convent, and "outstanding events."

At first Snowden feared the study would not yield a single interesting nugget. But then the sisters began to die—and what the neuropathologist found in their brains capsized prevailing scientific thought. A substantial proportion of the sisters whose brains revealed moderate Alzheimer's disease had, in fact, shown no symptoms during their annual cognitive tests. Even some nuns with the most advanced pathology remained mentally acute right to the end.

Snowden called them "escapees." One sister in particular stood out. Sister Bernadette cruised through her cognitive tests at ages eighty-one, eighty-three, and eighty-four, before dying of a heart attack at eighty-five. When the neuropathologist autopsied her brain, he discovered tangles riddling her neocortex and hippocampus. He scored her at Braak VI, the most severe level of Alzheimer's pathology.

"We were so dumbfounded by her lack of symptoms that we feared UPS had shipped us the wrong brain," Snowden later wrote (p. 134).

Snowden and his colleagues turned to the autobiographies written in 1930 for clues about the sisters' unlikely cognitive health. In analyzing their prose, the researchers found that "idea density" (the number of individual ideas expressed per ten words) strongly predicted who would slip into dementia fifty-eight years later and who would remain sharp—even if their brains showed the pathology of Alzheimer's disease. Sentence complexity would also predict their mental acuity, to a lesser extent. It turns out that being cheerful did not preserve their minds but did lengthen their lives: The most positive sisters lived, on average, seven years longer than the most negative (p. 116).

3. R. S. Wilson, J. A. Schneider, S. E. Arnold, J. L. Bienias, and D. A. Bennett, "Conscientiousness and the Incidence of Alzheimer's Disease and Mild Cognitive Impairment," *Archives of General Psychiatry* 64, no. 10 (2007): 1204–12.

4. P. A. Boyle, A. S. Buchman, L. L. Barnes, and D. A. Bennett, "Effect of Purpose in Life on Risk of Incident Alzheimer's Disease and Mild Cognitive Impairment in Community-Dwelling Older Persons," *Archives of General Psychiatry* 67, no. 3 (2010): 304–10.

5. For a great overview of *eudaimonic* well-being—what it is, who has it, who doesn't, how it matters for health, and, importantly, what can be done to improve it—see C. D. Ryff, "Psychological Well-being Revisited: Advances in the Science and Practice of Eudaimonia," *Psychotherapy and Psychosomatics* 83, no. 1 (2014): 10–28.

6. Research by psychologist Roy Baumeister at Florida State University landed squarely on the side of *eudaimonia*. He surveyed nearly four hundred American adults, measuring their levels of (hedonic) happiness and (eudaimonic) meaning. Then he examined which forms of happiness correlated with moods, behaviors, relationships, health,

and stress. "Happiness without meaning," Baumeister concluded, "characterizes a relatively shallow, self-absorbed or even selfish life, in which things go well, needs and desires are easily satisfied, and difficult or taxing entanglements are avoided." Whereas "the meaningful but unhappy life is in some ways more admirable than the happy but meaningful life."

Of course, Baumeister found that most people seek both (hedonic) happiness and (eudaimonic) meaning. But tipping the seesaw one way or the other makes all the difference. What distinguishes us from animals, he says, is meaning. How are our hedonic instincts better than those of, say, a jaguar, a rattlesnake, or (it pains me to say it) my Labrador retriever, Sandra Day? They involve satisfying immediate needs, such as food and sex and other forms of fun; taking rather than giving; thinking exclusively about the present (*Let us eat and drink, for tomorrow we die!*) rather than linking present actions with the past or the future. See R. F. Baumeister, K. D. Vohs, J. L. Aaker, and E. N. Garbinsky, "Some Key Differences Between a Happy Life and a Meaningful Life," *Journal of Positive Psychology* 8, no. 6 (2013): 505–16; quotation from 515–16.

7. C. P. Niemiec, R. M. Ryan, and E. L. Deci, "The Path Taken: Consequences of Attaining Intrinsic and Extrinsic Aspirations in Post-College Life," *Journal of Research in Personality* 43, no. 3 (2009): 291–306.

8. Researchers at University College London, Princeton University, and Stony Brook University surveyed 9,050 British people over age sixty-five. Questionnaires measured "eudaimonic well-being," including one's sense of control, feeling that what one does actually matters, and having a sense of purpose in life. After adjusting for age, sex, wealth, education, physical health, depression, smoking, physical activity, and alcohol consumption, they found that people with highest eudaimonic well-being were 30 percent less likely to die over the eight-and-a-half-year study period than those with low eudaimonic well-being. On average, they lived two years longer than the least eudaimonic group. See A. Steptoe, A. Deaton, and A. A. Stone, "Subjective Wellbeing, Health, and Ageing," *Lancet* 338 (February 2015): 640–48.

9. E. M. Friedman, M. Hayney, G. D. Love, B. H. Singer, and C. D. Ryff, "Plasma Interleukin-6 and Soluble IL-6 Receptors Are Associated with Psychological Well-being in Aging Women," *Health Psychology* 26, no. 3 (2007): 305–13.

10. This was one of the earliest studies to show how potent and vast the benefits of eudaimonic well-being are. MIDUS researchers found that older women who reported higher levels of eudaimonic well-being (especially personal growth and purpose in life) had better neuroendocrine regulation, as was evidenced by lower levels of the stress hormone cortisol throughout the day. They were protected against the inflammatory marker interleukin-6. They also showed higher levels of HDL cholesterol (the "good" cholesterol). On top of that, they showed better control of their blood sugar, and they slept better. See C. D. Ryff, B. H. Singer, and G. D. Love, "Positive Health: Connecting Wellbeing with Biology," *Philosophical Transactions of the Royal Society of London, Series B: Biological Sciences* 359 (2004): 1383–94.

11. Cole says this is a throwback to our ancestors. Back when the men were hunting lions and not personal data from your Facebook account, bacterial infection from a wound posed the greatest threat to health. Viruses posed a smaller threat in times of immediate danger. Antiviral responses are more appropriate for those living in larger, more peaceful societies, where they have contact with many people. Today, a spreading virus pre-

sents more of a threat to our health than a wound from a lion or a rival tribesman's spear. But our bodies have yet to adjust. When people are dealing with modern threats, turning on that caveman threat response is a cure worse than the disease.

12. B. L. Fredrickson, K. M. Grewen, K. A. Coffey, et al., "A Functional Genomic Perspective on Human Well-being," *Proceedings of the National Academy of Sciences* 110, no. 33 (2013): 13684–89.

13. P. A. Boyle, L. L. Barnes, A. S. Buchman, and D. A. Bennett, "Purpose in Life Is Associated with Mortality Among Community-Dwelling Older Persons," *Psychosomatic Medicine* 71, no. 5 (2009): 574.

14. Researchers surveyed some six thousand people in MIDUS, from their mid-twenties to their mid-seventies. They answered questions assessing their purpose in life (for example, "Some people wander aimlessly through life, but I am not one of them"). The researchers checked back fourteen years later. Across all age categories, people high in purpose in life (and positive relations with others) were more likely to be alive. See P. L. Hill and N. A. Turiano, "Purpose in Life as a Predictor of Mortality Across Adulthood," *Psychological Science* 25, no. 7 (2014): 1482–86.

15. E. S. Kim, J. K. Sun, N. Park, L. D. Kubzansky, and C. Peterson, "Purpose in Life and Reduced Incidence of Stroke in Older Adults: 'The Health and Retirement Study,'" *Journal of Psychosomatic Research* 74, no. 5 (2013): 427–32.

16. The researchers followed 1,618 Japanese men and women, ages forty to seventy-four, for thirteen years, and found that men who scored high in purpose were far less likely to die of cardiovascular disease or stroke, or for any reason, for that matter. Women showed no effect. See M. Koizumi, H. Ito, Y. Kaneko, and Y. Motohashi, "Effect of Having a Sense of Purpose in Life on the Risk of Death from Cardiovascular Diseases," *Journal of Epidemiology* 18, no. 5 (2008): 191–96.

17. This was a huge study of 73,000 Japanese adults over a twelve-year period. Having purpose lowered the risk of death over that period significantly, protected men from cardiovascular disease, and reduced the likelihood of extreme types of death for both men and women. See K. Tanno, K. Sakata, M. Ohsawa, et al., "Associations of *Ikigai* as a Positive Psychological Factor with All-Cause Mortality and Cause-Specific Mortality Among Middle-aged and Elderly Japanese People: Findings from the Japan Collaborative Cohort Study," *Journal of Psychosomatic Research* 67 (2009): 67–75.

18. Following 7,168 people over the age of fifty, the researchers found that those high in purpose were more likely to undergo cholesterol tests and colonoscopies. Women were more likely to get mammograms or Pap smears, and men to get prostate exams. Purposeful people spent 17 percent fewer nights in the hospital. See E. S. Kim, V. J. Stretcher, and C. D. Ryff, "Purpose in Life and Use of Preventive Health Care Services," *Proceedings of the National Academy of Sciences* 111, no. 46 (2014): 16331–36.

19. As people get older, they accumulate chronic conditions and have higher levels of IL-6 and C-reactive protein. A MIDUS study of 998 older people with chronic medical conditions showed that if a person had strong purpose in life and good relations with others, they had lower levels of inflammation. See E. M. Friedman and C. D. Ryff, "Living Well with Medical Comorbidities: A Biopsychosocial Perspective," *Journals of Gerontology, Series B: Psychological Sciences and Social Sciences* 67, no. 5 (2012): 535–44.

20. In this longitudinal investigation, Ryff found that higher-income women had better glycemic control than those with low income. But if women in lower income brackets had

higher well-being (particularly purpose in life, but also personal growth and positive emotions), they had better glycemic control than other low-income women without positive emotional dispositions. See V. K. Tsenkova, G. D. Love, B. H. Singer, and C. D. Ryff, "Socioeconomic Status and Psychological Well-being Predict Cross-Time Change in Glycosylated Hemoglobin in Older Women Without Diabetes," *Psychosomatic Medicine* 69 (2007): 777–84.

21. The researchers studied 1,028 men and women, ages thirty-five to eighty-six, and found that those with lower levels of education had higher levels of the inflammatory marker interleukin-6. But those with a higher psychological profile, including environmental mastery, positive relations with others, purpose in life, self-acceptance, and positive affect, showed less elevated levels of interleukin-6 compared with others of their education level. Moreover, for those with a high school education or less but scoring high in psychological well-being, the level of the inflammatory marker was comparable to that in college-educated adults. See J. A. Morozink, E. M. Friedman, C. L. Coe, and C. C. Ryff, "Socioeconomic and Psychosocial Predictors of Interleukin-6 in the MIDUS National Sample," *Health Psychology* 29 (2010): 626–35.

22. Carstensen told me she became interested in the disparities of aging "by accident" when she was twenty-one years old. "I was in a terrible auto accident and I ended up, with many broken bones, on an orthopedic ward for about four months," she said. "And because I was there for so long, I got to know the nurses and they put me in a four-bed ward, surrounded by older women. The [nurses] said, 'Your job is to talk to these older folks and try to keep them entertained and oriented.'" Carstensen noticed some of the older patients were clearly the matriarchs of their families: Their children visited all the time, and their grandchildren would climb on the bed and talk. These women recovered well. Other women languished, alone, day in and day out. They fared more poorly. "It made me wonder how much of aging is a biological process and how much of that process is actually steered by the social world in which we live," she said. "And so I became a psychologist to study the interactions between biology and behavior."

23. L. L. Carstensen, B. Turan, S. Scheibe, et al., "Emotional Experience Improves with Age: Evidence Based on over Ten Years of Experience Sampling," *Psychology and Aging* 26, no. 1 (2011): 21–33.

24. Carstensen notes that her findings about the emotional brain differ from the U-curve of happiness that economists have identified. She told me that psychologists (including her) and economists are measuring two different things. "When you ask people how satisfied they are with their lives, it's a cognitive question. It's really not emotional." They think about all they have yet to achieve, all of their obligations, and voilà! Middle-aged people have slipped to the nadir of the U-curve. But, she says, "if you are focused on more purely emotion, you see this line upward across adulthood."

25. S. T. Charles, M. Mather, and L. L. Carstensen, "Aging and Emotional Memory: The Forgettable Nature of Negative Photos for Older Adults," *Journal of Experimental Psychology* 132, no. 2 (2003): 310–24.

26. M. Mather, T. Canli, T. English, et al., "Amygdala Responses to Emotionally Valenced Stimuli in Older and Younger Adults," *Psychological Science* 15, no. 4 (2004): 259–63. Other researchers, too, have found older people regulate their emotions more effectively than the young. One group at Duke University's Center for Cognitive Neuroscience scanned the brains of young and older adults while they looked at photos. The older

adults remembered fewer unhappy photos, as predicted. Once again, all roads lead to the amygdala. The emotional center of the brain interacted less with the memory center (the hippocampus) and more with the front part of the brain involved with controlling emotions. In other words, the older brain kept emotions in check. See P. L. St. Jacques, F. Dolcos, and R. Cabeza, "Effects of Aging on Functional Connectivity of the Amygdala for Subsequent Memory of Negative Pictures: A Network Analysis of Functional Magnetic Resonance Imaging Data," *Psychological Science* 20, no. 1 (2009): 74–84.

27. Carien van Reekum also found that people who have high purpose in life and psychological well-being process negative information differently from how others do. Van Reekum, who is now a neuroscientist at the University of Reading, in England, scanned the brains of twenty-nine women as they looked at negative images (a person with a disfiguring tumor, a car crash) and neutral ones (a cup, a scene in a workplace, a face). When they were viewing the tumors and car crashes, the people who scored low on purpose in life showed a strong and immediate response in their amygdala, the part of the brain associated with emotions such as fear and anxiety. Those who scored high in psychological well-being showed more activity in the prefrontal cortex—the part of the brain that handles reasoning, planning, and higher-order thinking. They did not react quickly or dramatically to the photos: It is as if the front part of their brain said, *Hold on, slow down, let's appraise this situation carefully.*

"They are more prone to also see a positive side of negative information," van Reekum told me when I reached her at the office at nine p.m. (making her the perfect person to study the effect of purpose in life, pushing past the momentary pleasures to reach a larger goal). "It's not that I think that people who are high in psychological well-being respond with less negative emotions to a stimulus. What I think is, they have this flexibility to turn it on or off, depending upon the context." See C. M. van Reekum, H. L. Urry, T. Johnstone, et al., "Individual Differences in Amygdala and Ventromedial Prefrontal Cortex Activity Are Associated with Evaluation Speed and Psychological Well-being," *Journal of Cognitive Neuroscience* 19, no. 2 (2007): 237–48.

Van Reekum worked on a follow-up study, which found that people who scored high on purpose in life also show this same neurological pattern, in which they somehow regulate the bad stuff and put it in a larger context. It is why future Olympians push through the pain of the moment for the shot at the gold and why new parents suffer through exhaustion to give baby a two a.m. meal. Van Reekum thinks of this ability to put bad things in a different perspective as resilience. When these people hit a bump in the road, "they will be the ones who will [take] a step back, and think, 'Well, that didn't work, but let's try it this way, then, again.'" See S. M. Schaefer, B. J. Morozink, C. M. van Reekum, R. C. Lapate, and C. J. Norris, "Purpose in Life Predicts Better Emotional Recovery from Negative Stimuli," *PLOS ONE* 8, no. 11 (2013): e80329.

"By the way," she adds, "that's also what I think is going on when people get older."

As it turns out, older people's brains also take bad events in stride, recruiting the very same brain regions as those psychologically healthy people—but for a different reason. "I think it's because of their experience built up in life," van Reekum says. "I think what older adults are better at than younger adults is adjustment. They adjust to situations a lot more, whereas younger adults want to problem-solve. They want to go do it. Whereas older adults, I think, they take it in, but they are more readily able to let go of it as well." See C. M. van Reekum, S. M. Schaefer, R. C. Lapate, et al., "Aging Is

Associated with Positive Responding to Neutral Information but Reduced Recovery from Negative Information," *Social Cognitive and Affective Neuroscience* 6, no. 2 (2011): 177–85.

Van Reekum noted that her results differ from those of Laura Carstensen and fellow researcher Mara Mather. Asked about this discrepancy, van Reekum said it's a puzzle, and it is early days in this sort of brain research.

28. For a critical analysis, see Robert R. Provine, *Laughter: A Scientific Investigation* (New York: Penguin Books, 2000), 189–207.

29. R. Mora-Ripoll, "The Therapeutic Value of Laughter in Medicine," *Alternative Therapies in Health and Medicine* 16, no. 6 (2010): 56–64. Dr. Mora-Ripoll sifted through nearly two hundred scientific studies on laughter. He concluded that laughter has emotional and some physiological benefits in the short term: that is, relaxing muscles, improving respiration, stimulating circulation, and decreasing stress hormones. He also concluded there was some evidence that laughter increases the immune system's defense. For a comprehensive account, see Table 3, 58–59.

30. R. I. M. Dunbar, R. Baron, A. Frangou, et al., "Social Laughter Is Correlated with an Elevated Pain Threshold," *Proceedings of the Royal Society B: Biological Sciences* 279, no. 1731 (2011): 1161–67.

31. Robin Dunbar came to this conclusion, along with other skeptics, including Robert Provine. Provine was persuaded by studies that found that healthy people put in a painful situation (for example, a tight blood pressure cuff) could tolerate a higher threshold of pain if they were watching, say, a Lily Tomlin video. He also found compelling a study of orthopedic surgery patients. Those who watched comedies *and* dramas asked for fewer painkillers. This shows the importance of distraction—although the researchers found the effect of comedy over and above the effect of distraction. Provine offered this caveat: "The desired comedy effect is lost if there is no choice—annoying comedy can increase the analgesic use. Bad drama is boring—bad comedy is obnoxious" (Provine, *Laughter*, 202).

32. See, for example, J. T. Buhle, B. L. Stevens, J. J. Friedman, and T. D. Wager, "Distraction and Placebo: Two Separate Routes to Pain Control," *Psychological Science* 23, no. 3 (2012): 246–53.

33. Just in case you want to know: Barbara Bradley Hagerty, *Fingerprints of God: The Search for the Science of Spirituality* (New York: Riverhead Books, 2009). I think you can get it on Amazon for 98 cents. Plus shipping.

34. One benefit of writing a book is that you can legitimately ask experts about your personal problems—in the interest of research. One pain specialist, who asked not to be identified, noted that for people with chronic pain, "their life revolves around pain. Talking about pain. Getting treatments from different providers because of the chronic pain. Sometimes they never get a good answer of why it's happening. That's why chronic pain is a mystery—because it's very difficult to treat, because once pain disrupts your quality of life, then it's hard to really be the person you used to be. Being that normal person, the regular person. You forgot who that person was."

He told me that vocal cord pain is very tricky. The nerves in that area are "overly responsive to minimal or no stimuli. They're just firing on their own without any stimulation."

Then he added, my heart sinking: "Hopefully, you can get to the point where you can keep the symptoms as manageable as possible for you to have a quality of life. A functional life where you are engaged in life to the best of your ability. Hopefully, you're happy enough with that."

"Wow. I was hoping to get rid of it."

"The pain may just disappear one day. You may just wake up one day and realize, *Wait a minute: I forgot I had pain*," he said. "The body is dynamic. It's always trying to heal itself. It's always trying to move on away from the pain." He tried to mask his doubt, but doubt was all that I could hear.

CHAPTER 6. THE DESERT OR OASIS OF MIDLIFE MARRIAGE

1. This meta-analysis of twenty-five studies found that romantic love exists in long-term marriages—but without the obsession of new love. In fact, it found obsession in long-term relationships correlated with unhappy marriages, whereas obsession was a big plus in new relationships. See B. P. Acevedo and A. Aron, "Does a Long-term Relationship Kill Romantic Love?" *Review of General Psychology* 13, no. 1 (2009): 59.
2. C. Reissman, A. Aron, and M. R. Bergen, "Shared Activities and Marital Satisfaction: Causal Direction and Self-Expansion Versus Boredom," *Journal of Social and Personal Relationships* 10, no. 2 (1993): 243–54.
3. A. Aron, C. C. Norman, E. N. Aron, C. McKenna, and R. E. Heyman, "Couples' Shared Participation in Novel and Arousing Activities and Experienced Relationship Quality," *Journal of Personality and Social Psychology* 78, no. 2 (2000): 273.
4. Boredom is also a cancer on the marriage. See I. Tsapelas, A. Aron, and T. Orbuch, "Marital Boredom Now Predicts Less Satisfaction 9 Years Later," *Psychological Science* 20, no. 5 (2009): 543–45.
5. M. N. Shiota and R. W. Levenson, "Birds of a Feather Don't Always Fly Farthest: Similarity in Big Five Personality Predicts More Negative Marital Satisfaction Trajectories in Long-term Marriages," *Psychology and Aging* 22, no. 4 (2007): 666.
6. "Joy to the World" was written by Hoyt Axton and made famous by the band Three Dog Night, who released the song in 1970 on their album *Naturally*. The song was copyrighted in 1970 by Irving Music, Inc.
7. I. F. Lin and S. L. Brown, "Unmarried Boomers Confront Old Age: A National Portrait," *Gerontologist* 52, no. 2 (2012): 153–65.
8. Boomers are also a robustly discontented lot: Not only are they divorcing in record numbers, but if they do stay married, they are ten percentage points unhappier than our parents' generation. See W. Bradford Wilcox, "When Marriage Disappears: The New Middle America," in *2010: The State of Our Unions: The Social Health of Marriage in America* (Charlottesville, VA: National Marriage Project at the University of Virginia and Center for Marriage and Families at the Institute for American Values, 2010), 13–53.
9. J. M. Gottman and R. W. Levenson, "The Timing of Divorce: Predicting When a Couple Will Divorce over a 14-Year Period," *Journal of Marriage and Family* 62, no. 3 (2000): 737–45.
10. See E. Finkel, "The All-or-Nothing Marriage," *New York Times*, February 14, 2014. Finkel cites statistics from Steven P. Martin: Of people who married between 1975 and 1979, the ten-year divorce rate for those without a high school diploma was 28 percent, versus 18 percent for those with at least a college degree. For people married between

1990 and 1994, the figures are 46 percent and 16 percent, respectively, a gap of thirty percentage points. http://ideas.repec.org/a/dem/demres/v15y2006i20.html.

11. The twenty-nine dimensions fall into several categories:

Emotional Temperament: How do you feel about yourself and about the world? These include: self-concept, emotional status, emotional energy, obstreperousness, and romantic passion.

Social Style: How do you relate to other people? These include: character, kindness, dominance, sociability, autonomy, and adaptability.

Cognitive Mode: How do you think about the world around you? These include: intellect, curiosity, humor, and artistic passion.

Relationship Skills: How much effort and skill do you devote to making a relationship work? These include: communication style, emotion management, and conflict resolution.

Values and Beliefs: How do you feel about spirituality, religion, family, and even politics? These include spirituality, family goals, traditionalism, ambition, and altruism.

Physicality: How do you relate physically with the world? These include: physical energy, sexual passion, vitality, security, industry, and appearance.

12. J. T. Cacioppo, S. Cacioppo, G. C. Gonzaga, E. L. Ogburn, and T. J. VanderWeele, "Marital Satisfaction and Breakups Differ Across On-line and Off-line Meeting Venues," *Proceedings of the National Academy of Sciences* 110, no. 25 (2013): 10135–40.

13. Bradbury and colleagues discovered that brides (though not grooms) had shrewd instincts: Those who had doubts before the marriage were 2.5 times as likely to be divorced four years later. If they were still married, they reported they were significantly less happy with their marriages. See J. A. Lavner, B. R. Karney, and T. N. Bradbury, "Do Cold Feet Warn of Trouble Ahead? Premarital Uncertainty and Four-Year Marital Outcomes," *Journal of Family Psychology* 26, no. 6 (2012): 1012.

14. Huston conducted some of the earliest longitudinal research. He tracked 168 couples for fourteen years, beginning two months after their wedding day. When Huston began his research in 1979, the prevailing wisdom held that most couples are giddy throughout their courtship and during the first two years of marriage but then become disillusioned or discontented. Huston debunked that notion, and his research has since been confirmed. See T. L. Huston, "What's Love Got to Do with It? Why Some Marriages Succeed and Others Fail," *Personal Relationships* 16, no. 3 (2009): 301–27.

15. I can't resist mentioning a few other intriguing insights from Huston's fourteen-year study. Men with "feminine" traits made better husbands. Couples who are particularly "lovey-dovey" as newlyweds are likely to divorce. Women who see future problems while they are courting should trust their instincts. Differences in tastes and ideas did not predict divorce: Brooding over those differences did. And having a child transforms their lifestyles but does not change their feelings for each other. For a good synopsis, see Kay Randall, "What's Love Got to Do with It?" at http://www.utexas.edu/features/archive/2003/love.html.

16. My gratitude to Russell Collins, marriage therapist and columnist, for bringing this to my attention: Russell Collins, "The Ultimate Relationship Tip," *Noozhawk*, May 18, 2011.

17. Physically, they suffered less cardiovascular arousal. See B. H. Seider, G. Hirschberger, K. L. Nelson, and R. W. Levenson, "We Can Work It Out: Age Differences in Relational

Pronouns, Physiology, and Behavior in Marital Conflict," *Psychology and Aging* 24, no. 3 (2009): 604.

18. Robert Levenson, interview by Kathleen Dunn, *Kathleen Dunn Show*, Wisconsin Public Radio, March 3, 2013.

19. Deborah Kirk, "The Science of Love," *Diablo Magazine*, February 2014, http://www .diablomag.com/February-2014/The-Science-of-Love/.

20. L. Bloch, C. M. Haase, and R. W. Levenson, "Emotion Regulation Predicts Marital Satisfaction: More Than a Wives' Tale," *Emotion* 14, no. 1 (2014): 130.

21. Kirk, "Science of Love."

22. C. M. Haase, L. R. Saslow, L. Bloch, et al., "The 5-HTTLPR Polymorphism in the Serotonin Transporter Gene Moderates the Association Between Emotional Behavior and Changes in Marital Satisfaction over Time," *Emotion* 13, no. 6 (2013): 1068.

23. D. Schoebi, B. M. Way, B. R. Karney, and T. N. Bradbury, "Genetic Moderation of Sensitivity to Positive and Negative Affect in Marriage," *Emotion* 12, no. 2 (2012): 208.

24. See R. B. Slatcher, "When Harry and Sally Met Dick and Jane: Creating Closeness Between Couples," *Personal Relationships* 17, no. 2 (2010): 279–97; Keith Walker and Richard Slatcher, presentation at the Society for Personality and Social Psychology, Wayne State University, February 10, 2014.

25. Geoffrey Greif and Kathleen Holtz Deal, *Two Plus Two: Couples and Their Couple Friendships* (New York: Routledge, 2012).

26. Carlin Flora, author of *Friendfluence: The Surprising Ways Friends Make Us Who We Are* (New York: Anchor, 2013), told me that friends relieve loneliness more than spouses. They provide an escape valve: I can consult with my friends about some of my work or family problems, which means Devin doesn't have to fill every role—husband, partner, soul mate, emotional and work confidant. She also found that friends are a good influence on a marriage, since they expect you to stay together.

27. Now let me state what I consider to be a glaring omission in the research: pets, or in our case, our dog, Sandra Day. She was just eight weeks old—not much older than our marriage—when we brought her home. Sometimes, during the early bouts, when I would wonder (within his earshot) why I married that guy, I would see Devin on the floor, cooing to Sandra, stroking her gently, and I would remember what I loved about him. She is as sensitive as a child—when our voices get a little edgy, she lowers her head and looks at us pleadingly—and more often than not, we resolve the quarrel peacefully. Devin has created a Sandra persona and voice, a wry, cynical running commentary on our lives, on me, on what she thinks about the neighbors. It's funny, it's endearing, it makes me love him more. This may sound crazy (although not to dog owners) but probably more than any other thing, Sandra Day has enriched our marriage. In that vein, scientists are now finding a chemical connection between dogs and their owners. We love our dogs, and our dogs love us. See M. Nagasawa, S. Mitsui, S. En, et al., "Oxytocin-Gaze Positive Loop and the Coevolution of Human-Dog Bonds," *Science* 348, no. 6232 (2015): 333–36.

28. Gottman and his Love Lab were catapulted to fame after Malcolm Gladwell featured his work in the book *Blink* (Boston: Little, Brown, 2005). See John Gottman, *Why Marriages Succeed or Fail* (New York: Simon & Schuster, 1994).

29. S. Carrere and J. M. Gottman, "Predicting Divorce Among Newlyweds from the First Three Minutes of a Marital Conflict Discussion," *Family Process* 38, no. 3 (1999): 293–301.

30. Northwestern University, "Twenty-one Minutes to Marital Satisfaction: Minimal Intervention Can Preserve Marital Quality over Time," *ScienceDaily*, February 5, 2013, www.sciencedaily.com/releases/2013/02/130205123702.htm (accessed August 8, 2015).

31. R. D. Rogge, R. J. Cobb, E. Lawrence, M. D. Johnson, and T. N. Bradbury, "Is Skills Training Necessary for the Primary Prevention of Marital Distress and Dissolution? A 3-Year Experimental Study of Three Interventions," *Journal of Consulting and Clinical Psychology* 81, no. 6 (2013): 949.

32. John Gottman asserts that a couple needs a five-to-one ratio: five positive statements for every negative statement. Barbara Fredrickson at the University of North Carolina, Chapel Hill, states that if a couple makes fewer than three positive statements to one critical statement, they're "headed for divorce." See S. Biali, "Want Lasting Love? Say These Words to Your Honey," *Psychology Today*, October 2, 2012, https://www.psychologytoday.com/blog/prescriptions-life/201210/want-lasting-love-say-these-words-your-honey.

33. I interviewed four couples suggested by Sue Johnson to learn a little more about rewiring the brain for vulnerability. Here is one case. In March 2010, Sarah Nunnink and Steve Agular had been married six years and together for eleven—long enough for them to (barely) survive the cataclysmic seven-year mark, but headed toward the disconnection that fells many midlife marriages around year 14. Steve was starting his residency in medical school in San Diego; he was exhausted by work, detached from Sarah, wanting only to be left alone. Sarah, a psychologist, was worried that she was becoming irrelevant to his life. One moment, on their vacation in New Zealand, captured the state of their marriage:

"We're driving in a bus on a tour to some cave and he's got his ear pods in, listening to music and reading medical journals," Sarah told me. "I am staring out the window at landscapes, and I just never felt so alone as I did in that moment."

"We lived together and were living very separate lives," Steve added. "On the surface, it was okay, but inside it was pretty empty. We actually talked about getting divorced because there was nothing really left. It felt like it'd run its course already."

As a last-ditch effort, they called a therapist who practiced Emotionally Focused Therapy. During the second session, Steve told the therapist, a little cockily, that he had never had to pursue relationships and that he felt lucky he had never risked being rejected.

"He said, 'I don't find that very lucky at all,'" Steve recalled. "The light went off in my head and everything just came flooding all at once. It sounds very trivial on the surface, but it was enough to really affect me."

Steve began to cry. Sarah had never seen him vulnerable before. At this point, diagnosis moved into treatment—that is, breaking old patterns of thought and behavior, and rewiring their brains. This was easier said than done, of course: Sarah and Steve had perfected a destructive routine, in which he would withdraw and she would pursue. After a few weeks in therapy, when Steve realized that Sarah merely needed assurance that he wasn't abandoning the marriage—and when he realized he could be vulnerable without being weak—the spiral began to loosen.

"I remember actually saying, 'I am here,'" Steve said. "I'm in this for the long haul. This is what I want and you're the most important thing to me."

"Once I started to finally feel like I'm number one and nothing mattered more to him in this world than me," Sarah recalled, "I actually started to *feel* it inside of me. I started to calm down and didn't need to ask any questions or a hundred questions."

Their brains were actually changing. Brain scans attest to that. Over the next few months, they realized that they could in fact be each other's shelter in the storm: Steve could find strength in vulnerability; Sarah would not need constant reassurance. As their attachment styles began to change, their marriage flourished.

Now, here is my one and only finding about sex. Everything I have read boils down to the same advice: Have sex, early and often, even when you don't feel like it. That's fine as far as it goes, but in distressed relationships, that can create more problems than it solves. Steve and Sarah had lost their spark by the time of the New Zealand vacation, and even after more than a year of therapy, even after their emotional connection had blossomed, Steve announced one day in therapy that he still felt little sexual attraction to his wife.

"We thought it would be this big, jaw-dropping moment right before commercial break," Steve said. The therapist did not. "He just glanced up and said, 'Oh, that makes total sense. This is all going to work itself out in the wash as we continue to go through this.'"

Although it took time, the therapist was spot-on: vulnerability led to sexuality.

In retrospect, Sarah says, they never had a terrible marriage. Just a typical one.

"I never felt like I married the wrong person," she said. "But I was only half fulfilled. There's a whole other realm that I wasn't even aware of that was possible with this emotional connection. After going through the process, wow, I can't believe we might have gone through our married life without ever having that."

Steve now tries to model his behavior after his toddler son. "He's open, he cries out, 'I want Mommy,' he puts his arms out to her or to me when he has an emotional need. Something scares him. He's insecure. He's hungry. He comes to all his people that he's attached to: Grandma, Mom, Dad. I see that and I think it's so natural." Steve laughs. "And he didn't have to go through therapy."

34. S. M. Johnson, M. B. Moser, L. Beckes, et al., "Soothing the Threatened Brain: Leveraging Contact Comfort with Emotionally Focused Therapy," *PLOS ONE* 8, no. 11 (2013): e79314. This was one of sixteen studies analyzing the effects of Emotionally Focused Therapy. According to those studies, couples not only reduced the amount of distress in their relationship but saw increases in measures of bonding and intimacy. See Sue Johnson, *Love Sense: The Revolutionary New Science of Romantic Relationships* (New York: Little, Brown, 2013).

CHAPTER 7. FINDING A LITTLE PURPOSE

1. S. J. Colcombe, K. I. Erickson, N. Raz, et al., "Aerobic Fitness Reduces Brain Tissue Loss in Aging Humans," *Journals of Gerontology Series A: Biological Sciences and Medical Sciences* 58, no. 2 (2003): M176–80.

2. S. J. Colcombe, K. I. Erickson, P. E. Scalf, et al., "Aerobic Exercise Training Increases Brain Volume in Aging Humans," *Journals of Gerontology Series A: Biological Sciences and Medical Sciences* 61, no. 11 (2006): 1166–70.

3. K. I. Erickson, R. S. Prakash, M. W. Voss, et al., "Aerobic Fitness Is Associated with Hippocampal Volume in Elderly Humans," *Hippocampus* 19, no. 10 (2009): 1030–39.

4. K. I. Erickson, M. W. Voss, R. S. Prakash, et al., "Exercise Training Increases Size of Hippocampus and Improves Memory," *Proceedings of the National Academy of Sciences* 108, no. 7 (2011): 3017–22.

5. Erickson says a pill would change molecules in the brain through a particular pathway such as a neurotransmitter, but that's where it stops. "You're changing a particular molecule and not others. And that's where it really differs from exercise, because exercise has a very large effect on many, many different molecules." The same is true for brain training. Cognitive training can strengthen specific skills—memorizing numbers, or seeing patterns among pictures, for example—and they strengthen specific networks in the brain. But exercise covers the waterfront, activating and connecting many regions of the brain. A pill, or brain training, is like putting one strand of Christmas tree lights on a tree. Exercise is like covering a tree with many strands. Now stand back and gaze at the two trees: Which would you prefer?

6. If you'll recall from the notes in chapter 3, Rutgers University researcher Tracey Shors found that when rats performed a challenging task—running on a rotorod, a rod poised over water that turns as in a log-rolling competition—the rats created new neurons, even though they were adults. Scientists believe that you and I create neurons in the same way. Other scientists have seen running perform similar feats. When some adult mice are given a wheel to run on, while others are given stimulating toys, only the running mice grow new brain cells four months later. And the athletic mice made cognitive gains as a result: Only the running mice become better at navigating a water maze. See M. L. Mustroph, S. Chen, S. C. Desai, et al., "Aerobic Exercise Is the Critical Variable in an Enriched Environment That Increases Hippocampal Neurogenesis and Water Maze Learning in Male C57BL/6J Mice," *Neuroscience* 219 (2012): 62–71. Earlier studies have shown that unless the rats exercised, the new brain cells just died. They were not put into the networks and used for all cognitive activities.

   We would be remiss if we forgot about monkeys; experiments showed that blood flow to the brain made them smarter. Researchers at the University of Pittsburgh taught monkeys how to use a treadmill. In a scene that reminds me of January at my own gym, one group of monkeys worked out five days a week, an hour a day. The other group sat immobile on the treadmill. Five months later, the workout monkeys, probably feeling cocky and superior, figured out which object covered a piece of fruit twice as quickly as the sedentary monkeys did. They were probably hungrier, too. See I. J. Rhyu, J. A. Bytheway, S. J. Kohler, et al., "Effects of Aerobic Exercise Training on Cognitive Function and Cortical Vascularity in Monkeys," *Neuroscience* 167, no. 4 (2010): 1239–48.

7. A. Z. Burzynska, L. Chaddock-Heyman, M. W. Voss, et al., "Physical Activity and Cardiorespiratory Fitness Are Beneficial for White Matter in Low-Fit Older Adults," *PLOS ONE* 9, no. 9 (2014): e107413.

8. As part of a continuing study at Washington University, the researchers examined 201 adults, ages forty-five to eighty-eight. They tested for plaques and for the APOE e-4 gene, which carries fifteen times the risk for Alzheimer's disease. Those who had jogged or walked at least thirty minutes a day, five times a week, had the same level of plaque accumulations as those who did not carry the high-risk gene. See R. Pizzie, H. Hindman, C. M. Roe, et al., "Physical Activity and Cognitive Trajectories in Cognitively Normal Adults: The Adult Children Study," *Alzheimer Disease & Associated Disorders*

28, no. 1 (2014): 50–57. Other researchers have found that exercise helped only those without the gene. But in all studies, exercise had a beneficial effect for one group or another. See Emilie Reas, "Exercise Counteracts Genetic Risk for Alzheimer's," *Scientific American*, October 16, 2014.

9. Sandra Aamodt and Sam Wang, "Exercise on the Brain," *New York Times*, November 8, 2007.

As long as we're going with the better-late-than-never theory, older women who walked regularly showed up to 30 percent less cognitive decline than their sedentary counterparts over an eight-year period. See Anne Underwood, "Can Memory Loss Be Prevented?" *New York Times*, June 11, 2009. Researchers at Rush University found that inactive older adults (the bottom 10 percent) were more than twice as likely to develop Alzheimer's disease as those who were the most active (top 10 percent). Researchers followed 716 older adults over three and a half years. This was the first study to use an objective measure (an actigraph) rather than relying on people's reports of how active they were.

10. S. Agrigoroaei and M. E. Lachman, "Cognitive Functioning in Midlife and Old Age: Combined Effects of Psychosocial and Behavioral Factors," *Journals of Gerontology Series B: Psychological Sciences and Social Sciences* 66, Suppl. 1 (2011): i130–40.

11. H. Naci and J. P. A. Ioannidis, "Comparative Effectiveness of Exercise and Drug Interventions on Mortality Outcomes: Metaepidemiological Study," *British Medical Journal* 347 (2013): f5577. In 2009, the Department of Health and Human Services committee on physical exercise found that people who completed a three-to-six-month exercise program dropped their levels of C-reactive protein (which indicates the risk of cardiovascular disease). By how much? By 30 percent on average—about the same effect as a statin drug. The committee also found that exercise does everything but make dinner and wash the car: Looking at the scientific evidence, it said that physical activity in adults lowers the risk of early death, stroke, type 2 diabetes, high blood pressure, high cholesterol, and colon and breast cancer. For a review, see C. Ballantyne, "Does Exercise Really Make You Healthier?" *Scientific American,* January 2, 2009, http://www.scientificamerican.com/article/does-exercise-really-make/. British researchers followed 2,400 British men and women across adulthood since March 1946, and they, too, found that exercise across these adults' lives meant that when they were older, they could perform activities more easily (getting up from chairs more quickly, standing and balancing, holding a strong grip). See R. Cooper, G. D. Mishra, and D. Kuh, "Physical Activity Across Adulthood and Physical Performance in Midlife: Finding from a British Birth Cohort," *American Journal of Preventive Medicine* 41, no. 4 (2011): 376–84.

12. About major depression, see J. A. Blumenthal, M. A. Bayak, K. A. Moore, et al., "Effects of Exercise Training on Older Patients with Major Depression," *Archives of Internal Medicine* 159 (1999): 2349–56. For mild to moderate depression, see K. A. Barbour, T. M. Edenfield, and J. A. Blumenthal, "Exercise as a Treatment for Depression and Other Psychiatric Disorders: A Review," *Journal of Cardiopulmonary Rehabilitation and Prevention* 27, no. 6 (2007): 359–67.

13. B. M. Hoffman, M. A. Babyak, A. Sherwood, et al., "Effects of Aerobic Exercise on Sexual Functioning in Depressed Adults," *Mental Health and Physical Activity* 2, no. 1 (2009): 23–28. Researchers at Duke University Medical Center studied two hundred

depressed adults, aged forty and over, who were generally sedentary and overweight. They divided them into three groups: One group walked, ran, or biked thirty minutes a day, three days a week. The two others received either an antidepressant or a placebo pill. After four months, they took the Arizona Sexual Experiences questionnaire. The exercisers reported better sex than the placebo group, and marginally better sex than the antidepressant group.

14. Because the study is blind—none of the researchers knows what group anyone is in—I cannot know for certain. But it was pretty obvious from the interview that Ron Becker is in the dieting group and Nancy Ley is in the exercise group. The researchers were not present during either interview.

15. Gary Marcus, *Guitar Zero* (New York: Penguin Books, 2012).

16. E. I. Knudsen and P. F. Knudsen, "Sensitive and Critical Periods for Visual Calibration of Sound Localization by Barn Owls," *Journal of Neuroscience* 10, no. 1 (1990): 222–32.

17. Marcus, *Guitar Zero*, 8.

18. B. A. Linkenhoker and E. I. Knudsen, "Incremental Training Increases the Plasticity of the Auditory Space Map in Adult Barn Owls," *Nature* 419 (6904): 293–96.

19. There is much evidence suggesting that learning a language as a child helps one stay mentally acute in later years, but almost no one has looked at the effect of learning a language as an adult. Thomas Bak at the Centre for Cognitive Aging and Cognitive Epidemiology (University of Edinburgh) looked at the IQ scores of 835 Scottish people who were tested at age eleven (in 1936) and again when they were in their seventies. Of those, 195 could speak a second language at age eleven. Another sixty-seven learned a second language as adults. When the researchers examined the cognitive tests of the septuagenarians—in particular, reading, verbal fluency, and general intelligence—they found that those who learned a second language as adults scored better on their IQ than would have been predicted from their IQ scores at age eleven. See T. H. Bak, J. J. Nissan, M. M. Allerhand, and I. J. Deary, "Does Bilingualism Influence Cognitive Aging?" *Annals of Neurology* 75, no. 6 (2014): 959–63.

20. See M. Antoniou, G. M. Gunasekera, and P. C. M. Wong, "Foreign Language Training as Cognitive Therapy for Age-Related Cognitive Decline: A Hypothesis for Future Research," *Neuroscience & Biobehavioral Reviews* 37, no. 10 (2013): 2689–98. Anecdotal evidence abounds that learning a new language can help an adult reverse the decline. When writer William Alexander studied French intensively for one year, some of his scores on memory tests catapulted from the lowest 10 percent to the top 20 percent. See William Alexander, *Flirting with French: How a Language Charmed Me, Seduced Me, and Nearly Broke My Heart* (Chapel Hill, NC: Algonquin Books, 2014).

21. K. Hakuta, E. Bialystok, and E. Wiley, "Critical Evidence: A Test of the Critical-Period Hypothesis for Second-Language Acquisition," *Psychological Science* 14, no. 1 (2003): 31–38.

22. T. A. Salthouse, "When Does Age-Related Cognitive Decline Begin?" *Neurobiology of Aging* 30, no. 4 (2009): 507–14.

23. Younger brains have millions more synapses (connections between brain cells) than older brains, and young brains are more plastic, or adaptable. Even the neurotransmitters are on the side of the young: Acetylcholine, which regulates new connections between brain cells (and thus memories), flows freely until around age twelve, and then the

neurotransmitter becomes more selective. However—and this is why learning new things helps as an adult—the brain switches on the neurotransmitter during "a novel situation, a shock, or intense focus, maintained through repetition or continuous application," as writer Robert Twigger put it. See Robert Twigger, "Master of Many Trades," *Aeon*, November 4, 2014, https://aeon.co/essays/we-live-in-a-one-track-world-but-any one-can-become-a-polymath.

24. P. Iverson, P. K. Kuhl, R. Akahane-Yamada, et al., "A Perceptual Interference Account of Acquisition Difficulties for Non-native Phonemes," *Cognition* 87, no. 1 (2003): B47–57.

25. K. A. Ericsson, "The Influence of Experience and Deliberate Practice on the Development of Superior Expert Performance," in K. A. Ericsson, N. Charness, P. Feltovich, and R. R. Hoffman, eds., *Cambridge Handbook of Expertise and Expert Performance* (Cambridge, UK: Cambridge University Press, 2006), 685–706.

26. See Malcolm Gladwell's 2008 book *Outliers* (New York: Little, Brown), which argued that talent is unnecessary as long as you practice ten years or ten thousand hours.

27. K. A. Ericsson, K. Nandagopal, and R. W. Roring, "Toward a Science of Exceptional Achievement," *Annals of the New York Academy of Sciences* 1172, no. 1 (2009): 199–217.

28. I had my own reservations about Ericsson's "practice, not talent" theory. Ericsson has studied writers and claims that IQ does not predict success in writing. I told him I wanted to believe his findings, but I didn't. I noted that a friend of mine is David Brooks, a columnist for *The New York Times*. David and I both have been journalists for about thirty years. I have done well enough, I told Ericsson, but I am not David Brooks—not only in terms of his success, but also in his ability to write elegantly and synthesize ideas.

"I think there's an IQ difference between David and me," I said. "I mean, we're in the same profession, we've both worked really hard, and we're both motivated to do well—so how do you explain the difference?"

Ericsson said the key for writers—as with, say, pianists—is that they begin early enough to develop their craft over many years.

"What is it that David Brooks can do that other people can't do?" he asked. "I would basically then go backward and try to see when was the first time he was writing and summarizing people's views, or commenting on things. And then maybe look at your life. When did you do the kinds of things that David Brooks is now doing? Did you have a period when you were politically interested, where you were addressing some of these issues, and would go out and read so you would be able to come up with a new viewpoint?"

"Interesting," I said, not wanting to admit my early paucity of interest in these areas. "I'll have to think about this." The next time I saw David, I asked him about his past.

"I knew I wanted to be a writer at age seven," he said. "When I read *Paddington Bear*, I wanted to be a fiction writer. I wrote for my elementary school newspaper. I couldn't understand why the girl I had a crush on liked another guy more than me, because I could write better than he could," he laughed. At the University of Chicago, David contributed reviews and satirical pieces to campus publications before trying his hand at news reporting and ultimately moving on to writing opinion pieces.

"Michael Oakeshott, a British philosopher, once said that it takes three generations to make a career," he told me. David's grandfather was a great writer, both his parents were published academics and fully supported his writing ambitions, and now David is one of the most prominent writers of his generation.

I, on the other hand, never scribbled a word for the school newspaper in high school or college. I had no particular passion for politics. I fell into journalism because I loved to write and I loved to tell stories, and a job at *The Christian Science Monitor* opened up after college. Nothing in my adolescence pointed to a career as a columnist or White House correspondent.

Ericsson has a point, but I still believe that David's early interests in writing and the support of his parents cannot completely explain why he has risen above almost everyone else in his generation. Somewhere in the mix is sheer talent.

29. The researcher found that both expert and amateur pianists in their sixties lagged behind younger pianists in mental processing speed. Moreover, older *amateur* pianists showed age-related declines in performing music-related tasks and in the speed of finger movements. But *expert* older pianists performed only slightly below young expert pianists. Why? Ericsson says it all depended on the amount of deliberate practice during the older pianists' adulthood. See R. T. Krampe and K. A. Ericsson, "Maintaining Excellence: Deliberate Practice and Elite Performance in Young and Older Pianists," *Journal of Experimental Psychology: General* 125, no. 4 (1996): 331.

30. This is precisely Joe Friel's message. Friel is a famous endurance sports coach and author of *The Cyclist's Training Bible* (Boulder, CO: Velo Press, 1996). He told me that the problem with older athletes is that they go on autopilot: "They begin to cut back on everything that's challenging, and do a lighter workout." True, some physical capacities begin to flag with time: Your aerobic capacity declines (the ability to process oxygen and thus your energy level), and so does your muscle mass, even as you gain body fat. But if you train hard, like a younger athlete, you can turn back the clock. He, at seventy, is almost as fast as he ever was.

"So the decline has as much to with lifestyle as it does with biology," I said.

"No question," Friel said. "In fact, some scientists believe it's forty percent biology and sixty percent lifestyle. I see it all the time. People make gigantic changes in their body structure, in their health and their fitness, just by changing exercise and nutrition."

CHAPTER 8. WHEN BAD STUFF HAPPENS

1. Those include: realistic optimism; the ability to face fear; having a moral compass and altruistic instincts; possessing some religious or spiritual sensibilities; having social support; knowing resilient role models; being physically fit; staying mentally acute; remaining cognitively and emotionally flexible; and retaining a sense of meaning, purpose, and growth. Most resilient people do not possess all of these characteristics. But Southwick, Charney, and others have singled out optimism and social support as particularly critical. See Steven Southwick and Dennis Charney, *Resilience: The Science of Mastering Life's Greatest Challenges* (Cambridge, UK: Cambridge University Press, 2012).

2. Charney and Southwick have also found a genetic basis for resilience. They conducted several studies involving U.S. Special Forces who were undergoing high-intensity training, looking at who performed better during intense interrogation and physical stress. They found that those soldiers who could bring the stress hormones back to baseline more quickly (chemicals including cortisol, adrenaline, and noradrenaline) earned the highest scores. One particular neurotransmitter seems to be an elixir: Neuropeptide Y

has been called the "resilience hormone," because it shuts down the alarm system quickly. The top-performing Special Forces soldiers had the highest level of neuropeptide Y in their bloodstream. In fact, neuropeptide Y is so good at reducing stress quickly that researchers are developing a nasal spray with the hormone, which could be given to people immediately following a traumatic event to prevent them from developing PTSD.

3. James Pennebaker, of the University of Texas in Austin, asked some people to write about their most traumatic experiences for fifteen minutes, four days in a row; he asked another group to simply write in a diary. Those who found meaning in the event were healthier in the long run: He checked the health records a year later and found that "meaning makers" went to the doctor and to the hospital fewer times than those who simply wrote about a nontraumatic event. See J. W. Pennebaker and C. K. Chung, "Expressive Writing and Its Links to Mental and Physical Health," in H. S. Friedman, ed., *Oxford Handbook of Health Psychology* (New York: Oxford University Press, 2011), 417–37.

4. Freud believed that talking about your depression would help lift it. In fact, the opposite appears to be true. Researchers Susan Nolen-Hoeksema and Jannay Morrow found that when they asked moderately depressed people to ruminate on their state for eight minutes, they grew more depressed. When they asked other depressed people to think about something else—that is, distracting their thoughts—those people became significantly less depressed. See S. Nolen-Hoeksema and J. Morrow, "Effects of Rumination and Distraction on Naturally Occurring Depressed Mood," *Cognition & Emotion* 7, no. 6 (1993): 561–70. For a great overview of the research, see Emily Esfahani Smith, "The Benefits of Optimism Are Real," *The Atlantic,* March 1, 2013, http://www.theatlantic.com/health/archive/2013/03/the-benefits-of-optimism-are-real/273306/.

5. For an excellent review, see Southwick and Charney, *Resilience*, 34–35. In one study of Israeli civilians who were exposed to Scud missile attacks during the first Gulf War, optimists developed fewer stress-related psychological illnesses (such as PTSD and depression) than did pessimists. They also used fewer medical services. See M. Zeidner and A. L. Hammer, "Coping with Missile Attack: Resources, Strategies, and Outcomes," *Journal of Personality* 60, no. 4 (1992): 709–46.

6. C. S. Carver, C. Pozo, S. D. Harris, et al., "How Coping Mediates the Effect of Optimism on Distress: A Study of Women with Early Stage Breast Cancer," *Journal of Personality and Social Psychology* 65, no. 2 (1993): 375–90. M. F. Scheier, K. A. Matthews, J. F. Owens, et al., "Dispositional Optimism and Recovery from Coronary Artery Bypass Surgery: The Beneficial Effects on Physical and Psychological Well-being," *Journal of Personality and Social Psychology* 57, no. 6 (1989): 1024–40.

7. The researchers followed a thousand elderly people in the Netherlands for fifteen years. Those who were optimists—and had high expectations before surgery—enjoyed better health after surgery. Optimists were less likely to be rehospitalized after coronary bypass surgery. And they had significantly lower risk of dying from cardiovascular problems over a fifteen-year period. See E. J. Giltay, M. H. Kamphuis, S. Kalmijn, F. G. Zitman, and D. Kromhout, "Dispositional Optimism and the Risk of Cardiovascular Death: The Zutphen Elderly Study," *Archives of Internal Medicine* 166, no. 4 (2006): 431–36.

8. This is one of the cooler—and most personally relevant—studies I have seen. Sheldon Cohen at Carnegie Mellon University infected subjects, both optimists and pessimists, with a cold virus and then quarantined them in a hotel for a week. Those with higher

positive emotions were less likely to develop colds. And the optimists who did catch a cold experienced much milder symptoms than those with more negative emotions. See S. Cohen, W. J. Doyle, R. B. Turner, C. M. Alper, and D. P. Skoner, "Emotional Style and Susceptibility to the Common Cold," *Psychosomatic Medicine* 65, no. 4 (2003): 652–57.

9. The thirty-seven negative events fell into seven categories: one's own illness or injury; a loved one's illness or injury; violence (e.g., physical assault, forced sexual relations); bereavement (e.g., parent's death); social/environmental stress (e.g., serious financial difficulties, living in or having lived in dangerous housing); relationship stress (e.g., parents' divorce); and disaster (e.g., major fire, flood, earthquake). See M. D. Seery, E. A. Holman, and R. C. Silver, "Whatever Does Not Kill Us: Cumulative Lifetime Adversity, Vulnerability, and Resilience," *Journal of Personality and Social Psychology* 99, no. 6 (2010): 1025.

10. One of the first people to show that a little stress is a good thing was Salvatore Maddi, a psychologist at UC Irvine and founder of the Hardiness Institute. Maddi, then at the University of Chicago, and colleagues began following 430 managers of the Illinois phone company in the 1970s, and were well positioned to track their mental and physical health when the phone company laid off half of its 26,000-person workforce. About two thirds of the employees in the study suffered significant performance, leadership, and health declines as a result of the extreme stress, including heart attacks, strokes, obesity, depression, substance abuse, and poor performance reviews. But the other third actually thrived during the upheaval, maintaining their health, happiness, and high performance. Looking into their backgrounds, the researchers found that the resilient people had endured difficult (though not abusive) childhoods: For example, one parent had struggled with alcoholism, or a father's military career had forced them to move frequently. Maddi concluded that these resilient (or "hardy") people had three key beliefs, which he dubbed the Three C's. "Commitment" motivated them to stay focused and engaged rather than become isolated. They felt in "control" of their fate, confident that their hard work would pay off, unlike the less resilient peers who felt powerless. And they viewed the stress as a "challenge," an opportunity for growth and learning, rather than a burden. See S. R. Maddi, "Hardiness Training at Illinois Bell Telephone," in J. P. Opatz, ed., *Health Promotion Evaluation* (Stevens Point, WI: National Wellness Institute, 1987), 101–15. In another study, Maddi found that adults coped with illness, spousal loss, and major accidents if they had previously experienced and coped with stress in childhood. See D. M. Khoshaba and S. R. Maddi, "Early Experiences in Hardiness Development," *Consulting Psychology Journal: Practice and Research* 51, no. 2 (1999): 106–16.

11. Silver found another clue to resilience in studying Israeli communities that were exposed to daily mortar fire for seven years: living in a close-knit community with shared values. She compared four communities. Two of them experienced no shelling. One rural community suffered daily shelling, as did a city in southern Israel. The residents of the rural community were homogenous, had a sense of belonging, and trusted the national and local government. On the other hand, people in the city—many of them immigrants from North Africa and Russia—felt isolated from their neighbors, dislocated from their culture, and distrustful of the government. The rural residents experienced about the same low levels of PTSD and stress as residents of communities that had not been shelled at all. In fact, only one resident experienced the symptoms of full-blown PTSD. By con-

trast, the city dwellers were traumatized: Over a quarter reported symptoms consistent with PTSD. They also suffered more than twice the number of symptoms of global distress, and went to the hospital nine times as often as did the residents of the rural community that was attacked. See M. Gelkopf, R. Berger, A. Bleich, and R. C. Silver, "Protective Factors and Predictors of Vulnerability to Chronic Stress: A Comparative Study of 4 Communities After 7 Years of Continuous Rocket Fire," *Social Science & Medicine* 74, no. 5 (2012): 757–66.

12. D. M. Lyons, K. J. Parker, M. Katz, and A. F. Schatzberg, "Developmental Cascades Linking Stress Inoculation, Arousal Regulation, and Resilience," *Frontiers in Behavioral Neuroscience* 3 (2009): 32.

13. Taylor Swift read Maya's blog, which eventually topped ten million hits. The singer wrote a song about Ronan. She made Maya coauthor and donated half the proceeds, $250,000, to the Ronan Thompson Foundation, whose aim was to find a cure for this childhood cancer.

14. Richard G. Tedeschi and Lawrence G. Calhoun, *Trauma and Transformation: Growing in the Aftermath of Suffering* (Thousand Oaks, CA: Sage Publications, 1995).

15. I wondered what sets one person on this unwanted trajectory of growth and another on a path to permanent despair. Some personality traits play a part. It helps to be an optimist who is able to focus on solutions and disengage from the problems that can't be solved. Social support can help, and religious or spiritual beliefs, although those are sometimes, as in Maya's case, the first to go. Calhoun and Tedeschi asked themselves the same question, and created a twenty-one-item inventory to ferret out whether a person has experienced posttraumatic growth or not. The items fall under five headings: If you feel personally stronger; if you have changed or developed your spiritual views; if you recognize new opportunities in your life; if you have a greater appreciation for life; and if your relationships with other people have changed, then you are a candidate for growth. I reflect on Maya, and think: *Check, check, check, check, and check*—maybe not in a Pollyanna way (discarding God, discarding friends), but there is no denying the transformation in her mission and seriousness of purpose.

16. The program was aimed at schoolchildren struggling with depression or school-related trauma. It was claimed that in nearly two dozen randomized controlled studies where the Penn curriculum was used, children who learned the skills were significantly less likely to get depressed—in some cases, the number of children suffering from moderate to severe depression was cut in half. Critics scoff at this, saying that the studies showed only tiny improvements and that they have never been tested in the far more hair-raising circumstances of driving in a tank bracing for an IED explosion.

17. I interviewed more than a dozen soldiers who had put the Army's resilience training into real-life practice. They found it helped them back away from the emotional precipice they were facing. Most of the soldiers were middle-aged, but my favorite story came from a twenty-three-year-old private named Ryan Whitt.

In 2011, Whitt was a nineteen-year-old college dropout who hoped the military would provide some direction to his life. On May 27, eight months into his Army career, Whitt splurged on a motorcycle, giddy as the teenager he was when he pulled onto the highway on his way back to Fort Hood, Texas. In a split second, he sensed a dark object to his left, and his world narrowed down to one stark fact.

"I went about fifty-five miles an hour into the side of a Suburban."

Broken ribs. Collapsed lung. Broken collarbone. Separated shoulder. Torn ligaments and tendons in the knees. Broken vertebrae. A heart that stopped twice on the way to the hospital. The doctors telling him he might never walk again.

"My first reaction was like, 'Well, there goes everything I wanted to do in my life,'" Whitt told me. "I had expected so much out of myself as a soldier and in my military career. And it was just over so fast."

A few weeks later, after being discharged from a rehabilitation facility, Whitt returned to Fort Hood. Because he could not manage stairs, he was put in an office in his barracks, an office staffed twenty-four hours a day, seven days a week. He could not get out of bed or walk without help. Sometimes he would go days without a shower.

"I would overmedicate myself at night to sleep, and overmedicate in the morning to not feel the pain," he said. "When you sit that long, helpless, your thoughts get the best of you. That was the worst part."

"He was in a very dark place," recalled Staff Sergeant Randall Traxler, the unit's Master Resiliency Trainer.

Subtly, without really telling Whitt, Traxler began employing some of the resilience techniques he learned from the Penn researchers. The two men set "little tiny goals"—small victories every day—to build up Whitt's optimism. "Or if he started to catastrophize," Traxler said, "I'd walk him through it and provide him the evidence" that things were not hopeless.

"Without me knowing it, he'd kind of coax me into using resiliency skills," Whitt said, laughing. "I started to teach myself how to counteract my own thoughts, like not letting myself fall into 'thinking traps' or thinking, *Why, why, why?* I started doing the goal setting. I started hunting the good stuff. The negative thinking, the thinking traps, all of that just immediately started to fall back on resiliency."

Every day, Whitt would write down what he wanted to accomplish. Little things—things you or I do in thirty seconds, such as sitting up in bed—required an hour.

"I had a game plan. I'd wake up, get myself mentally prepared because it was going to suck and it was going to hurt," Whitt recalled. "I'd wait for the medicine to kick in and do its thing. I'd roll over on my left side, push myself up, use what little ab muscles I had to push up. I'd sit there for thirty or forty minutes, and then swing myself up to the edge of the bed. I think it took me an hour and twenty minutes to put one sock and one boot on. It was a process, but it kept me busy, kept me from thinking all the terrible things, so I can't really complain."

Whitt's first attempt to put on his uniform required more than four hours. Whitt and Traxler texted and talked every day, and soon Whitt started borrowing books and exercises on resiliency. They both realized that even if Whitt weren't medically discharged, he would never lead a unit in Afghanistan or anywhere else. So the two men set a new sort of goal. Whitt decided to enter a competition called "Soldier of the Unit," which required knowing military history, how to lead soldiers, how to handle situations on base and in war. This young man who left college after one semester decided to reinvent himself—in his eyes and the eyes of others—into a scholar.

"A big part of being in the Army is physical fitness, and I wasn't going to excel in that," he conceded. "So I had to do things that other soldiers weren't good at, which was memorizing the Army-by-the-books type of things. And I went into my first board [competition], and I guess, from what everyone has told me, I absolutely rocked it."

Whitt aced the next competition, and the next, eventually becoming the top soldier in the brigade. Ryan Whitt was not medically discharged. He was promoted to sergeant. When I spoke with him, he was lifting weights every day and running twice a week—this, for a man who was told he probably would live out his days in a wheelchair. He fell in love and married.

"I don't want to say that I'm glad that it happened, because I wouldn't wish what I went through on my worst enemy," Whitt said. "But before, I was young, dumb, and ignorant, you know. I am ten times better of a man now than I ever could have been before."

Of course, Sergeant Whitt is a data point of one: Maybe he would have thrived without the resilience training. Maybe all it took was a friend, one sergeant who could buck him up when no one else would. Maybe, but he doesn't think so. He had to learn resilience. He had to build that muscle.

"I can tell you right now, before my accident, I really don't think I had any resiliency. Whatever happened, I was the 'Woe is me' guy. But once I noticed the change in how I was thinking about things, it was one of those *Holy crap* moments: This really does work."

18. For his seminal article that shifted the thinking on resilience, see G. A. Bonanno, "Loss, Trauma, and Human Resilience: Have We Underestimated the Human Capacity to Thrive After Extremely Aversive Events?" *American Psychologist* 59, no. 1 (2004): 20–28.

19. In his TED talk on October 2, 2012, Bonanno listed some of the tragedies that he and others have chronicled, and what percentage of the victims are "resilient" (maintaining their psychological functioning within a few days of the event) and what percentage suffered psychopathology (experiencing chronic depression or PTSD). Here are some examples:

Losing a spouse. Resilient: 58.5 percent. Chronic: 21 percent
Spinal cord injury. Resilient: 53–59 percent. Chronic: 12 percent
Bereavement. Resilient: 41–50 percent. Chronic: 0–21 percent
Breast cancer surgery. Resilient: 66 percent. Chronic: 15 percent
Hereditary cancer test. Resilient: 67–77 percent. Chronic: 9–13 percent
Job loss. Resilient: 69 percent. Chronic: 4 percent
Divorce. Resilient: 72 percent. Chronic: 19 percent
Combat deployment. Resilient: 83–85 percent. Chronic: 5–7 percent

20. Bonanno and his colleagues surveyed more than 2,700 New York residents during the six months after the attacks. On average, 65 percent bounced back within that time. People who were close to, or in, the World Trade Center buildings when they were hit exhibited more symptoms of posttraumatic stress disorder. But even among those highly exposed groups, within six months one third were functioning normally. See G. A. Bonanno, S. Galea, A. Bucciarelli, and D. Vlahov, "Psychological Resilience After Disaster: New York City in the Aftermath of the September 11th Terrorist Attack," *Psychological Science* 17, no. 3 (2006): 181–86.

21. G. A. Bonanno, A. D. Mancini, J. L. Horton, et al., "Trajectories of Trauma Symptoms and Resilience in Deployed U.S. Military Service Members: Prospective Cohort Study," *British Journal of Psychiatry* 200, no. 4 (2012): 317–23.

22. https://www.authentichappiness.sas.upenn.edu/testcenter.
23. Here are the descriptions of my strengths. Let's hope you fare better than I.

Industry, diligence, and perseverance: You work hard to finish what you start. No matter the project, you "get it out the door" in timely fashion. You do not get distracted when you work, and you take satisfaction in completing tasks.

Gratitude: You are aware of the good things that happen to you, and you never take them for granted. Your friends and family members know that you are a grateful person because you always take the time to express your thanks.

Spirituality, sense of purpose, and faith: You have strong and coherent beliefs about the higher purpose and meaning of the universe. You know where you fit in the larger scheme. Your beliefs shape your actions and are a source of comfort to you.

Fairness, equity, and justice: Treating all people fairly is one of your abiding principles. You do not let your personal feelings bias your decisions about other people. You give everyone a chance.

Humor and playfulness: You like to laugh and tease. Bringing smiles to other people is important to you. You try to see the light side of all situations.
24. Richard J. Davidson with Sharon Begley, *The Emotional Life of Your Brain* (New York: Hudson Street Press, 2012).
25. I. Molton, M. P. Jensen, D. M. Ehde, et al., "Coping with Chronic Pain Among Younger, Middle-aged, and Older Adults Living with Neurological Injury and Disease," *Journal of Aging and Health* 20, no. 8 (2008): 972–96.
26. M. Goyal, S. Singh, E. M. S. Sibinga, et al., "Meditation Programs for Psychological Stress and Well-being: A Systematic Review and Meta-analysis," *JAMA Internal Medicine* 174, no. 3 (2014): 357–68.
27. The studies indicated that Mindfulness-Based Stress Reduction, a program developed by Jon Kabat-Zinn at the University of Massachusetts Medical Center, lowered pain by between 5 and 8 percent, and significantly more—30 percent—for irritable bowel syndrome. See S. Schmidt, P. Grossman, B. Schwarzer, et al., "Treating Fibromyalgia with Mindfulness-Based Stress Reduction: Results from a 3-Armed Randomized Controlled Trial," *Pain* 152, no. 2 (2011): 361–69; C. R. Gross et al., "Mindfulness-Based Stress Reduction for Solid Organ Transplant Recipients: A Randomized Controlled Trial," *Alternative Therapies in Health and Medicine* 16, no. 5 (2010): 30–38; N. E. Morone, B. L. Rollman, C. G. Moore, L. Qin, and D. K. Weiner, "A Mind-Body Program for Older Adults with Chronic Low Back Pain: Results of a Pilot Study," *Pain Medicine* 10, no. 8 (2009): 1395–1407; S. A. Gaylord, O. S. Palsson, E. L. Garland, et al., "Mindfulness Training Reduces the Severity of Irritable Bowel Syndrome in Women: Results of a Randomized Controlled Trial," *American Journal of Gastroenterology* 106, no. 9 (2011): 1678–88. This last study found that mindfulness-based stress reduction reduced pain by 30 percent.
28. It's sometimes called a "wind-up syndrome," according to Susan Gaylord, who directs the Program on Integrative Medicine at the University of North Carolina, Chapel Hill. Gaylord's study (cited in the preceding note: "Mindfulness Training Reduces the Severity of Irritable Bowel Syndrome in Women") found that mindfulness training reduced the pain of irritable bowel syndrome by 30 percent. Gaylord launched this study in part for personal reasons. Years ago, she suffered from serious abdominal pain and began practicing mindfulness meditation. To her surprise, as she progressed, her pain flickered

on and off, and eventually—once she had removed the emotional overlay—the pain dissipated completely. (If you'll recall, this is the precise phenomenon that Madhav Goyal at Johns Hopkins experienced.) "The wind-up is sort of a physiological version of the body's catastrophizing," Gaylord told me. "Stress leads to more pain, which leads to more stress, which leads to more pain—that's a wind-up syndrome. Mindfulness can help us unwind and unravel that whole syndrome to the point where we can ask: What is there? What is actually there? Which may be a lot less than what we have built it up to be."

29. Doctors have recognized the placebo effect for centuries, but it was Dr. Henry Beecher's experience during World War II that gave "placebo" a place in modern medicine. During one battle, Beecher found himself on a beach, cut off from supplies and running out of morphine for the wounded men. He observed that he was able to reduce their pain simply by giving them a saltwater injection. Thus was born the serious study of the placebo effect. "Thirty-five percent of the time, the *belief* that you're going to get better is just as good as the best medication," says Dr. James Gordon, who studied under Beecher at Harvard Medical School. "Now what researchers are looking at is: Okay, how does this work psycho-physiologically? And if it works, how do we maximize it? Why deprecate it and say it's 'just' a placebo effect? You should say, 'It's a placebo effect, fantastic! This is what we want.'"

30. My thanks to Madhav Goyal, who brought these papers to my attention. Placebos have reduced blood pressure and hypertension: R. A. Preston, B. J. Materson, D. J. Reda, and D. W. Williams, "Placebo-Associated Blood Pressure Response and Adverse Effects in the Treatment of Hypertension: Observations from a Department of Veterans Affairs Cooperative Study," *Archives of Internal Medicine* 160, no. 10 (2000): 1449–54. This review suggests that placebos can reduce pain and increase appetite for cancer patients, but not reduce tumor size or improve quality of life: G. Chvetzoff and I. F. Tannock, "Placebo Effects in Oncology," *Journal of the National Cancer Institute* 95, no. 1 (2003): 19–29.

31. S. Kam-Hansen, M. Jakubowski, J. M. Kelley, et al., "Altered Placebo and Drug Labeling Changes the Outcome of Episodic Migraine Attacks," *Science Translational Medicine* 6, no. 218 (2014): 218ra5.

32. When given fake acupuncture and warm words from a sympathetic acupuncturist, 62 percent of the subjects suffering from irritable bowel syndrome said their symptoms improved. Only 28 percent on the wait list felt better. And in a measure of how much bedside manner plays into beliefs and pain, only 44 percent who received just the acupuncture (without a sympathetic practitioner) improved. See T. J. Kaptchuk, J. M. Kelley, L. A. Conboy, et al., "Components of Placebo Effect: Randomised Controlled Trial in Patients with Irritable Bowel Syndrome," *British Medical Journal* 336, no. 7651 (2008): 999–1003.

33. Deborah Kotz, "Can Chronic Medical Conditions, Including Depression, Be Treated with Placebos?" *Boston Globe,* March 7, 2011.

34. For the studies, see T. D. Wager, J. K. Rilling, E. E. Smith, et al., "Placebo-Induced Changes in fMRI in the Anticipation and Experience of Pain," *Science* 303, no. 5661 (2004): 1162–67; T. D. Wager, D. J. Scott, and J. Zubieta, "Placebo Effects on Human μ-Opioid Activity During Pain," *Proceedings of the National Academy of Sciences* 104, no. 26 (2007): 11056–61.

35. Judy Peres, "Sometimes Physical Pain Can Be Traced to Memory," *Chicago Tribune*, July 3, 2007.

36. A. R. Mansour, M. N. Baliki, L. Huang, et al., "Brain White Matter Structural Properties Predict Transition to Chronic Pain," *Pain* 154, no. 10 (2013): 2160–68.

37. Researchers in Germany found that people who worked on a difficult memory task reported less pain when they were exposed to a painful level of heat than did people who were given an easy memory task. More intriguingly, a brain scan detected less activity in the spinal cord during the difficult mental task, meaning that fewer pain signals were being relayed to the brain. The researchers hypothesize that distraction may release natural opioids; when they repeated the study but gave participants a drug that blocked the effects of the opioids, distraction was much less effective (40 percent less) in reducing the pain. See C. Sprenger, F. Eippert, J. Finsterbusch, et al., "Attention Modulates Spinal Cord Responses to Pain," *Current Biology* 22, no. 11 (2012): 1019–22.

38. Schwartz told me that DiCaprio learned his part so thoroughly that he actually developed OCD symptoms that persisted for months after the filming was completed.

CHAPTER 9. GIVING IT AWAY

1. Erik H. Erikson, *Identity and the Life Cycle* (New York: W. W. Norton, 1980). See also Joan M. Erikson, *The Life Cycle Completed* (New York: W. W. Norton, 1987).

2. I am happy to report that researchers find childless people are just as generative as those with kids. Researchers surveyed 289 childless people and 2,218 people with kids (biological, adopted, stepchildren) who were part of the Midlife in the United States (MIDUS) database. They found that parents do not have an advantage when it comes to generativity and that childless people enjoyed the same level of psychological well-being as those with children: They have plenty of opportunities to contribute to the next generation or to invest outward. "Parenthood also appears to be no more important to women's than men's development, contrary to popular assumptions," the authors wrote (much to my relief). "Our findings indicated no differences for childless women and mothers and for childless men and fathers in the link between generativity and psychological well-being. This finding is inconsistent with stereotypical perceptions of childless adults, especially women, as being maladapted, having psychological disorders, and being immature, unhappy, and unfulfilled. Apparently, childless adults can rise above pervasive negative attitudes about their lifestyle and create purposeful and meaningful lives, supporting the notion that human development is diverse and heterogeneous. This shift may be especially strong for women today, as their career pursuits outside the home are considered legitimate and generally beneficial." See T. Rothrauff and T. M. Cooney, "The Role of Generativity in Psychological Well-being: Does It Differ for Childless Adults and Parents?" *Journal of Adult Development* 15, no. 3–4 (2008): 148–59; quotation from 155.

3. G. Stanley Hall was a pioneering psychologist who died in the early twentieth century. His exact quote is: "We rarely come to anything like a masterly grip till the shadows begin to slant eastward, and for a season, which varies greatly with individuals, our powers increase as the shadows lengthen."

4. Also, the donors showed stronger white matter connection between the temporal lobe and the amygdala, and the prefrontal cortex, suggesting that there may be better com-

munication between the parts of the brain that involve emotion and decision making. See A. A. Marsh, S. A. Stoycos, K. M. Brethel-Haurwitz, et al., "Neural and Cognitive Characteristics of Extraordinary Altruists," *Proceedings of the National Academy of Sciences* 111, no. 42 (2014): 15036–41.

5. J. Zaki and J. P. Mitchell, "Equitable Decision Making Is Associated with Neural Markers of Intrinsic Value," *Proceedings of the National Academy of Sciences* 108, no. 49 (2011): 19761–66. A follow-up study is: J. Zaki, G. López, and J. P. Mitchell, "Activity in Ventromedial Prefrontal Cortex Covaries with Revealed Social Preferences: Evidence for Person-Invariant Value," *Social Cognitive and Affective Neuroscience* 9, no. 4 (2013): nst005.

6. J. Moll, F. Krueger, R. Zahn, et al., "Human Fronto-mesolimbic Networks Guide Decisions About Charitable Donation," *Proceedings of the National Academy of Sciences* 103, no. 42 (2006): 15623–28.

7. D. Tankersley, C. J. Stowe, and S. A. Huettel, "Altruism Is Associated with an Increased Neural Response to Agency," *Nature Neuroscience* 10, no. 2 (2007): 150–52.

8. Y. Morishima, D. Schunk, A. Bruhin, C. C. Ruff, and E. Fehr, "Linking Brain Structure and Activation in Temporoparietal Junction to Explain the Neurobiology of Human Altruism," *Neuron* 75, no. 1 (2012): 73–79.

9. M. Zanon, G. Novembre, N. Zangrando, L. Chittaro, and G. Silani, "Brain Activity and Prosocial Behavior in a Simulated Life-Threatening Situation," *NeuroImage* 98 (2014): 134–46.

10. German researchers, including psychologist Sebastian Markett at the University of Bonn, found that altruism was linked to a specific gene variation. The researchers asked 101 men and women to give them a DNA sample and then play a game. They received a reward (five euros) for memorizing a set of numbers, and they could increase that reward by gambling with the proceeds. Finally, the participants were shown a picture of an impoverished little girl named Lina, from Peru, and a bracelet she had knitted. The participants were told they could donate any amount of money they earned, anonymously. Then the experimenters left the room. The researchers looked at variations of the COMT gene, which influences how neurotransmitters (including dopamine) are activated in the brain. Those transmitters have been linked to social behaviors such as bonding. It turned out that people with two variations (Val/Val or Val/Met) donated twice as much money as those with a third variation (Met/Met). This was true regardless of gender. In fact, more than 20 percent of those people with the altruistic variations donated all their money. In the white Caucasian population as a whole, 75 percent have the altruistic combination (25 percent Val/Val, 50 percent Val/Met) and 25 percent carry the nonaltruistic combination. Identical twin studies have led researchers to believe that altruism has genetic roots. But this is the first study that has linked it to a specific gene. See M. Reuter, C. Frenzel, N. T. Walter, S. Markett, and C. Montag, "Investigating the Genetic Basis of Altruism: The Role of the COMT Val158Met Polymorphism," *Social Cognitive and Affective Neuroscience* (2010): nsq083.

In another study, nearly two hundred people submitted DNA samples and then took question-and-answer tests measuring empathy. Researchers zeroed in on a particular gene that is a receptor for oxytocin, a hormone associated with trust, empathy, and social bonding. People have one of three variations of the gene receptor: AA, AG, or GG. People with GG variation scored significantly higher on empathy tests than people with the other two. They were also less reactive to stress (measured by heart rate after a loud burst of noise). The study indicates some people may be naturally more empathetic than others. However, researchers caution that gene variation is not destiny, since people's experience and habits can make them more or less empathetic. See S. M. Rodrigues, L. R. Saslow, N. Garcia, O. P. John, and D. Keltner, "Oxytocin Receptor Genetic Variation Relates to Empathy and Stress Reactivity in Humans," *Proceedings of the National Academy of Sciences* 106, no. 50 (2009): 21437–41.

11. This is in contrast to Endal, a Labrador retriever and British wonder dog. According to—wait for it—Endal's Wikipedia page: "Endal came again to national attention in a 2001 incident, when Allen [his owner] was knocked out of his wheelchair by a passing car. Endal pulled Allen, who was unconscious, into the recovery position, retrieved his mobile phone from beneath the car, fetched a blanket and covered him, barked at nearby dwellings for assistance, and then ran to a nearby hotel to obtain help." https://en.wikipedia.org/wiki/Endal.

12. C. Zahn-Waxler, B. Hollenbeck, and M. Radke-Yarrow, "The Origins of Empathy and Altruism," in M. W. Fox and L. D. Mickley, eds., *Advances in Animal Welfare Science* (Washington, DC: The Humane Society, 1984), 21–41.

13. R. M. Joly-Mascheroni, A. Senju, and A. J. Shepherd, "Dogs Catch Human Yawns," *Biology Letters* 4, no. 5 (2008): 446–48.

14. For the monkey that went without food, see J. H. Masserman, S. Wechkin, and W. Terris, "'Altruistic' Behavior in Rhesus Monkeys," *American Journal of Psychiatry* 121, no. 6 (1964): 584–85. For the monkey CPR video, see http://www.telegraph.co.uk/news/newsvideo/viral-video/11306466/Watch-Monkey-saves-dying-friend-at-train-station-in-India.html.

15. G. S. Wilkinson, "Reciprocal Food Sharing in the Vampire Bat," *Nature* 308 (1984): 181–84.

16. I. B. A. Bartal, J. Decety, and P. Mason, "Empathy and Pro-social Behavior in Rats," *Science* 334, no. 6061 (2011): 1427–30.

17. Here are some of Paul Zak's findings about his favorite hormone: Oxytocin increases trusting behavior in men. In a seminal study, the researchers found that when oxytocin is turned into a nasal spray, it can pass through the blood-brain barrier, allowing researchers to raise the level of hormone in a participant's brain and thus test whether the hormone increases pro-social activities. It does, to a certain extent. Zak has found that higher levels of oxytocin are associated with more giving to charity; in women, they are associated with having more friends, better romantic relationships, and more sex. See M. Kosfeld, M. Heinrichs, P. J. Zak, U. Fischbacher, and E. Fehr, "Oxytocin Increases Trust in Humans," *Nature* 435 (7042): 673–76. Later, Zak asked sixty-eight men to play an economic game where they could give money to a charity. Half the men received a nasal spray of oxytocin; half received a placebo. Zak found that those who received oxytocin were 80 percent more generous than those given the placebo. He says that oxytocin receptors reside disproportionately in areas associated with emotions and social behavior, such as the amygdala, hypothalamus, and anterior cingulate. See P. J. Zak, A. A. Stanton, and S. Ahmadi, "Oxytocin Increases Generosity in Humans," *PLOS ONE* 2, no. 11 (2007): e1128. In still another study, Zak and others found that oxytocin does increase the likelihood that people would donate money to a charity. Of those who chose to donate, those who received a spray of oxytocin donated 48 percent more. See

J. A. Barraza, M. E. McCullough, S. Ahmadi, and P. J. Zak, "Oxytocin Infusion Increases Charitable Donations Regardless of Monetary Resources," *Hormones and Behavior* 60, no. 2 (2011): 148–51.

18. Oxytocin is a boon for committed relationships. In one study, researchers at the University of Zurich found that when men and women were given a nasal spray of oxytocin and then asked to talk about a sore subject, both men and women improved their communication, and their cortisol (stress) levels dropped. See B. Ditzen, M. Schaer, B. Gabriel, et al., "Intranasal Oxytocin Increases Positive Communication and Reduces Cortisol Levels During Couple Conflict," *Biological Psychiatry* 65, no. 9 (2009): 728–31.

In a second study, the researchers took a saliva sample and looked specifically at an enzyme linked to social stress. Surprisingly, when people received oxytocin, men and women responded differently. The women showed a decrease in the stress enzyme, while the men saw an increase and reported feeling more intense emotions. Yet the outcome was the same: Both men and women became better at communicating during a conflict; they smiled more and were more open about their feelings. But women were more relaxed and men were more engaged. See B. Ditzen, U. M. Nater, M. Schaer, et al., "Sex-Specific Effects of Intranasal Oxytocin on Autonomic Nervous System and Emotional Responses to Couple Conflict," *Social Cognitive and Affective Neuroscience* 8, no. 8 (2012): nss083.

Researchers at the Karolinska Institutet in Stockholm found that oxytocin seems to affect the tenor of one's relationships. The researchers looked at twins studies and discovered the women with one variation in an oxytocin receptor gene had a more difficult time maintaining long-term relationships, kissed their partners less, did not desire physical proximity, and were more likely to report a marital crisis. See H. Walum, P. Lichtenstein, J. M. Neiderhiser, et al., "Variation in the Oxytocin Receptor Gene Is Associated with Pair-Bonding and Social Behavior," *Biological Psychiatry* 71, no. 5 (2012): 419–26.

Some researchers, such as Adam Guastella at the University of Sydney's Brain and Mind Research Institute, believe oxytocin could become the next-best thing in couples therapy. Why? Oxytocin increases trust, generosity, and our ability both to identify emotion in facial expressions and to communicate. He believes that couples who receive oxytocin give partners the benefit of the doubt and are less critical of their partners. This, he believes, could amplify one's ability to take the other person's perspective, reduce blame, and smooth problem solving. See O. A. Wudarczyk, B. D. Earp, A. Guastella, and J. Savulescu, "Could Intranasal Oxytocin Be Used to Enhance Relationships? Research Imperatives, Clinical Policy, and Ethical Considerations," *Current Opinion in Psychiatry* 26, no. 5 (2013): 474–84.

And, in more evidence that pair bonding rules, researchers at the University of Bonn found that when they sprayed oxytocin into the noses of men, those in a monogamous relationship maintained four to six inches more space between them and an attractive woman in a crowd. Single men edged just as close, regardless of whether they received oxytocin or not. Men who received oxytocin also approached pictures of attractive women more slowly. This suggests oxytocin may promote faithfulness in men in committed relationships. See D. Scheele, N. Striepens, O. Güntürkün, et al., "Oxytocin Modulates Social Distance Between Males and Females," *Journal of Neuroscience* 32, no. 46 (2012): 16074–79.

19. Jennifer Bartz, Jamil Zaki, and others have found it intensifies memories, for good or for ill. When the researchers gave men a nasal spray dose of the hormone, they found that men who had warm relationships with their mothers remembered them as even warmer and more caring. But those who had distant relationships with their mothers remembered them as even colder and less caring. See J. A. Bartz, J. Zaki, K. N. Ochsner, et al., "Effects of Oxytocin on Recollections of Maternal Care and Closeness," *Proceedings of the National Academy of Sciences* 107, no. 50 (2010): 21371–75.

In another study, researchers found that a whiff of oxytocin can either decrease or increase trust, depending on the wiring and history of the person being tested. They gave a dose of oxytocin to people playing an economic game that required cooperation and trust. They found that oxytocin actually *decreased* trust in highly anxiously attached people (people with borderline personality disorder who tend to have volatile relationships). In fact, the researchers estimated that much of oxytocin's effect (some 60 percent) is influenced by the person's personality or the social context. In some people, the hormone makes a person happier, more generous, and more trusting; in other people, the opposite occurs. See J. A. Bartz, J. Zaki, N. Bolger, and K. N. Ochsner, "Social Effects of Oxytocin in Humans: Context and Person Matter," *Trends in Cognitive Sciences* 15, no. 7 (2011): 301–09.

Oxytocin also seems to increase jealousy and gloating among men in competitive situations. Fifty-six men, half of whom received a shot of oxytocin spray, were asked to play a competitive game. Those with oxytocin felt more envy and gloating. Later, however, the researchers said they believe the hormone is "an overall trigger for social sentiments." That is, when the person's association is positive, the hormone increases pro-social behavior, and when it is negative, it makes the negative sentiments worse. See S. G. Shamay-Tsoory, M. Fischer, J. Dvash, et al., "Intranasal Administration of Oxytocin Increases Envy and Schadenfreude (Gloating)," *Biological Psychiatry* 66, no. 9 (2009): 864–70.

And for all those mice reading this book, beware: The hormone could increase your emotional pain. Northwestern University researcher Jelena Radulovic and colleagues found that during a stressful social experience, oxytocin is released and activates a part of the brain that intensifies the memory. In addition, it seems to increase the tendency to feel fearful and anxious during stressful events going forward. See Y. F. Guzmán, N. C. Tronson, V. Jovasevic, et al., "Fear-Enhancing Effects of Septal Oxytocin Receptors," *Nature Neuroscience* 16, no. 9 (2013): 1185–87.

20. Oxytocin altered Paul Zak's behavior, and subsequently his life. "I'm an introvert, and I noticed that I wasn't spending a lot of time building social relationships," he confesses. One day, he realized, *Hey, I'm the connection guy and I'm not connecting to people as I would like.* He tried an experiment. Knowing that touch releases oxytocin, he decided to hug people instead of shaking their hands. "It's like a brain hack!" he says, delighted. "Not only do I appear safe and nice and okay to be around, but I made your brain recognize me as part of your community, your family. And what I find is, after the hug, the richness of the interaction is greatly increased. Somehow the hug does that. It's stupid but it works."

21. Here is Paul Zak's hypothesis about how the hormone makes us more generous: If I see someone in distress, I begin to share those emotions—whether they come from a friend, or images on television of Hurricane Katrina or the earthquake in Haiti. That engage-

ment likely releases oxytocin in my system. I take on the distress, and the way to relieve my new distress is to do something to help—to give blood, to volunteer for Habitat for Humanity, to send a check. "So one reason I'm generous is because I want to relieve my own distress," Zak says. "If I do that, at the same time, I get a little [dopamine] reward response. And so, if you've been on the planet more than twenty or twenty-five years, you've had enough of these situations to go, 'Oh, apparently when humans are in pain and suffering, they like to be helped and it makes me feel good, too.'"

22. Zak created a two-minute video clip in which a father described his young son's cancer, over images of the dad playing with his little boy. People who watched the video experienced a spike in two hormones: cortisol, which is associated with focused attention and indicates distress, and oxytocin. The observers were then given the opportunity to donate money toward finding a cure for childhood cancer, either through the father's foundation or through another charity. The more oxytocin a person released, the more likely he or she was to donate money. The researchers found that empathy was associated with a 47 percent increase in oxytocin from baseline (before a person watched the video). The increase in empathy and oxytocin was higher in women than in men. Higher levels of empathy were also associated with more generous monetary offers toward strangers in an ultimatum game. Zak and others concluded that this is evidence that oxytocin is a physiologic signature for empathy, and that empathy mediates generosity. See J. A. Barraza and P. J. Zak, "Empathy Toward Strangers Triggers Oxytocin Release and Subsequent Generosity," *Annals of the New York Academy of Sciences* 1167, no. 1 (2009): 182–89. Zak told me that in a subsequent study funded by the Defense Advanced Research Projects Agency (DARPA), he tested heart rate and skin conductance of people watching the video. He identified the stress response and empathetic response, and could predict with 80 percent accuracy who would donate. He also scanned people's brains while they watched the video and found that the most active areas of the brain were associated with "theory of mind"—that is, the ability to understand others, as well as areas of the brain rich in oxytocin receptors.

23. In one large survey of people over seventy, participants reported less depression and better health, and were one third less likely to die over the two-year period of the study (1998–2000) if they volunteered a hundred hours a year. But more than that, the benefits begin to tail off or lead to burnout. See S. G. Post, "It's Good to Be Good: 2011 5th Annual Scientific Report on Health, Happiness and Helping Others," *International Journal of Person Centered Medicine* 1, no. 4 (2011): 814–29 (see p. 817). See also M. C. Luoh and A. R. Herzog, "Individual Consequences of Volunteer and Paid Work in Old Age: Health and Mortality," *Journal of Health and Social Behavior* 43 (2002): 490–509.

24. C. D. Batson, B. D. Duncan, P. Ackerman, T. Buckley, and K. Birch, "Is Empathic Emotion a Source of Altruistic Motivation?" *Journal of Personality and Social Psychology* 40, no. 2 (1981): 290–302.

25. P. Condon, G. Desbordes, W. B. Miller, and D. DeSteno, "Meditation Increases Compassionate Responses to Suffering," *Psychological Science* 24, no. 10 (2013): 2125–27.

26. One group learned compassion meditation. Another practiced "cognitive reappraisal," in which a person learns to reframe a bad situation—recalling a stressful event, for example, and then thinking about it in a new, less upsetting way. Both methods are used for emotional regulation. But only compassion meditation increased people's altruistic

behavior. See H. Y. Weng, A. S. Fox, A. J. Shackman, et al., "Compassion Training Alters Altruism and Neural Responses to Suffering," *Psychological Science* 24, no. 7 (2013): 1171–80.

27. J. S. Mascaro, J. K. Rilling, L. T. Negi, and C. Raison, "Compassion Meditation Enhances Empathic Accuracy and Related Neural Activity," *Social Cognitive and Affective Neuroscience* (2012): nss095.

28. The researchers reviewed thirteen randomized trials and found that when nurses and doctors had better relationships with patients, the patients receive as much beneficial effect as from taking an aspirin a day to prevent heart attacks. Other studies of patients with diabetes, hypertension, and osteoarthritis arrived at the same conclusion: A good relationship with one's doctor brought about better health outcomes, such as weight loss, lower blood pressure, stable blood sugar and lipid levels, and reduced pain. In these studies, the "interventions" were pretty basic: Patients flourished if the doctor made more eye contact with them, paid close attention to their emotions, or conducted "motivational interviewing" and goal setting to address issues. See J. M. Kelley, G. Kraft-Todd, L. Schapira, J. Kossowsky, and H. Riess, "The Influence of the Patient-Clinician Relationship on Healthcare Outcomes: A Systematic Review and Meta-analysis of Randomized Controlled Trials," *PLOS ONE* 9, no. 4 (2014): e94207.

29. Singer recruited sixteen couples and scanned the wives' brains when they saw their husbands receive a shock. When they heard their husbands receiving a shock, the women felt their pain, in an emotional but not a *sensory* way: The regions of the brain relating to affective pain lit up, but the areas associated with physical pain did not. See T. Singer, B. Seymour, J. O'Doherty, et al., "Empathy for Pain Involves the Affective but Not Sensory Components of Pain," *Science* 303, no. 5661 (2004): 1157–62.

30. C. D. Marci, J. Ham, E. Moran, and S. P. Orr, "Physiologic Correlates of Perceived Therapist Empathy and Social-Emotional Process During Psychotherapy," *Journal of Nervous and Mental Disease* 195, no. 2 (2007): 103–11.

31. H. Riess, J. M. Kelley, R. W. Bailey, E. J. Dunn, and M. Phillips, "Empathy Training for Resident Physicians: A Randomized Controlled Trial of a Neuroscience-Informed Curriculum," *Journal of General Internal Medicine* 27, no. 10 (2012): 1280–86. Residents continued to be more empathetic one year later. See M. Phillips, A. Lorie, J. Kelley, S. Gray, and H. Riess, "Long-Term Effects of Empathy Training in Surgery Residents: A One-Year Follow-up Study," *European Journal of Person Centered Healthcare* 1, no. 2 (2013): 326–32.

32. For a comprehensive overview of the physical, psychological, and neurological benefits of volunteering or giving (time or money), see S. G. Post, "It's Good to Be Good." Here are some specific studies:

    How volunteering prolongs your life: A. H. Harris and C. E. Thoresen, "Volunteering Is Associated with Delayed Mortality in Older People: Analysis of the Longitudinal Study of Aging," *Journal of Health Psychology* 10, no. 6 (2005): 739–52; D. Oman, C. E. Thoresen, and K. McMahon, "Volunteerism and Mortality Among the Community-Dwelling Elderly," *Journal of Health Psychology* 4, no. 3 (1999): 301–16; S. L. Brown, R. M. Nesse, A. D. Vinokur, and D. M. Smith, "Providing Social Support May Be More Beneficial Than Receiving It: Results from a Prospective Study of Mortality," *Psychological Science* 14, no. 4 (2003): 320–27; P. Moen, D. Dempster-McClain, and R. M. Williams, "Social Integration and Longevity: An Event History

Analysis of Women's Roles and Resilience," *American Sociological Review* 54, no. 4 (1989): 635–47.

How volunteering boosts happiness and well-being: N. G. Choi and J. Kim, "The Effect of Time Volunteering and Charitable Donations in Later Life on Psychological Wellbeing," *Ageing and Society* 31, no. 4 (2011): 590–610; E. A. Greenfield and N. F. Marks, "Formal Volunteering as a Protective Factor for Older Adults' Psychological Well-being," *Journals of Gerontology Series B: Psychological Sciences and Social Sciences* 59, no. 5 (2004): S258–64; C. Schwartz, J. B. Meisenhelder, Y. Ma, and G. Reed, "Altruistic Social Interest Behaviors Are Associated with Better Mental Health," *Psychosomatic Medicine* 65, no. 5 (2003): 778–85.

How it protects you from depression: M. A. Musick and J. Wilson, "Volunteering and Depression: The Role of Psychological and Social Resources in Different Age Groups," *Social Science & Medicine* 56 (2003): 259–69; T. Y. Lum and E. Lightfoot, "The Effects of Volunteering on the Physical and Mental Health of Older People," *Research on Aging* 27, no. 1 (2005): 31–55.

How being "other oriented" reduces the risk of heart attack: L. Scherwitz, R. McKelvain, C. Laman, et al., "Type A Behavior, Self-involvement, and Coronary Atherosclerosis," *Psychosomatic Medicine* 45, no. 1 (1983): 47–57.

How volunteering keeps you sober: M. E. Pagano, B. B. Zeltner, J. Jaber, et al., "Helping Others and Long-Term Sobriety: Who Should I Help to Stay Sober?" *Alcoholism Treatment Quarterly* 27, no. 1 (2009): 38–50; M. E. Pagano, K. B. Friend, J. S. Tonigan, and R. L. Stout, "Helping Other Alcoholics in Alcoholics Anonymous and Drinking Outcomes: Findings from Project MATCH," *Journal of Studies on Alcohol* 65, no. 6 (2004): 766–73.

How empathy and volunteering boost the immune system (the "Mother Teresa effect"): D. C. McClelland and C. Kirshnit, "The Effect of Motivational Arousal Through Films on Salivary Immunoglobulin A," *Psychology and Health* 2, no. 1 (1988): 31–52.

How volunteering cures burnout: L. N. Dyrbye, F. S. Massie, A. Eacker, et al., "Relationship Between Burnout and Professional Conduct and Attitudes Among U.S. Medical Students," *JAMA* 304, no. 11 (2010): 1173–80; C. Campbell, D. L. Campbell, D. Krier, et al., "Reduction in Burnout May Be a Benefit for Short-term Medical Mission Volunteers," *Mental Health, Religion and Culture* 12, no. 7 (2009): 627–37.

How volunteering reduces chronic pain: P. Arnstein, M. Vidal, C. Wells-Federman, B. Morgan, and M. Caudill, "From Chronic Pain Patient to Peer: Benefits and Risks of Volunteering," *Pain Management Nursing* 3, no. 3 (2002): 94–103; A. Luks, "Helper's High: Volunteering Makes People Feel Good, Physically and Emotionally," *Psychology Today* 22, no. 10 (1988): 34–42.

33. There are piles of studies, mainly of older people; here are a few of my favorites on longevity: Stanford researchers followed some 7,500 people over seventy between January 1984 and December 1991. They found that those who occasionally volunteered were 25 percent less likely to have died over that period. Those who frequently volunteered were 31 percent more likely to be alive at study's end. See A. H. Harris and C. E. Thoresen, "Volunteering Is Associated with Delayed Mortality in Older People: Analysis of the Longitudinal Study of Aging," *Journal of Health Psychology* 10, no. 6 (2005): 739–52.

Doug Oman and colleagues followed 2,025 people over fifty-five between 1991 and

1995. He discovered that people who volunteered were 44 percent less likely to die over the four-year period. He also found that volunteering reframed people's life purpose and brought meaning into their lives. See D. Oman, C. E. Thoresen, and K. McMahon, "Volunteerism and Mortality Among the Community-Dwelling Elderly," *Journal of Health Psychology* 4, no. 3 (1999): 301–16.

Stephanie Brown at the University of Michigan followed more than four hundred older couples. Those who helped others (including their spouses) had lower risk of mortality. Interestingly, those who *received* help did not live longer. The types of help included providing child care and assisting with transportation, errands, and shopping for friends, family, and neighbors in the past four months. All these were related to lower death rate. See S. L. Brown, R. M. Nesse, A. D. Vinokur, and D. M. Smith, "Providing Social Support May Be More Beneficial Than Receiving It: Results from a Prospective Study of Mortality," *Psychological Science* 14, no. 4 (2003): 320–27.

Researchers at Cornell University followed 427 wives and mothers in upstate New York for thirty years. Regardless of number of children, marital status, occupation, education, or social class, women who volunteered once a week lived longer and had better physical functioning. See P. Moen, D. Dempster-McClain, and R. M. Williams, "Social Integration and Longevity: An Event History Analysis of Women's Roles and Resilience," *American Sociological Review* 54, no. 4 (1989): 635–47.

34. Older adults volunteering ten or fewer hours per week experienced improved psychological well-being (feeling more satisfied with life, having good relations with others, liking yourself). Interestingly, those who volunteered *more* than ten hours a week did *not* experience a positive effect on well-being, perhaps because more time commitments and responsibilities created stress. Also, making charitable donations of any size was linked with greater well-being, and donating more than a hundred dollars per month showed a more positive effect. See N. G. Choi and J. Kim, "The Effect of Time Volunteering and Charitable Donations in Later Life on Psychological Wellbeing," *Ageing and Society* 31, no. 4 (2011): 590–610. See also E. A. Greenfield and N. F. Marks, "Formal Volunteering as a Protective Factor for Older Adults' Psychological Well-being," *Journals of Gerontology Series B: Psychological Sciences and Social Sciences* 59, no. 5 (2004): S258–64. See also C. Schwartz, J. B. Meisenhelder, Y. Ma, and G. Reed, "Altruistic Social Interest Behaviors Are Associated with Better Mental Health," *Psychosomatic Medicine* 65, no. 5 (2003): 778–85.

As to depression: Researchers find that people twenty-five or older experience less depression when they volunteer—especially those over the age of sixty-five. This is true even adjusting for baseline depression, demographics, employment status, socioeconomic status, health and functioning, and religious attendance. See M. A. Musick and J. Wilson, "Volunteering and Depression: The Role of Psychological and Social Resources in Different Age Groups," *Social Science & Medicine* 56 (2003): 259–69.

In a large survey of people over seventy, people who volunteered reported less depression and better health, and they were two thirds less likely to die over the two-year period of the study (1998–2000). See T. Y. Lum and E. Lightfoot, "The Effects of Volunteering on the Physical and Mental Health of Older People," *Research on Aging* 27, no. 1 (2005): 31–55.

35. Researchers at UCLA analyzed speech patterns of type A personalities, defined as always in a hurry, easily moved to hostility and anger, and having high levels of competi-

tiveness. (Uh-oh.) The incidence of heart attack and other stress-related illnesses was highly correlated with the level of self-reference (using words such as *I, me, my, mine, myself* during a structured interview). Many references correlated with heart disease. Being self-obsessed and self-preoccupied adds stress and stress-induced physical illness, such as coronary disease. See L. Scherwitz, R. McKelvain, C. Laman, et al., "Type A Behavior, Self-Involvement, and Coronary Atherosclerosis," *Psychosomatic Medicine* 45, no. 1 (1983): 47–57.

36. Maria Pagano led a study of alcoholics in the group Alcoholics Anonymous. Those who helped other people were more likely to be sober than those who did not; but those who helped *other AA members* were most likely to be sober a year later. Of the 8 percent who helped others, 40 percent remained sober over the next year, compared with 22 percent of those who did not help anyone. In other words, helping doubled the likelihood that you would stay sober. See M. E. Pagano, B. B. Zeltner, J. Jaber, et al., "Helping Others and Long-term Sobriety: Who Should I Help to Stay Sober?" *Alcoholism Treatment Quarterly* 27, no. 1 (2009): 38–50. See also M. E. Pagano, K. B. Friend, J. S. Tonigan, and R. L. Stout, "Helping Other Alcoholics in Alcoholics Anonymous and Drinking Outcomes: Findings from Project MATCH," *Journal of Studies on Alcohol* 65, no. 6 (2004): 766–73.

37. Just thinking about giving seems to have a physiological impact. In the 1980s, the renowned Harvard behavioral psychologist David McClelland discovered that subjects who watched a film about Mother Teresa's work tending to orphans in Calcutta—an example of profound compassion—showed significant increases in a protective antibody (salivary immunoglobulin A, or S-IgA) over those watching a neutral film. McClelland termed this the "Mother Teresa effect." Moreover, this antibody remained high for an hour after the film in those subjects who were asked to focus their minds on times when they had loved or been loved. See D. C. McClelland and C. Kirshnit, "The Effect of Motivational Arousal Through Films on Salivary Immunoglobulin A," *Psychology and Health* 2, no. 1 (1988): 31–52.

38. Burnout plagues medical students in the United States, but those who undertook two-week medical mission trips in South America scored lower burnout rates after they returned. They continued to feel less burnout six months later. See L. N. Dyrbye, F. S. Massie, A. Eacker, et al., "Relationship Between Burnout and Professional Conduct and Attitudes Among U.S. Medical Students," *JAMA* 304, no. 11 (2010): 1173–80. See also C. Campbell, D. L. Campbell, D. Krier, et al., "Reduction in Burnout May Be a Benefit for Short-term Medical Mission Volunteers," *Mental Health, Religion and Culture* 12, no. 7 (2009): 627–37.

39. People suffering from chronic pain report decreased intensity, and less disability and depression, when they reach out to others in similar pain. In one study, pain was reduced by 13 percent. Scientists believe the release of endorphins explains the phenomenon. See P. Arnstein, M. Vidal, C. Wells-Federman, B. Morgan, and M. Caudill, "From Chronic Pain Patient to Peer: Benefits and Risks of Volunteering," *Pain Management Nursing* 3, no. 3 (2002): 94–103. Other researchers discovered the benefits of "helper's high" after surveying thousands of people: Thirteen percent said they experienced fewer aches and pains, and 22 percent said they felt less depressed. See A. Luks, "Helper's High: Volunteering Makes People Feel Good, Physically and Emotionally," *Psychology Today* 22, no. 10 (1988): 34–42.

40. If you volunteer for unselfish reasons (to help others), you are about 60 percent less likely to die in a given period (in this case, fifty years) than if you volunteer for selfish reasons (to feel good about yourself) or do not volunteer at all. Researchers from the University of Michigan and Stony Brook University Medical Center followed more than ten thousand Wisconsin high school students from their graduation in 1959 to 2008. The average age was sixty-nine years. In 2004, respondents reported whether they had volunteered within the past ten years and how regularly. They reported their reasons for volunteering by answering ten questions. Overall, 4.3 percent of 2,384 nonvolunteers had died four years later, in 2008. This was about the same percentage as those who volunteered for self-oriented reasons (4 percent). However, only 1.6 percent of those who volunteered for selfless motives had died over the same period. In other words, volunteering for the right reasons cut one's risk of death by 60 percent. See S. Konrath, A. Fuhrel-Forbis, A. Lou, and S. Brown, "Motives for Volunteering Are Associated with Mortality Risk in Older Adults," *Health Psychology* 31, no. 1 (2012): 87.

41. Aaron Hurst, "Being Good Isn't the Only Way to Go," *New York Times*, April 19, 2014.

42. For an exhaustive account of the families' journey, see Lawrence Wright, "Five Hostages," *The New Yorker,* July 6, 2015.

43. In June 2015, the White House revised its policy with Presidential Policy Directive (PPD) 30, "U.S. Nationals Taken Hostage Abroad and Personnel Recovery Efforts." While the U.S. government itself will not pay ransom money to hostage-takers, it will no longer threaten families with criminal prosecution if they try to raise money on their own. The government will share more information with families, and will serve as a go-between between hostage-takers (or their intermediaries) and the families, to increase the chances that the hostages will return home safely. See https://www.whitehouse.gov/the-press -office/2015/06/24/presidential-policy-directive-hostage-recovery-activities.

44. I thought of something Abigail Marsh at Georgetown had said to me: "People define altruism out of existence." David (and other altruistic people, such as Harold Mintz) do this out of modesty; psychologists do it out of reductionism. Marsh points out that anytime you have a goal and you accomplish it—running a marathon, losing ten pounds, finishing a book—you will take pleasure in it. It's natural to get pleasure out of a selfless act. But claiming that pleasure you receive cancels out the selfless nature of the act is "ridiculous," she says. "You have made altruism impossible at that point. The real question is: Why do some people decide this selfless thing is what they want to do—that this is their goal?" Why do some people attend baseball games for pleasure, while others give away their kidney? Why did other media companies and other private citizens who had the money, the research capabilities, and the connections choose *not* to help, while David did?

CHAPTER 10. THE MEANING OF WORK

1. I am borrowing this idea from John Davis, a senior lecturer at Harvard Business School. Davis says we create a trajectory early in our adult lives with some "big bets": what career you pursue, whom you marry (and whether you marry), where you live, what lifestyle you choose. Then there are "a thousand little choices" that reinforce your trajectory: the friends you make, or the daily patterns you create, such as regular exercise or eighty-hour workweeks. And finally, he says, there are the "unconscious influences,"

the voices of your parents or society, saying we should follow this path, we should climb this hill. "People are so focused on doing what they're doing, there could be another hill, right next to them, that is a *better* hill for them, at least at a certain point in their life," Davis says. "They might not see it, or if they do see it or suspect that it's there, they may not know how to jump from their hill to the other hill." Davis says the key, midway through a career, is to try to broaden people's perspectives "so that they can understand that those interests are in them and are yearning for expression and that here's a pathway to the other hill."

2. Marci Alboher, *The Encore Career Handbook: How to Make a Living and a Difference in the Second Half of Life* (New York: Workman, 2013).

3. Let me tell you about another, fascinating message delivered to the Class of '77 by Thomas DeLong, a professor of organizational behavior. By way of background, De-Long offers an unusual course for Harvard Business School, one that forces students to reflect on the personal cost of success, primarily, privileging ambition and career advancement above family, friends, and other passions. DeLong told me the origin of the course: The companies hiring HBS graduates had complained that they "weren't the most reflective bunch, and many of them want to keep everything on a superficial level, and you need to address that," DeLong said. It's not clear that challenging the culture of achievement for one semester will provide enough corrective, but it is a start.

   In his lecture to the Class of '77, DeLong presented case studies—with a few details changed—of the lives of six alumni from the Class of 1976. He walked the audience through the analyses of how their lives were performing, in much the way that these very alumni had analyzed case studies of company performance thirty-five years earlier. Among the six were two divorces, one separation before death, and two people who had decided to exit the achievement track for personal passions. The sixth case was heartbreaking.

   "The man is going to work in the morning," DeLong begins, "and his young son grabs hold of his leg and starts to sob. He doesn't want his dad to go to work, and he cries, 'Dad, you spend too much time at work!' The dad finally gets out the door and this seven-year-old chases the car halfway down a block, yelling for his dad."

   Later, in an interview, DeLong described another chilling case. An alumnus was mowing his lawn, and his young daughter stood in front of the lawn mower to get his attention. "The dad weaves around her, pushes her to the side, backs up to make sure that he leaves a perfect diagram in the grass and continues, looks back, and sees his daughter with eyes huge—huge—looking stunned," he told me.

   The most powerful part of the lecture was DeLong's personal story. In 2003, he had just received an endowed chair at the business school and felt he needed to overperform to justify the prestigious position. On March 11, DeLong's twenty-three-year-old daughter called him. She told him she had just been diagnosed with lymphoma. While talking to his daughter, "I was thinking, 'Well, this is really going to disrupt my schedule,'" DeLong admitted, wincing at the memory. "I'm having this internal conversation and it's like, 'Wait a second, excuse me?'"

   The next morning, DeLong flew out to see his daughter, but those moments of internal debate cut him to the quick, as it appeared to affect the Class of '77, if their sad silence was any measure.

   "I was addicted to the need for achievement and to cross things off my list," he said.

"I'm thinking to myself on the plane, 'So, Tom, do you really need your twenty-three-year-old to get cancer for you to gain perspective?'"

DeLong is not saying that all the graduates of Harvard Business School live craven, loveless lives of teeming ambition. Many enjoy balanced lives, still in love with their first spouse, still connected to, not alienated from, their children. But DeLong says when he reviews the letters that alumni send in before their tenth and twenty-fifth reunions, he often sees "a gradual deadening in relationships." He witnesses an emptiness and a boredom that spawns restlessness as people invest shallowly, not deeply. "The rut just gets deeper and deeper," he told the crowd, "and it reinforces your addiction and then you buy new and different kinds of smart phones that are even more sophisticated that will feed your addiction."

His stories are not all this sad, but his message seemed to reverberate among this driven crowd.

4. C. Strenger and A. Ruttenberg, "The Existential Necessity of Midlife Change," *Harvard Business Review* 86, no. 2 (2008): 82–89. See also C. Strenger, "Paring Down Life to the Essentials: An Epicurean Psychodynamics of Midlife Changes," *Psychoanalytic Psychology* 26, no. 3 (2009): 246.

5. Strenger suggests there is a Goldilocks aspect to the timing as well. You shouldn't leap out of a paying job before you know where you want to land. Don't just quit to "find yourself." In Strenger's experience, it generally takes five years from the moment a person realizes he needs to change his career to the time he finds a satisfying job. Research by Encore.org puts the number at eighteen months; still, that is a long time to be in limbo without a paycheck. Also, you should test the waters before committing. Encore suggests internships or volunteer work.

6. Now, let me be clear: Strenger is not saying that people cannot reinvent their careers. Laurie Duperier did, and so have many others. Rather, he argues that people cannot become anything they want beginning at midlife: I will never be an astronaut and, as much as he would like to, my husband will never be a baseball announcer. The reinvention stories may appear to be a radical midlife do-over, but we do not know the backstory. Perhaps that attorney turned chef grew up in a family of restaurateurs. Maybe the doctor who became an organic farmer actually grew up on a farm. Certainly it appears that Laurie Duperier made a radical leap into the world of dog therapy. But she is melding her love of dogs with a wealth of experience: making shrewd legal decisions, understanding the business climate, and seeing an opportunity with a market she knows well—dog lovers with disposable income.

7. C. Strenger, "*Sosein*: Active Self-Acceptance in Midlife," *Journal of Humanistic Psychology* 49 (2009): 46–65.

8. Even in these professions, there is an asterisk. For example, there may be a demand for college professors who teach marketing but not English literature.

9. To that end, Freedman created Encore Fellowships, which match private-sector professionals with nonprofit organizations and government agencies that need those skills but can't afford them. Usually these places tend to the poor, elderly, or sick, or work for the social good, such as improving schools or preserving the environment. The money is modest compared with corporate salaries (usually $25,000 for half-time work), but the fellows I talked to did not join for the money. To dramatize the fact that experience can be parlayed into astounding achievements, Freedman has created the Purpose Prize.

The $100,000 award is given to people who have accomplished an extraordinary feat after the age of sixty. Tom Cox, who is profiled in this chapter, is plowing his prize money into building a network of pro bono attorneys. Other Purpose Prize winners have created a disaster relief organization with thousands of volunteers, an organization that transfers to food banks fresh fruit and vegetables that were headed for disposal, and a network of therapeutic riding centers for children with disabilities.

10. Here are a few studies on overcoming fear. Cognitive reappraisal can reduce fear: See A. Hermann, T. Keck, and R. Stark, "Dispositional Cognitive Reappraisal Modulates the Neural Correlates of Fear Acquisition and Extinction," *Neurobiology of Learning and Memory* 113 (2014): 115–24. Distraction and reappraisal can help reduce claustrophobia: See J. H. Kamphuis and M. J. Telch, "Effects of Distraction and Guided Threat Reappraisal on Fear Reduction During Exposure-Based Treatments for Specific Fears," *Behaviour Research and Therapy* 38, no. 12 (2000): 1163–81. Cognitive behavioral therapy helps with anxiety disorders: See J. Blechert, F. H. Wilhelm, H. Williams, et al., "Reappraisal Facilitates Extinction in Healthy and Socially Anxious Individuals," *Journal of Behavior Therapy and Experimental Psychiatry* 46 (2015): 141–50. Cognitive reappraisal helps with phobias: See A. Hermann, V. Leutgeb, W. Scharmüller, et al., "Individual Differences in Cognitive Reappraisal Usage Modulate the Time Course of Brain Activation During Symptom Provocation in Specific Phobia," *Biology of Mood & Anxiety Disorders* 3 (2013): 16. Therapy can help reduce or eliminate panic disorders for those who fear being in crowds or public spaces: See T. Hahn, T. Kircher, B. Straube, et al., "Predicting Treatment Response to Cognitive Behavioral Therapy in Panic Disorder with Agoraphobia by Integrating Local Neural Information," *JAMA Psychiatry* 72, no. 1 (2015): 68–74; B. G. Dias, S. B. Bannerjee, J. V. Goodman, and K. Ressler, "Towards New Approaches to Disorders of Fear and Anxiety," *Current Opinion in Neurobiology* 23, no. 3 (2013): 346–52. Here is a famous overview of the neural basis for fear: J. LeDoux, "Fear and the Brain: Where Have We Been, and Where Are We Going?" *Biological Psychiatry* 44, no. 12 (1998): 1229–38.

11. The most innovative way to test the waters comes courtesy of Brian Kurth, who founded VocationVacations, now called PivotPlanet. One day he was stuck in Chicago traffic and began to daydream. What kind of work would he really enjoy? He thought, *I love dogs, why not be a dog day-care owner?* After work that night, he surfed the Internet for a company that provided a service where you can try out your dream job without quitting your day job. He came up with a blank. So he called up a dog day-care owner and asked if he could shadow her for two or three days.

"The first day, I knew I didn't want to be a dog day-care owner because as much as I love dogs, I didn't want to spend the day spraying down mats and picking up poop," he told me, laughing. "Two days in, I'm thinking, Oh, my gosh. Thank God I did this, because seriously I was thinking of leasing space and starting to get certified."

From this experience sprang VocationVacations. Kurth grew a stable of mentors who would allow the client to shadow them for three days. Want to be an actor? Own a restaurant? Run a brewery? Ranch bison? Kurth matched hundreds of mentors with clients in a vast array of businesses. Some of the clients took the plunge into their dream careers—but not the ones Kurth expected. "The people who made changes were the Millennials and the Gen-Xers," he said, referring to people born in the 1980s to early 2000s, and the mid-1960s to early 1980s, respectively. "They were not the baby boomers."

"Why do you think that is?" I asked.

"Why? Money. *Money money money money money,*" Kurth said. "The Gen-Xers and the Millennials can take a risk and, if they fail, still have enough time to make their money back. Baby boomers don't. And so they're going to wait until they're retired or semiretired from their cubicle-land day job that they don't enjoy. They're going to hang tight. Then the recession happened and they sure as hell were going to hang tight."

Kurth has changed his business model and renamed it PivotPlanet. After the 2008 recession, business dropped off precipitously. If people were nervous about leaving their safe jobs before, now they were terrified. PivotPlanet provides the same matching service for clients—but generally via video conferencing, which eliminates the travel expense. In addition to the consumer product, PivotPlanet, the company offers Revere, a private-label online platform that easily and efficiently connects internal knowledge seekers with internal subject-matter experts within university alumni associations, trade associations, nonprofits, and companies.

12. Some people volunteer strategically, but for others, like Valerie Sowa, a new career simply offered itself up as a result of her largesse. Valerie had served on the board of the Montessori school her children attended in River Falls, Wisconsin, for years. She owned her own direct sales business, and one day when she was around fifty, Valerie realized she was bored and needed a change: "My children no longer needed me at home, my business only seemed to serve myself, and I was ready to contribute to something larger than just my own personal gain." Valerie set an end date for her business, and as she daydreamed about where she could serve, she realized she was happiest when serving on the Montessori school board. Three days later, her phone rang: The head of the school was leaving; would she be interested in applying? Her years of volunteering, without an agenda, led straight to her most fulfilling career.

13. "Initially I liked advertising a lot," Roger McDorman told me. "But it's a business focused on youth, and you're only as good as your last great idea." He looked down the road, ten, fifteen, twenty years, and realized this was not sustainable. The threat of hiring a younger, cheaper replacement would only grow more unsettling, like a buzz saw inching toward his head in an action-hero movie. He did glean one valuable insight from his years of advertising. He was fascinated by trademark and copyright issues.

At forty-two, with a two-year-old son and another soon to come, Roger entered law school at the University of North Carolina. His family pared down to a spartan lifestyle—no vacations, no eating out—while it accumulated tens of thousands of dollars in debt. All he could do was hope for the best.

"'I'm going to work hard and apply myself,' I told myself, 'and then there will be a job that will make everything okay waiting for me on the other side.'"

"Was that true?"

"No."

Roger collected his diploma in 2010 and stepped into a disastrous job market. For two "lean and scrappy years," he performed contract work in intellectual property law, before landing a job at the U.S. Patent and Trademark Office. It's gloriously steady work, "like Lucy in the chocolate factory."

"I sometimes describe myself as a pound rescue," he said, laughing. "You're never going to hear me complain about this, because however difficult a case might be and however screwed-up an application might be, it's trademarks all day, all night, in stereo. I'm like a pig in the mud. I absolutely never get tired of it. My worst day at the PTO is better than my best day in advertising."

Roger says the process was more evolutionary than revolutionary: Like many others, in retrospect, he could see how his interests—first, for journalism, then for advertising, then for intellectual property issues—overlapped and guided him, like runners handing off a baton.

"Maybe the best part of all this is that, mentally and emotionally, I've done a complete one-eighty from where I was in those last, dour days in advertising," he wrote me later. "Not only does the work I'm doing and the satisfaction I get from it seem sustainable, it's practically unlimited. I can easily see myself doing this and loving it into my dotage. Retirement? Pfft. They'll have to drag me out of here."

With his six-figure debt to pay off, I asked him what advice he has for someone miserable in his work and considering starting over in school.

"I would say, don't allow yourself to fall in the trap of 'I'm too old to do X,'" he said. "I would say, don't look at it too hard, because if you just look at the numbers and crunch the data, that's a surefire recipe for talking yourself out of it."

14. I related my story to Carlo Strenger, the Israeli psychiatrist, during our Skype interview. I confided my thoughts about making a mid-career leap, thoughts I had voiced to no one except my husband and a few close friends. I watched him absorb this, him and his large, impatient dog who kept nudging him for a walk. When I finished, Strenger, who looks a little like Mr. Clean, broke into a delighted grin. "Your story really exemplifies the kind of processes I'm talking about," he said. "You didn't become a fashion designer, okay? You took an ability that you had—well honed, well developed—and you vaulted with it in a different direction." I still recall the relief that swept over me. *See, I am not crazy,* I thought. *A psychiatrist as much as said so!* I filed away the image of Strenger's grin; over the next few months, I would call it up, just for reassurance.

15. "Pill for Poverty," by Robert Bidney (© Robert Bidney, reprinted by permission):

> They've got a pill when you feel depressed
> They've got a pill when there's heartburn in your chest
> They've got a pill to heal most anything
> Almost anything
> Just about everything
>
> I need a pill for poverty
> Living a life that's killing me
> I need a job
> Gotta feed my family
> I need a pill, give me a pill . . .
>
> I used to feel satisfied
> I had a house and a little money put aside
> Taken away, yeah, that's all history

When will it end
Oh all this misery
I need a pill for poverty

What I've become is killing me
Losing my pride
My dignity
I need a pill, give me a pill . . .
Over the counter or under the table
I need a remedy with hope on the label
God only knows, I'm willing and able

I need a job
Gotta feed my family
I need a pill, give me a pill
I need a pill for poverty
What I've become is killing me
Losing my pride
My dignity
I need a pill, give me a pill
I need a pill, someone give me a pill
I need a pill . . . for poverty.

16. In the year since Nancy wrapped up her work with Bev, she has launched her consulting business, adding another client in the health policy field. Two clients keeps her busy (although she has feelers out for more), given her other commitments. Along with continuing as director of graduate studies for the environmental resource policy program at GW, she is developing and leading an online master's degree for her program. "I'm getting the opportunity to build something from the ground up," she says. "I love this stuff!" As to her "mission" to make the world a better place: "In a small way, I am working to make higher education more accessible [to people who are not in the position to move to D.C. but want the quality education]. It's a decent start, and I'll take it."

AFTERWORD: SIXTEEN SUGGESTIONS FOR MIDLIFE

1. Credit goes to C. S. Lewis, who advised: "Aim at Heaven and you will get Earth 'thrown in': aim at Earth and you will get neither." See C. S. Lewis, *Mere Christianity* (New York: Macmillan, 1943), 104.
2. My thanks to Chris Dionigi, one of my midlife e-mailers. The full quotation is: "I think that it is vitally important that a person is always a rookie at something. And if that something is of service to people and things you care about, you can lead an extraordinary life."

INDEX

READERS GUIDE

1. Have you ever had a midlife crisis? If so, what happened? Was there something that triggered it? How did you emerge from it (if you did)?

2. The author suggests that midlife *crisis* is rare. But she says that a midlife slump in happiness is nearly universal. Does this ring true to you? If so, is there anything you did to help you move past the slump, or did that happen naturally?

3. Researchers say that one key to happiness at midlife is to shift from seeking external achievement and acquisition (a more prestigious job, more money, a larger house) to focusing on other people and a purpose or cause that is important to you. Have you seen this shift in yourself or others?

4. Many people at midlife think they've lost their cognitive edge—they forget names, or the reason they've walked into the living room. But research suggests the midlife brain is operating at its cognitive peak. What is your experience?

5. Studies show that eudaimonia—pleasure derived from long-term, often hard, and yet meaningful endeavors—makes people happier and healthier in the long run than shorter-term pleasures. Have you found this to be true?

6. Researchers have determined that a psychological trait called "purpose in life" can actually protect people from the symptoms of Alzheimer's disease. What might more "purpose in life" look like for you?

7. Research indicates that friends—even more than family—can help people stay healthy and keep their memory. What kinds of benefits do you draw from the friendships you have?

8. What surprised you most about the marriage research presented in the book? Did you learn anything that you might incorporate into your own marriage?

9. Psychologists believe that we are more resilient than we think—and that even after disasters, we return to our "set point." When was the last time you experienced a rough patch in your life, and what helped you cope and move beyond it?

10. The author proposes ways to think about a mid-career shift, including volunteering, getting another degree, and moving to a different position in one's organization. Which resonates with you? How might you change your career, or just the manner in which you approach your present occupation, to take better advantage of your natural talents, proclivities, personality traits, and skills?

11. If you were to make three changes as a result of the research and stories in this book, what would they be?

12. What did you think of the sixteen suggestions at the end of the book? Do you intend to act on any of them?

Barbara Bradley Hagerty asks new questions.

As an award-winning journalist and broadcaster, Barbara Bradley Hagerty knows how to ask important questions that prompt surprising—and heartening—answers.

In *Fingerprints of God*, she uses these skills to explore what science is learning about human spiritual experience: how faith can affect us physically, emotionally, and psychically.

From the biological underpinnings of belief to science's hunt for the "God gene," the answers Hagerty unearths shed exciting new light on how and why we believe.

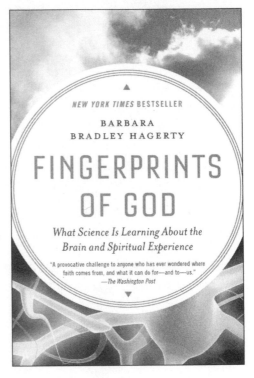

NEW YORK TIMES BESTSELLER

BARBARA
BRADLEY HAGERTY

FINGERPRINTS
OF GOD

*What Science Is Learning About the
Brain and Spiritual Experience*

"A provocative challenge to anyone who has ever wondered where
faith comes from, and what it can do for—and to—us."
—The Washington Post

"A provocative challenge to anyone who has ever wondered where faith comes from, and what it can do for—and to—us." **—The Washington Post**

"Hagerty writes with touching candor and honesty, but also with a journalist's skeptical eye that demands facts and data. . . . Hagerty treads some fascinating territory." **—The Christian Science Monitor**

"Ambitious . . . [A] fascinating trek through the burgeoning scientific field of the study of spirituality." **—New York Post**